Black Girls and Adolescents

Black Girls and Adolescents

Facing the Challenges

Catherine Fisher Collins, Editor

Foreword by Marian Wright Edelman

 PRAEGER

AN IMPRINT OF ABC-CLIO, LLC

Santa Barbara, California • Denver, Colorado • Oxford, England

Library of Congress Cataloging-in-Publication Data

Collins, Catherine Fisher.
  Black girls and adolescents : facing the challenges / Catherine Fisher Collins.
    pages cm
  ISBN 978-1-4408-3053-2 (hardback) — ISBN 978-1-4408-3054-9 (ebook)
  1. African American teenage girls.   2. African American teenage girls
—Social conditions.   3. African American teenage girls—Health and
hygiene.   4. African American young women.   I. Title.
  E185.86.C58167   2015
  305.235′20896073—dc23   2014033029

ISBN: 978-1-4408-3053-2
EISBN: 978-1-4408-3054-9

19 18 17 16 15   1 2 3 4 5

This book is also available on the World Wide Web as an eBook.
Visit www.abc-clio.com for details.

Praeger
An Imprint of ABC-CLIO, LLC

ABC-CLIO, LLC
130 Cremona Drive, P.O. Box 1911
Santa Barbara, California 93116-1911

This book is printed on acid-free paper (∞)

Manufactured in the United States of America

This book is dedicated to the Fisher family—my parents, the late Herman and Catherine Fisher; my brother, the late Herman A. Fisher; my sister, Fay Austin; and brother, David Fisher. My daughter, Principal Laura Harris, and my son, Clyde Collins, MD; also my grandchildren, Crystal Harris, Kenneth Harris, Caiden Collins, Cara Collins, Cayla Collins, Zaire Harris, Dylan Harris, Mia Harris, and Jayden Hunter.

This book is also dedicated to the late Marcia C. Jordon of Niagara Falls, New York, a very dear friend and godmother to Dr. Clyde Collins of Texas.

This book is also dedicated to the late Dr. Lorraine E. Peeler, my dear friend and colleague.

Contents

PART II: PARENTING

PART III: EDUCATION

PART IV: CRIMINAL JUSTICE

Foreword

I am grateful for this comprehensive new collection of scholarship and research devoted to Black girls. I have always felt blessed to be born who I was, where I was, when I was. As a Black girl child growing up in a small segregated town, I could never take anything for granted and never for a moment lacked a purpose worth fighting, living, and dying for, or an opportunity to make a difference if I wanted to. Caring Black adults were buffers against the segregated and hostile outside world that told us we weren't important, and long before the phrase was popular our mothers and grandmothers took their time braiding our hair, neatly pressing our clothes, and reminding us every day that Black was beautiful. Yet there is a sense that for as many strides forward as we have made, Black children today are under dangerous assault—while at the same time the fabric of community that was so critical in sustaining Black children for so long has frayed.

The most dangerous place in America for a child to grow up is at the intersection of race and poverty, and racial disparities which run through every major child-serving system in our nation too often impact Black girls' life chances: limited health and mental health care; lack of access to a high quality early childhood continuum that includes home visiting, Early Head Start and Head Start, child care, preschool, and kindergarten; an overburdened child welfare system; and failing schools with harsh zero tolerance discipline policies that too often push children out of school and into juvenile detention and adult prison.

Children of color are already a majority of all children under age two and in five years children of color will be the majority of all children in America. All of our children—including all of our Black children—truly must be ready in critical mass to take their place among the workers, educators, members and leaders of the military, and political leaders of tomorrow. America is going to be left behind if our children are not enabled and empowered to get ahead. But when nearly two in five Black children are poor; when Black babies are more than twice as likely as White babies to die before their first birthdays and Black children are twice as likely as White children to die before their 18th birthdays; when more than 80 percent of fourth and eighth grade Black public school students cannot read or compute at grade level; when a Black public school student is suspended every four seconds of the school day and a Black child is arrested every 68 seconds; and when gun violence is the leading cause of death among Black children ages 1–19, we are in grave danger—and it is critical that we examine what we can do to improve our children's chances.

Much of the public attention paid to our nation's racial disparities focuses on their profound impact on Black boys and Black men, but Black girls are also deeply at risk. For example, Black girls are suspended from school at higher rates than girls of any other race or ethnicity and higher rates than most boys; and while twice as many boys as girls are arrested, girls are the fastest growing segment of the juvenile justice system. At the same time Black girls and all girls often face a unique set of challenges. Considering again the juvenile justice system, almost three quarters of girls in the system have been sexually or physically abused. Many are arrested for nonviolent offenses which can often be linked to abuse and neglect such as truancy, running away, or alcohol and substance use— most offenses that would not be considered offenses for an adult. Yet once arrested these girls are often even more at risk when placed in detention facilities without the health, mental health, or educational supports they need. Cycles like these are a vicious snare for far too many Black girls. From the juvenile justice system to education policy, health to mental health, body image to substance abuse, poverty to teenage pregnancy, the chapters in this book are a much-needed examination of many of the unique challenges Black girls face—and they offer welcome prescriptions for solutions.

The hand that rocks the cradle rocks the future, and Black women from Sojourner Truth and Harriet Tubman to Rosa Parks, Septima Clark, Fannie Lou Hamer, and Ella Baker have rocked history. We must prepare today's Black girls to do the same. It is up to us to do everything we can to make sure every Black girl is healthy, well educated, valued, safe, and hopeful. Understanding the potential risks and challenges Black girls face will help us better support them and put the next generation of Black girls on a path to successful adulthood. *Black Girls and Adolescents: Facing the Challenges* is an invaluable resource.

Marian Wright Edelman
Founder and President, The Children's Defense Fund

Preface

America is in critical condition when it comes to providing needed services for all children, particularly African American adolescent girls. There are four sections in this text that include chapters dealing with health, parenting, education, and criminal justice issues. Each chapter addresses a major concern for these girls, examining not only the problems they face, but also potential solutions. The chapters also reveal areas in which there exists a need for further investigation, public scrutiny and additional financial resources.

The first section addresses health issues. Chapter 1 deals with HIV, a life-changing illness that, for young people, involves a threat to self-esteem and perhaps a day-to-day struggle with secrecy, increasing the risk of spreading the virus. Therefore, HIV prevention strategies are crucial. This chapter highlights how HIV prevention programs have the ability to build self-esteem, foster maturity, and nurture responsibility among adolescent Black girls.

Chapter 2 presents the challenges to physical and mental health experienced by African American adolescent females. Beginning with a discussion of obesity and other health-related issues, it continues with a discussion of mental health issues, focusing on depression and suicide, and concludes with suggestions on effective programs for African American adolescent females.

In Chapter 3, the focus is on adolescents with sickle-cell anemia, and the many challenges they face as they leave the pediatric stage and enter the adolescent stage (ages 13–21). The chapter will present how hematologists, physicians who specialize in the "red cells," appear not to be interested in providing care for this population of patients. Also addressed are the stigmatization, racism and negative labeling (such as "drug seeker," "frequent flyer" and "bad blood") these adolescents face, as well as the need for further research and funding.

Pelvic inflammatory disease is discussed in Chapter 4. PID, an asymptomatic or symptomatic infection of the upper genital tract, is very common among adolescents, especially those who are racial minorities. The sexually transmitted infections chlamydia and gonorrhea are implicated in most cases of PID. Also, African American adolescents are exposed to unique circumstances that increase their risk factors for PID. Adolescence is a time of rapid growth and development, ambivalence and a quest for independence, as well as engagement in high-risk behaviors and experimentation. All of these factors combined place the African American adolescent at risk for PID. This cycle, as presented, can be affected by early identification and treatment, education, and appropriate interventions.

Chapter 5 presents how the reality of African American adolescent girls—one of the groups least likely to abuse illicit drugs, alcohol, and cigarettes—conflicts with stereotypes in American culture. This chapter will present the national statistics, past and current, documenting the rates of alcohol and illicit drug abuse and dependence in African American adolescent girls. It will also explore potential explanations for disproportionately poor outcomes, despite lower abuse rates.

Chapter 6 turns our attention to the impact of poverty. It examines the United States, which, despite being one of the wealthiest countries in the world, has a high amount of poverty and one of the highest rates of childhood poverty in comparison to other industrialized nations. In this chapter, an overview is presented on economic policies and social attitudes in the United States that have, over time, perpetuated structural inequalities. Also discussed are policies implemented during the 1970s and 1980s that have drastically limited social and economic opportunities for many, particularly those in urban areas. Further, this chapter presents the unspoken burden Black adolescent girls face in a way that redirects myths of voluntary poverty to the truth about structural poverty and its consequences in the lives of far too many young Black girls.

The final chapter in the first section, Chapter 7, addresses the national epidemic of obesity. For over the past three decades, the rate of obesity in this nation has increased markedly, with the African American female population existing as the most at-risk group. Also presented in this chapter is a review of the particular circumstances, causes, and current environment in which the overweight and obesity epidemic has developed among African American female children and adolescents, as well as recommendations to resolve this crisis.

The second section examines the impact of parenting on adolescent girls. Chapter 8 focuses on biracial challenges to mental health and looks at the identity development of people with multiple racial heritages. In this discussion of multiracial individuals, the influence of the racialized American culture is considered as a significant factor; that is, the problem of the color line remains. Although the research in this area is equivocal, anxiety, depression, and cognitive and emotional dissonance have been related to psychosocial challenges experienced by this population.

Chapter 9 explores the causes and risk factors for the high rate of teenage pregnancy among the African American community. In addition, the chapter focuses on the consequences of teenage pregnancy on the child, parent(s), and society. Lastly, the chapter discusses some of the ways to combat teenage pregnancy, including identifying pregnancy prevention programs that have been shown to be most effective.

Chapter 10 addresses the impact of poverty on lifestyle patterns of the Black community, including diets high in salt, fat, and sugar. Further, there are sociocultural barriers and facilitators to physical activity among Black teens. In this chapter the reader will find compelling evidence of the impact of socioeconomics, parental influence, and body image perception among Blacks.

Chapter 11 covers normal growth and development of adolescent girls, as well as the risk factors to which they are exposed during the process of adolescence. It explores the role of parents in educating their girls about their emerging sexuality, yet acknowledges the ambivalence that parents may experience because of their own upbringing, values, and beliefs. The chapter offers objective information on risk modification and approaches to engaging both parents and teens in an ongoing dialogue.

The section's final chapter, Chapter 12, addresses how young Black women develop the perseverance to handle loss at an early age and to prepare for a life of wholeness, goodness, healthy self-regard, and productivity, where their personal, professional, and family lives are characterized by strength and vitality.

Section three addresses education. Chapter 13 deals with how adolescents, including African American females, engage in non-intercourse sexual behaviors, such as oral sex, in the mistaken belief that these behaviors are safe and without risk. To them, oral sex is not sex because virginity, as it is traditionally defined, is not lost, and the likelihood of pregnancy is removed. However, sexually transmitted infections can be acquired through oral sex, including human papilloma virus–related oral cancer. Sex education must emphasize safe sexual behaviors other than vaginal intercourse and pregnancy prevention.

Chapter 14 addresses barriers to mental health treatment for African American girls and teens. The chapter explores both extra- and intracultural challenges impacting accessibility, clinical joining, and treatment adherence issues. The chapter also addresses the issue of caregivers' cultural competence and how being culturally competent influences the aforementioned counseling barriers.

Chapter 15 addresses how, each year, tens of thousands of youths age out of the U.S. foster care system, leaving the majority of them unprepared for what lies ahead as they transition to adulthood. The chapter focuses on the conditions and major challenges many of these youth—specifically Black adolescent females, who are extremely vulnerable—will face. Best practices to inform policy and important factors for successful program development that effectively meet the needs and improve outcomes of foster care youth are also offered.

Chapter 16 presents the thoughts and life experiences of two groups of Black adolescent females as they create and enact their class, race, and gender identities at urban and suburban high schools. Unfortunately, little research exists that solely focuses on Black teenage girls' gender and racial identity construction within the context of educational institutions. When Black females have been included in studies, it has been in relation to their Black males and White female counterparts, and is often presented from a White scholar's viewpoint.

Chapter 17 focuses on the treatment of suicidality among African American females attending elite schools and the relevance of diminished community support. It explores the impact of racism, and identifies specific cultural factors that may contribute to depression and suicidal behavior. It suggests that by incorporating ideas from a social justice viewpoint, integrating the intergenerational legacy of slavery, and combining clinical coping strategies with family and community support systems, there is a different way for thinking about how we provide treatment for this population. Anecdotally, there appears to be evidence suggesting that reconnecting students to a supportive community helps to strengthen their sense of self-worth and mitigate suicidality.

Chapter 18 looks at sex trafficking of minors. Admittedly, sex trafficking is a global issue. However, of the estimated 20.9 million human trafficking victims, reportedly 1.5 million are in "developed" economies such as the European Union and the United States (*USA Today*, Thursday, September 27, 2012, p. 1A). Using snowball sampling, we were able to identify six respondents that provided us with an in-depth understanding of human sex trafficking from a personal account as women who were in law enforcement, social workers, and victors who are now providing services to support survivors. The scope of this problem is immeasurable; identification of victims is essential for their survival, as this chapter will present.

Chapter 19 connects research placing adolescent girls of African descent at profoundly greater sexual health risks to the imperative that they be prepared for life though exploration of their lives prompted by poetry presentations. The author believes that students can be empowered by engagement with adults who use tenets of Critical Literacy and Critical Health literacy. She describes some of the strategies she uses to engage students in conversations of self- and societal empowerment, as related to sexual health and well-being, using poetry and tenets of critical literacy, critical health literacy, and poetry as pedagogy.

In Chapter 20, the focus is on the development of self-identity in African American female adolescents. Utilizing informal conversations and written evaluations, the article demonstrates how natural mentoring positively impacts the development of their self-identity.

Chapter 21 explores the nature of education for Black girls in the 21st century. The plight of Black girls involves growing up in a system that facilitates invisibility and subversion, and one that fails to provide a realistic depiction of Black girls, although experience intersects with single interpretations and representations. In order to mold more resilient Black girls who grow up resolute with a positive self-identity, service (i.e., mentoring) needs to function as the catalyst for designing effective leadership in Black girls.

The fourth and final section deals with the impact of the criminal justice system on adolescent African American girls. Chapter 22 explores the dynamics of African American girls who are violated and victimized by the juvenile justice system. Because of their unique circumstances that contribute to their involvement in the juvenile justice system, this chapter will take a critical look at the various risk factors associated. It also covers controversial issues in juvenile delinquency and analyzes how race and gender play an integral role in their victimization and the violation of their due process.

Chapter 23 investigates the growing prevalence of antisocial and criminal behavior among adolescent girls. Specifically, there is a focus on the racial disparities present in the juvenile justice system that disproportionately impact Black girls. After examining the contexts associated with the deviance and criminality of Black girls—including family, neighborhoods, schools, and abuse—the chapter ends with several proposed solutions to this very important social problem.

Chapter 24's focus is on the 13 characteristics of an at-risk African American girl. Using Bloom's at-risk model, the chapter demonstrates how young African American adolescent girls are drawn into criminal behavior. Also included is research from the Children's Defense Fund, which depicts the intersection of many factors that contribute to young African American girls entering the juvenile justice system.

Chapter 25 raises the ancient question, "How old should a person be in order to be treated as an adult for purposes of criminal prosecution?" This issue has taken center stage in the current debate on criminal responsibility in New York, one of only two states that treats adolescents as young as 16 as adults. In her writing, "Raising the Age of Criminal Responsibility in New York: A Judge's Observation," a 27-year-veteran New York trial judge discusses the history of the decision to treat adolescents as adults, the pitfalls and consequences of that decision on the lives of children, the developing brain science which informs issues of culpability, and the special concerns for adolescent girls. As New York policymakers tackle this important issue, Judge Bing Newton's chapter provides observations that inform those who are concerned about both public safety and the lives of children.

Chapter 26 offers a sociological perspective on different pathways of aggression among African American girls through elementary school years leading into their teenaged years. It explores sociocultural and structural influences that inhibit physical, verbal, and relational aggression. Intervention options and directions for future research are included.

The final chapter, Chapter 27, addresses the unique challenges that African American adolescent females in the criminal and juvenile justice systems face that affect their status and treatment. A historical perspective of the roles, functions and responsibilities of the courts in these systems, as well as perceptions and assumptions about African American adolescent females in this country, is included to aid in understanding said challenges and how they relate to crime and delinquency.

Acknowledgments

There are so many to thank.

This book would not have been possible without the assistance from so many individuals who care about a segment of America's forgotten population—children, particularly African American girls. To the dedicated contributors to this work: Sheila Aird, Funmi Aiyegbo-Ohadike, Te Cora Ballom, Ursuline Bankhead, Lindamichelle Baron, Virginia Batchelor, Juanita Bing Newton, Betty Boyle-Duke, Kellie Bryant, Tomasina Cook, Cassandra E. Dobson, Hope E. Ferguson, Aquilla Frederick, Gloria Gibson, Mary Harley Gresham, Yvette Harris, Chiquita Howard-Bostic, Portia Johnson, Jessica Jones, Illana Lane, Denise Linton, Byron Miller, Jamesetta A. Newland, E. Jeannette Ogden, Marianne Partee, Caryn R.R. Rodgers, Leslie R. Walker, and Yvonne Wesley, this project wouldn't have been possible without you.

My children, Principal Laura Harris and Clyde A. Collins, MD. You are the love of my life. How do I thank you for being my children?

My sincere appreciation is extended to the following:

- My colleagues at State University of New York's Empire State College: Your support is truly appreciated.

- Dr. Maxine Sellers: As my professor, you encouraged me to investigate women's issues.

- The Rev. Darius Pridgen, pastor of True Bethel Church: Thank you for your friendship and support.

- Marian Wright Edelman, President and Founder, Children's Defense Fund, for your contribution to this work and your continued work to make the voices and needs of our nation's children heard.

A heartfelt thank you to the members of Jack and Jill of America Inc.; For Women Only (FWO), Far North Region members; The Buffalo Chapter of Links Inc.; WWWS1400 AM staff, Surely Worthington and Kevin Carr and Naomi Chapter #10, Order of the Eastern Star.

And, finally, to everyone that I missed: Know that you are all very special in my life and this book.

Part I

Health

Chapter 1

HIV/AIDS in Adolescent Black Girls

Yvonne Wesley

INTRODUCTION

Young, gifted, female and Black; how will today's young Black ladies face numerous ordeals and opportunities? Adolescence is a time of physical, emotional, and cognitive change. It is a time of magical thinking that says, "Oh no, that would never happen to me." It is a time that includes exploring, which involves risky behaviors. These may include sexual activity and/or substance use as major themes.

In the United States women and adolescents accounted for 21 percent of new HIV diagnoses in 2011. Half of all the new HIV cases occurred among youth ages 13–25 worldwide. For adolescent girls of African descent, the risk of HIV infection is more than quadruple that of White teens. According to U.S. statistics, African Americans have a greater burden of HIV than any other racial groups, so that puts Black adolescent girls at higher risk of infection. The rate of HIV/AIDS diagnosis for Black women was more than 19 times that of White women in 2011.

HIV is a life-changing illness, and for a teenager that is only half the battle. The day-to-day struggles of medications and secrecy are heart-breaking. When an adolescent gets infected with HIV she stays infected and affected for life. Therefore, prevention must be the first line of defense. Key prevention strategies include: 1) awareness of one's HIV status, 2) knowledge that drug use is associated with increased risk of HIV, and

3) behaviors that acknowledge the need for consistent condom use among young, gifted Black females.

HIV prevention programs with fresh materials that reflect current fashion, language, and HIV/STD information are most helpful. Comparing HIV prevention programs and demonstrating how some programs provide adolescent Black girls with more than the facts, this chapter shows that HIV prevention programs have the ability to build self-esteem, foster maturity, and nurture responsibility among adolescent Black girls.

HIV 101

In 1981, five previously healthy young men living in Los Angeles died from pneumonia. This marked the first cases of acquired immunodeficiency syndrome (AIDS) in the United States. New York and San Francisco immediately reported pneumonia deaths in healthy young men that same year. Considered a disease acquired through sexual contact, at that time, the Centers for Disease Control (CDC) began to track the need for medication to treat a very specific type of pneumonia called pneumocystis carinii pneumonia (PCP). According to government documents, in 1983, the CDC issued recommendations to prevent the spread of AIDS via sexual intercourse, drug use, and occupational transmission. This brief history of AIDS in the United States started in men; however, due in part to sexual transmission, the AIDS virus quickly spread to women.

Understanding the difference between HIV and AIDS is fundamental to discussions of HIV. Known as the human immunodeficiency virus, HIV is just that, it is a virus. However, once the virus enters a person's body it will replicate and destroy the immune system. If untreated, the person will ultimately die of an illness such as pneumocystis carinii pneumonia. AIDS, on the other hand, is a diagnosis given when a person with HIV has a combination of multiple illnesses that may lead to death. CDC classifications of HIV and AIDS are based on the lowest CD4 cell count and/or HIV-related illnesses. The definition of AIDS includes all HIV-infected persons with CD4 counts of less than 200 cells/ml as well as those with certain HIV-related illnesses or symptoms.

CD4 is a type of White blood cell that helps a person's body fight off diseases. Unfortunately the AIDS virus attaches itself to that very specific White blood cell and destroys it as the virus reproduces itself. The more virus a person has, the more CD4 cells are destroyed. Therefore, it is very important to take medication to prevent the virus from reproducing itself. It is also important to prevent more virus from entering one's body. Simply stated, there are tests that can determine whether the virus has entered a person's body. There are other tests that determine how much virus is in a person's body. Further still, there are tests that can determine how many CD4 cells a person has. Being HIV infected does not mean a person has

AIDS; however if the person continues to: 1) have unprotected sex, 2) share needles, and/or 3) avoid anti-retroviral medications, the virus will replicate and cause AIDS-defining illnesses.

This brief overview of HIV is intended to clarify a basic understanding of HIV and AIDS. Detailed information can be found at U.S. government websites such as www.CDC.gov or www.HRSA.gov. Most important to this chapter are the following points: young Black females are at increased risk of becoming HIV infected, and prevention is the best strategy.

ADOLESCENCE: THE DEVELOPMENTAL PHASES

Prior to a discussion of the prevention programs that work best among Black adolescent females, this section providers the reader with a brief overview of adolescent developmental phases. Adolescence is commonly defined as ages 13 to 19 years old. However, there are some authors that use the word adolescence to refer to the time period beginning with menses for girls and signs of puberty in boys. These events can start as early as age 9 or as late as age 16. The age at which adolescence begins is therefore somewhat blurry and so is the age at which adolescence ends. Some government data include persons up to age 25 while other reports suggest that adolescence ends at the legal age of 21. For the purpose of this chapter, ages will be given to clarify which age group is being discussed.

Specific to adolescence, there are three developmental phases. The early phase has been defined as the time when the adolescent is less than 15 years old. During the middle phase the adolescent is between ages 15 and 17, and in the late phase, the adolescent is between ages 17 and 19. However, other researchers have defined the three phases with different age categories: ages 9 to 12 years corresponding to Phase I as early adolescence, Phase II ages 13 to 16 years as middle adolescence, and Phase III ages 17 to 22 years as late adolescence. Data show that Black and Hispanic girls continue to mature faster than White girls, on average. Despite the variation in the onset and ending of each phase, there are developmental tasks that need to be completed successfully to produce healthy individuals. These include:

i.   Acceptance of and comfort with one's body image
ii. Internalization of sexual identity and role
iii. Personal value system
iv. Sense of productivity
v.   Sense of independence

During the early developmental phase, the adolescent is a concrete thinker with little foresight for consequence and the adolescent has an external locus of control. In other words, teens in early adolescence make careless decisions and are easily influenced by people around them. Within the middle phase, the adolescent is prone to experimentation, seeks support from peers and has the ability to do some abstract thinking. This group of teens is willing to try new things and has some understanding of consequences, but mainly wants to be a part of a group. It is during the late or final phase of adolescence that a teen begins to gain a sense of individuality, has the ability to anticipate the consequences of his or her behavior, and most of all the adolescent has the ability to do some problem solving.

HIV prevention programs for adolescents must first address an adolescent's cognitive ability and development task as these have great influence on his or her behavior. Specific to persons of African descent there is scant literature that suggests issues of respect, responsibility, and self-development are essential when developing healthy attitudes, values, and behaviors among African American adolescents. Specific to Black female teens, the limited literature highlights the point that they are chatty but not communicative about their real romantic love feelings.

GEOGRAPHY OF HIV

The 2010 U.S. census reports that 13.6% of the 308,745,538 U.S. population is Black (Rastogi, Johnson, Hoeffel, and Drewery, 2012). Approximately 24% of the Black population in the United States is between the ages of 10 and 24 years old. Eight percent of the Black population is between the ages 10 and 14 years old, while another 8.4% are between the ages 15 and 19. Most of the Black population in the United States is over age 24.

The U.S. census data also show that there are certain regions of the United States that have larger populations of Blacks than others. When divided into four regions: 1) Northeast, 2) Midwest, 3) South, and 4) West, the South region has the greatest population of Black people. However, the states with the greatest population of Black people include California, New York, Florida, Texas, and Georgia. The top ten cities with the largest number of Black people in rank order are as follows: New York, NY, Chicago, IL, Philadelphia, PA, Detroit, MI, Houston, TX, Memphis, TN, Baltimore, MD, Los Angeles, CA, Washington, DC, and Dallas, TX. However, the top ten cities with the largest percentage of Black people in ranked order are as follows: Detroit, MI, Jackson, MS, Miami Gardens, FL, Birmingham, AL, Baltimore, MD, Memphis, TN, New Orleans, LA, Flint, MI, Montgomery, AL, and Savannah, GA. This demographic information is shared because the spread of HIV among Black adolescent females is related to geography.

In 2013 the Centers for Disease Control reported that between 2008 and 2011 rates greater than 30 infected persons per 100,000 adults and adolescents were found in Washington, DC (117.9), Louisiana (36.6), Maryland (36.4), Florida (33.2), Georgia (31.4), and New York (30.1).

Products of the Environment: Nature or Nurture

Meditz and colleagues (2011) clearly link the spread of HIV to geography, that is, it is a product of one's environment. Fried and Kelly (2011) also note how race, gender, and neighborhood, which serve as economic indicators, drive health inequities such as HIV transmission rates. They make the point that laws, policies, and practices in places such as Mississippi, Tennessee, and the District of Columbia elevate sexual behavior charges from misdemeanor to felony. This places the poorest and most underserved communities at greater risk of HIV infection by causing people with HIV to avoid the health care system and/or avoid disclosure of their HIV status. Moreover, Fried and Kelly discuss how many young Black women lack access to nonjudgmental, adequate sexual and reproductive health care in places like Washington, DC, which has been known to be the city with the highest HIV rates per capita in the United States. They also share that young Black women need to feel safe to inquire about reproductive choices and techniques to reduce their risk of HIV infection.

Floyd and Brown (2012) also addressed the concern of drug use within geographic areas where there is a large percentage of Black people. They noted that high rates of sexually transmitted infections and HIV/AIDS are inextricably linked to the drug epidemic in the United States. The connection between drugs and sexual behavior places young Black women at increased risk as they are disproportionately affected by sexually transmitted infections (STIs), including HIV (Floyd and Brown, 2012). These authors also noted that in disadvantaged Black communities, socioeconomic conditions are linked to drug activity and are likely to influence: 1) partner selection, 2) the sexual availability of women, and 3) the types of male sexual behaviors that are tolerated by women.

Floyd and Brown (2012) contend there is a growing body of literature suggesting that sexual partner characteristics contribute to factors that lead to the disproportionately high rates of STIs among Black females. Key characteristics of a sexual partner are that the male sexual partner has a history of incarceration, substance use/abuse, and concurrent sexual partners. All three characteristics increase the risk of the spread of HIV.

Describing an interesting path to HIV infection, Floyd and Brown highlight the neighborhood as a starting point for what ends up at the finish line of HIV. However, they make the argument that drug use within a socioeconomically depressed neighborhood is a mediator between neighborhood and HIV infection. In other words, the association of neighborhood with HIV infection is mediated by drug use. When drug use enters the picture, the equation changes and HIV spreads faster in geographic places where drug use flourishes. Floyd and Brown explain that drug use and drug dealing occur in all socioeconomic levels of society, and transcends races; however, visibility of drug dealing is primarily concentrated in socioeconomically deprived Black communities. The authors go so far as to suggest that in many urban disadvantaged Black neighborhoods, the drug epidemic has changed social structures, norms, and behaviors. In fact, sexual partners of drug users include non–drug-using residents.

Floyd and Brown (2012) posit that young adult Black females living in socioeconomically disorganized neighborhoods are at increased risk for adverse health and social outcomes by virtue of where they live. By becoming a product of their environment, Floyd and Brown assert, young people tend to obtain sexual partners from their direct environment, and these networks influence other networks. To test this point, Floyd and Brown studied attitudes and the prevalence of sexual partners of 120 non–drug-using Black females ages 18–30 living in a socioeconomically disadvantaged neighborhood. Twenty-five percent of the participants were between the ages of 18 and 20. Seventy-three percent had a high school education and 60% were unemployed. Twenty-eight percent of the participants reported having an STI in their lifetime. Most of the participants (82%) reported that drug activity was a major problem in their neighborhood. In addition, more than half (58%) of women studied indicated having sex with a man who sold drugs, and 48% reported having sex with a man who had been incarcerated for selling drugs.

Data from Floyd and Brown's (2012) study support their notion that young Black females have sex with men who sell drugs and have been incarcerated, despite the fact that the young Black women do not use drugs themselves. The point to be made here is that many young Black women become a product of their environment. Their sense of self and self-expression are linked to their neighborhood. The drug epidemic in Black communities appears to impact norms, behaviors, and sex partners of non–drug-using females, thereby increasing their risk for STIs. With this understanding, HIV prevention programs need to address the knowledge, attitude, and behavior of young Black females.

Self-Expression—Gender and Sexuality

Studying the etiological pathway of condom use and sexual risk behaviors among Black and White female adolescents with a mean age of 15.09 years old ($SD = 1.16$) residing in a detention center, Lopez and colleagues (2011) found that higher self-esteem was associated with lower rates of non-condom use. Moreover, strong depressive self-concept—which was a construct built from the overlap of six items from Roseberg's Self-Esteem Scale with nine items from the Center for Epidemiological Studies' Depression Scale—was related to decreased condom use. Accordingly,

Lopez and colleagues found that the path from child abuse to no condom use was mediated by depressive self-concept and the use of alcohol for sexual enhancement among the Black female adolescents. In other words, African American girls residing in a detention center utilized substance use coping.

Working from the notion that females' sense of self-worth and identity are rooted in relationships with others, Lopez and colleagues (2011) found support for their hypothesis that dysfunctional relationships with significant others lead to feelings of helplessness and impaired self-worth, which then yields decreased self-efficacy and problematic behaviors such as drug abuse. They argue that parent-child relationships are crucial indicators of risk for female teens as the parent-child relationship sets the stage for how the female teen will approach, answer, and navigate relationships during adolescence. According to Lopez and colleagues (2011) female children respond to abuse in gendered ways such as internalizing self-blame, low self-worth, and depression when they become adolescences, and males act out in aggression. These authors explain that, due to a greater reliance on relationships, girls can be at greater risk of engaging in sexual relationships as a way of coping with feelings of low self-worth or depression. Low self-worth and/or depression may lead to lack of condom use because the female adolescent may be less concerned about her health due to symptoms of depression (Lopez et al., 2011). In addition, these authors note that poor self-worth may contribute to feelings of helplessness, preventing a girl from negotiating condom use with her partners. Lopez and colleagues also suggest that HIV prevention strategies that enhance self-esteem promote condom use. In fact, their study found self-esteem and condom self-efficacy to be mediators between child abuse and the lack of condom use among these adolescents. Simply put, condom use among female teens increases if they have positive self-esteem and condom self-efficacy.

HIV Prevention Programs

With an understanding of factors that influence HIV prevention behaviors, such as condom use among Black female adolescents, Chin and colleagues (2012) conducted a systematic review of group-based interventions to determine their effectiveness. Specifically the authors examined whether comprehensive risk reduction was effective in preventing pregnancy, HIV, and other STIs. While describing how the number and percentage of STIs within the Black community can be seen as a state of emergency, Chin and colleagues highlighted the importance of behavioral theory–based interventions that increase the adolescent's knowledge. In addition, Chin and colleagues noted that theory-based interventions must influence attitudes/beliefs and create supportive norms that help build relevant communication and decision-making/practical skills among Black females, ages 15–19. This group of teens was found to have had the highest gonorrhea rates in 2010.

Findings from Chin and colleagues' meta-analysis of 62 studies revealed positive effects and significant primary outcomes. Specifically, the following decreases occurred: sexual activity by 12%, number of sex partners by 14%, unprotected sexual activity by 25%, and prevalence of STIs by 31%. In addition, the use of protection increased 13%. Gender differences were noted among the studies that found a greater effect on boys compared to girls. This may be due in part to the notion that boys are more sexually active than girls.

The authors concluded there is evidence from numerous studies that shows comprehensive risk-reduction interventions for adolescents ages 10–19 years are effective. However, despite the favorable outcome from the studies, there was considerable intervention variation across the 62 studies. The interventions varied in terms of focus, length, and intensity.

There were no key characteristics of the effective interventions that would allow the investigators to explain the wide range in the magnitude of the interventions' effects. Furthermore, the investigators could not identify any one specific variable that accounted for the effectiveness of an intervention across the 62 studies. For example, interventions in a school setting were more effective for some outcomes, whereas interventions in the community were associated with greater effectiveness for other outcomes.

Chin and colleagues' (2012) systematic review and meta-analysis of 62 studies utilizing group-based interventions showed the interventions to be effective in reducing sexual activity, number of sex partners, unprotected sex, and prevalence of STIs. However, the group-based interventions varied considerably, making it impossible for Chin and colleagues to make recommendations beyond the need for theory-based interventions that change attitudes, and increase knowledge and skills. The authors' inability to recommend specific activities based on scientific evidence is troublesome as it limits funding to provide effective focused interventions that prevent the spread of HIV. On the other hand, it appears the literature is clear: theory-based group interventions that 1) provide knowledge, 2) improve attitudes, and 3) increase skills yield favorable outcomes.

Aside from group interventions, a more recent study by Jones, Hoover, and Lacroix (2013) found that episodes of unprotected anal and vaginal sex decreased significantly ($p < .001$) in a sample of 238 Black women (mean age 22 years) living in urban areas of New Jersey after receiving text messages ($n = 121$) or watching 20-minute videos ($n = 117$) of episodes of a soap opera on their smartphone.

Despite the disadvantages of smartphone use such as cost, findings from Jones and colleagues' study show that today's technology can be helpful in changing young women's attitudes and behaviors toward sex. The mean age of Jones and colleagues' participants was somewhat older (mean age 22 years) than the target of this chapter; however, Jones's approach of viewing episodes of a soap opera video to reduce HIV risk behavior in a relatively homogeneous sample utilizing a smartphone is promising as young children of today embrace technology. The issue of the cost of a smartphone among low-income families may become a thing of the past as communication technology allows developing countries to utilize smartphones. In other words, the evolving wireless environment is becoming more readily available in populations/countries where clean drinking water is still an issue (World Bank, 2012). Communication technology may be an innovative way to reach today's and tomorrow's adolescents. A report released by the World Bank highlights the importance of mobile health: "Health now encompasses any use of mobile technology to address health care challenges such as access, quality, affordability, matching of resources, and behavioral norms [through] the exchange of information" (p. 45). Being part of a wave that sees a patient as a consumer, health services and public health promotion messages are ready for mobile health software. Mobile phone applications that deliver health information in the form of a game or quiz are now reality in developing countries. In fact, health prevention and education campaigns have been successful in Uganda (Vital Wave, 2011). In fact, short message service (SMS) texting has become a prominent mode of sharing health messages for those with a mobile usage culture (Gombachika and Monawe, 2011).

As it is well understood that prevention is less costly compared to lifelong treatment of HIV for an adolescent, the use of mobile health has the potential to transform health care systems in low-income economies (World Bank, 2012). Mobile health holds the potential for great savings and more effective health care delivery with limited resources. Public health messages that are as educational as they are entertaining offer much promise. Today's HIV prevention programs can benefit from mobile health technology, and may be more appealing to today's youth.

Take-Home Message

HIV is a life-changing disease, and for the younger generation the disease is only half the problem. The other half is the day-to-day struggle that comes with HIV care. Despite the fact that being HIV infected is not the same as having AIDS, the stigma of being HIV infected still carries a heavy weight. No longer the death sentence of the 1980s, HIV-infected teens are faced with emotional changes, self-identity issues, and peer pressure. Sexual exploration and a spirit of invisibility join to complicate HIV care which may still include numerous pills per day depending on the youth's health insurance plan. Therefore, HIV prevention strategies are crucial.

HIV prevention can start simply by knowing one's HIV status, as approximately one in five HIV-infected people are unaware of their HIV status. This places them at greater risk for spreading the virus to others. Unfortunately, one-fourth of Americans living with HIV/AIDS are women, and women of color are disproportionately impacted. In fact, the HIV/AIDS diagnosis rate for African American/Black women is more than 19 times the rate for Caucasian/White women. Moreover, government data trends show the average age at the time of HIV diagnosis is within the 20–24-year-old age category. This may suggest most people become infected as a teenager.

Approximately 70% of people age 13–19 diagnosed with HIV are Black, despite the fact that Black teens are a small proportion of the U.S. teen population. Of these teens, most (80%) are males and were infected from male-to-male sexual contact. However, almost 90% of teen females are infected from heterosexual contact. In addition, the southeastern region of the United States, specifically, Florida, South Carolina, and Louisiana had the highest concentrations of HIV diagnoses among teens.

In conclusion, most authors and scientists agree that comprehensive risk-reduction programs for teens that promote behaviors that prevent or reduce the risk of pregnancy, HIV, and other STIs are best. Whether a curriculum-based teen intervention conducted in schools or community settings, or a video on a smartphone, both have been shown to have a positive effect on teens' sexual behaviors.

REFERENCES

Chin, H. B., Sipe, T. A., Elder, R., Mercer, S. L., Chattopadhyay, S. K., Jacob, V., et al. (2012). The effectiveness of group-based comprehensive risk-reduction and abstinence education interventions to prevent or reduce the risk of adolescent pregnancy, human immunodeficiency virus, and sexually transmitted infections: Two systematic reviews for the guide to community preventive services. *American Journal of Preventive Medicine, 42*(3), 272–294. doi:http://dx.doi.org/10.1016/j.amepre.2011.11.00

Floyd, L. J., & Brown, Q. (2012). Attitudes toward and sexual partnerships with drug dealers among young adult African American females in socially disorganized communities. *Journal of Drug Issues, 43*(2), 154–163.

Fried, S. T., & Kelly, B. (2011). Gender, race + geography = jeopardy: Marginalized women, human rights and HIV in the United States. *Women's Health Issues, 21*(6, Suppl), S243–S249. doi:10.1016/j.whi.2011.07.008

Gombachika, H., & Monawe, M. (2011). Correlation analysis of attitudes towards SMS technology and blood donation behavior in Malawi. *Journal of Health Informatics in Developing Countries, 5*(2).

Jones, R., Hoover, D. R., & Lacroix, L. J. (2013). A randomized controlled trial of soap opera videos streamed to smartphones to reduce risk of sexually transmitted human immunodeficiency virus (HIV) in young urban African American women. *Nursing Outlook, 61*(4), 205–215.

Lopez, V., Kopak, A., Robillard, A., Gillmore, M. R., Holliday, R. C., & Braithwaite, R. L. (2011). Pathways to sexual risk taking among female adolescent detainees. *Journal of Youth Adolescence, 40*, 945–957.

Meditz, A. L., MaWhinney, S., Allshouse, A., Feser, W., Markowitz, M., Little, S., et al. (2011). Sex, race, and geographic region influence clinical outcomes following primary HIV-1 infection. *Journal of Infectious Diseases, 203*, 442–451.

Rastogi, S., Johnson, T. D., Hoeffel, E. M. & Drewery, M. P. (2012). The Black Population: 2010, U.S. Census Bureau, 2010 Census Briefs C2010BR-06 available at http://www.census.gov/prod/cen2010/briefs/c2010br-06.pdf

U.S. Department of Health and Human Services, Office of Adolescent Health. (2012). June 2012: Teens and the HIV/AIDS Epidemic. Retrieved from http://www.hhs.gov/ash/oah/news/e-updates/june-2012.html#Book mark_3

Vital Wave Consulting. (2011). "Mobile Applications Laboratories Business Plan." *info*Dev. http://www.infodev.org/en/Publication.1087.html

World Bank. (2012). *Information and Communications for Development 2012: Maximizing Mobile.* Washington, DC: World Bank. doi: 10.1596/978-0-8213 -8991-1; website: http://www.worldbank.org/ict/IC4D2012. License: Creative Commons Attribution CC BY 3.0

Chapter 2

African American Adolescent Females: Physical Health and Mental Health Issues

Yvette R. Harris

The goal of this chapter is to describe the physical health and mental health issues that African American adolescent females encounter. The chapter is divided into four sections. Section One discusses African American adolescent females and physical health issues. Section Two presents information on sexual behavior and African American adolescent females. Section Three addresses the mental health challenges of African American adolescent females. The chapter concludes with Section Four, Suggestions for Next Steps and Future Directions.

SECTION ONE: PHYSICAL HEALTH ISSUES

This section describes the physical health issues that are persistent and common in the lives of African American adolescent females. The section begins with a discussion of obesity and other weight-related issues and continues with information on lesser known physical issues, such as lupus and sickle-cell disease, that are prominent in the lives of African American adolescent females. The section also includes descriptions of intervention programs designed to improve the physical health and well-being of African American adolescent females.

African American Adolescent Females and Weight Issues

According to data released by the Youth Risk Behavior Survey YRBS (2012), 13.0% of U.S. adolescents are obese. Statistically, the prevalence of obesity is higher among African American adolescent females. Table 2.1 provides comparative data on the occurrence of obesity among African American adolescent females and their counterparts from other racial and ethnic groups. As the table illustrates, in the past twenty years for all adolescent females there has been an increase in the percentage classified as obese; however, the percentage of change or increase in obesity has been greater for African American adolescent females.

Although obesity is the major national concern, the rise in the number of adolescents identified as overweight is becoming a growing concern for health care professionals. This is due to the current estimates indicating that 15.2% of U.S. adolescents are considered overweight (YRBS, 2012). Unfortunately, the incidence is much higher among African American adolescent females (19.6%) than Hispanic females (18.0%) or White females (13.8%).

What factors account for the differences in the obesity rates and other weight-related issues among the adolescents? Although there is no general consensus, health care professionals and other researchers argue that it may be the complex relationship between genetic and environmental factors (Adkins, Sherwood, Story & Davis, 2004). However, the majority of research has focused on exploring the modifiable environmental factors contributing to obesity. For example, Hess-Biber, Howling, Leavy & Lovejoy (2004) examined cultural attitudes toward body weight and body image and observed that African American adolescent females in comparison to White adolescent females express more positive attitudes about having a heavier body weight. Furthermore, in

Table 2.1.
Prevalence of obesity among girls age 12–19 years, by race and ethnicity, United States 1988–1994 and 2009–2010

	1988–1994	2009–2010
White	8.9%	14.7%
Black	16.3%	24.8%
Latina	13.4%	18.6%

Source: Centers for Disease Control National Center for Health Statistics/National Health and Nutrition Examination Survey III.

contrast to White adolescent females, African American adolescent females are less likely to describe themselves as being overweight (YRBS, 2012). While both African American and White adolescent females indicate a desire to be thinner, African American adolescent females are more likely to discuss positive aspects of their current bodies and adopt heavier body image ideals. Others have explored level of physical activity and found that African American adolescent females are less likely to engage in physical activity than are their counterparts from other racial and ethnic groups. Additional data from the YRBS (2012) indicate that 26% of African American adolescent females, in comparison to 13% of White females and 21% of Hispanic females, do not participate in 60 minutes of daily physical activity. McNutt, Hu, Schreiber, Crawford, Obarzanek & Melinn (1997) focused on healthy eating habits and observed that African American adolescent females in comparison to White adolescent females and Hispanic adolescent females are less likely to engage in healthy eating and less likely to make healthy eating choices.

In light of these findings, health care professionals and researchers have developed intervention programs specifically targeting African American adolescent females. These programs are quite diverse with respect to goals and target behavior. For example, there are programs that target adolescents and focus on encouraging healthy eating and encouraging participation in exercise, such as *Butterfly Girls* (see Thompson et al., 2013 for a complete description of the program). Similarly *Black Girls Run* is a grassroots program designed to promote physical activity among African American adolescent females. In contrast, there are programs which include the adolescent and their families, and employ a multi-focused approach which includes providing the family information on healthy eating, physical activity, and ways in which to incorporate these changes within the family context. A comprehensive review of family-focused programs found that participation in the programs resulted in short-term weight reduction for the adolescents. Lastly, there are programs that are embedded in ongoing community support programs for adolescents. One such program, *Lively Ladies,* is a ten-week after-school program with a specific focus on increasing the physical activity of African American adolescent females through mentoring, modeling, and reinforcement.

While some African American adolescent females participate in the structured programs described above, 55% of African American adolescent females make attempts to lose weight on their own. Such methods include refraining from eating as opposed to taking diet pills, laxatives, or vomiting.

African American Adolescent Females and Asthma

Asthma is the most common chronic illness of childhood and adolescence (Harris & Graham, 2007). The number of children and adolescents diagnosed with moderate to severe asthma has increased in the past several decades and unfortunately, a disproportionate number of these children and adolescents are African American. The incidence of asthma is higher in African American adolescent females than in White or Hispanic adolescent females. African American adolescents who suffer from severe asthma are more likely to miss school, experience frequent hospitalizations, and suffer from severe disability. They are also four to six times more likely to die from asthma than are their White age mates. African American children and African American adolescents have an annual rate of hospitalization of 199.2 per 10,000 compared to 54.8 per 10,000 for White children (see National Asthma Association Web site for more information: www.lungusa.org).

According to many health care professionals, it is difficult to treat adolescents with asthma. This is due in part to their cognitive level, as they deny the disease has a serious impact on their functioning, and due in part to their tendency to underreport symptoms, as well as resistance to adhere to a medical regimen and treatment program. Furthermore, they engage in risk-taking behaviors that at times exacerbate their symptoms.

Varied interventions have been designed to focus on the specific developmental needs and level of adolescents. Capitalizing on adolescents and their use of technology, some researchers have developed reminder apps to remind them to take their medication. Other interventions have focused on the adolescents and educating their caregivers about warning signs of asthma (American Psychological Association, 2008).

African American Adolescent Females and Lupus

Lupus is classified as an autoimmune disease with symptoms that include fatigue, fever, rashes, and joint pain. Lupus can lead to serious organ damage, and occurs more often in women than in men. It strikes 1 in 500 African American females compared to 1 in 1,000 White females. According to the results of a recent study, African American women are more likely to be diagnosed with lupus at younger ages, especially during adolescence and during childbearing years, and experience greater rates of kidney failure and other neurological problems. Thus physicians recommend that adolescents with lupus refrain from taking high dose estrogen birth control because estrogen intensifies the symptoms of lupus. Adolescents with lupus are also discouraged from smoking and drinking alcohol. It seems that alcohol and nicotine minimize the effectiveness of drugs used to treat lupus. Adolescents are also cautioned against engaging in high-risk activities such as tattooing and body piercing due to the increased risk of infection. Some medications prescribed for lupus suppress the immune system, and consequently the body cannot effectively fight infections that might result from tattooing and body piercing.

While there are few programs specifically targeting African American adolescent females, health care professionals maintain that there is a continued need to understand the etiology and course of the disease in African American females in general and African American adolescent females in particular, given the early onset of the disease and given its impact on reproductive health. The Lupus Foundation of America provides resources and outreach to women and adolescents affected with lupus.

African American Adolescent Females and Sickle-Cell Disease

Sickle-cell disease (SCD) is a generic term applied to a group of genetic disorders characterized by the production of abnormal hemoglobin molecules (Harris & Graham, 2007). Normal blood cells are oval or round in shape; the red blood cells of those with the disease are sickled in shape and vascular occlusion occurs when sickled red blood cells create blockages in the capillaries (Galloway & Harwood-Nuss, 1988). The disease primarily affects individuals of African and Mediterranean ancestry, and current estimates indicate that 1 out of 400 African American adolescent females are affected with the disease. There are a host of physical, cognitive, and social complications experienced by adolescents as a consequence of the disease. Many are at risk for stroke, and some experience continual episodes of pain, which necessitate frequent hospitalizations, while others encounter cognitive and learning problems. Perhaps the most challenging aspect of the disease for African American adolescent females is the experience of delayed puberty. Maturing off time brings with it a host of psychological challenges; however for African American adolescent females, maturing off time, coupled with the persistent debilitating effects of the disease, may bring a different set of mental health problems.

Fortunately, in the past twenty years medical researchers and psychologists have turned their attention to designing effective medical treatment protocols, and psychologists are developing new approaches to treat the mental health challenges associated with SCD. For more information on the disease visit the SCD website.

SECTION TWO: AFRICAN AMERICAN ADOLESCENT FEMALES AND SEXUAL BEHAVIOR

This section discusses the sexual behavior of African American adolescent females. The section begins with a discussion on the number of

African American adolescent females engaging in sexual behavior, continues with a discussion of contraceptive use, sexually transmitted disease, pregnancy outcomes, and sexual violence, and concludes with a discussion of intervention programs for safe sexual behavior designed for African American adolescent females.

Engagement in Sexual Activity

In the last twenty years, the percentage of African American adolescents in general and the percentage of African American adolescent females engaging in sexual activity has decreased. In 1991, 78% of African adolescent females engaged in sexual activity and this percentage decreased to 60% in 2011. There has also been a decline in the last twenty years in the percentage of African American adolescent females reporting having multiple sexual partners, a rise in the percentage reporting that they delay engaging in sexual activity, and a drop in the percentage who report that they are currently sexually active (falling from 55% to 37% in 2011).

Contraception Use

The percentage of African American adolescent females using contraceptives has increased in the last twenty years. The change has been most obvious in their use of condoms. In 1991 only 40% of African American female adolescents used a condom and that percentage rose to 54% in 2011. Currently 64% of sexually active African American female adolescents report using condoms during sexual intercourse. In fact using condoms seems to be their preferred birth control method. That is, in contrast to White adolescent females, they are less likely to use birth control pills as a contraceptive method.

Sexually Transmitted Diseases

Approximately 3 million adolescents acquire a sexually transmitted disease each year (Bachanas et al., 2002). Unfortunately African American adolescents, especially those who reside in urban areas, have the highest rates of sexually transmitted infections (STIs). African American females are more likely than White adolescent females to become infected with an STD. According to the CDC, African American female adolescents between the ages of 15 and 19 have the highest rates of syphilis and gonorrhea.

African American adolescent females are also considered to be the fastest growing group of adolescents diagnosed with HIV/AIDS. They comprise 73% of the 13–19-year-olds diagnosed with HIV, and 66% of those diagnosed with AIDS between the ages of 13 and 19. Why is this rate higher for African American adolescent females? Many researchers have attempted to address and answer this question. Miller-Johnson and colleagues (1999) propose that African American females, in comparison to those who don't experience emotional or behavior problems, are more likely to engage in high-risk sexual behavior. This places them at risk for acquiring the virus, and other sexually transmitted diseases. Alternately others maintain that there are social and other environmental factors that place African American adolescent females at risk for acquiring the virus and other sexually transmitted diseases. Social support seems to serve as a buffer. That is, African American adolescent females with social support are less likely to engage in risky sexual behavior; however, those who have peers who engage in risky sexual behavior are more likely to engage in high-risk sexual behavior as well (Black, Ricardo & Stanton, 1997). Others have observed that African American adolescent females who are substance abusers are at risk for acquiring an STI or HIV/AIDS. Some researchers have noted that a traumatic experience such as rape is correlated with the engagement in risky sexual behavior for African American adolescent females (Lang et al., 2011). Lastly, it may be lack of knowledge about the manner in which STIs and HIV/AIDS are acquired. Data suggest that only 12.9% of African American adolescents report receiving HIV/AIDS education. Consequently efforts have been introduced by several community groups, health care professionals, and organizations which specifically target African American adolescent females.

Pregnancy and Outcomes

Table 2.2 provides information on the pregnancy rates for all U.S. adolescent females including information about pregnancy outcomes for 2011.

In general, the pregnancy rate for U.S. adolescent females independent of ethnic background has declined and the rate for African American adolescent females has decreased by 51% from 1991 to 2009. The current rate for African American adolescent females is 110 per 1,000 and this compares to 40 per 1,000 for White adolescent females, and 102 per 1,000 for Hispanic adolescent females.

Table 2.2.
Pregnancy Outcomes by Ethnicity (2011)

	Pregnancy	Live Birth	Abortion	Fetal Loss
White, Non-Hispanic	40	30	10	5
Black, Non-Hispanic	115	60	50	15
Hispanic	100	70	12	15

Source: Centers for Disease Control and Prevention.

The table also illustrates that while African American adolescent females have the highest pregnancy rates, they do not have the highest live birth rates. Hispanic adolescent females have the highest live birth rates, whereas African American adolescent females have the highest abortion rates.

Sexual Violence

Sexual assault and violence are far too common in the lives of African American adolescent females. According to Lang and colleagues (2011), approximately one in three African American adolescent females report encountering some form of sexual assault. Hence they are at risk for experiencing a host of mental health problems that sometimes go untreated as a result of their reluctance to report and discuss their rape.

Prevention/Intervention Programs

Many programs designed to reduce sexual activity in teens have surfaced in the last twenty years. A sampling of those programs, the three discussed below, were selected for discussion in the chapter because they employ creative and integrative approaches to discussing issues and consequences of sexual behavior with the adolescents, and each program provides information on the effectiveness of their program. Additional information on prevention and intervention programs designed for African American adolescent females can be obtained from the Centers for Disease Control Website.

Becoming a Responsible Teen (BART) is a community-based program designed primarily for African American teens aged 14–18. The program consists of eight sessions with a focus on HIV/AIDS prevention and pregnancy prevention. The adolescents are involved in group discussion and role-playing activities to develop their communication and decision-making skills about such issues as sexual behavior, HIV/STD, and pregnancy prevention. Evaluation of the program indicates that one year after program completion, participants delayed having sexual intercourse, increased their use of condoms, and there was a decrease in pregnancy rates as well as STI rates.

The *Preventing AIDS through Live Movement and Sound (PALMS) Project* advocates for practicing safe sex. The program was facilitated by peers, and program participants engaged in role playing and group discussion activities. Six months after the program, participants had increased knowledge about HIV and condom use.

Sisters Saving Sisters is a clinic-based program designed for urban African American and Latina female adolescents with the goals of providing them with information on STIs, HIV/AIDS, and safe sexual practices.

Follow-up evaluation data suggest that program participants increased their condom use, decreased the number of sexual partners, and there was a decrease in the rates of reported STIs.

SECTION THREE: AFRICAN AMERICAN ADOLESCENT FEMALES AND MENTAL HEALTH ISSUES

Adolescent mental health has received considerable attention in the media. This is due in part to the recent waves of school shootings, mall shootings, and theater shootings and due in part to the realization and the acknowledgment that the stigma associated with mental health problems and other social and economic barriers prevents many families from seeking treatment. Consequently there has been a collective effort by politicians, researchers, and health care professionals to find ways to reduce the stigma, and to increase accessibility to mental health care for adolescents and their families.

There is also growing interest in the mental health functioning and well-being of African American adolescents in general and African American adolescent females in particular. This may be the result of the recent findings released by YRBS (2012) suggesting that African American females in comparison to African American adolescent males report frequently experiencing episodes of sadness and depression. Evidence suggests that the suicide rate among African American preteens and teens age 10–14 has increased by 233% over the past fifteen years. In the particular case of African American adolescent females, they express more suicidal ideation than White adolescent females and African American adolescent males. That is, African American adolescent females are more likely than White adolescent females and African American adolescent males to make a suicide plan and more likely to have seriously considered a suicide attempt.

Researchers have begun to explore this trend in depression and suicide ideation in African American females and observed that these mental health problems tend to co-occur with body dissatisfaction, sexual assault, experiences with community violence, and such physical illnesses as sickle-cell anemia and lupus.

Treatment approaches for African American adolescent females are diverse in nature. Some focus on individualized counseling using a cognitive behavioral orientation. One such program is called *Seeking Safety*, which shows promise in working with African American adolescent females diagnosed with either PTSD (post-traumatic stress disorder) or a substance use disorder. This form of psychotherapy involves assisting the clients in developing new cognitive tools, adopting new behaviors, and working on interpersonal relationships. Other approaches have been community-based efforts. *Rise Sister Rise* (Frazier et al., 2011) located in Dayton,

Ohio, is an example of such an effort. This program pairs the adolescents with community women who serve as mentors and sounding boards. The program also offers information on mental health service providers in the community.

SECTION FOUR: CONCLUSIONS AND NEXT STEPS

There is compelling evidence to suggest that obesity is the number one health concern for African American adolescent females. Therefore any health goals for the twenty-first century for this population must focus on developing ecologically valid, culturally anchored, and developmentally centered prevention and intervention programs. That is, those programs must be designed to take into account their cognitive and social levels, and their cultural attitudes toward weight. The programs must also be tailored to their unique environmental constraints and challenges.

There have been impressive changes in the sexual behavior of African American adolescent females. However, they are the fastest growing group of adolescents diagnosed with STIs and HIV/AIDS. Research must be devoted to determining and disentangling the environmental, attitudinal, and situational factors that are related to these findings.

There are also few comprehensive studies providing detailed information on the mental health challenges unique to African American adolescent females. One area in particular ripe for investigation is suicide ideation. Research should be designed to identify the precise proximal and distal factors that influence suicidal ideation in African American adolescent females. In addition, as Joe and colleagues (2009) recommend, there needs to be better training for clinicians in identifying suicidal behavior in African American adolescent females.

REFERENCES

Adkins, S., Sherwood, N., Story, M., & Davis M. (2004). Physical activity among African American Girls: The role of parents and the home environment. *Obesity Research*, 12, 38S–45S.

American Psychological Association. (2008). Risk and resilience in African American children. Washington, DC: APA.

Bachanas, P., Morris, M., Lewis-Gess, J., Sarett-Cuasay, E., Sirl, K., Ries, J., & Sawyer, K. (2002). Predictors of risky sexual behavior in african american adolescent girls: implications for prevention interventions. *Journal of Pediatric Psychology*, 6, 519–530.

Black, M., Ricardo, I., & Stanton, B. (1997). Social and psychological factors associated with AIDS risk behaviors among low income urban, African American adolescents. *Journal of Research on Adolescence*, 7, 173–195.

Boyington, J., Cater-Edwars, L., Piehl, M., Hutson, J., Langdon, D., & McManus, S. (2008). Cultural attitudes toward weight, diet and physical activity among overweight African American girls. *Preventing Chronic Disease: Public Health Research, Practice and Policy*, 5, 1–9.

Frazier, F. C., Belliston, L. M., Brower, L. A., & Knudsen, K. (2011). Placing Black girls at promise: A report of the Rise Sister Rise study. Executive Summary. Columbus, OH: Report from the Ohio Department of Mental Health.

Galloway, S., & Harwood-Nuss, A. (1988). Sickle-cell anemia: A review. *Journal of Emergency Medicine*, 6, 213–226.

Harris, Y. R., & Graham, J. A. (2007). *The African American Child Development and Challenges*. New York: Springer Publishers.

Hesse-Biber, S., Howling, S., Leavy, P., & Lovejoy, M. (2004). Racial identity and the development of body image issues among African American adolescent girls. *The Qualitative Report*, 9, 49–79.

Joe, S., Baser, R., Neighbors, H., Caldwell, C., & Jackson, J. (2009). 12-month and lifetime prevalence of suicide attempts among Black adolescents in the National Survey of America Life. *Journal of the American Academy of Child & Adolescent Psychiatry*, 48, 271–282.

Lang, D., Sales, J., Salazar, L., Hardin, J., DiClemente, R., Winggood, G., & Rose, E. (2011). Rape victimization and high risk sexual behaviors: longitudinal study of african american adolescent females. *Western Journal of Emergency Medicine*, 12, 333–342.

McNutt, S., Hu, Y., Schreiber, G., Crawford, P., Obarzanek, E., & Mellin, L. (1997). A longitudinal study of the dietary practices of Black and White girls 9 and 10 old at enrollment: the NHLBI Growth and Health Study. *Journal of Adolescent Health* 20, 27–37.

Miller-Johnson, S., Winn, D., Cole, J., Maumary, G., Hyman, C., Terry, D., & Lochman, J. (1999). Motherhood during the teen years: A developmental perspective on risk factors for childrearing. *Development and Psychopathology*, 11, 85–100.

Thompson, D., Mahabir, R., Bhatt, R., Boutte, C., Cantu, D., Vasquez, I., Callender, C., Cullen, K., Baranowki, T., Liu, Y., Waler, C., & Buday, R. (2013). Butterfly Girls: Promoting healthy diet and physical activity to young African American girls online: rational and design. *BMC Public Health*, 13, 709.

Youth Risk Behavior Surveillance (2012). Morbidity and Mortality Weekly Report, 61, 1–168.

Chapter 3

The Challenges Facing Sickle-Cell Disease (SCD) Patients during the Transitional Period from Adolescence to Adulthood

Cassandra E. Dobson

INTRODUCTION

Transitional care from adolescence to adult care for Sickle-Cell Disease (SCD) patients has been challenging over the last few decades, despite the fact that SCD has achieved notable success in the progress of the treatment, care, and research. Medical science has come a long way in improving the lives of patients with SCD since the discovery of the sickle-cell gene over 110 years ago, yet these patients were given a check that was returned marked insufficient treatment and insufficient funding. One of the successes is that patients with SCD are living longer. In 1910, Dr. James Herrick first described the "sickle-shaped cell" from a blood sample of a dental student. Dr. Herrick was intrigued by what he had seen under the microscope and wrote about the "peculiar elongated and sickle-shaped red blood corpuscles" (Herrick, 2001).

Since Dr. Herrick's findings of the "sickled cell," many other discoveries have impacted the study and treatment of the disease. The development of neonatal screening in 1973 allowed early and preventive care for SCD patients. In addition, other innovative treatments for SCD allowed children who have SCD to have improved quality of life and, most importantly, increased life spans (National Institutes of Health [NIH], 2012). The innovative treatments began to emerge with bone marrow transplants in 1984. In 1986, the use of penicillin was shown to reduce the incidence of Streptococcus pneumonia infection, which has been reported to be a major cause of death for SCD children from birth to age 3–5 (Quinn, Rogers, McCavit & Buchanan, 2010; United States Department of Health and Human Services [USDHHS], 2010). In 1995, Hydroxyurea (HU) was first used for the management of sickle-cell crises pain. The use of HU was approved by the Federal Drug Administration (FDA) and has been reported to be effective to increase fetal hemoglobin which can decrease the frequency of pain crises (Deepika & Panepinto, 2012). There was initially some concern over the use of HU by sickle-cell patients, which resulted from lack of education regarding the drug, safety, and efficacy data for younger patients with SCD (Department of Health and Human Services: National Institute of Health [DHHS:NIH] News, 2008). Some patients are aware that the drug is a chemotherapeutic medication and have refused to take the medication based on that premise. Other patients are afraid of the side effects that HU may have on them, since it has been linked with the treatment for cancer patients. As a result, only a small percentage of SCD patients are currently reported to be taking HU. However, those patients taking HU have reported it to be beneficial in increasing hemoglobin F (HgbF). As a result, HU has shown significant decrease in painful crises (International Association of Sickle-Cell Nurses and Physician Assistants, 2008; DHHS & NIH News, 2008).

Due to these incredible scientific innovations for the treatment of SCD, children's life spans have improved tremendously. Children who were expected to die before their teenage years are now living past their eighteenth birthdays and way beyond into their forties and fifties (NIH, 2012; Koshy & Dorn, 1996). Patients with SCD are surviving into adulthood and their life expectancy has increased greatly. The mean age has increased for patients with Hgb (SS), the most severe form of sickle-cell disease, from age 10 to age 45, and has increased to age 60 in Hgb (SC), a milder form of sickle-cell disease (Platt, 1992; Athale & Chintu, 1994). As a result of the change in the life expectancy for the SCD patients where their survival rate has increased from pediatrics to adolescence and as children grow out of their pediatrician's care, it seems that the care they once received that has allowed them to reach adolescence is now no longer available. Some adolescents continue to visit their pediatrician for health care way into adulthood, causing further delay in the transitional process (Fortuna, Halterman, Pulcino & Robbins, 2012), while others are found without appropriate physicians who know and care about treating SCD patients.

PURPOSE

This chapter will provide some insight into some of the challenges faced by SCD adolescent patients who now have grown out of the pediatrician care and are thrown into a world where no preparation has been made for transitional care. Most importantly, there are few hematologists interested in caring for sickle-cell patients. Society has placed these patients in a box and has formulated a culture of ethnic stigmatization against this population. Such patients have been labeled as "drug seekers" and "frequent flyers." Most damaging of all is to label the disease as a "black disease" or "bad blood." These labels are just a few, but they have caused tremendous physical and psychological pain in the SCD population.

Etiology of Sickle-Cell Disease

SCD is an inherited chronic blood disorder that results from a defective hemoglobin gene that is referred to as hemoglobin S (HbS). This inherited hemoglobin gene can range from the benign form sickle-cell trait to the debilitating and often fatal sickle-cell anemia (Ellison, 2012). The hallmark of the disease is severe, recurrent painful episodes that are a result of occlusions of small blood vessels by the red cells that are sickled, resulting in anemia (Children's Hospital and Regional Medical Center, 2006; Ballas, 2007; Fosdal & Wojner-Alexandrov, 2007). However, there are many other complications associated with SCD, such as severe infections, acute chest syndrome, pneumonia, and strokes (Vichinsky et al., 2000). These conditions can be life-threatening if left untreated, but when detected early some conditions can be managed or even prevented (Charache, Lubin & Reid, 1992). According to the National Institutes of Health (NIH, 2002), the presentation of the disease and its symptoms may change with age, and the course of the disease may vary between patients, which makes treating SCD more challenging.

Sickle-cell disease affects primarily African Americans (AA) in the United States; however, it is not uncommon for SCD to be found in other cultures and ethnicities, such as the Mediterranean, the Caribbean, South and Central American, Chinese, Middle Eastern, and Indian (Newland, 2008). Sickle-cell disease also affects all ages on the health spectrum (Charache, Lubin & Reid, 1992).

Transitional Care for SCD Adolescents

The average sickle-cell patient is identified early in life with a serious illness and is placed in a high-risk group. Such a patient is given aggressive medical care initially; however, as the child reaches adolescence, certain changes such as social, emotional, and behavioral problems occur, which interfere with his or her ability to receive appropriate health care (Adedoyin, 1992). As the adolescent reaches adulthood even more devastating emotional and psychosocial changes occur that interrupt health care or even terminate it.

Transitional care is essential to facilitate the progression of health-centered care from adolescence to adulthood for the patient with sickle-cell disease as well as to maximize functioning and well-being (Scal et al., 1998). The desired outcome of the transitional period is to assure that each adolescent with sickle-cell disease continues to receive uninterrupted health care that is designed to meet his or her growing needs. For the adolescent with sickle-cell disease, early placement into a transitional program will provide complete comprehensive care, thus providing the health care provider with the knowledge vital in the treatment and management of this complex disease, especially when the patient continues to live longer.

Transitional Period

The transitional period is defined as the purposeful, planned movement of adolescents and young adults with a chronic condition from pediatric to adult health care (Musumadi, Westerdale & Appleby, 2012). The age may vary during this period and can range from age 16 to 25. The identified ages that were established for transitional care are 13 through 20. These ages were decided upon based on the scientific review of the literature that takes into account the cognitive and developmental stages of the adolescent.

A review of the growth and developmental constructs provided insights into this complex topic. A useful foundation for understanding adolescents' transition challenges and for developing strategies for assisting them and their families is made clear through such theorists as Erikson (1959), Rutter (1989), and Bandura (1997).

The transitional period is the stage in life when persons move from late adolescence to young adulthood (Davis & Stoep, 1997). This age may range from 14 to 25 depending on the developmental age of the adolescent (Davis & Stoep, 1997; Betz, 1998). The transitional period is a very challenging period for the adolescent who is faced with many developmental changes. The changes that occur during the developmental stages are commonly divided into three phases. The first stage is known as early adolescence which is characterized by the onset of puberty. The age ranges from 13 to 14 and there is notable growth spurt during this stage. The adolescent's primary concern revolves around body image and same-sex friendships. These two concepts are very important to the adolescent (Larson, 1990; Eccles, 1999; Erikson, 1959). During this stage the adolescent may want to separate from the family; however, he or she may continue to rely on the family for decision making or to intercede on his or her behalf (Larson, 1990; Erikson, 1959).

Middle adolescence, the ages between 14 and 16, is the most difficult as the adolescent growth is almost complete and there is the struggle for independence and conflict with sexual identity. The adolescent looks for approval in behavior and appearance from the opposite sex (Eccles, 1999). The adolescent can be characterized by several attributes during this stage. One such attribute frequently associated with the mid-adolescent is commonly referred to as the "seesaw personality" where the adolescent exhibits infantile dependency on one end of the spectrum to complete independence on the other end. This frequent flip in personality often causes confusion and conflict in the family. At this stage, however, the adolescent is said to be secure and is able to make most of his decisions. Due to the adolescent's need to strive for independence, sickness and hospitalization are not tolerated well and pose the greatest threat because body integrity and peer group relations are threatened during this stage. The power of control is lost and the dependency role is overbearing (Larson, 1990; Erikson, 1959).

The third stage is known as late adolescence and is between the ages 16 and 21. The adolescent is characterized by maturity and the major concern that surrounds the adolescent is his future plans. The adolescent is making his own decisions during this period, and is now more likely to take advice from parents and other adults (Larson, 1990; Erikson, 1959). The age for when a child becomes an adolescent may vary from author to author, but the underlying meaning remains the same, which is the period where the individual passes from childhood into adulthood (Kinney & Ware, 1996). The normal course that the adolescent will face can be very challenging, having to deal with many issues that confront him/her such as peer pressure, violence, and sexual identity. When the adolescent has a chronic disease those challenges are even more devastating. The adolescent with a chronic disease like sickle-cell disease may have a difficult time navigating the process of transition into adult life (Shultz & Liptak, 1998). There are common concerns, such as race and having a "black disease," high rates of morbidity, mortality, and other poor social and health outcomes (Telfair, Myers & Drezner, 1994; Kinney & Ware, 1996).

Challenges Facing SCD Adolescents during the Transitional Period

Lack of Readiness

Although the evidence shows that patient readiness should be the first step in the transitional process, it is often avoided and it is rare that the pediatric providers take the appropriate steps in preparing the adolescent

(Lebensburger, Bemrich-Stolz & Howard, 2012). There is often no individual assessment for readiness during the transitional period, but rather the transitional phase is based on the chronologic age of the child. It is not uncommon for adolescents with SCD to be unprepared for the transitional process. McPherson, Thaniel, and Minniti (2009) reported that insufficient knowledge and anticipatory guidance were barriers to the transitional process. The assessment of patient readiness is determined by how well the patient understands her medical history, feelings about the transitional process, and where medical care will be received. However, little evidence is found on how to engage patients successfully in transition and the enhancement of patients' ability to initiate specific behavioral change (Lebensburger, Bemrich-Stolz & Howard, 2012). The readiness assessment score ranked the lowest on the five components of readiness assessment with a mean score of 0.88 out of a possible score of 4 points (95%, CI= 0.66–1.09). Patients with SCD continue to show insufficient readiness for transition during adolescence. The adolescent and family must be identified for readiness before the transition process is started (Cappelli, MacDonald & McGrath, 1989). The adolescent must first begin to accept health care responsibility from his/her parent and guardian, as well as accept the concept of transitional care, which is a critical part of behavioral change (Lebensburger, Bemrich-Stolz & Howard, 2012; Schidlow & Fiel, 1990).

Inadequate Planning

Interventions must be carefully planned. The planning phase is essential to provide needed information about the adolescent/family. Because the SCD patients are rarely prepared to be transitioned from adolescent to adult care, there is a sense of inadequate planning. There must be a timely transfer of records and other documents for the patient. Education must be provided to the personnel who will be directly involved with the patient, especially emergency room staff. Patients should be assessed for disease knowledge as well. The social workers', genetic counselors', and registered nurses' roles will be significant during this phase. Patients must gradually learn how to take part in their own health care. Early intervention should be provided when maladaptive behaviors are identified. Certain barriers must be identified and resolved if the transition is to be successful (Shultz & Liptak, 1998). Research has shown that when conflicts are identified and interventions are provided early, the results are often positive (Shultz & Liptak,1998).

Locating Adult Health Care Providers

There continues to be a lack of adult health care providers who are knowledgeable or comfortable in caring for young adolescents with SCD.

In the transitional period there have to be some strategies that will promote an increase in provider expertise and commitment to care for the SCD patients (Lebensburger, Bemrich-Stolz & Howard, 2012). Due to the increase in life span, many patients are without adequate medical care and psycho-social support. It is reported that many adult patients with SCD have difficulty gaining access to the adult medical care system (Athale & Chintu, 1994). As the sickle-cell patient gets older, health care providers often feel poorly prepared to care for these patients. This is a direct result of the unexpected increased life expectancy for the sickle-cell patients and other disparity in health care when it comes to caring for patients with SCD. Many patients are not adequately prepared mentally, emotionally, and financially to live with a chronic disease (Platt, 1992; Gil, Wilson & Edens, 1997). There are reports of sickle-cell patients having difficulties receiving age-appropriate care outside of pediatric sickle-cell centers (Blum & Okinow 1993; Rosen, 1994). These patients have difficulty living functional adult lives and set few or no accomplishable goals, while other patients exhibit passive coping skills and are reported to have limited insights into their disease. Sickle-cell patients are stigmatized by their disease, are often disrespected by the health care team, and are often said to be non-compliant with treatment regimens (Telfair, Myers & Drezner, 1994; Haywood, 2013). Although the need for transitional programs for chronic diseases and other disabilities has received increased attention over the last few decades, there has been an inadequate focus in this area for patients with sickle-cell disease (Fortuna, Halterman, Pulcino & Robbins, 2012).

Obtaining Appropriate Health Insurance

Since SCD is considered a chronic disability, oftentimes the health insurance that is provided for SCD is social security benefits, which include Medicaid. The quality of care that is essential for the SCD patients can be affected by the type of insurance they have. Having Medicaid has placed the SCD patients in a low socioeconomic status, which locks such patients out when it comes to receiving quality health care. Some patients fall short of having comprehensive health care and often fall into the health care gaps without appropriate health care. It is reported that African Americans (AA) experience health care differently than other groups in the United States (Byrd & Clayton, 2003). This evidence is still being seen in the SCD population today. There continues to be differential treatment of SCD versus other chronic diseases. People with diseases that affect the "white cells," which affect more Caucasians than AA, continually get more appropriate medical treatment, financial support, and are respected by the medical team, despite their bouts with severe and chronic pain. The disease of the "red cells," on the other hand, which affects mostly AA as well as other ethnic groups from different cultures, seems to experience continual struggles to receive the same treatments and respect.

IN SUMMARY

There are many challenges that continue to face adolescents with SCD who are in the transitional period. Despite the innovation in the treatment, care, and research of SCD, there seems to be very little attention that is placed on the adolescents' ability to transition to adult care. The adolescents with SCD are often faced with stigmatization. Very little respect is given to the SCD patients by the health care team. In addition, there are very few hematologists who understand the disease process of SCD. There is rarely any preparation provided to the adolescent before transitioning occurs. Many adolescents lack readiness and continue to receive care from their pediatrician far into their adult years. Due to the chronicity of the disease, adolescents are rarely able to hold long-lasting employment, which further places them in the position of not receiving the appropriate quality of health care that is required and necessary to maintain quality of life. Most commonly the insurance of choice that the SCD patient will be qualified for is Medicaid, which leaves the adolescent without the appropriate health care.

RECOMMENDATION

It is of utmost importance for hospitals and community health care centers to design appropriate transitional programs, starting from pediatric care in order to aid in assisting the adolescent in overcoming many of the challenges that he/she will face during the crucial adolescence period. The adolescent should be given the opportunity to prepare, adapt, adjust, and cope with the new challenges that he/she will need to combat in order to meet his/her present and future health needs. More research is needed to investigate the best evidence in preparing and transitioning adolescents to adult care effectively. Additional funding needs to be directed specifically for the transitional period that is essential to the care for the SCD patients.

In 2004 a comparison was made between funding for sickle-cell disease and cystic fibrosis (CF). At that time, there were an estimated 80,000 patients with sickle-cell disease and 30,000 patients with cystic fibrosis. However, NIH and the private sector funding agencies provided funding that was disproportionate to that for SCD: CF received a total funding of $128 million versus SCD, which received $90 million. The private sector funding for SCD was $0.5 million and $152.2 million for CF. In essence, patients with SCD received only 12% of the funding per person compared to CF. Only 32% of the total funding was awarded to SCD compared to CF.

There has been consistent underfunding for SCD in both the public and private sectors (Smith, Oyeku, Homer & Zuckerman, 2006).

Sickle-cell disease has been labeled as a "cultural" and "ethnic" disease because the vast majority of people that are affected with SCD are of African descent. Health disparity continues to exist in the treatment and quality of care which has posed some unequal treatment that is directly linked to the majority of AA who have the disease. However, as the trend continues where there is an increase in bi-cultural and bi-racial relationships, over the next decade or so, the faces of SCD will not be able to be defined; there will be a "bi-blood" mixture. The fear of "contaminated" or "Negro blood" in the White community because of "intermarriage" relationships with AA will no longer be a fear of the past, but a reality (Wailoo, 1997). There will be a shift in how the clinical presentation manifests itself, and the faces of SCD will no longer be stigmatized against. Hopefully, this evolution will change the trajectory of care for the SCD population towards better treatment and respect. The only questions that will need to be asked are: Will the treatment of the disease change? Will the funding increase? Will the population at large, especially the health care team, take the patients more seriously when they are calling out in pain? And will doctors find the disease more challenging to treat?

Lastly, many adolescents are not given respect from the health care team, causing further insult to their self-esteem, which may cause disturbances in the stages of development, where identity and role confusion are being resolved. The health care system provisions lack uniformity and continuity of care, especially for the adolescents who are transitioning through the growth spectrum. There continues to be a lack of education, counseling, research, support, community outreach programs, and trained physicians who are needed to meet the growing demands of the adolescent health care needs. The adolescent with SCD deserves the appropriate, individualized care that meets his unique yet complex needs. Many adolescents are not given the appropriate resources during the transitional period that is vital to live a long and healthy life.

It is pertinent that more research be done that will generate funding for adolescents with SCD in order to provide appropriate transitional care. Since these populations of patients are often neglected and are not given the skills needed to navigate the health care system, these patients are left to fend for themselves in the health care arena. A collaborative approach is needed to tackle all of the aspects of transitional care that will be necessary to change the status quo of the adolescent with SCD who requires transitional care.

REFERENCES

Adedoyin, A. M. (1992). Psychosocial effects of sickle cell disease among adolescents. *East African Medical Journal*, July, 370–372.

Athale, H. U., & Chintu, C. (1994). The effect of sickle cell anemia on adolescents and their growth and development—Lessons from the sickle cell clinic. *Journal of Tropical Pediatrics*, 40, 264–252.

Ballas, S. K. (2007). Current issues in sickle cell pain and its management. *American Society of Hematology*, 1, 97–105. doi:10.1182/asheducation-2007.1.97

Bandura, A. (1997). Self-efficacy: Towards a unifying theory of behavioral change. *Psychological Review*, 84, 191–215.

Betz, C. (1998a). Facilitating the transition of adolescents with chronic conditions from pediatric to adult health care and community settings. *Issues in Comprehensive Pediatric Nursing*, 21, 97–115.

Betz, C. (1998b). Adolescent Transitions: A nursing concern. *Pediatric Nursing*, 24:1, 23–29.

Blum, R. W., & Okinow, N. A. (1993). Teenagers at risk: A national perspective of state level services for adolescents with chronic illness of disability: Executive Summary. In: *Connections: The Newsletter of the National Center for Youth with Disabilities*, 3:1(Supplement).

Butler, D. J., & Beltran, L. R. (1993). Functions of an adult sickle cell group: Education, task orientation and support. *Health Social Work*, 18:1, 49–56.

Byrd, W. M., & Clayton, L. (2003). Racial and ethnic disparities in health care: A background history. In *Unequal Treatment: Confronting Racial and Ethnic Disparities in Health Care*, ed. B. D. Smedley, A. Y. Smith, and A. Nelson, 455–527. Washington DC: National Academies Press.

Cappelli, M., MacDonald, N. E., & McGrath, P. J. (1989). Assessment of readiness to transfer to adult care for adolescents with cystic fibrosis. *Children Health Care*. Fall, 18:4, 218–224.

Charache, S., Lubin, B. H., & Reid, C. D. (1992). Management and therapy of sickle cell disease. U. S. Department of Health and Human Services, Public Health Service Publication, No. 84-2117, Washington, D.C., National Institutes of Health.

Children's Hospital and Regional Medical Center. (2006). Sickle cell disease: critical elements of care. 4th ed. www.cshen.org. Retrieved 5/12/2012.

Committee on Children with Disabilities and Committee on Adolescence. (1996). American Academy of Pediatrics: Transition of care provided for Adolescents with special health care needs. *Pediatrics*, 98:6, 1203–1206.

Davis, M., & Stoep, A. (1997). The transition to adulthood for youth who have serious emotional disturbance: Developmental transition and young adult outcomes. *Journal of Mental Health Administration*, Fall, 24:4, 400–426.

Deepika, S. D., & Panepinto, J. A. (2012). What is the evidence that hydroxyurea improves health-related quality of life in patients with sickle cell disease? *American Society of Hematology*, 290–291.

Department of Health and Human Service (DHHS): National Institute of Health News (2008). Panel Finds Hydroxyurea Treatment Is Underutilized for Sickle Cell Disease, *Improved access to care and education about the treatment are deemed priorities*. http://www.nih.gov/news/health/feb2008/od-27.htm. Retrieved 11/2013.

Eccles, J. S. (1999). The development of children ages 6 to 14. The future of children. *When School Is Out*, 9(2), 30–44.

Ellison, A. (2012). Sickle cell disease: Advice on handling emergencies. *Contemporary Pediatrics*, 29 (9), 18–28.

Erikson, E. H. (1959). Identity and the Life Cycle. *Psychological Issues*, 1, 1–71.

Fortuna, R. J., Halterman, J. S., Pulcino, T., & Robbins, B. W. (2012). Delayed transition of care: A national study of visits to pediatricians by young adults. *Academic Pediatrics*, 12 (5), 405–407.

Fosdal, M. D., & Wojner-Alexandrov, A. W. (2007). Events of Hospitalization Among Children with Sickle Cell Disease. *Journal of Pediatric Nursing*, 342–346.

Gil, K., Wilson, J. J., & Edens, J. L. (1997). The stability of pain coping strategies in young children, adolescents, and adults with sickle cell disease over an 18-month period. *Clinical Journal of Pain*, 13:2, 110–115.

Haywood, C. (2013). Disrespectful care in the treatment of sickle cell disease requires more than ethics consultation. *American Journal of Bioethics*, 13 (4), 12–14.

Herrick, J. B. (2001). Peculiar Elongated and Sickle-shaped Red Blood Corpuscles in a Case of Severe Anemia. *Yale Journal of Biology and Medicine: Classics of Biology and Medicine*, 74, 179–184.

International Association of Sickle-Cell Nurses and Physician Assistants. (2008). Nursing Practice Guidelines: Care of the patient with sickle cell disease receiving hydroxyurea. http://www.iascnapa.org. Retrieved 5/23/11.

Kinney, T. R., & Ware, E. R. (1996). The adolescent with sickle cell disease. *Hematology/Oncology Clinics of North America*, 10:5, 1255–1264.

Koshy, M., & Dorn, L. (1996). Continuing care for adult patients with sickle cell disease. *Hematology/ Oncology Clinics of North America*, 10:5, 1265–1273.

Larson, L. A. (1990). The adolescent with chronic illness and hospitalization. *Adolescent Medicine*, 18:3, 56–60.

Lebensburger, J. D., Bemrich-Stolz, C., & Howard, T. H. (2012). Barriers in transition from pediatrics to adult medicine in sickle cell anemia. *Journal of Blood Medicine*, 3, 205–212.

McPherson, M., Thaniel, L., & Minniti, C. P. (2009). Transition of patients with sickle cell disease from pediatric to adult care: Assessing patient readiness. Pediatric Blood Cancer, doi:10.1002/pbc.21974. www.interscience.wiley .com. Retrieved 5/11/11.

Musumadi, L., Westerdale, N., & Appleby, H. (2012). An overview of the effects of sickle cell disease in adolescents. *Nursing Standard*, 26(26), 35–40.

National Institutes of Health. (2002). What is sickle cell disease? http://www .nhlbi.nih.gov/health-topics/topics/sca. Retrieved 10/31/2011.

National Institutes of Health: News in Health. (2012). When blood cells bend: Understanding sickle cell disease. http://newsinhealth.nih.gov/issue/ apr2012/feature2. Retrieved 5/20/2013.

Newland, J. A. (2008). Factors influencing independence in adolescents with sickle cell disease. *Journal of Child and Adolescent Psychiatric Nursing*, 21, 177–185. doi:10.1111/j.1744-6171.2008.00149.x

Platt, O. S. (1992). The national history of sickle cell disease: Life expectancy. Paper presented at the Bone Marrow Transplantation for Hemoglobinopathies Workshop, sponsored by the National Heart, Lung and Blood Institute, NIH, Bethesda, Maryland.

Quinn, C. T., Rogers, Z. R., McCavit, T. L., & Buchanan, G. R. (2010). Improved survival of children and adolescents with sickle cell disease. *Blood*, 115(17). 3447–3452, doi:10.1182/blood-2009-07-233700. Retrieved 10/18/2012.

Rosen, D. S. (1994). Transition from pediatric to adult-oriented health care for the adolescent with chronic illness or disability. *Adolescent Medicine. State of the Art Reviews*, 5:2, 241–248.

Rutter, M. (1989). Pathways from childhood to adult life. *Journal of Child Psychology and Psychiatry*, 30, 23–51.

Scal, P., Evans, T., Blozis, S., Okinow, N., & Blum, R. (1998). Trends in transition from pediatric to adult health care services for young adults with chronic conditions. *Society for Adolescent Medicine*, 24, 254–264.

Schidlow, D., & Fiel, S. B. (1990). Life beyond pediatrics: Transition of chronically ill adolescents from pediatric to adult health care systems. *Adolescent Medicine*, 74:5, 1113–1120.

Shultz, A., & Liptak, G. (1998). Helping adolescents who have disabilities negotiate transitions to adulthood. *Issues in Comprehensive Pediatric Nursing*, 21, 187–210.

Smith, L. A., Oyeku, S. O., Homer, C., & Zuckerman, B. (2006). Sickle Cell Disease: A Question of Equity and Quality. *Pediatrics*, 117, 1763, doi:10.1542/peds.2005-161, pediatrics.aappublications.org. Retrieved 09/2013.

Telfair, J., Myers, J., & Drezner, S. (1994). Transfer as a component of the transition of adolescents with sickle cell disease to adult care: Adolescent, adult, and parent perspectives. *Journal of Adolescent Health*, 15, 558–565.

U.S. Department of Health and Human Services: National Institutes of Health: National Heart, Lung and Blood Institutes. (2010). Publication No. 10-7657.

Vichinsky, E., Neumayr, L., Earles, A., Williams, R., Lennette, E., Dean., D., Nickerson, B., Orringer, E., McKie, V., Bellevue, R., Daeschner, C., & Manci, E. (2000). Causes and outcomes of the acute chest syndrome in sickle cell disease. *New England Journal of Medicine*, 342:25, 1855–1909.

Vichinsky, E. P., Hurst, D., & Lubin, B. H. (2000). Sickle cell disease: Basic concepts. *Hospital Medicine*, 128.

Wailoo, K. A. (1997). *Drawing blood: Technology and disease identity in twentieth-century America*. Baltimore, MD: Johns Hopkins University Press.

Chapter 4

The Never-Ending Pelvic Inflammatory Disease among Adolescents

Denise Linton

INTRODUCTION

Our adolescents are our future; therefore, it is imperative that as a community we seek opportunities to educate them about preventable diseases with the goal of protecting them against such diseases. And, health care providers need to identify and treat diseases which are prevalent among adolescents in their early stages in order to prevent long-term complications. One such disease or condition is pelvic inflammatory disease (PID), which is an infection of the uterus (womb), fallopian tubes (tubes or oviducts), and ovaries with one or more microorganisms (Mackay & Woo, 2014). Additionally, according to Jadack and Georges (2010), PID "is any acute, subacute, recurrent, or chronic infection of the oviducts and ovaries with involvement of the adjacent reproductive organs. . . . It includes inflammation of the cervix (cervicitis), uterus (endometritis), oviducts (salpingitis), and ovaries (oophoritis)" (p. 776). Consequently, the manifestation of the disease varies according to the affected area, but whatever the affected area(s), abdominal pain and vaginal discharge are common complaints.

Infective agents that cause STDs enter the vagina during sexual activity and from there they migrate to the cervix (entrance to the uterus or womb), uterus, fallopian tubes (tubes that carry fertilized eggs from the ovaries to the uterus), and cause pelvic inflammatory disease (PID) (CDC, 2012). In acute PID, clinical manifestation or symptoms may be sudden and severe but they may be less abrupt and less severe in subacute PID. On the other hand, in recurrent PID there are repeated episodes of infection and inflammation, and in chronic PID there are prolonged infection and inflammation. Symptoms may resolve then recur in the former while they persist in the latter. Approximately 750,000 to 1 million cases of PID occur in the United States every year and there is an annual estimated treatment cost of $3.5 to $5 billion (Callahan & Caughey, 2013).

If PID is not treated and/or is recurrent it can result in chronic pelvic pain, infertility (difficulty or inability to get pregnant), and/or ectopic pregnancy (pregnancy outside the uterus or womb) (CDC, 2012). "Twenty-five percent of all women who have had PID eventually experience . . . long-term health problems. Infertility is present in 20% of women who have had PID, and the incidence of ectopic pregnancy is increased six to ten times" (Jadack & Georges, 2010, p. 776). It is apparent that the cycle of "never ending pelvic inflammatory disease among adolescents" needs to be broken.

RISK FACTORS FOR PELVIC INFLAMMATORY DISEASE

PID is more common among females who are 25 years of age and younger and those who are minority (MacKay & Woo, 2014). Additionally, females who douche, have had an intrauterine device (IUD) inserted, surgery in the pelvic area, abortion, who have sex at an early age, multiple sex partners, and/or sexually transmitted infections (STIs) are more likely to have PID (Jadack & Georges, 2010; Livengood & Chacko, 2012). Other vaginal infections such as bacterial vaginosis increase the risk or likelihood for PID (Mete, Yenal, Tokat & Secekus, 2012). Bacterial vaginosis is more common among females who douche. Females douche by introducing a solution, for example vinegar solution, into the vagina in order to cleanse the vagina and/or reduce malodor in the vaginal area. This practice tends to be cultural, but unfortunately douching alters the protective acidic environment in the vagina and increases the possibility of infections (Mete, Yenal, Tokat & Secekus, 2012). PID is less common among women who use barrier and oral contraception (Callahan & Caughey, 2013).

PID among Adolescents

PID is a serious issue among our adolescents because they engage in high-risk behaviors. Furthermore, "despite the high rates of infections documented in the adolescent population, providers frequently fail to inquire about sexual behaviors, assess STD risks, provide risk reduction counseling, and ultimately, fail to screen for asymptomatic infections during clinical encounters" (CDC, 2010, p. 10). And, the adolescent female is at increased risk of being infected with STDs and subsequently PID because of her immune system and her anatomy. The immune system of the adolescents is unaccustomed to STIs so they succumb to diseases when they become infected (Browner-Elhanan & Coupey, 1999; Steele, Yen & Wang, 2013). Additionally, their immature cervical cells are more susceptible to STIs, especially chlamydia and gonorrhea, compared to their adult counterpart who possesses mature cervical cells (Browner-Elhanan & Coupey, 1999; Steele, Yen & Wang, 2013). The latter is especially true for the five years prior to the first menstruation [menarche] (Browner-Elhanan & Coupey, 1999) which usually occurs between nine years of age and 16 years of age (Bickley & Szilagyi, 2013); that is, early to middle adolescence.

There are three stages of adolescence: early, middle, and late (Bickley & Szilagyi). Early adolescence is the period from 10 to 14 years of age, middle adolescence is ages 15 to 16, and late adolescence refers to the period from 17 through 20 years of age. Each stage of adolescence is characterized by physical, cognitive, social, and emotional development that varies in "onset and duration" (Bickley & Szilagyi, 2013, p. 857). Consequently, individualized appropriate education and interventions must occur in order to reduce and prevent the cycle of PID among adolescents.

PID and African American Adolescents

African American adolescents engage in high-risk behaviors and they have unfortunate life experiences that increase their likelihood of being diagnosed with PID. Sexual activity at an early age and having multiple sex partners increase the possibility of PID. African American adolescents who experience high levels of psychological distress, have been abused, have low educational level, low socioeconomic status, and who do not have support from their family are more likely to have PID because of a history that includes STIs (Browner-Elhanan & Coupey, 1999; Champion et al., 2005; DiClemente et al., 2004; Hall et al., 2008; Seth et al., 2009).

Seth and colleagues (2009) conducted a study to examine "the association of psychological distress with a biologically confirmed STI, risky sexual practices, self-efficacy and communication" (p. 292). The researchers found that STI was present among those who experienced very high levels of psychological distress; they were also more likely to inconsistently use condoms, engage in sexual activity while intoxicated with alcohol and/or on drugs, and they were afraid of communicating with their partners. Champion and colleagues (2005) found that African American adolescents between 14 to 18 years of age who had been sexually and physical abused were at an increased risk of PID because they began having sex at an early age, had more sex partners, had high rates of recurrent STD, and they did not seek health care early. The latter was thought to be due to embarrassment, shame, the perception that it was not necessary to be evaluated by a health care provider, and unsupportive family (Champion et al., 2005).

Prior to settling in long-term relationships, young adolescents tend to have multiple short-term sexual relationships that expose them to pathogens that cause STDs compared to more mature females who can wait to engage in sexual activities (Browner-Elhanan & Coupey, 1999). Furthermore, adolescents engage in high-risk behaviors due to their inexperience and giving in to their strong desire to experiment (Browner-Elhanan & Coupey, 1999; Hall et al., 2008).

DiClemente et al. (2004) conducted a research study in order to assess STD prevalence among 170 pregnant African American females who attended an urban hospital clinic for their first prenatal clinic visit. The study participants were 14 to 20 years of age and their average age was 17.5 years. The findings were remarkable: "more than 50% reported a history of STD infection and nearly one-quarter of the adolescents tested positive for at least one of four STDs assessed on study enrollment" (p. 382). The average age of their first sexual experience was 14, 3% had more than one partner in the past 30 days, approximately one-third believed that their significant other was having sex with another female at the same time, and 9% of them reported having sex with a male partner who was not their significant other after they thought that they were pregnant. This is definitely evidence of engaging in multiple high-risk behaviors and infection with STDs that can result in recurrent PID.

Pelvic Inflammatory Disease and Sexually Transmitted Infections

Although multiple microorganisms cause PID, sexually transmitted infections, primarily Chlamydia trachomatis and Neisseria gonorrhoeae, are the causative agents in most cases of PID (CDC, 2010). This is unfortunate because both infections are preventable and treatable. Adolescents between 15 to 19 years of age have the highest rates of chlamydia and gonorrhea in the United States (CDC, 2010). Therefore, it is apparent that any discussion about PID among adolescents has to include information about chlamydia and gonorrhea.

Chlamydia trachomatis is the microorganism that causes chlamydia, which is the most common STI in the United States; an estimated 2.86 million infections occur yearly and 1,412,791 cases of chlamydia were reported to the CDC in 2011 (CDC, 2012). "It is estimated that 1 in 15 sexually active females aged 14–19 years has chlamydia" (CDC, 2012, p. 1). On the other hand, Neisseria gonorrhoeae are the bacteria that cause gonorrhea, which is the "second most commonly reported infectious disease in the United States; . . . the CDC estimates that more than 800,000 Americans still become infected with gonorrhea every year; . . . fewer than half of these infections (321,849 in 2011) are diagnosed and reported to CDC" (CDC, 2013, p. 2). Coinfection with both infections is implicated in an estimated 40% of all cases of PID (Callahan & Caughey, 2013).

Complications of PID

It is important to note that "approximately one third to one half of women with symptomatic PID develop chronic pelvic pain" (Champion et al., 2005, p. 234). Furthermore, PID is the primary risk factor for ectopic pregnancy because chronic infections result in scarring and distortion of the fallopian tubes (Rolle et al., 2006). And, ectopic pregnancy can occur when infection with chlamydia and gonorrhea affect the cilia within the cells of the fallopian tube. Subsequently there is slowing of the ovum (egg) as it travels to the uterus, and fertilization of the ovum with the sperm occurs in the fallopian tube (Rolle et al., 2006). Adolescents who become infected with Chlamydia trachomatis may be unaware of the reproductive consequence of infertility because they may not be planning a pregnancy (Haggerty et al., 2010).

Rolle et al. (2006) presented a case study in which a 24-year-old patient who was diagnosed with twin ectopic pregnancy had a history of first sexual activity at 14 years of age, 15 sexual partners, illegal drug use, a diagnosis of chlamydia, gonorrhea, Type 2 herpes simplex, and syphilis on four separate occasions over a six-year period. She reported adherence with treatment for all four infections, and present testing for chlamydia, gonorrhea, and syphilis was negative. Adolescents often think and say that "it will never happen to me or it has not happened to me." The aforementioned case study depicts the consequence of earlier actions occurring many years later. The individual engaged in high-risk behaviors during adolescence probably had recurrent PID, and ectopic pregnancy is the sequel.

EVALUATION OF ADOLESCENTS WITH PELVIC INFLAMMATORY DISEASE

Health care providers who provide services to adolescents should take into consideration the fact that "adolescence is a tumultuous time, marked by the transition from family-dominated influences to increasing autonomy and peer influence. The struggle for identity, independence, and eventually intimacy leads to stress, health-related problems, and often, high-risk behaviors" (Bickley & Szilagyi, 2013, p. 857). Family, friends, and the African American community should also be mindful of the aforementioned challenges of this period. The social developmental tasks of the adolescent, their characteristics, and the recommended approaches that health care providers who provide services to adolescents can use are depicted in Table 4.1. The specific social tasks of identity and independence have been selected because of their relevance to PID. Family, friends, and the African American community should also be mindful of the information in Table 4.1.

The information can be used to assist with communication with adolescents, in addition to guiding and supporting them.

> Sexual health discussions should be appropriate for the patient's developmental level and should be aimed at identifying risk behaviors (e.g., unprotected oral, anal, or vaginal sex and drug-use behaviors). Careful, nonjudgmental, and thorough counseling is particularly vital for adolescents who might not feel comfortable acknowledging their engagement in behaviors that place them at high risk for STDs. (CDC, 2010, p. 10)

A comprehensive history is conducted by a health care provider in order to determine whether the adolescent has PID or is at risk for having PID. Personal questions related to sexual activity are unavoidable because they provide information that will allow the provider to arrive at the correct diagnosis and offer individualized appropriate treatment and

Table 4.1.
Social Development Tasks of the Adolescent and Recommended Approaches by Health Care Providers

	Stages of Development		
Concepts	Early	Middle	Late
➢ Age	10–14 years old	15–16 years old	17–20 years old
➢ Identity	Concerned about being normal. Peers are important	Asks who she is and becomes introspective	She thinks about her sexuality, the future, and her role
➢ Independence	Ambivalent about herself, her family, and her peers	Tests limits, experiments, and dates	She separates from her family in order to become more independent
➢ Approaches by health care providers	Reassure her and be positive Support her	Accept her and do not judge her	Encourage, support, and guide

Source: Adapted from Bickley, L. S., & Szilagyi, P. G. (2013). *Bates' nursing guide to physical examination and history taking* (11th ed.). Philadelphia: Wolters Kluwer/Lippincott Williams & Wilkins.

prevention strategies. The sexual history includes questions related to the age of first sexual activity, number of sex partners to date, whether sexually active at the moment and duration of the present relationship. The adolescent should be asked questions regarding the use of contraception, hormones (pills, patch, injection, intrauterine device—IUD) or barrier (condom), and a history of PID, STD, and/or exposure to STI. Adolescents who are infected with Chlamydia trachomatis may have symptoms but the majority of them may not have symptoms and will not seek testing and treatment for chlamydia.

It is very important that health care providers inquire about STDs in adolescents and evaluate them for STD at least annually. The following case study demonstrates the importance of screening adolescents for STDs since they are implicated in most cases of PID. According to Adler (2008) a 19-year-old female obtained a physical examination in order to be a summer camp counselor. Unfortunately, three months after being informed of a normal physical examination she was evaluated and diagnosed with PID. She returned to her health care provider because of cervical tenderness and a tender uterus, and her diagnostic tests were positive for chlamydia. Her history revealed that she was sexually active for one year and during that time she had three sexual partners and her present one was of two months duration (Adler, 2008). She was not assessed or evaluated for STD at her initial visit.

Physical Examination

A physical examination (PE) is typically conducted after the history is obtained in order to assess for signs of PID. The PE includes an examination of the abdomen, external genital area, and the pelvis. Abdominal examination may reveal tenderness in the lower abdomen. The practitioner assesses the external genital area for signs of infections such as discharge, swelling, and pain. The discharge that is associated with chlamydia and gonorrhea may or may not be foul smelling while that associated with bacterial vaginosis (a risk factor that is common among adolescents who douche) tends to possess a "fishy" odor. In order to conduct the pelvic examination the practitioner has to insert a speculum into the vagina in order to examine the vagina and the cervix. The classic signs of PID include tenderness of the cervix (cervical motion tenderness [CMT]) and tenderness on either side of the lower abdomen where the tubes are located (adnexal tenderness). These signs are elicited when the provider uses his or her hand to examine the cervix, tubes, and ovaries internally.

Both Chlamydia trachomatis and Neisseria gonorrhoeae can be identified by obtaining an endocervical (inside the opening to the cervix) swab during the pelvic examination. Urine testing can also be used to detect both infections; it should be performed on the first urine of the day (Steele,

Yen & Wang, 2013). The PE can be a very painful experience for the adolescent who has PID, especially acute PID. The experience can be more tolerable if the practitioner is gentle and the adolescent conducts distraction activities such as deep breathing exercises and imagery.

Diagnosis and Management of Pelvic Inflammatory Disease

The diagnosis of PID among adolescents, like adults, is a difficult one to make. Generally, treatment is recommended for adolescents who complain of abdominal pain for which other causes have been eliminated or are unlikely, are sexually active and/or at risk for STD (CDC, 2010). "Laparoscopy can be used to obtain a more accurate diagnosis; . . . its use is not easy to justify when symptoms are mild or vague. Moreover, laparoscopy will not detect endometritis and might not detect subtle inflammation of the fallopian tubes" (CDC, 2010, p. 63). Adolescents should be treated for PID if they manifest the signs and symptoms that are depicted in Table 4.2 because of the complications of untreated PID (CDC). The treatment of PID may take place in the hospital setting or in a community clinic with antibiotics that are given orally or by injection. The decisions are based on the standard of care that providers are held to and include

Table 4.2.
Signs and Symptoms of Pelvic Inflammatory Disease

➢ Pelvic pain or lower abdominal pain in addition to ≥ one of the following "minimum criteria"
➢ Pelvic examination resulting in tenderness of the
  ○ Cervix
  ○ Uterus or
  ○ Adnexa

Signs of inflammation
➢ Vaginal secretions that contain White blood cells
➢ Exudates around the cervix
➢ Friable cervix

Additional criteria
➢ Fever of more than 101 degree Fahrenheit (oral temperature)
➢ Discharge (mucus and pus) in the vagina and cervix
➢ Multiple White blood cells in vaginal secretions during microscopic examination
➢ Higher than normal erythrocyte sedimentation rate (ESR)
➢ Higher than normal C-reactive protein (CRP) and
➢ Infection of the cervix with Neisseria gonorrhoeae and Chlamydia trachomatis

Source: Centers for Disease Control and Prevention. (2010). Sexually *transmitted disease treatment guidelines, 2010*. Retrieved from http://www.cdc.gov/std/treatment/2010/STD-Treatment-2010 -RR5912.pdf

the adolescent's history, PE, the result of diagnostic test(s), and treatment guidelines set forth by the CDC.

Patient education includes abstaining from sex until after completing treatment and notification and treatment of partners, including those from the previous 60 days since an individual can be exposed to an STI but not know until weeks after the exposure (CDC). Some providers may provide medication for partner(s); this is referred to as expedited partner therapy (EPT), but they should still be evaluated by a provider (CDC). The adolescent should return to her health care provider for follow-up within 48 to 72 hours for re-evaluation because symptoms usually improve within 72 hours.

CONCLUSION

Pelvic inflammatory disease, a preventable disease, is prevalent among our adolescents. Most cases of PID are caused by Chlamydia trachomatis and/or Neisseria Gonorrhoeae. "The surest way to avoid chlamydia is to abstain from vaginal, anal, and oral sex or to be in a long-term mutually monogamous relationship with a partner who has been tested and is known to be uninfected" (CDC, 2012, p. 2). Many adolescents do not realize that they have PID because they do not have symptoms. On the other hand, adolescents may present with severe symptoms that include pain in the lower abdomen, fever, malodorous vaginal discharge, pain during sex, and/or bleeding between periods (Callahan & Caughey, 2013; CDC, 2013). It is very important for adolescents to visit their practitioner if they experience any of the above symptoms. However, since PID may be asymptomatic and the STDs that may cause PID may be asymptomatic, adolescents should obtain annual examination and testing for chlamydia and gonorrhea.

REFERENCES

Adler, S. (2008). Preventing PID: the case for routine STD screening. *Cortlandt Forum*, 30–35.

Bickley, L. S., & Szilagyi, P. G. (2013). *Bates' nursing guide to physical examination and history taking* (11th ed.). Philadelphia: Wolters Kluwer/Lippincott Williams & Wilkins.

Browner-Elhanan, K. J., & Coupey, S. (1999). Pelvic inflammatory disease in adolescents. *AIDS Patient Care and STDs, 13*(10), 601–607.

Callahan, T. L., & Caughey, A. B. (2013). *Blueprints: Obstetrics & Gynecology.* Baltimore, MD: Lippincott Williams & Wilkins.

Centers for Disease Control and Prevention. (2010). *Sexually Transmitted Disease Treatment Guidelines, 2010.* Retrieved from http://www.cdc.gov/std/treatment/2010/STD-Treatment-2010-RR5912.pdf

Centers for Disease Control and Prevention. (2012). *Chlamydia—Fact Sheet.* Retrieved from http://www.cdc.gov/std/chlamydia/stdfact-chlamydia .htm

Centers for Disease Control and Prevention. (2013). *CDC Fact Sheet: Gonorrhea Treatment Guidelines.* Retrieved from http://www.cdc.gov/nchhstp/ newsro om/docs/Gonorrhea-Treatment-Guidelines-FactSheet.pdf

Champion, J. D., Piper, J. M., Holden, A. E., Shain, R. N., Perdue, S., & Korte, J. E. (2005). Relationship of abuse and pelvic inflammatory disease risk behavior in minority adolescents. *Journal of the American Academy of Nurse Practitioners, 17*(6), 234–241.

DiClemente, R. J., Wingood, G. M., Crosby, R. A., Rose, E., Lang, D., Pillay, A. P., et al. (2004). A descriptive analysis of STD prevalence among urban pregnant African American teens: Data from a pilot study. *Journal of Adolescent Health, 34*(5), 376–383. doi:10.1016/j.jadohealth.2003.08.010

Haggerty, C. L., Gottlieb, S. L., Taylor, B. D., Low, N., Xu, F., & Ness, R. B. (2010). Risk of sequelae after chlamydia trachomatis genital infection in women. *Journal of Infectious Diseases, 201*(S2), S134-155. doi:10.1086/652395

Hall, T., Hogben, M., Carlton, A. L., Liddon, N., & Koumans, E. H. (2008). Attitudes toward using condoms and condom use: Differences between sexually abused and nonabused African American female adolescents. *Behavioral Medicine, 34:*45–52

Jadack, R. A., & Georges, J. M. (2010). Alteration in female genital and reproductive function. In L. C. Copstead & J. L. Banasik, *Pathophysiology* (4th ed., pp. 776–777). St Louis: Saunders.

Livengood, C. H., & Chacko, M. R. 2012. *Clinical features and diagnosis of PID.* Retrieved from http://www.uptodate.com/contents/clinical-features -and-diagnosis-of-pelvic-inflammatory-disease?source=search_result&sea rch=pelvic+inflammatory+disease&selectedTitle=2%7E150

MacKay, H. T., & Woo, J. (2014). Gynecologic disorders. In M. A. Papadakis & S. J. McPhee (eds.), *2014 current medical diagnosis & treatment* (53rd ed., pp. 741– 742). New York: McGraw-Hill Education.

Mete, S., Yenal, K., Tokat, M. A., & Secekus, P. (2012). Effects of vaginal douching on Turkish women's vaginal douching practice. *Research and Theory for Nursing Practice: An International Journal, 26*(1), 41–53.

Rolle, C. J., Wai, C. Y., Bawdon, R., Santos-Ramos, R., & Hoffman, B. (2006). Unilateral twin ectopic pregnancy in a patient with a history of multiple sexually transmitted infections. *Infectious Diseases in Obstetrics and Gynecology,* pp. 1–3. doi:10.1155/IDOG/2006/10306

Seth, P., Raiji, P. T., DiClemente, R. J., Wingood, G. M., & Rose, E. (2009). Psychological distress as a correlate of a biologically confirmed STI, risky sexual practices, self-efficacy and communication with male sex partners in African American female adolescents. *Psychology, Health & Medicine, 14*(3), 291–300. doi:10.1080/13548500902730119

Steele, B. J., Yen, S., & Wang, N. E. (2013). Gynecologic complaints in the adolescent female. *Practical Journal of Pediatric Medicine, 18*(2), 13–22.

Chapter 5

African American Girls and Substance Use

Leslie R. Walker and Caryn R. R. Rodgers

THE PARADOX

There really should not be much of a story here. African American adolescent girls are among the least likely groups to use alcohol and illicit drugs in the country, second only to the lower use of drugs in the Asian adolescent female community (Johnston, O'Malley, Bachman & Schulenberg, 2013). This is true despite the fact that drugs and alcohol are promoted disproportionately in African American communities (Gil, Vega & Turner, 2002). It is also true despite African American girls being exposed to more statistically defined "risk factors" (Gil et al., 2002; Wallace Jr. & Muroff, 2002).

This reality is in direct conflict with the all-too-common images of drug-using African American women and teens that can be seen in popular media. One can always conjure the image of the crack-using Black young woman with a baby that was so popularized in the media of the 1990s. Even during that era, Black women and teens used less cocaine and fewer other drugs than the general population. It is time the Black community changed the stereotype that we ourselves cling to, despite evidence to the contrary.

This chapter will present the national statistics, past and current, that document the rates of alcohol and illicit drug abuse and dependence in

African American adolescent girls. Secondly, the chapter will focus on exploring existing and potential explanations for disproportionately poor outcomes, despite lower use. Also presented are factors that contribute to drug use as well as factors that protect against and prevent initiation of drug use. Although few prevention and treatment interventions have been evaluated specifically for this adolescent population, what has been developed will be discussed.

STATE OF AFRICAN AMERICAN ADOLESCENT FEMALE SUBSTANCE USE IN THE UNITED STATES

According to available 2012 adolescent drug use data as well as historical data, compared to White and Hispanic adolescent females, African American adolescents have persistently used the least amount of alcohol and illicit substances with the exception of marijuana (Johnston et al., 2013). It is important to note the trends over the last decade as shown on Tables 5.1 and 5.2; regular drug use has remained relatively constant for the last decade with the exception of marijuana and prescription drugs. These have increased over the last five years but the increase is still lower than the increase in the larger United States population of adolescents.

The two most commonly used drugs for all adolescents are alcohol and marijuana. It is interesting to note that while it is not statistically significant, there is an increasing trend for females to report drinking more than males. This is unique to the United States. In contrast, marijuana is used significantly more by males than females. African American adolescents report trying marijuana at statistically the same rate as other youth. See Table 5.3.

Table 5.1.
Trends in Past Month Substance Use among Blacks Aged 12–17 (in percent): 2002–2010

	Alcohol Use	Cigarette Use	Marijuana Use	Nonmedical Use of Prescription-Type Drugs
2002	10.9	6.6	6.9	3.0
2003	10.1	6.9	5.9	3.4
2004	9.8	6.0	6.4	2.6
2005	11.6	6.5	7.2	3.3
2006	10.5	6.0	6.5	3.1
2007	10.1	6.1	5.8	3.1
2008	10.1	5.0	5.9	2.1
2009	10.6	5.1	7.3	3.5
2010	10.8	4.5	7.5	2.6

Source: 2002 to 2010 SAMHSA National Survey on Drug Use and Health (NSDUHs).

Table 5.2.
Past Month Substance Use among Blacks Aged 12 to 17 Compared with National Average (in percent): 2004 to 2009

	Alcohol Use	Cigarette Use	Marijuana Use	Nonmedical Use of Prescription-Type Drugs
Blacks	10.5	5.8	6.5	2.9
National Average	16.0	10.2	6.9	3.3

Source: 2004 to 2009 SAMHSA National Survey on Drug Use and Health (NSDUHs).

Table 5.3.
Adolescent High School Report of Ever Using Marijuana or Alcohol, 2011 YRBS (in percent)

Drug	U.S. Total	All Females	AA Female	All Males	AA Male
Alcohol	70.8	70.9	66.1	70.6	60.9
Marijuana	39.9	37.2	37.7	42.5	48.5

Source: Developed by authors from the 2011 Centers for Disease Control, Youth Risk Behavioral Survey.

MARIJUANA (CANNABIS SATIVA, BLUNT, POT, MARY JANE)

When we look within African American adolescents as a group, female marijuana use is significantly lower than that of males. Some gender differences in risk have been found recently (Schepis et al., 2011) that highlight some interesting factors for adolescent girls in general. It appears that extracurricular activities are more protective for the girls than boys, but having a job in high school made it significantly more likely an adolescent girl would have used marijuana. Just being an African American adolescent female conferred some protection against marijuana use, but if marijuana was used, alcohol was consumed as well. Only 14% of marijuana-using teens reported not using alcohol (PATS, 2012). It was also found that those who smoked marijuana had increased odds of smoking cigarettes, but this correlation was stronger in males than females (PATS, 2012). In both African American females and males, better grades decreased the chance of drug use, but having a depressed mood increased the chance of drug use. Further study is needed with African American adolescent females in particular, to better understand what protective factors have prevented the higher use of drugs seen in the general adolescent population. It is also important to take into account the recent increases in overall use of marijuana since the introduction of state medical marijuana laws in the 2000s.

Marijuana is an illicit drug for adolescents; however, consistent with the recent decrease in perception of risk, marijuana's use has increased in all adolescent groups, including African American youth. In the last five years African American youth have increased their marijuana use to the national average. The recent relaxation of laws for medicinal use of marijuana and its legalization for recreational use in Washington and Colorado state are likely to continue to decrease the perception of risk for the drug, which could in turn further increase marijuana use rates. This is a concern, considering marijuana dependence is the most common reason adolescents in the United States attend drug treatment programs.

In the last decade, marijuana has been increasingly perceived by the general public as a risk-free high with many perceived benefits ranging from help for anxiety and depression, chronic pain, and weight management to ADHD. None of these claims have been proven true for adolescents by scientific research. It has been difficult to study all of the effects of marijuana and its derivatives, since research on this highly controlled substance has rarely been approved for study by the federal government; therefore, there is little proof for the many claims found on the internet and in popular culture. This fact has not stopped many youth from using marijuana for perceived medicinal reasons and for recreational reasons.

Regardless of the scientific data and lack of dosing information, despite no federal regulation for consistency or quality control and lack of oversight by the Federal Drug Administration, twenty states and the District of Columbia have created medical marijuana laws legalizing its use for their residents. In 2012, two states, Colorado and Washington, became the first places in the world to legalize recreational marijuana for people over 21 years of age. In 2013 the U.S. government agreed not to prosecute its use in those states as long as certain rules are adhered to. No access to and no use by minors is one of the rules that the federal government will be watching closely.

Alcohol is one of the most widely accepted drugs in American society. Over 70% of twelfth grade high school students report drinking alcohol (CDC, 2012). If you refer back to Table 5.3 you will remember that 66% of African American girls report using alcohol—less than White American girls but more use than African American adolescent males (60%). Despite less overall use compared to the general adolescent population, there are significant disparities in alcohol-related problems with African Americans experiencing more than White Americans. Although we do not have specific data on adolescents, African American adults were found to have more drunk driving arrests, more likely to report alcohol dependence, and more likely to experience social stigma with drinking compared to White Americans who are reporting the same level of drinking (Mulia, Ye, Greenfield & Semore, 2009). Alcohol use contributes to the three leading causes of death (homicide, unintentional injuries [including car crashes], and suicide) among African Americans 12 to 20 years old (CDC, 2012).

FACTORS RELATED TO AFRICAN AMERICAN ADOLESCENT GIRLS' SUBSTANCE USE

The story of African American girls' substance use continues to be complicated and it does not appear that we are telling the whole story. Despite the lower rates of use statistically, there seems to be a limited focus on understanding substance use or the absence of use among African American adolescent girls. There is a dearth of articles focusing solely on African American girls and substance use. It is possible to find articles on African American youth but not as easy to find articles solely on African American girls and substance use.

In a literature search using search terms such as "African American adolescent girls and substance use," a great deal of articles were generated, reporting on the relationship between substance use and sexual risk behavior, despite the fact that sexual behavior, sex, and sexual risk behavior were not at all in the search terms. In fact, it was difficult to find articles with the generic search terms that did not have to do with sexual behavior. Articles on African American girls' mental health and substance use seemed almost absent. Clinically we find that African American girls are reporting use of marijuana to regulate emotion and mood. The story of African American girls living outside of urban neighborhoods is completely absent from the literature. When considering all of the numbers and outcomes examined and reported at this point, there continue to be huge gaps in the work. If we want to truly understand the role of substance use in the lives of African American girls, we need to examine the issue. In light of these gaps there are definitely some investigators who are examining those factors that may be specifically related to African American girls' substance use or abstinence, both risk and protective factors.

In examining the 55 risk factors identified by Hawkins and colleagues (Hawkins, Catalano & Miller, 1992) it was found that there are differences in how factors such as neighborhood disorganization and associating with drug-using peers influence substance use among African American girls and White girls (Wallace Jr & Muroff, 2002). Using data from the Monitoring the Future Study, authors reviewed contextual factors, namely laws and norms, availability of substances and economic deprivation/neighborhood disorganization. Individual level factors include family, academic performance and commitment, alienation and rebellion, early and persistent problem behaviors, attitudes favorable toward drug use, association with drug-using peers, early onset of drug use, and physiological factors (Wallace Jr & Muroff, 2002). It was concluded that African American youth were exposed to more important contextual risk factors and White youth were more likely to be exposed to individual level risk factors. This study focused on a national data set, but did not solely focus on girls.

Factors contributing to use are important, but it is also necessary to understand the ways in which substances, when they are used, are being used. According to the AdHealth survey, it was found that there are differences in alcohol use patterns between African American and White girls and different typologies of use. There were also differences in those factors related to the different alcohol use patterns. One such factor, mother's education, differed significantly, such that there was higher maternal education among African American girls who abstained from use than that of experimenters (Dauber, Hogue, Paulson & Leiferman, 2009). This study focused on girls, and in particular mother-daughter pairs but did not focus solely on African American girls.

Using data from the Woodlawn study, a longitudinal study of 1,242 African American first grade children in Chicago that began in 1966, investigators identified trajectories of marijuana use from childhood to age 32 separately for men and women (Juon, Fothergill, Green, Doherty & Ensminger, 2011). Four trajectories were identified for women. They found that based on adolescent predictors, those classified as abstainers were more likely to finish high school compared to those identified as persistent users. Persistent users were those who began using marijuana in late childhood/early adolescence and continued to use through age 32. In adulthood, persistent users who had the highest prevalence of substance use disorder, were more likely to have been incarcerated in the past 10 years and had a reported higher rate of lifetime major depressive disorder. For girls in particular, low adolescent social bonds related to persistent marijuana use. This study looked at the relationship between use trajectories and adult outcomes. It focused solely on African American youth, looked at factors over time, and although it did not focus solely on girls, it reported outcomes for women.

In a longitudinal study of 681 African American adolescents in a large Midwestern city, all participants were in the ninth grade (Zimmerman & Schmeelk-Cone, 2003). Data collection included both a 50- to 60-minute structural interview as well as self-administered paper-and-pencil survey. Investigators found low school motivation contributed to continued drug use, but drug use did not contribute to decreasing school motivation. Alcohol and marijuana use during high school increased the likelihood of not completing high school. This study did not report on the qualitative methods in this paper but did incorporate a mixed method approach in collecting the data.

A relatively large cross-sectional study in central Alabama focused solely on African American youth, grades 5 through 12 (Wright & Fitzpatrick, 2004). The focus of this study was to identify risk and assets and examine the relationship between risk and assets on substance use outcomes. The sample was 52% female with a median age of 14 years, with respondents from high school (ninth grade through twelfth grade, 45%), middle school (seventh and eighth grade, 22.1%) and elementary school (fifth through sixth grade, 32.5%). Risk factors included physical assault by a family member or adult residing in the child's home, gang membership, and peer attitudes toward substance use. Assets were a subjective account of grades, self-esteem, and whether or not the respondents felt their parent(s) knew where they went with their friends; respondents were asked to identify if they felt there was someone at their school who cared about them. All of the risk variables were significantly correlated with alcohol use. Grades received in school and parental monitoring were the assets that were significant. In examining these factors as they relate to marijuana use, significant risk factors were family abuse and deviant peers, and again significant assets were parental monitoring and grades. When gender was entered into the model, the type of substance determined whether it was the assets or the risk factors that affected gender's significance. The authors suggested gender-specific prevention and intervention programs.

In a study of middle school–aged African American and Latina girls, there were differences found in factors that were related to abstaining from alcohol and cigarette use (Rodgers, Nichols & Botvin, 2011). African American girls were more likely to abstain from alcohol and cigarette use than Latina girls. For African American girls, factors associated with not using alcohol or cigarettes included household structure, mother's use, father's use, perception of friends' use, and access to drugs. African American girls were more likely not to use substances if their parents did not use substances, if they had lower perception of friends' use, and had greater difficulty obtaining drugs.

In a study conducted in New York City of 781 mother-daughter pairs, with daughters aged 11–14, with a mean age of about 12, approximately 47% of whom were African American, it was found that with unstructured after-school activities, higher levels of depression, mother's alcohol use, and indication that their best friends used substances, they were more likely to use alcohol. Conversely, positive body image, mother's knowledge of daughter's whereabouts, mother's knowledge of daughter's companions, ability to always contact mother, families that had rules against substance use, and parents who encouraged their children to abstain from substance use (Schinke, Fang & Cole, 2008) were factors in less use of alcohol. Again these findings were not related solely to African American girls; however, there was a large sample of African American girls included in this study.

A rare longitudinal study, including African American girls, examining the relationship between substance use and depressive symptoms and/or anxiety (Marmorstein et al., 2010) took place in Pittsburgh. A total of 2,451 girls participated over several waves. This particular study focused on the first six waves of the study, which included ages 5 through 13. At wave one, of the girls who were either age 5, 6, 7, or 8, 52% were African

American. At the sixth wave, girls were ages 10–13. These authors found that initial marijuana use was associated with a specific increase in depressive symptoms among girls who were already experiencing high levels of depressive symptoms. Initial marijuana use was also associated with decreases in social anxiety among girls experiencing increasing levels of social anxiety. In this study differences by race/ethnicity are not examined, so it is not clear what this relationship means specifically for African American girls, but African American girls are a large proportion of the study and the study focuses solely on girls.

This is by no means intended to be an exhaustive list of all factors or all studies that incorporate some focus on African American girls' substance use. These are some of the studies that have begun to examine substance use among African American girls by better understanding the factors contributing to use, factors contributing to abstaining from use, and different ways substances may be used by African American girls. There is also an example of a study that took place in central Alabama as opposed to a northeast urban community; there are some others (Clark, Belgrave & Abell, 2012). However, as you can see, all except one of these studies focused solely on African American girls. It seems that overall, the factors that appear to contribute are expected or make sense, for example parental monitoring, having after-school activities, peer use and norms, availability of substances, grades; however, in these studies there may be some missing factors, particularly when considering intervention development and prevention. Despite these seemingly expected components and factors related to use or abstaining from use, there is also another component that some investigators suggest would give us the most impact in addressing substance use within communities, cultural factors and community strengths.

STRENGTHS OF THE AFRICAN AMERICAN COMMUNITY AND INTERVENTION

Interestingly enough, despite the statistical acknowledgment of lower use among African American girls, there remains a deficit model approach to examining substance use within the population. It could potentially mean that African American girls could be a source for understanding how a group, many of whom are considered to be living in adverse environments, whether it be related to neighborhood context, poverty, or the complexities of being an African American female in the United States, refrain from using substances, when many young people are "normatively" experimenting with substances. African American girls are "normatively" abstaining from substance use. As a society and as investigators we might gain a lot from understanding this paradox.

There are identified strengths within the African American context. Strengths include a spiritual reverence or training, self-reliance, supportive extended family and family network, and teaching of cultural values (Brook & Pahl, 2005; Doswell & Braxter, 2002). Having an Afrocentric worldview is also conceptualized as a strength. An Afrocentric worldview is predominantly defined by an emphasis on community and group relationships, interdependence, spirituality, and cooperation.

These strengths incorporate factors like familism. In a longitudinal study of youth grades 7 to 10 living in New York City, at the third wave of the study the mean age of the participants was 14.6. Familism, defined as a strong attachment to family both nuclear and extended, as well as having high regard for family interventions, was found to be a significant protective factor in relation to substance use (Brook & Pahl, 2005).

Focusing on community strengths and building on the impact of parents within the African American community could be and have been found to be extremely valuable. In other communities the role of peers can seem to diminish the influence of parents; however, in African American communities it seems that parents continue to play an extremely influential role (Clark et al., 2012). More specifically, factors like parent attitudes toward substance use and parents' awareness of where their child is, what their child is doing, and who their child is with, contribute to African American girls abstaining from substance use.

There are researchers who advocate greatly for using culturally relevant and culturally subscribed factors; some investigators believe it is not possible to create and implement prevention programs for African American girls without an understanding of Afrocentric values (Corneille, Ashcroft & Belgrave, 2005). Attributes identified as valuable include strong ethnic and racial identity, positive feelings about the self, good health, positive peer group norms, pro-social behavior, and the use of adaptive coping strategies (Corneille et al., 2005). Research is growing in this area (Belgrave, Brome & Hampton, 2000; Belgrave, Reed, Plybon & Corneille, 2004).

In a review of the Center for Substance Abuse Prevention cross-site evaluation of 47 programs, 12 served African American youth (Chipungu et al., 2000). The authors concluded in their review that most of the programs incorporated some Afrocentric component and that this contributed to youths' satisfaction and program engagement. Others subscribe to using cultural variables to adapt existing evidence-based interventions (Castro & Alarcón, 2002). Others describe techniques and types of cultural sensitivity in tailored interventions (Resnicow, Soler, Braithwaite, Ahluwalia & Butler, 2000).

SUMMARY

There is a need for research to better understand the etiology of substance use among African American adolescent girls. There is a wealth of information missing that could also assist in better understanding the etiology of substance use among adolescents in general. The idea that there is lower use within this population may be a factor that limits resources or funding associated with studying substance use in this population and necessitates the melding of behaviors such as substance use and sexual behavior in order to examine substance use; however, this approach may be causing a limited understanding of the true issue and calls for the need of creativity and unconventionality.

Further, existing methodologies of collecting longitudinal survey data or even cross-sectional data can be enhanced through more qualitative and mixed-method approaches which would facilitate a greater understanding of the dynamic experiences and phenomenological experience of African American girls. Also in this work it seems imperative to include samples of African American girls living in suburban communities as well as rural communities and those places in between, not just urban/inner-city communities. Understanding the within-group ethnic and cultural diversity would enhance current knowledge as well. It is likely that there are differences in use according to differences in heritage, whether someone is a first or second generation immigrant from a specific African country, Dominican Republic, Puerto Rico, British Honduras, and so on. Religious identification could also play a role in understanding dynamic experiences African American adolescent girls have with licit and illicit substances.

In looking at what is available to conceptualize African American adolescent girl drug use, the literature comes up short. We are then left with supposition that can be filled in with stereotypes and unsubstantiated beliefs. The lack of accurate tools to prevent early substance use in this population of young adolescent women is the outcome of lack of commitment to this small but significant population. This leaves us guessing why African American adolescent girls do not fit the typical American model of adolescent initiation of drug use. Why, in fact, do young African American adolescent girls have low drug use but by adulthood have increased drug and alcohol use to national levels? There is a story there and better defining what is happening will better inform how to craft effective prevention models for these young adults.

It is comforting that these young adolescent women on average are using mind-altering substances less when their brains are most vulnerable and when it would have the greatest impact on attaining a high school degree. Having more African American health researchers who want to explore is also crucial, as well as having people begin to ask direct questions, to see value in expanding beyond describing African American female substance use as correlated with sexuality; having prevention interventions developed that address treatment in a culturally effective manner, and knowing what would revolutionize our impact in the community throughout the life course.

REFERENCES

Belgrave, F. Z., Brome, D. R., & Hampton, C. (2000). The contribution of Afrocentric values and racial identity to the prediction of drug knowledge, attitudes, and use among African American youth. *Journal of Black Psychology, 26*(4), 386–401.

Belgrave, F. Z., Reed, M. C., Plybon, L. E., & Corneille, M. (2004). The impact of a culturally enhanced drug prevention program on drug and alcohol refusal efficacy among urban African American girls. *Journal of Drug Education, 34*(3), 267–279.

Brook, J. S., & Pahl, K. (2005). The protective role of ethnic and racial identity and aspects of an Afrocentric orientation against drug use among African American young adults. *The Journal of Genetic Psychology, 166*(3), 329–345. doi:10.3200/GNTP.166.3.329–345

Castro, F. G., & Alarcón, E. H. (2002). Integrating cultural variables into drug abuse prevention and treatment with racial/ethnic minorities. *Journal of Drug Issues, 32*(3), 783–810. doi:10.1177/002204260203200304

Centers for Disease Control and Prevention (CDC, 2012). Youth Risk Behavior Surveillance—United States, 2011. MMWR 2012;61 (No. SS-4).

Chipungu, S. S., Hermann, J., Sambrano, S., Nistler, M., Sale, E., & Springer, J. F. (2000). Prevention programming for African American youth: A review of strategies in CSAP's national cross-site evaluation of high-risk youth programs. *Journal of Black Psychology, 26*(4), 360–385.

Clark, T. T., Belgrave, F. Z., & Abell, M. (2012). The mediating and moderating effects of parent and peer influences upon drug use among African American adolescents. *Journal of Black Psychology, 38*(1), 52–80. doi: 10.1177/0095798411403617

Corneille, M. A., Ashcroft, A. M., & Belgrave, F. Z. (2005). What's culture got to do with it? Prevention programs for African American adolescent girls. *Journal of Health Care for the Poor and Underserved, 16*(4), 38–47.

Dauber, S., Hogue, A., Paulson, J. F., & Leiferman, J. A. (2009). Typologies of alcohol use in White and African American adolescent girls. *Substance Use & Misuse, 44*(8), 1121–1141. doi:10.1080/10826080802494727

Doswell, W. M., & Braxter, B. (2002). Risk-taking behaviors in early adolescent minority women: Implications for research and practice. *Journal of Obstetric, Gynecologic, & Neonatal Nursing, 31*(4), 454–461. doi:10.1111/j.1552-6909.2002 .tb00068.x

Durr, M., Small, L., & Dunlap, E. (2010). Inner-city African-American women's adolescence as stressful life events: Understanding substance abusing behavior. *Journal of African American Studies, 14*(2), 202–219. doi:10.1007/ s12111-009-9113-6

Gil, A. G., Vega, W. A., & Turner, R. J. (2002). Early and mid-adolescence risk factors for later substance abuse by African Americans and European Americans. *Public Health Reports, 117*(Suppl 1), S15.

Hawkins, J. D., Catalano, R. F., & Miller, J. Y. (1992). Risk and protective factors for alcohol and other drug problems in adolescence and early adulthood: implications for substance abuse prevention. *Psychological Bulletin, 112*(1), 64.

Johnston, L. D., O'Malley, P. M., Bachman, J. G., & Schulenberg, J. E. (2013). *Monitoring the future national survey results on drug use, 1975–2012: Secondary school students* (Vol. 1). Ann Arbor: Institute for Social Research, The University of Michigan.

Juon, H.-S., Fothergill, K. E., Green, K. M., Doherty, E. E., & Ensminger, M. E. (2011). Antecedents and consequences of marijuana use trajectories over the life course in an African American population. *Drug and Alcohol Dependence, 118*, 216–223.

Marmorstein, N. R., White, H., Chung, T., Hipwell, A., Stouthamer-Loeber, M., & Loeber, R. (2010). Associations between first use of substances and change in internalizing symptoms among girls: Differences by symptom trajectory and substance use type. *Journal of Clinical Child & Adolescent Psychology, 39*(4), 545–558. doi:10.1080/15374416.2010.486325

Mulia, N., Ye, Y., Greenfield, T. K., & Semore, S. E. (2009). Disparities in alcohol-related problems among White, Black and Hispanic Americans. *Alcoholism: Clinical and Experimental Research, 33*(4), 654–662.

Partnership Attitude Tracking Study (PATS, 2012). Sponsored by MetLife Foundation. Retrieved from http://www.drugfree.org/wp-content/uploads/2013/04/PATS-2012-FULLREPORT2.pdf

Resnicow, K., Soler, R., Braithwaite, R. L., Ahluwalia, J. S., & Butler, J. (2000). Cultural sensitivity in substance use prevention. *Journal of Community Psychology, 28*(3), 271–290. doi:10.1002/(SICI)1520-6629(200005)28:3<271::AID-JCOP4>3.0.CO;2-I.

Rodgers, C. R. R., Nichols, T. R., & Botvin, G. J. (2011). Alcohol and cigarette free: Examining social influences on substance use abstinence among Black non-latina and latina urban adolescent girls. *Journal of Child & Adolescent Substance Abuse, 20*(4), 370–386.

Schepis, T. S., Desai, R. A., Cavallo, D. A., Smith, A. E., McFetridge, A., Liss, T. B., & Potenza, M. N. (2011). Gender differences in adolescent marijuana use and associated psychosocial characteristics. *Journal of Addiction Medicine, 5*(1), 65–73.

Schinke, S. P., Fang, L., & Cole, K. C. A. (2008). Substance use among early adolescent girls: Risk and protective factors. *Journal of Adolescent Health, 43*(2), 191–194. doi:http://dx.doi.org/10.1016/j.jadohealth.2007.12.014

Wallace, J. M., Jr., & Muroff, J. R. (2002). Preventing substance abuse among African American children and youth: Race differences in risk factor exposure and vulnerability. *Journal of Primary Prevention, 22*(3), 235–261.

Wright, D. R., & Fitzpatrick, K. M. (2004). Psychosocial correlates of substance use behaviors among African American youth. *Adolescence, 39*(156), 653–667.

Zimmerman, M. A., & Schmeelk-Cone, K. H. (2003). A longitudinal analysis of adolescent substance use and school motivation among African American Youth. *Journal of Research on Adolescence, 13*(2), 185–210.

Chapter 6

Black Girls in Poverty

Marianne E. Partee[1]

INTRODUCTION

The United States has one of the highest rates of poverty in the developed world at 21% according to the 2012 U.S. Census Bureau. As poverty in the United States was placed in an international context, it was reported that in 2007 the U.S. relative poverty rate was nearly three times higher than that of Denmark, which had the lowest rate (6.1%), and about 1.8 times higher than the peer country average of 9.6% (Gould & Wething 2012). Many of the U.S. poor do not have enough income to afford the basic necessities to sustain a healthy life. Households with income below the poverty line do not have enough income to maintain a nutritional diet, or afford decent housing, or adequate medical care. Absolute poverty is easy to see in areas of high unemployment, or low wages, high rates of crime, high rates of drug abuse, and low high school graduation rates. Many Americans see poverty to be a problem that is more widespread than the government. In a public opinion survey published by the Center for American Progress, when asked what percentage of their fellow Americans were living in poverty the average guess was 39%—a sharp

---

[1] To Jamie and Baba. Always remember that of all my life's accomplishments, the one I am most proud of is being your mother. Love you, Mom.

rise from the official (government) estimate of 15% (Carpenter, 2014). Mark Rank (2013), a columnist for the *New York Times,* reported that the dispersion of poverty has been increasing over the past two years, particularly within suburban areas. Further, according to the latest Census Bureau numbers, two-thirds of those below the poverty line identify themselves as White (Rank, 2013). Poverty as a national issue currently is being viewed as a mainstream concern that considers poverty a temporary relative result of macroeconomic fluctuations. Most people have been poor for some portion of their lifetime and are uplifted out of poverty during economic expansions. Short-term relative poverty is perceived to be a state that generates widespread support for government intervention. Yet many Americans do not know much about the poor that exist in absolute poverty. Middle-class Americans that experience relative poverty tend to be geographically separated, living in suburbs or in areas divided by highways from those that live in persistent poverty. Poverty in America is grossly misunderstood, with little differentiation between relative poverty that may be temporary and absolute poverty that is long term and persistent. The distinction between levels of poverty needs to be understood and myths about persistent poverty must be debunked.

America's poor are a diverse group that reaches from coast to coast (Bishaw, 2013). Absolute poverty is concentrated geographically and racially in the United States. In Appalachia and the Dakotas it is White, in the western part of the country it is Hispanic, and in the eastern urban areas it is Black. While poverty cuts across racial lines the cut is not even. The United States also has one of the highest percentages of child poverty at 23%. The more disconcerting news according to the Center for Children in Poverty is that Black children tend to live in poverty more than any other group. The rate of living in poverty for Black children is 38% and 37% for Black females ages 15 to 24. It means that nearly 40% of adolescent Black females live in households who cannot meet their basic needs for food, clothing, and shelter. Black females, like other groups living in absolute poverty, are not visible to most Americans that experience temporary relative poverty. Literature addressing the existence of relative poverty has been researched and written in academia, discussed in politics and the general public, as well as by social scientists continuously. However literature discussing the young Black female in absolute poverty and her state of mind does not have a voice. In fact absolute poverty as an urban problem has its very own social category, the Black underclass. The ghetto Black underclass are impoverished living in the nation's urban centers that experienced an exodus of the Black middle class from the Black ghetto (Wilson, 1987, p. 143). Those left behind are the most disadvantaged of the Black community, living as welfare dependents, lacking the skills to be employed, or have dropped out of the labor force and become individuals that engage in high volumes of crime. Consequently, too often Americans

overwhelmingly believe that absolute persistent poverty is an urban problem of poor Blacks and blame the poor Blacks for being poor. Myths about
the young Black females basking in poverty are espoused. In turn there
was a lack of demand for public policy to address absolute poverty, economic inequality, or educational reform. The issues of poverty must be
revisited by considering the structural forces that have perpetuated and
exacerbated urban poverty over time. Strategies and policies need to be
formulated to uplift households out of poverty. The nation must acknowledge the poverty of the mind that has emerged over the past four decades
and be honest as to how it has hurt young impoverished Blacks (Patterson,
2006).

BORN POOR, BLACK, AND FEMALE IN THE 1990s

The issues of race, urban income inequality, and poverty in the United
States have been discussed mainly with the focus of "when work disap-
pears" the outcome is central, and the impact of limited or lack of income
on African American families portrays characteristics of relative poverty, a
temporary state that fiscal policy should address. Fiscal policy is one of
the tools available that allows policy makers to re-shape the environment
where households and business make transactions. The environmental arrangement of people in cities and their quality of life has been a major
concern for members dating back to the industrial revolution (Partee,
2009). The economic prosperity in the United States during the 1970s and
1980s generated a perception that institutional racism that had barred
Blacks from advancing in America no longer existed in large measures
(Wilson, 1980). Middle class American Whites and Blacks appeared to
have equal access and opportunity. The War on Poverty had been won and
in a Gallup poll taken in 1998 only 5% of Americans felt that poverty was
an important issue. The Black underclass left behind was not counted.
This chapter aims to address the unspoken persistent absolute poverty of
the Black underclass as well as the culture of poverty for the Black girls
from the 1990s. The work here will acknowledge the unspeakable truth
about how structural forces reinforced income inequality and absolute
poverty in urban areas in the United States where the concentration of
Blacks have lived since the migration patterns from the south to the north-
ern urban centers during the 1950s (Partee, 2003). Poverty for anyone is
harsh; the snapshot of time presented here addresses the economic, political, and social structure from the 1990s. The forces to be considered have
affected Blacks in America, creating persistent unemployment, or at best
underemployment and limited economic opportunity, with Black girls of
the 1990s inheriting the plague of poverty. A poverty that through unspoken methods has de-feminized the image of the young Black urban
woman. The impoverished life that these girls endured was a

socioeconomic downward spiral creating poverty of the mind. A mind shaped by racially isolated communities, with high unemployment, high crime, poor schools, and marginal government subsidy. The underclass Black girl of the 1990s is categorized as "wanna be welfare queens." The welfare queen negative stereotype grew in popularity when it was used by Ronald Reagan. This is just one myth; there are several others that stigmatize and blame females for the economic conditions to which they were born.

Poverty of the mind must be introduced into mainstream conversations. What it is, how it came to be, and how it impacts young Black females needs to be understood. The urban 1990s girl cannot be viewed as a welfare queen or any other stereotype that sees her as a willing participant in her limited lot in life. The poverty that the 1990s girl has endured must be understood through the context of the structural arrangements in the United States that allow for poverty to persist in urban areas where the Black underclass is concentrated. Poverty of the mind diminishes one's self-worth and human capital. It is not an ideology that society can allow to persist. The inheritance of devalued human capital is too terrible to pass along.

Brief Historical Overview of Trends of Poverty in the United States

Poverty in the capitalist United States was at a national alarming rate during the Great Depression. Millions of Americans were out of work and without income. Up to the 1930s the U.S. government was not involved with social welfare. The Federal government for the first time under President Franklin Roosevelt and the New Deal provided protection to households from financial disaster. The federal government expanded its social welfare programs in the 1960s under President Lyndon Johnson's Great Society with the creation designed to bring the poor into the economic mainstream. These policies did more than help the poor. In fact, the increased government spending expanded economic activity by providing resources to households; the households in turn spent more, and when households spend more businesses do better. Overall, what was observed was the success of government expansionary fiscal policy. Expansionary policies and increase in government spending was an acceptable rationale for nearly fifty years. Who benefitted and how it was distributed was not much of a concern for most Americans.

During the 1960s and 1970s movements began that demanded more than government spending to secure economic growth and stability. The social movements demanded government involvement in correcting injustices based on gender, race, and religion. The success of the movements is evidenced by the Civil Rights Act of 1963 and Affirmative Action of 1972. Awareness of social injustice and economic inequality brought attention to discriminatory practices against Blacks and women. The nation was on a path that was to correct past practices that limited economic resources and fostered social segregation. The nation's welfare state programs and policies were on a path to minimize poverty along with continued responsibility for the nation's economic stability, health, education, housing, and working conditions for all citizens rich and poor. The welfare state, government doling out money, seemed to have created prosperity, equality, and opportunity for all individuals and was the law of the land. Unfortunately the economic and social gains of the 1960s and 1970s movements found an attitude of apathy in most during the 1980s (Wilson, 1980). Individuals pursuing their own best interest in capitalist United States enjoyed the newfound legal equality. Upper- and middle-class Black Americans benefited by equal opportunity in employment, education, and housing. Poverty that persisted for Blacks was concentrated in urban areas as advantaged Black families were allowed to move, separating themselves from the less fortunate Black underclass (Moynihan, 1965). For the first time in large measure middle-class Blacks were not confined to social space occupied by the poor. The Black middle class or the Black Bourgeoisie who were economically viable and had owned businesses in segregated Black neighborhoods left the poor Blacks behind and moved into White communities. The middle-class Black men and women could find jobs in industry and manufacturing and the growing service sector as the nation's economy experienced expansion. The poor underclass was left behind and soon was perceived as a people that voluntarily remained poor in the 1980s.

The Reagan Years

President Ronald Reagan put into effect a number of policies that had strong negative impacts on the lives and aspirations of many African Americans. The ideology of the conservative president changed the direction of the country's attitudes that existed during the Civil Rights and Affirmative Action movements of the 1960s and 1970s. This chapter is not one that is about the critique of Reagan's presidency, rather a brief overview that shows the latent consequences of the minimal state government and persistent urban Black poverty, and ultimately their effects on the lives of the Black girls of the 1990s. To start, it is best to consider the attitudes that reflect Reagan's views toward race and Blacks through his actions. A 2004 edition of *The Progressive* magazine published an article on Ronald Reagan stating:

He delivered his first major campaign speech for the presidency in 1980 in Philadelphia, Miss., the town where Klansmen murdered three civil-rights workers in 1964 during "Freedom Summer." By delivering a speech in a town that was once a hotbed of racial hatred, he upset African-Americans and emboldened old-guard segregationists. Second, he opposed the Civil Rights Act of 1964 and the Voting Rights Act of 1965. When he was running for governor of California in 1966, Reagan assailed the Fair Housing Act, saying, "If an individual wants to discriminate against Negroes or others in selling or renting his house, it is his right to do so." William Rehnquist, an ardent foe of desegregation efforts, was on the Supreme Court, and Reagan elevated him to chief justice in 1986. . . . Reagan adopted the Republican Party's Southern Strategy of winning over the votes of Southern Whites who opposed civil rights. *Time* magazine writer Jack White wrote in November 2002 that Ronald Reagan "set a standard for exploiting White anger and resentment" over the years. Reagan did not hesitate to perpetuate an ugly myth about single Black mothers receiving government assistance with the phrase "welfare queens." Nor did he shy away from using the word "quota" to fight moves toward affirmative action that help people of color and women obtain fairness in education and in the workforce. (Gilmore, 2004)

With Reagan's philosophy of "Government is not the solution to our problem, government is the problem," actions and choices for government reflected a dedication to a free society, not an integrated society. Maybe one could discount the former president's views as ones that caused the onset of a downward spiral for Blacks if it were not for the economic policies that took place during his administration along with the restrictive social climate.

Ronald Reagan was the first conservative U.S. president in more than 50 years. His presidency began with the tall task of combating the worst recession since the Great Depression. The economy was experiencing stagflation, an economic downturn coupled with double-digit inflation. Ronald Reagan's administration's economic actions became known as Reaganomics. Reagan implemented expansionary fiscal policy by tax reform aimed at economic recovery. According to data published in the Urban Institute and Brookings Institution and illustrated in Figure 6.1, Reagan cut federal income taxes rates from 70% to 28% for the top income bracket, from 49.875% to 20% for capital gains maximum marginal tax rate, while taxes on the bottom 80% of the country stayed the same or increased slightly.

He reduced government regulations. He also promised to reduce government spending. His goal was to promote business—business would demand workers, households would receive income, and household income would be spent. The way to stimulate the economy was not by increasing demand with government spending; instead it was to increase the supply of

Figure 6.1

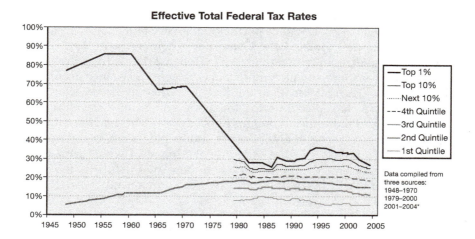

capital by lowering taxes. Lowering taxes would free up private wealth for investment. This practice became known as supply-side economics and for the general public became a transaction known as "trickledown economics." The advances to big business would eventually generate enough value that sufficient income would trickle down to the poor. The War on Poverty according to Reagan had been won. The government had an obligation to help the needy but handouts to able-bodied individuals would perpetuate the cycle of poverty. The impoverished Black urban underclass requirements to prove need became more restrictive and states were allowed to limit the services they offered to the poor.

President Reagan's laissez-faire philosophy was pro–big business and small government. He eliminated many price controls. Price controls were believed to have caused inflation. The Reagan administration deregulated industries for oil and gas, cable television, long-distance phone services, interstate bus services, and ocean shipping. Bank regulations were eased and many attribute the Savings and Loans crisis of 1989 to the removed restrictions. The policies of Reagan were aimed at reducing the economic downturn by alleviating the burden to government and stimulating the private sector. The trend continued under both Bushes and Clinton. The free market continued to yield increased wealth for big business and the government continued to reduce or at least attempted to reduce government spending for welfare programs aimed at poverty. The market was to provide jobs and income for all that were willing to work.

Meanwhile it has been shown the 1980s saw pervasive racial discrimination by banks, real estate agents, and landlords, unmonitored by the Reagan administration. When community groups uncovered blatant redlining, Reagan's HUD and Department of Justice failed to prosecute or sanction banks that violated the Community Reinvestment Act, which prohibits racial discrimination in lending (Dreier, 2011). During the 1980s cities began to decline and government anti-poverty assistance decreased by nearly 60%. The cuts included funding for public service jobs and job training, federal legal services for the poor, community development block grants, and reduced funding for public transit. This had devastating outcomes for urban schools and libraries; municipal hospitals and clinics; and sanitation, police, and fire departments; many of which shut their doors. Many cities have not recovered and these are the urban areas that the majority of Black girls of the 1990s have been born in and live in (Reich, 2011).

Reaganomics, the contractionary fiscal policy, increased the concentration of wealth in America and dismantled jobs and services and property value for the urban classes. Americans were sold into the ideology that big government was bad, the free-market was good, and everyone was left to stand on their own. The gains that African Americans were beginning to acquire since the 1960s and 1970s were spiraling down. The 1980s' economic laissez-faire policies proved successful with deregulation, tax cuts, and there was a decline of industry in the United States. Free market policies gave way to free trade. High-paying manufacturing jobs were lost as multinationals did business outside the physical borders of the United States. The wealth for capital owners remained concentrated while jobs for the middle class were lost. The growth in jobs was for lower paying jobs in the service industry. The working middle class was shrinking, income inequality was increasing, and poverty was on the rise. Antagonistic views about race relations were on the rise as middle class workers squabbled to get a smaller piece of the economic pie, and surely the crumbs from the pie would not trickle down to the impoverished Black urban underclass.

The 1990s Black Girls of Today

Many Black girls from the 1990s were born into the Black underclass. These girls exist in an isolated sector in society where hope for many is unthinkable as the socioeconomic conditions have led to a shrinking of the middle class with loss of income, particularly for Blacks in America who have had the greatest increase in poverty rates since the economic losses of the 1990s. According to the poverty and income data report for 2012 by the Census Bureau, income inequality remained historically high in 2012. The top 5% is the only group to have recovered its prerecession

(2007) income levels; all other groups have even lost further ground in the 2009–2012 recovery. Racial and ethnic disparities have increased substantially since 2000, as racial and ethnic minorities have seen larger income declines, with 14.8% less for the median Black household.

In spite of the increasing income inequality and persistent poverty America is getting tough with anti-welfare sentiments of the 1990s. Democrats and Republicans at both the national and state levels seem to have agreed that paying public funds to the poor—particularly to single mothers and their children—perpetuates dependency and undermines self-sufficiency and the work ethic. National experts on welfare have pointed out the fallacies in the current proposals for welfare reform, arguing that they merely recycle old remedies that have not worked (Handler & Hasenfeld, 2007). As Handler and Hasenfeld remind readers, America still maintains the prejudice that has historically existed against "the undeserving poor," and to the stereotype of Black women in urban areas who have children in order to stay on welfare is untrue. Keep in mind the "welfare queen" dating back to the Reagan years is a prejudice label for urban Black women, the mothers of the Black girls of the 1990s, which consequently is a plague for 1990s young Black girls to overcome. In truth most welfare mothers are in the labor market, a condition of welfare reform from the Clinton years. The work that is available to them is mostly low-wage, part-time employment with no benefits. Poverty affects achievement. As described by Ravitch (2013) in her discussion on poverty and academic achievement, the same factors certainly pertain to life achievement in general. Ravitch (2013) points out the effects of poverty on a child's well-being emotionally and motivationally as well as on the ability to concentrate on anything other than day-to-day living. Some children are able to rise above it but most do not.

> It is easy for people who enjoy lives of economic ease to say that (absolute) poverty doesn't matter. It doesn't matter to them. It is an abstraction. For them it is a hurdle to overcome, like having a bad day or a headache or an ill-fitting jacket. But for those who live in a violent neighborhood, in dingy surroundings, it is a way of life, not an inconvenience. Children who have seen a friend or relative murdered cope with emotional burdens that are unimaginable to the corporate leaders who want to reform their schools or close them. (Ravitch, 2013, p. 94)

Poverty matters before a child is born and between 1990 and 2006 premature births increased by 20% according to the American Congress of Obstetricians and Gynecologists. According to the Centers for Disease Control poverty is one of the most important predictors of insufficient prenatal care. Women with incomes below the federal poverty level consistently show higher rates of late or no prenatal care than women with larger incomes. The underclass Black girls of the 1990s are a part of this category through no fault of their own.

Young Black girls have been living at the margins of socioeconomic poverty while being exposed to the materialistic inequalities that seem unexplainable. How is a young poor Black girl to reconcile her reality to that of the visible consumption-lavishing lifestyle the media portrays? The media provides the reference groups for young Black woman and girls that are isolated from the middle-class Blacks. Where are they to turn when a generation of unemployment or underemployment has been the characteristic of their households throughout their young lives? When they have not in large measure seen personal success by education and employment, how are they to understand the value of schooling? When American society values material goods to determine people's worth and achievements, why are young Black girls criticized for desiring external possessions? In America consumption is conspicuous. In the United States material possessions reflect economic status and successes. When people are poor they cannot engage in competitive consumption so they have babies. The birthrate for young Black girls in poverty is a very rational choice given their realities. The young Black girl who does not graduate from high school is making a rational choice when graduating does not provide any tangible rewards. The young Black girl that does not hope for a different life from poverty is rational if that life seems unattainable.

Absolute Poverty and the Absolute Truth

Blaming the victim does not address the need for a change in public views to support public policy to reduce poverty by increased labor market opportunities and legislation that promotes more things such as the Earned Income Tax Credit. Unless there are more jobs paying higher income, poverty will not be lessened nor will there a reduction in the need for welfare assistance (Moynihan, 1973). The aspirations for young Black girls will remain distorted. Hope in their economic aspirations will be limited at best and the value for schooling will not exist. If schooling does not provide the knowledge to be marketable, enabling graduates to receive a living wage in the labor market, there will not be an increase in motivation or an attitude that values schooling. Many think that the poor are irrational, yet their choices seem to be quite rational. Due to factors that contribute to social instability such as diminished family income, the deterioration of quality schools, increased incidence of crime, along with the destructive media images to which they are exposed, their choices are fairly reasonable. The likelihood of them escaping poverty is fairly slim. They do not live in an environment that plans for the future because it is uncertain, and the past is too painful so they live in a culture that values having a good

time now. The poor do not have material possessions so they value people. Young Black girls will sacrifice the uncertainty of attempts at success
for relationships. People are prized possessions. It is amazing how the
perpetual negative stereotypes of Black women have remained intact in
American society from pre–civil rights with a hold that still reigns. The
Black women in America have been considered the Jezebels as well as the
welfare queens. These stereotypes certainly impact the aspirations and
self-esteem of young Black girls. The poor in America are devalued and
this is a burden for the urban Black girl of the 1990s.

Social theory has taught us that self-fulfilling prophecies emerge according to the looking-glass self. Cooley clearly explained that one becomes what one believe's oneself to be. So if society portrays young Black
girls negatively it is not unreasonable that they internalize that belief.
They far too often become underachievers both socially and economically. The social class of Black female marginalization and hence poverty
is reproduced. It is reproduced by the power of the mind that has been
shaped and reshaped by the narrow pathology of America's social and
economic institutions that denigrate the Black female—a truth that is
unspeakable.

Remedies to Reduce Urban Poverty: Self-Empowerment

If America wants to reduce poverty for young Black girls it must begin
by acknowledging how systematic economic downturns eroded resources,
and that has translated into failing schools, along with the 1980s deregulation of media that mass-produces negative images. Juilet Schor (2003)
very eloquently describes the power of the media, reference groups, and
materialism in American culture. Over the past three decades American
society has changed drastically, as the girl of the 1990s only knows.

> All forms of the media have pushed the limits of social acceptabil-
> ity. Television programs have become more daring and suggestive
> both in language and in the content of their story line. . . . Many
> young students rush home after school to catch the latest episode of
> their favorite and increasingly risqué soap opera. Popular music
> artists such as Madonna have pushed sexuality into the forefront of
> their music and concerts. Certain rap artists, especially those per-
> forming gangsta rap, express defiance of widely accepted standards
> of behavior. The words to some rap songs promote disrespect and
> violence toward women and encourage violence toward police and
> authority figures. Television's music channels such as MTV have
> established fame and fortune for many rock groups who sometimes
> focus on disturbing and violent scenes within their videos. (Bosch,
> 1997, p. 21)

The impact of television on the minds of young people is widely debated. Business spends millions of dollars a year on media advertisement to influence consumer spending, an influence surely not doubted. So if media can be respected for its powerful influence in generating value, we must also accept when it is responsible for generating the devaluing of moral attitudes in society. Violence in society is reflected in schools. The violence in schools became a national concern in the 1990s. In 1990, the U.S. Congress passed the Gun-Free School Zones Act, and in 1994 Congress passed the Gun-Free Schools Act that was signed by President Bill Clinton (Reicher, 1995, pp. 32–38). Hence by the 1990s the violence in schools was so prevalent Congress had to act and legislation to keep schools safe was passed. The 1994 law made it mandatory for any school accepting federal dollars to implement policies ensuring that violent acts and carrying of weapons would result in automatic suspension.

Marketing and mass media for profit drive messages that devalue personal pride and private lives, promoting a culture of fun at any cost. They promote a desire for materialism to be marketed to children. The desensitizing of young Blacks to the value of life and the precious sacredness of their bodies and minds coincides with Reagan's practice of deregulation, allowing the media to freely provide images of intimacy that were glamourized in sexual imagery. For example, during the 1970s there were clear guidelines about the nature of sexual content and use of profanity in the media. By the 1990s sexual encounters on primetime television were the norm, chaos in loving relationships and violence were popular, and physical exposure was rapid. The young minds of Americans in the 1990s were saturated with images that a mere decade before were unthinkable. The media created false images of how success is measured and acquired. Young people no longer were faced with an image of what to be in terms of work but were instead faced with images of what they should want to acquire materialistically. Consumerism expanded in the American economy and defined the social structures, presenting an unrealized eroding desire that warped the minds and goals of the young, and this impact on the minds of Black girls in poverty is no exception. The reference groups that the media portrays are far-reaching and have generated a negative bar to reach that is empty of substance and character.

Young Black girls need to be able to be grounded, to come to understand deferred gratification. This message must be adopted by the public at large, the professors, teachers, clergy, economic advisors, politicians, and everyone that is concerned about the state of the urban Black girl in poverty. This message by any means necessary must be passed on to young girls as a new motto and creed. Expose young girls to the truth of the past and give them hope and the tools for economic success. Personal responsibility must become popular. Young Black girls in poverty must be told to learn that you are not what you own, but you are a superior being that does not have to be confined to the limited spaces carved by negative stereotypes, past practices of failed political policies, and economic corrosion. Keep in mind that there was a time when it was illegal for Blacks in America to read. Young girls must be given incentives to read, shown the value of individuality, and shown how to plan to be the best that one can be. It is essential for young Black girls to develop the desire to empower the mind and be at peace. Being at peace does not mean not being around noise; it means being at peace in its midst. The truth is that where the mind is the body will follow. It is necessary for young Black girls to be taught to be courageous and claim what is good, and good will follow. Young Black girls must be exposed to the historical paths of the African American women. The strength of the Black woman has always been instrumental in the advancement of the Black family, for she did not walk behind the Black man, she always walked beside him. When there was no man, the Black female walked proudly alone and this is a history that must be remembered. When the young Black underclass female is allowed to be reminded that she is a Black pearl, the circle of poverty can begin to be broken. The acceptance of a life in poverty will not be acceptable. The desire to overcome the structural barriers that perpetuate poverty will begin to be broken. As America has once again begun a discussion about poverty in America for middle class Whites and Blacks, it is an opportune time to push for individual responsibility at the same time. America must change the macroeconomic policies as well as the microeconomic policies on the structural institutions, particularly the economic institution as it relates to the Black underclass and the Black girls of the 1990s.

REFERENCES

Addy, S., Engelhardt, W., & Skinner, C. (January 2013). Basic Facts about Low-income Children Under 18 Years, 2011. New York, NY: National Center for Children in Poverty, Columbia University.

Bishaw, A. (2013). Poverty 2000–2012. In *American Census Survey Brief Report*, February 13.

Bosch, C. (1997). *Schools under Siege; Guns Gangs and Hidden Dangers*. Springfield, NJ: Enslow Publishers.

Carpenter, Z. (2014). Eighty-six percent of Americans think the government should fight poverty. *The Nation*. www.thenation.com

Dreier, Peter. (2011). Why not let Reagan rest in peace?: Because many of the most serious problems facing America today began on his watch, *The Nation*, *www.thenation.com*. February 4, 2011.

Duncan, J., & Magnuson, K. (2011). The long reach of early childhood poverty, *Pathways*, Winter 2011.

Gilmore, Brian. Nostalgia for Reagan distorts his policies against Blacks. *The Progressive*. www.progressive.org. June 8, 2004.

Gould, E., & Wething, H. (2012). U.S. poverty rates higher, safety net weaker than in peer countries. Washington, DC: Economic Policy Institute.

Handler, J., & Hasenfeld, Y. (2007). *Blame Welfare: Ignore Poverty and Inequality*. New York: Cambridge University Press.

Moynihan, P. (1965). Employment, income and the ordeal of the negro family. In *The Negro American*. Edited by T. Parsons and K. B. Clark. Boston: Beacon Press.

Moynihan, P. (1973). *The Politics of a Guaranteed Income*. New York: Random House.

Partee, M. (2003). *The History of the State University of New York at Buffalo Department of Economics 1917–2000: The Rise and Fall of the Once Promising Department*. Ann Arbor, MI: Pro Quest Company.

Partee, M. (2009) *The Industrial Revolution in Encyclopedia of Time*. Ed. J. Birx. Thousand Oaks, CA: Sage Publications.

Patterson, O. (2009). A poverty of the mind. *New York Times*, March 26.

Price, R. G. (2010). How Reagan sowed the seeds of america's demise (March 30, 2010). www.rationalrevolution.net

Rank, M. (2013). Poverty in America is mainstream. *New York Times*, November 2.

Ratcliffe, C., & McKernan, S. (2012). *Child Poverty and Its Lasting Consequence*. Urban Institute.

Ravitch, D. (2013). *Reign of Error: The Hoax of the Privatization Movement and the Danger to America's Public Schools*. New York: Random House.

Reich, R. (2011). *After Shock: The Nest Economy & America's Future*. New York: Vintage Books.

Reicher, M. (1995). American school board journal, pp. 32–38, in C. Bosch (1997), *Schools Under Siege: Guns, Gangs and Hidden Dangers*. Springfield, NJ: Enslow.

Schor, J. (2003). *The Overspent American: Why We Want What We Don't Need*. Northampton, MA: Media Education Foundation.

Schor, J. (2011). *True Wealth: How and Why Millions of Americans Are Creating a Time-Rich, Ecologically Light, Small-Scale, High-Satisfaction Economy*. New York: Penguin.

Sowell, T. (1981). *Markets and Minorities*. New York: Basic Books.

Teen Health and the Media. http://www.depts.washington.edu/thmedia/view .cgi?

Urban Institute and Brookings Institution. (2004). Effective Total Federal Tax Rates. http://www.taxpolicycenter.org/briefing-book/key-elements/business/what-is.cfm

Wacquant, L. (2013). *Urban Outcast: A Comparative Sociology of Advanced Marginality*. Hoboken: Wiley Books (eBook).

Wilson, W. J. (1980). *The Declining Significance of Race*. Chicago: University of Chicago Press.

Wilson, W. J. (1987). *The Truly Disadvantaged: The Inner City, the Underclass, and Public Policy*. Chicago: University of Chicago Press.

Chapter 7

Prevention of Overweight and Obesity among African American Girls

Te Cora Ballom

If you watch any television programs, you are likely to see lots of fit young people. They are actors in television commercials, movie actors, athletes, and performers of one kind or another and are overwhelmingly height and weight proportionate or at least conform to the generally accepted concept of fitness. This is a sharp contrast to what you will see if you tune in to a news broadcast when everyday people are being filmed or interviewed. The next time you attend a junior high school sporting event, take notice of the adolescents in the stands or the cheerleaders or even the athletes. You will quickly begin to see the literal spread of an epidemic. In America, childhood obesity rates have tripled during the past thirty years and today, nearly one in three children is overweight or obese (Ogden, 2014). Consider the result of studies indicating that 5% of adolescents aged 12 to 19 years old were obese in 1980 and that number had soared to 20.5% by 2012 (Ogden, 2014). The statistics that gave me real grief were that, in African American and Hispanic communities, approximately 40% of the children are overweight or obese and African American females aged 12–19 years old are overweight or obese at a rate of 42.5% (Ogden, 2014).

It isn't difficult to understand the progression of the overweight and obesity problem afflicting America's children. There was a time when more children walked to school, played outdoors, and had regular gym class during school. The child's family ate meals at home, the portion sizes were smaller, and vegetables had their place on the dinner plate. Fast-food restaurants weren't as prolific and there were no soft drink machines in schools. Imagine a time when there were only three television networks, no cable television, no satellite television, and no Internet streaming. Programming for children was only aired a couple of hours a day. Times change, programming has changed, eating behaviors have changed, and the weight range of the population has also changed (Epstein, 2008; Kaur, 2003).

Obesity has long been a clinical issue and the rapid spread of the problem prompted the American Medical Association to take action, officially recognizing obesity as a disease in 2013. Excess body weight leads to metabolic abnormalities associated with increased morbidity and mortality. The minority community has higher rates of overweight and obesity and as a result suffers disproportionately the associated maladies. The problem is compounded by some other issues plaguing the minority community, including disparities in health care, socioeconomic condition, and education level. There is interrelation between these problems. It has been suggested that there is a correlation between educational attainment, poverty, and health (Aber, 1997). Statistics indicate that African Americans are likely to be poor, have less education, suffer from sickness, and not have health insurance (African American Profile—The Office of Minority Health, n.d.). Given the correlation of these issues, it is not surprising that a trend analysis performed as part of a study forecast that over 86% of non-Hispanic Black women will be overweight or obese by 2015 (Wang, 2007). The figure most often cited at this time comes from the National Center for Health Statistics (2012), which found that African American girls were an astounding eighty percent more likely to be obese than non-Hispanic White girls.

About 1994 or 1995, twenty years ago at the time of this writing, a woman called my medical office and the receptionist referred her to the office manager to help her with a question about her adolescent daughter's health. The office manager listened as the woman, who was not a patient and whose daughter was not a patient, explained her concern about her daughter's obesity. She was very distraught and wanted a referral or a lead on some type of program that could help her daughter. The office manager left a message for me and I returned the woman's call when I finished seeing the day's patients. Although I did not know the woman, she knew of me through friends who were patients and she worked in the bank building across the parking lot from my office. I had seen her before going to and leaving work and knew she was African American.

I listened as the woman talked at length about her daughter. She talked about the effect her weight was having on her social life and her self-perception and it was obvious she was desperate to help her. She was certain that somewhere there was a program that addressed this problem and could help her daughter.

I was at a loss. On a daily basis, marketing representatives from every imaginable health agency or company traipsed into my office in an effort to make me aware of what services they could provide my patients. I received a truckload of advertisement material every month from different ancillary health providers, and I stayed well informed on the resources available that might be a benefit for my patients. Yet the best I could offer this woman was a referral to a pediatrician. I didn't hold much hope that the pediatric doctor could offer more. After informing the woman that she was right to be concerned and of the potential health problems that obesity could pose for her daughter in the future, I gave her a name and a phone number and hopefully she found the help she was seeking.

Twenty years have passed and I am reminded of that woman and her daughter frequently, every time I read about the obesity epidemic in America and the disproportionate rate of obese and overweight African Americans and especially African American adolescent females. What has changed in twenty years and what needs to change in the next twenty years to curb the spread of this disease? What could be done to prevent so many other young African American adolescents from being in the position of the daughter of the woman who called my office?

The Centers for Disease Control and Prevention (CDC) defines overweight and obesity as the accumulation of excessive adipose tissue or "ranges of weight that are greater than what is generally considered healthy for a given height" (Obesity and Overweight for Professionals, n.d., p. 1). The most accepted measure of excess fat is known as the Body Mass Index (BMI). It is a measurement tool that approximates excess fat accumulation and though it does not actually measure body fat, it is a less expensive and simpler tool than other methods. Using the BMI as a measure, adults who are overweight have a BMI within the range 25 to 29.9, adults with a BMI greater than 30 are considered obese, and a BMI of greater than 40 is considered extremely obese (Obesity and Overweight for Professionals, n.d.).

Pediatricians utilize growth charts for children and adolescents (aged 2–19 years) to determine weight status by age and sex, and a specific percentile. The CDC defines obesity in children as a BMI at or above the growth chart criteria of the 95th percentile based on gender and age standards. Overweight is defined as a BMI at or above the CDC criteria of the 85th percentile, but lower than the 95th percentile based on gender and age standards (Obesity and Overweight for Professionals, n.d.).

Obesity can have a detrimental effect on the body, and in fact some studies estimate that 300,000 deaths annually can be attributed to obesity

(Reilly, 2003; Allison, 1999). Obese children and adolescents are at risk for developing multiple chronic diseases at an early age such as high blood pressure, high cholesterol, type 2 diabetes, sleep apnea, joint problems, gallstones, and gastroesophageal reflux (i.e., heartburn), which are usually suffered by adults (Reilly, 2003). The ill effects of these disease processes can have long-standing consequences or can curtail their lives during early adulthood (Daniels, 2006).

In addition, obese children and adolescents are at risk for developing long-term psychological problems, such as the effects of stigmatization and poor self-esteem (Puhl, 2007). Clinical evidence supports that obese children are more likely to become obese adults and that there is a higher incidence for Black women (The, 2010). These findings suggest that in order to avert the likelihood that the obese adults are subject to comorbidities and chronic diseases associated with obesity, intervention to reduce the progression of obesity at the adolescent stage is appropriate.

The U.S. government program responsible for producing the nation's health statistics is the National Health and Nutrition Examination Survey (NHANES). NHANES uses surveys and physical examinations to generate an assessment of the health and nutrition status of the population.

The NHANES 2011–2012 survey results revealed 16.9% of all children and adolescents aged 2–19 years are obese. During that same time interval 20.5% of children and adolescent African American girls aged 2–19 were obese compared with non-Hispanic White children and adolescents girls (aged 2–19) at 15.6% (Ogden, 2014). The prevalence rate for obesity increased among African American adolescent girls (age 12–19) from 16.3% to 22.7% during the survey periods 1988–1994 through 2011–2012 (Ogden, 2014). These figures offer a dire outlook for the health status of the U. S. population in coming years.

The childhood overweight and obesity epidemic presents a serious problem. We cannot afford to sit by idly and watch it progress. It is imperative that we find a solution to this epidemic which is devastating the health of all Americans and especially more predisposed African American female adolescents.

Some years ago, I was watching a television broadcast of a program that looked at the lives of a group of young African American female college students matriculating at a southern historically Black college. There were seven or eight young women all of whom appeared happy and well adjusted. I noticed that nearly every one of the women was overweight; most of them would probably have a BMI that classify them as obese.

At one point during the show, the group goes to the campus cafeteria and the cafeteria manager proudly points out all of the indulgences prepared daily for the nourishment of the college's students. There was practically every southern soul food delicacy you might ever desire: thick with cheese, swimming in butter or animal fat, covered with gravy, sugary, or breaded and fried, in abundance at the serve yourself buffet. The girls gleefully piled their plates high without giving any discernible consideration as to what the health consequences might be for consuming the decadent delights.

Were these eating habits learned in college? It is often speculated that new college students are apt to gain weight in their first year (Butler, 2004). I suspect that habits are formed much sooner than college age. The college girls mentioned previously undoubtedly have a predilection for the foods traditionally considered as "soul food," but what is soul food and is it the real cause of the weight disparity among African American adolescent females and other ethnic groups of the same age?

I once saw a video clip where an older male television personality was quizzing his younger African American female cohost about her holiday meal. He asked her what mac and cheese was as if he had never heard of it before and he wanted to know if it was some sort of secret African American epicurean delight. I am certain that macaroni pasta or cheese did not originate with African Americans. Wikipedia states that President Thomas Jefferson is responsible for popularizing macaroni and cheese in the United States sometime around 1802 after enjoying the dish in France and in Italy. He had it served at a White House state dinner. It is likely that African Americans worked in the kitchen preparing this dish and later in Southern eating establishments preparing and serving macaroni and cheese. The dish is most often prepared with copious amounts of butter, cheese, and eggs.

The derivation of some other soul food recipes is attributed to slave times when ingredients and seasonings brought from Africa were combined with the less desirable foods or parts of animals to which slaves had access (Gibbs et al., 1980; Whitehead, 1992). A combination of African, European, and Native American foods and cooking methods was used. In a study conducted by Tony L. Whitehead, it was documented that the method or style of preparation of foods distinguished them as traditional southern African American core foods (Whitehead, 1992). Among the primary preparation styles documented were frying meat in some form of fat, often pork fat, stewing vegetables in pork fat, preparation of cornbread with pork fat, and desserts or drinks made with excessive amounts of sugar (Whitehead, 1992).

The foods prepared by slaves and passed down to later generations were, and are today, enjoyed at family meals, family gatherings, and other African American social events, an example being the Friday or Saturday night fish fry. As African Americans shared the distinctly identifiable foods while experiencing the company of friends and family who all shared traditional eating habits, the cultural aspect of "soul food" was shaped. A cultural identity formed from the association of the foods with African American life and events (Kosoko-Lasaki, 2009). As noted in

Cultural Proficiency in Addressing Health Disparities, by Kosoko-Lasaki, Cook, and O'Brien (2009), "blacks living under the oppression of slavery with very few options, gathered at the end of the day for a communal meal with friends and family. They most likely found spiritual strength and regeneration through eating and camaraderie. This experience over generations became part of the culture."

African Americans may historically have been accustomed to a less than optimally healthy diet; that still does not mean they were overweight. To understand what has transpired to bring about the current state of epidemic, we must look at a host of factors. One very significant factor is the shift in Americans' eating habits away from meals prepared from scratch with fresh ingredients to a diet consisting primarily of higher calorie and processed foods, foods that are fat laden, foods higher in cholesterol and sugar (Smith, 2013).

Adolescent obesity among African American girls is a multifactorial problem in which a variety of determinants combine forming a complex mixture which is flavored with cultural, genetic, psychological, societal, and environmental ingredients. Blend in media influence, socioeconomic status, sedentary lifestyle, and larger portion sizes, and the mixture thickens. The scientific definition of being overweight or being obese is often not as much a concern in the African American community. The community commonly accepts a greater degree of plumpness as an accepted cultural difference. Being "big boned" or "thick" is accepted and even desirable as a cultural identification among segments of the minority population (Stockton, 2009; Gluck, 2002). The denial or unawareness of the risk associated with the overweight condition places the health of affected individuals at risk (Williams, 2013).

A 2009 study, "Self-Perception and Body Image Associations with Body Mass Index among 8–10-year-old African American Girls," concluded, "girls with higher BMI had greater body image discrepancy and were less confident in abilities to be active and eat healthy. Findings may inform the development of obesity interventions for preadolescents" (Stockton, 2009). Other studies have pointed to inconsistencies in the perceptions and behaviors associated with racial/ethnic differences in body image and weight (Gluck, 2002).

Body dissatisfaction was similar for Black and White girls in a weight-loss program. Ninety-nine percent of girls reported dissatisfaction with their current body size. Black girls reported larger body size ideals (Kelly, 2011). Significant weight misperceptions were evident among most girls (Kelly, 2011).

A study performed in 2013 entitled "Do Depression, Self-Esteem, Body-Esteem, and Eating Attitudes Vary by BMI among African American Adolescents?" concluded, "Among a community sample of predominantly African-American adolescents, obesity, not overweight, was associated with poor psychosocial health. Findings suggest that overweight may be perceived as normative, and that weight-related intervention programs consider adolescents' psychosocial functioning" (Witherspoon, 2013). The study suggests that perception of being overweight is relative to racial/ethnic perspective.

Bias and stigma associated with being overweight or obese can have adverse social consequences for children and adolescents. Consequences can come in the form of teasing, taunting, name-calling, or isolation. Weight bias is a form of prejudice whereby obese or overweight children may be viewed negatively by their teachers, physicians, parents, and friends (Washington, 2011). Obese children are often thought of as untidy, unambitious, lacking in self-discipline, or lazy.

The media plays a major role in promoting weight bias by associating positive messages with thin characters and negative messages with obese characters. Weight bias toward adolescents can have emotional consequences including low self-esteem, negative body image, and clinical depression (Puhl, 2007). It is important in searching for a solution to the childhood obesity epidemic, not to blame the children for this problem, but emphasize environmental conditions which contribute to this epidemic.

Frederick's study, "Increasing socioeconomic disparities in adolescent obesity," analyzed data from the NHANES 1988–2010 and 2003–2011 National Survey of Children's Health. The study reported a stabilization in the prevalence rate of obesity among youth with the exception of adolescents age 12–17 from low income and from less educated families (Frederick, 2014). Disadvantaged children are at far greater risk of not benefiting from intervention efforts.

Within the same week, I recently had the occasion to visit two convenience stores, one in an upscale, suburban community and another convenience store that was part of the same national chain located in a lower socioeconomic urban community populated by mostly Blacks and Hispanics. I was taken aback by the variety and preponderance of fruits and vegetables at both stores. A substantial portion of space was dedicated to healthful foods at both stores, which has not always been the case for this store chain. While this would appear to be progress, are there differences? The cost of convenience store food is significantly more than supermarket prices and this would be a greater deterrent to persons in the lower socioeconomic group. There are also social and cultural considerations. These differences are possibly significant in understanding why the trend of obesity prevalence of adolescents has diverged in direction in recent studies. While studies indicate a slight decline in the prevalence of obesity among adolescents from families with higher education level and/or higher socioeconomic level, the reverse is true for other adolescents whose prevalence level increased during the same time frame. Parental education level and similarly income level were the differentiating factors in the decline or increase in obesity prevalence (Frederick, 2014).

Lower socioeconomic status neighborhoods tend to have obesogenic (obesity-promoting) environments in which common circumstances include limited opportunities for physical activity, poor nutritional options, greater usage of electronic media (video games, social media, and television), which encourage a sedentary lifestyle (Lovasi, 2009). The contribution of the obesogenic environment to the current state of the overweight and obesity epidemic cannot be discounted. We should ask ourselves whether, if we could place today's African American female adolescents in the past about thirty years, they would have the same prevalence rates of overweight and obesity that they currently have or the rate that was prevalent during that time period and what environmental changes account for the difference.

The increase in media face time leads to a decrease in sleep duration (Lumeng, 2007). Advertising on electronic media influences food choice decisions by promoting food choices with less than adequate nutrition. Fruit and vegetable producers aren't flooding the airwaves with advertisements like the marketers of sugary beverages and processed foods. Advertising targets children, contributing to this ongoing complex problem (Harris, 2010). Lower socioeconomic status neighborhoods are frequently also food deserts. Food deserts are areas with limited availability of healthful foods at affordable cost, usually found in lower socioeconomic urban and rural areas—conditions which are exploited by the fast-food industry.

In 1970 there were about 30,000 fast-food outlets in the United States. By 1980 there were 140,000, and the estimate for 2001 was about 222,000, generating over $125 billion in sales (Paeratakul, 2003; French, 2000). The portion size changes are part of the "supersizing" phenomenon seen at fast-food establishments and at restaurants (Nielson, 2003). Portion sizes and energy intake for specific food types have increased markedly. The study, "Fast-food habits, weight gain, and insulin resistance (the CARDIA study); 15-year prospective analysis," by Pereira and colleagues followed 3,031 Black and White adults age 18–30 years old in 1985–86 using dietary assessments. The findings suggested that fast-food consumption increases the risk of obesity and type 2 diabetes (Pereira et al., 2005).

The U.S. Department of Health and Human Services recommends that children and adolescents aged 6–17 years old should have 60 minutes or more of physical activity each day as outlined in its publication, *The Physical Activity Guidelines for Americans* (Physical Activity Guidelines, n.d.). The study, "Decline in Physical Activity in Black Girls and White Girls During Adolescence," by Kimm and colleagues followed 1,213 Black girls and 1,166 White girls from the ages of 9 to 19 years old, for a 10-year period (Kimm et al., 2002). The findings suggest decreased physical activity in both Black and White girls during adolescence with a greater decline among Black girls. Cited in the study were determinants associated with decreased physical activity by the adolescent girls, including lower level of parental education, pregnancy, cigarette smoking, and high BMI (Kimm, et al., 2002).

This decline in physical activity promotes a sedentary lifestyle among African American adolescent girls. Increasing physical activity at school and at home is a key factor in preventing obesity in African American adolescent girls. A study supported by the National Institutes of Health, "The Associations Between Family Support, Family Intimacy, Neighborhood Violence and Physical Activity in Urban Adolescent Girls," revealed that family intimacy is very important to adolescent girls' attitudes toward physical activity (Kuo, 2007).

The 2013 Fast Facts Survey conducted by the Rudd Center for Food Policy and Obesity concluded that African American children and teens are targeted by fast-food television marketing and view 60% more fast-food ads than White children and teens (Boyland, 2011). Considering the dilemma facing the African American population, the deliberate targeting of African American children by fast-food marketers is unconscionable in light of the data available that children are responsive to advertisements and choose their food products accordingly (Boyland, 2011).

The Institute of Medicine committee of the National Academy of Sciences, under direction from Congress, completed a review in 2004 which found that children were influenced by television advertising and that food and beverage companies marketed products that were unhealthful. The Committee stated that "current marketing practices are out of balance with a healthful diet and create an environment that puts young people's health at risk" (Kraak, 2011). The fast-food industry has shown reluctance to enforce restrictions on themselves when it comes to marketing to children (Kraak, 2011).

A remarkable moment occurred in 2013, when the CEO of the fast-food giant McDonald's was confronted at the annual corporate shareholders' meeting by of all persons, a nine-year-old girl who questioned the propriety of McDonald's targeting children in their advertising for unhealthy foods. McDonald's CEO Don Thompson, who is African American, disputes any assertion that the company targets African American children; however the company maintains websites which are aimed specifically at the African American market, namely, McDonalds:365Black, (http://www.mcdonalds.com/365black/en/home.html).

It is nearly impossible to go to a store in America and see items which cannot be associated with a celebrity. Items from lipstick and lingerie to bedspreads and cookware bear the name of a celebrity from entertainers to athletes. Obviously marketers have figured out this is a method that works. The general public is persuaded by associating products with celebrity endorsers and fast-food items are no exception (Bragg, 2013).

When was the last time you saw an overweight celebrity endorse a fast-food product? Usually the celebrity endorsers are slender or athletic specimens, the picture of health and vitality, and often they are hawking the supersized product. It is unlikely that these celebrities consume much of the products they are promoting. Not unless their personal chefs are permitted to plate Burger King or McDonald's.

Alarm amid the scientific community over the obesity epidemic has generated research opportunities during the past twenty to twenty-five years. The acknowledgment that the growing overweight and obesity epidemic is a major public health issue is fueling a surge in discussion and focusing attention on the issue. A growing aggregation of data is being amassed regarding the causes of the obesity epidemic. The data may provide direction in developing future intervention strategies.

It is clear that if the past history is any guide the solution to the childhood obesity epidemic may lie in societal prevention intervention. The conclusion of some studies is that obesity has replaced smoking as the number one avoidable cause of premature deaths (Jia, 2010; Hennekens, 2013). Remember when we discuss obesity we are speaking about the associated cardiovascular disease, hypertension, diabetes, and other related diseases. In examining the case of smoking tobacco products, we can learn that from 1993 to 2008 while the proportion of adult smokers was declining, the proportion of obese people grew 85% (Jia, 2010). The decline in smoking over the last several years can be attributed to a variety of different interventions. Probably they were prompted by government action when in 1964, Dr. Luther Terry, then surgeon general of the United States, introduced the report that outlined clearly and unequivocally the hazards of smoking. The influence of the U.S. Surgeon General's office fixed public attention squarely on this issue.

Almost fifty years later, when asked about the tremendous decline in teen smoking rates, Danny McGoldrick, Vice President for Research, Campaign for Tobacco-Free Kids, told the *Los Angeles Times* newspaper that prevention programs combined with government interventions contributed to the teen smoking rate decline. Mr. McGoldrick commented, "We need to invest in more of what has worked in the past to accelerate these declines" (Alpert, 2013; Childstatsgov, n.d.).

The progress in prevention of African American adolescent female overweight and obesity may hinge on replicating some of the same methods and interventions that have been effective in reducing smoking rates. When public awareness and national policy converge, social change is actualized to make the necessary modifications, as in the case of seat belt or tobacco use (Hill, 2005).

Attention has been focused on the obesity epidemic by the U.S. government and First Lady Michelle Obama. The government efforts have been comprehensive, ranging from enacting policies which influence the nutritional value of foods served in schools to supporting initiatives that promote exercise and nutrition education.

Michelle Obama has led the charge, devoting countless hours to the effort with appearances in every imaginable venue or media type. Her association with the fight against the overweight and obesity epidemic carries with it significant recognition and media interest. At this stage it would probably be fair to say that no single person has brought any more awareness to the critical need to forestall the spread of this epidemic than Michelle Obama. She has also been successful in enlisting celebrities to join her in promoting healthy eating and exercise among children and adolescents.

Some African American parents of an adolescent female will feel the need to call their family physician or pediatrician with concerns about the weight of their child. With the spread of this epidemic, probably many more calls are placed than twenty years ago when I received the call at my office from the concerned women regarding her child's obesity issue.

With the increased recognition, health care practitioners and policy makers are trying to improve the treatment and prevention of the disease and progress is being made. More attention is being paid to intervention and treatment in adolescent and childhood overweight and obesity; however, studies show that there is still the necessity for improvement in attitudes and advancement of prevention (Force, 2005). It was in 1998 that a *Journal of Pediatrics* editorial written by Evan Chaney, MD, of the Pediatrics Department at the University of Massachusetts Medical Center, proclaimed that "Until we have a more sophisticated understanding of the hazards of childhood obesity and better intervention, 'primum non nocere' (first do no harm) remains, as always, the most prudent advice" (Rosner, 1998). In 2007, *Pediatrics* published new recommended Clinical Practice Guidelines for the Management of Obesity in Children and Adolescents, revised in 2009, and 2010 (Spear, 2007). The guidelines call for screening and referral to comprehensive and intensive intervention programs. The prevalence rate of overweight and obese children has grown; however, so have our awareness and resolve to face this issue (Baker, 2005).

There is an old joke about the patient who walks into the doctor's office and when the doctor asks, "What seems to be the problem?" the patient raises his arm and says, "Doctor, it hurts when I do this." The doctor responds, "Well, don't do that." Yes, this is a joke, but let's look at what is wrong with this advice. Obviously, it disregards the etiology of the patient's complaint, fails to illicit relieving or aggravating factors and consider possible treatment options. This may be likened to the advice that is often offered by society to individuals that are overweight or obese. We fail to perform a comprehensive evaluation on a complex problem. The recommendation given to obese individuals is to consume fewer calories and exercise more. This obviously is on the surface the correct advice. However, as we have explored in this chapter, the overweight and obesity issue is much more complex, serious, and the consequences are too great and it deserves a more considered response.

In writing on the subject of African American female adolescent obesity, it occurred to me that the writing vaguely reflected the method of documentation used by medical care providers called a SOAP note. SOAP is an acronym for subjective, observation, assessment, and plan and the method is used in patient charting. If we wanted to accept the SOAP note analogy and assume that our patient is the United States population of African American female adolescents, then at this point we have completed a history and physical on the patient, we have assessed behaviors and attitudes, assessed medical risks, taken measurements, reviewed test results, diagnosed the patient's problem, and we have explained the problem and explored the patient's options (Fitch, 2013). We are now ready to outline a treatment plan, provide a prescription for the patient, and instructions for follow-up.

Research and investigation into interventions and the prevention of childhood adolescent obesity are ongoing. There have been some successful efforts, and expanding those efforts and adapting them for the particular nature of African American female adolescents might be a good start point. Care must be taken to consider the cultural aspect or appropriateness of the intervention. Melnyk's study, *Preventing Obesity in Black Women by Targeting Adolescents*, cautions that attempts to adapt programs that may be successful for non–African Americans and only make superficial changes are not likely to work.

The solution to the obesity epidemic will require collaboration between all aspects of society, including federal entities via national policies, state government, local community, schools, health care industry, parents, other family members or caregivers, and the kids. The impact of national policy is crucial in maintaining momentum toward decreasing childhood obesity. The policies enacted by federal agencies can have a significant impact on state and local communities. For example, the United States Department of Agriculture (USDA) publishes dietary recommendations for Americans. The USDA has tremendous influence on food served at schools through these programs:

- National School Lunch Program
- School Breakfast Program
- Child and Adult Care Food Program
- Summer Food Service Program
- Fresh Fruit and Vegetable Program
- Special Milk and Smart Snack in School Program (CDC website)

The U.S. Department of Education offers grants to promote physical activity in schools. The CDC offers grants to states to develop programs which address childhood obesity. Among the private efforts, the Robert Wood Johnson Foundation, the nation's largest philanthropy, awarded grants to three colleges to develop community-based programs on childhood obesity. In addition, the foundation established a collaboration with the American Heart Association in 2012 to curb childhood obesity in low income communities by 2015 (Kelly, 2013). All levels of government should seek opportunities to partner with private national agencies in forming coalitions to develop policies that create safe environments and encourage a healthy lifestyle.

The CDC reports the obesity rate declined in 19 out of 43 States. Seven states declined to participate in data collection. Mississippi was one of the states that observed improvements in the prevalence rates of childhood obesity. Mississippi accomplished the goal through setting school vending machine nutrition standards in 2006, passing the Healthy Students Act of 2007, securing funding to make streets safer for walking and bicycling in 2010, and initiating the Move to Learn program in 2012 in which teachers lead students in short physical activity breaks. These efforts produced the drop in the state's childhood obesity rate from 43% in 2005 to 37.3% in 2011.

Local communities must make the commitment to seek out opportunities to promote healthy lifestyles and retrieve funding from national, state, and private entities towards accomplishing their goals. Communities should identify obesogenic environments and develop plans to provide safe environments which promote physical activity and offer healthy food options. The development of health advisory boards or task forces can assist in local policy implementation and support local school health and physical activities. Development of methods to endorse and support local farmers and community gardeners has had some success. Community gardens can be found at some schools, or churches, and others have posted on internet sites that they have a vacant lot and no time to plant a garden but are willing to share the produce with someone who will tend a garden.

The Healthy, Hunger-Free Kids Act (HHFKA) of 2010 under the purview of USDA takes aim at eliminating childhood obesity (Text of S. 3307, n.d.). The major focus of the act is to improve child nutrition. Schools that participate in the National School Lunch Program will be required to follow HHFKA policy. Dietary Guidelines for School Meals and implementation of a local school wellness policy are two of the major components of the HHFKA. The National School Board Association has made recommendations to assist in implementing the development of local school wellness policies. It is vital for schools to actively pursue opportunities to provide children education in nutrition and physical education. Some of the ideas being discussed as methods for schools to promote healthy lifestyles are:

- provide more fruits and vegetables at schools not associated with meals
- provide physical activity programs, provide health promotion and nutritional courses
- provide healthier options in the vending machines
- ban sugar-sweetened beverages and fast-food establishments within the schools
- ban the sale of candy for fund-raiser events
- plant a school garden
- form a teacher–parent health advisory group to promote healthy lifestyles and environments for the students

A successful example of a school district making an impact on childhood obesity in their community can be found in Kearney, Nebraska (Kearney, Nebraska: Signs of Progress, 2014). The school district received a three-year $900,000 grant awarded by the U.S. Department of Education for the purpose of providing assistance to the schools in improving their physical education programs. As a result, the community had a 13.4% decline in childhood obesity rates for elementary aged children from 2006 to 2011.

Health care providers must take an active leadership role in nutritional education and promoting lifestyle modification to parents and children during clinical appointments. Establishment of a multi-disciplinary approach to obesity prevention involving registered dietitian nutritionists, chefs, and recreation specialists may be necessary. All are involved in the care continuum, promoting wellness not just during the time allotted for the office visits. Of course this is a difficult idea to implement considering time and financial constraints and this is where the federal government has to incentivize.

The health care industry can make effective use of electronic medical records to flag at-risk patients who are overweight or obese so a treatment plan can be developed to address the issue. Medical care providers must consider BMI a vital sign. Providers should encourage breast-feeding, prescribe fresh fruits, vegetables, and physical activity for at least 60 minutes a day.

Parents will need to focus on developing healthy lifestyles with their children at an early age. Breast-feeding infants, healthy eating habits, and increased physical activity are some of the possibilities that parents may initiate. Less emphasis should be placed on dieting and body image. Studies have revealed healthy lifestyle habits, including healthy eating and physical activity, can lower the risk of becoming obese and developing related diseases (Taber, 2013).

A study entitled "Eating Behaviors Among Early Adolescent African American Girls and Their Mothers," published in the May 2013, issue of *The Journal of School Nursing*, looked at the nutritional intake of African American girls age 10–12 and their mothers in an urban community (Chicago, IL) and revealed a strong correlation between mother and daughter eating habits (Reed, 2013). A comparison of eating habits including frequency and location of meals, whether meals were consumed with the family, and the nutritional value of meals were examined for the girls and their mothers. The BMI was calculated for the mother-daughter pairs. The study found that 67.4% of the girls were in the overweight or obese range. Ninety-three percent of the mothers weighed in at the overweight or obese range (Reed, 2013). The study also found that 32.6% of the girls and 44.2% of the mothers indicated that they had consumed no meals with their family in the previous week. It was concluded that the girls and their mothers shared similar eating habits. Any intervention efforts should focus on educating both the mother and daughter to adopt healthier eating habits and make healthier food selections. If the current trend continues, it is possible that the girls could exceed the overweight and obese percentages of their mothers.

I hardly think many people would dispute that parents need to be role models for their children. But what if the parents are themselves facing overweight or obesity issues? Parents or caregivers can first make a commitment to their children, change their unhealthy eating habits, and adopt a healthy lifestyle by taking the following steps:

1. Encourage more fruits and vegetables at each meal.
2. Decrease media face time (to include televisions, computers, all video games, and all mobile devices).
3. Cook at home more often and eat family meals together without television, computers, or mobile devices.
4. Decrease consumption of meals away from home, sugar-sweetened beverages, fast foods, convenience foods, and snack foods in school vending machines.
5. Hold eating establishments responsible for offering healthy options and ask for nutritional information.
6. Increase physical activity to at least 60 minutes a day. Encourage walking, bicycling, and stair climbing.
7. Ensure sleep duration of 8 hours nightly.
8. Create media-free bedrooms.
9. Plant a vegetable garden.

10. Establish a relationship with a health care provider who practices prevention and promotes healthy lifestyle changes for kids.

Obesity remains a public health issue with one third of the children in the U.S. population being obese. Eradicating this epidemic will take collaboration, participation, and commitment from every facet of society. The approach to the problem has to view and treat it as a confirmed "epidemic." Public health officials should be actively involved in high risk areas and in Health Professional Shortage Areas, training individuals on those strategies proven successful in helping combat this disease.

If you believe there is a giant asteroid hurtling on a collision course with the country and predicted to obliterate a quarter of the continental United States, would you enact urgent measures? Would you declare a state of emergency? This is the mind-set and level of alarm necessary to fuel the type of urgent intervention required to prevent the future catastrophic consequences to the nation's health and economy presented by the overweight and obesity epidemic.

A critical point has been reached in the overweight and obesity epidemic and more so for African American female children and adolescents. Our nation has the responsibility to realize that drastic measures are needed to prevent continuing cases and control the epidemic. It will take a commitment financially and politically at all levels. A realization of the potential consequences of inaction or insufficient response must be had and the courage to act as if we are in a state of emergency.

As was the case with smoking, federal guidelines may need to be imposed regulating advertising of unhealthy products to children or risk the advertising images' negating efforts. A coordinated multidisciplinary approach centered and administered locally can ensure that cultural sensitivity needs are incorporated into all intervention. The collaboration of the intervention teams should take the form of public health emergency response teams, just as in combating other epidemics.

One plan of action to consider would be to assign the United States Public Health Service (USPHS) Commissioned Corp Officers, who respond to our nation's disasters such as Hurricane Katrina, to work at high-risk, disadvantaged schools, building community relationships and collaborating with school officials in developing a curriculum for the school's nutrition program. Students would have the opportunity to be a part of a newly legislated Junior Reserve United States Public Health Service Commissioned Corps similar to the current Junior ROTC. The student USPHS CORP would promote a healthy lifestyle among their classmates. There would be required nutrition and health courses in schools beginning in primary school through high school. Students would be required to take classes which meet the course requirement established by school districts to graduate from high school. The students would be trained by public health officials and in return train other students and develop response units, community mobilization projects, and youth peer counseling programs. Consider the impact of a fifteen-year-old African American female instructing a 10-year-old African American girl from the same cultural background to eat vegetables and fruits. The students would participate in weekly farmer's market visits and plant gardens at school and in the community. The causes of obesity are complex and multi-factorial and it will take decades to remedy the causes and behaviors which have contributed to bringing about the current circumstances. Our children's, and consequently, our country's future relies on a commitment from everyone to combat the obesity epidemic.

"The physical and emotional health of an entire generation and the economic health and security of our nation are at stake," as said by First Lady Michelle Obama at the Let's Move! Launch on February 9, 2010 (Let's Move, www.letsmove.gov, 2011).

REFERENCES

Aber, J. L., Bennett, N. G., Conley, D. C., & Li, J. (1997). The effects of poverty on child health and development. *Annual Review of Public Health, 18*, 463–483. doi:10.1146/annurev.publhealth.18.1.463

African American Profile—The Office of Minority Health—OMH. (n.d.). Retrieved March 30, 2014, from http://minorityhealth.hhs.gov/templates/browse .aspx?lvl=2&lvlID=51

Allison, D. B., Fontaine, K. R., Manson, J. E., Stevens, J., & Van Itallie, T. B. (1999). Annual deaths attributable to obesity in the United States. *JAMA, 282*(16), 1530–1538. doi:10.1001/jama.282.16.1530

Alpert, E. (2013, July 11). Cigarette smoking at new low among youths, survey finds. *Los Angeles Times*. Retrieved from http://articles.latimes.com/2013/ jul/11/local/la-me-0712-kids-wellbeing-20130712

Baker, S., Barlow, S., Cochran, W., Fuchs, G., Klish, W., Krebs, N., . . . Udall, J. (2005). Overweight children and adolescents: A clinical report of the North American Society for Pediatric Gastroenterology, Hepatology and Nutrition. *Journal of Pediatric Gastroenterology and Nutrition, 40*(5), 533–543.

Boyland, E. J., Harrold, J. A., Kirkham, T. C., Corker, C., Cuddy, J., Evans, D., . . . Halford, J. C. G. (2011). Food commercials increase preference for energy-dense foods, particularly in children who watch more television. *Pediatrics, 128*(1), e93–100. doi:10.1542/peds.2010-1859

Bragg, M. A., Yanamadala, S., Roberto, C. A., Harris, J. L., & Brownell, K. D. (2013). Athlete endorsements in food marketing. *Pediatrics*, 2013–0093. doi:10.1542 /peds.2013-0093

Butler, S. M., Black, D. R., Blue, C. L., & Gretebeck, R. J. (2004). Change in diet, physical activity, and body weight in female college freshman. *American Journal of Health Behavior, 28*(1), 24–32.

Childstats.gov—America's Children: Key National Indicators of Well-Being, 2013— Introduction. (n.d.). Retrieved April 1, 2014, from http://www.childstats .gov/americaschildren/

Daniels, S. R. (2006). The consequences of childhood overweight and obesity. *The Future of Children, 16*(1), 47–67. doi:10.1353/foc.2006.0004

Epstein, L. H., Roemmich, J. N., Robinson, J. L., Paluch, R. A., Winiewicz, D. D., Fuerch, J. H., & Robinson, T. N. (2008). A randomized trial of the effects of reducing television viewing and computer use on body mass index in young children. *Archives of Pediatrics & Adolescent Medicine, 162*(3), 239–245. doi:10.1001/archpediatrics.2007.45

Fitch, A., Fox, C., Bauerly, K., Gross, A., Heim, C., Judge-Dietz, J., Kaufman, T., Krych, E., Kumar, S., Landin, D., Larson, J., Leslie, D., Martens, N., Monaghan-Beery, N., Newell, T., O'Connor, P., Spaniol, A., Thomas, A., & Webb, B., Institute for Clinical Systems Improvement. Prevention and Management of Obesity for Children and Adolescents. Published July 2013.

Florida Atlantic University. (2013, January 31). Obesity approaching cigarette smoking as leading avoidable cause of premature deaths worldwide. Science Daily. Retrieved April 1, 2014 from www.sciencedaily.com/releases/2013/01/130131083755.htm

Force, U. P. S. T. (2005). Screening and Interventions for Overweight in Children and Adolescents: Recommendation Statement. *Pediatrics, 116*(1), 205–209. doi:10.1542/peds.2005-0302

Frederick, C. B., Snellman, K., & Putnam, R. D. (2014). Increasing socioeconomic disparities in adolescent obesity. *Proceedings of the National Academy of Sciences, 111*(4), 1338–1342. doi:10.1073/pnas.1321355110

French, L. H. (2000). Fast food restaurant use among women in the Pound of Prevention study: dietary, behavioral and demographic correlates. *International Journal of Obesity and Related Metabolic Disorders: Journal of the International Association for the Study of Obesity, 24*(10), 1353–9. doi:10.1038/sj.ijo.0801429

Gibbs, T., Cargill, K., Lieberman, L. S., & Reitz, E. (1980). Nutrition in a slave population: An anthropological examination. *Medical Anthropology, 4*(2), 175–262. doi:10.1080/01459740.1980.9965868

Gluck, M. E., & Geliebter, A. (2002). Racial/ethnic differences in body image and eating behaviors. *Eating Behaviors, 3*(2), 143–151.

Harris, J., Schwartz, M., & Brownell, K. Fast Food FACTS: Evaluating Fast Food Nutrition and Marketing to Youth, 2010. http://www.rwjf.org/files/research/20101108fffactsreport.pdf (accessed January 2013).

Hennekens, C. H., & Andreotti, F. (2013). Leading avoidable cause of premature deaths worldwide: Case for Obesity. *The American Journal of Medicine, 126*(2), 97–98. doi:10.1016/j.amjmed.2012.06.018

Hill, J. O., Catenacci, V., & Wyatt, H. R. (2005). Obesity: overview of an epidemic. *Psychiatric Clinics of North America, 28*(1), 1–23. doi:10.1016/j.psc.2004.09.010

James, D. C. S. (2009). Cluster analysis defines distinct dietary Patterns for African-American men and women. *Journal of the American Dietetic Association, 109*(2), 255–262. doi:10.1016/j.jada.2008.10.052

Jia, H., & Lubetkin, E. I. (2010). Trends in Quality-Adjusted Life-Years Lost Contributed by Smoking and Obesity. *American Journal of Preventive Medicine, 38*(2), 138–144. doi:10.1016/j.amepre.2009.09.043

Kaur, H., Choi, W. S., Mayo, M. S., & Harris, K. J. (2003). Duration of television watching is associated with increased body mass index. *The Journal of Pediatrics, 143*(4), 506–511.

Kearney, Nebraska: Signs of Progress. (2014, March 15). *RWJF*. Retrieved March 15, 2014, from http://www.rwjf.org/en/about-rwjf/newsroom/newsroom -content/2013/07/kearney-nebraska--signs-of-progress.html

Kelly, A. S., Barlow, S. E., Rao, G., Inge, T. H., Hayman, L. L., Steinberger, J., & Daniels, S. R. (2013). Severe Obesity in Children and Adolescents: Identification, Associated Health Risks, and Treatment Approaches—A Scientific Statement from the American Heart Association. *Circulation, 128*(15), 1689–1712. doi:10.1161/CIR.0b013e3182a5cfb3

Kelly, N. R., Bulik, C. M., & Mazzeo, S. E. (2011). An Exploration of Body Dissatisfaction and Perceptions of Black and White Girls Enrolled in an Intervention for Overweight Children. *Body Image, 8*(4), 379–384. doi:10.1016 /j.bodyim.2011.05.003

Kimm, S. Y. S., Glynn, N. W., Kriska, A. M., Barton, B. A., Kronsberg, S. S., Daniels, S. R., . . . Liu, K. (2002). Decline in Physical Activity in Black Girls and White Girls during Adolescence. *New England Journal of Medicine, 347*(10), 709–715. doi:10.1056/NEJMoa003277

Kosoko-Lasaki, S., Cook, C., & O'Brien, R. (2009). *Cultural Proficiency in Addressing Health Disparities*. Jones & Bartlett Learning.

Kraak, V. I., Story, M., Wartella, E. A., & Ginter, J. (2011). Industry progress to market a healthful diet to American children and adolescents. *American Journal of Preventive Medicine, 41*(3), 322–333; quiz A4. doi:10.1016/j.amepre.2011 .05.029

Kuo, J., Young, D. R., Voorhees, C. C., & Haythornthwaite, J. A. (2007). Associations Between Family Support, Family Intimacy, and Neighborhood Violence and Physical Activity in Urban Adolescent Girls. *American Journal of Public Health, 97*(1), 101–103. doi:10.2105/AJPH.2005.072348

Let's Move! (n.d.). Retrieved March 31, 2014, from http://www.letsmove.gov/

Lovasi, G. S., Hutson, M. A., Guerra, M., & Neckerman, K. M. (2009). Built Environments and Obesity in Disadvantaged Populations. *Epidemiologic Reviews, 31*(1), 7–20. doi:10.1093/epirev/mxp005

Lumeng, J. C., Somashekar, D., Appugliese, D., Kaciroti, N., Corwyn, R. F., & Bradley, R. H. (2007). Shorter sleep duration is associated with increased risk for being overweight at ages 9 to 12 years. *Pediatrics, 120*(5), 1020–1029. doi:10.1542/peds.2006-3295

McDonalds Home:365black.com. (n.d.). Retrieved March 31, 2014, from http:// www.mcdonalds.com/365black/en/home.html

Mississippi: Signs of Progress. (n.d.). *RWJF*. Retrieved April 1, 2014, from http:// www.rwjf.org/en/about-rwjf/newsroom/newsroom-content/2013/07/ mississippi--signs-of-progress.html

National Center for Health Statistics (US). (2012). *Health, United States, 2011: With Special Feature on Socioeconomic Status and Health*. Hyattsville (MD): National Center for Health Statistics (US). Retrieved from http://www.ncbi.nlm.nih .gov/books/NBK98752/

NHANES—National Health and Nutrition Examination Survey Homepage. (n.d.). Retrieved April 1, 2014, from http://www.cdc.gov/nchs/nhanes.htm

Nielsen, S., & Popkin, B. M. (2003). Patterns and trends in food portion sizes, 1977–1998. *JAMA, 289*(4), 450–453. doi:10.1001/jama.289.4.450

Obesity and Overweight for Professionals: Adult: Defining—DNPAO—CDC. (n.d.). Retrieved March 30, 2014, from http://www.cdc.gov/obesity/adult/defining.html

Ogden, C. L., Carroll, M. D., Kit, B. K., & Flegal, K. M. (2014). Prevalence of childhood and adult obesity in the United States, 2011–2012. *JAMA, 311*(8), 806–814. doi:10.1001/jama.2014.732

Paeratakul, S., Ferdinand, D. P., Champagne, C. M., Ryan, D. H., & Bray, G. A. (2003). Fast-food consumption among US adults and children: Dietary and nutrient intake profile. *Journal of the American Dietetic Association, 103*(10), 1332–1338. doi:10.1016/S0002-8223(03)01086-1

Pereira, M. A., Kartashov, A. I., Ebbeling, C. B., Van Horn, L., Slattery, M. L., Jacobs, D. R., Jr., & Ludwig, D. S. (2005). Fast-food habits, weight gain, and insulin resistance (the CARDIA study): 15-year prospective analysis. *The Lancet, 365*(9453), 36–42. doi:10.1016/S0140-6736(04)17663-0

Physical Activity Guidelines. (n.d.). Retrieved March 23, 2014, from http://www.health.gov/paguidelines/default.aspx

Prevention and Management of Obesity for Children and Adolescents. (n.d.). Retrieved from https://www.icsi.org/_asset/tn5cd5/ObesityChildhood.pdf

Puhl, R. M., & Latner, J. D. (2007). Stigma, obesity, and the health of the nation's children. *Psychological Bulletin, 133*(4), 557–580. doi:10.1037/0033-2909.133.4.557

Reed, M., Dancy, B., Holm, K., Wilbur, J., & Fogg, L. (2013). Eating Behaviors Among Early Adolescent African American Girls and Their Mothers. *The Journal of School Nursing, 29*(6), 452–463. doi:10.1177/1059840513491784

Reilly, J., Methven, E., McDowell, Z., Hacking, B., Alexander, D., Stewart, L., & Kelnar, C. (2003). Health consequences of obesity. *Archives of Disease in Childhood, 88*(9), 748–752. doi:10.1136/adc.88.9.748

Rosner, B., Prineas, R., Loggie, J., & Daniels, S. R. (1998). Percentiles for body mass index in U.S. children 5 to 17 years of age. *The Journal of Pediatrics, 132*(2), 211–222. doi:10.1016/S0022-3476(98)70434-2

Smith, L. P., Ng, S. W., & Popkin, B. M. (2013). Trends in US home food preparation and consumption: analysis of national nutrition surveys and time use studies from 1965-1966 to 2007-2008. *Nutrition Journal, 12*, 45. doi:10.1186/1475-2891-12-45

Spear, B. A., Barlow, S. E., Ervin, C., Ludwig, D. S., Saelens, B. E., Schetzina, K. E., & Taveras, E. M. (2007). Recommendations for Treatment of Child and Adolescent Overweight and Obesity. *Pediatrics, 120*(Supplement), S254–S288. doi:10.1542/peds.2007-2329F

Stockton, M. B., Lanctot, J. Q., McClanahan, B. S., Klesges, L. M., Klesges, R. C., Kumanyika, S., & Sherrill-Mittleman, D. (2009). Self-perception and Body Image Associations with Body Mass Index among 8–10-year-old African American Girls. *Journal of Pediatric Psychology, 34*(10), 1144–1154. doi:10.1093/jpepsy/jsp023

Taber, D. R., Chriqui, J. F., Powell, L., & Chaloupka, F. J. (2013). Association between state laws governing school meal nutrition content and student weight status: Implications for new USDA school meal standards. *JAMA Pediatrics, 167*(6), 513–519. doi:10.1001/jamapediatrics.2013.399

Text of S. 3307 (111th): Healthy, Hunger-Free Kids Act of 2010 (Passed Congress/ Enrolled Bill version). (n.d.). *GovTrack.us.* Retrieved March 17, 2014, from https://www.govtrack.us/congress/bills/111/s3307/text

The, N. S., Suchindran, C., North, K. E., Popkin, B. M., & Gordon-Larsen, P. (2010). The Association of Adolescent Obesity with Risk of Severe Obesity in Adulthood. *JAMA : The Journal of the American Medical Association, 304*(18), 2042–2047. doi:10.1001/jama.2010.1635

U.S. Department of Health. (2000). *Healthy people 2010.* Government Printing Office.

Wang, Y., & Beydoun, M. A. (2007). The Obesity Epidemic in the United States— Gender, Age, Socioeconomic, Racial/Ethnic, and Geographic Characteristics: A Systematic Review and Meta-Regression Analysis. *Epidemiologic Reviews, 29*(1), 6–28. doi:10.1093/epirev/mxm007

Washington, R. L. (2011). Childhood obesity: issues of weight bias. *Preventing Chronic Disease, 8*(5), A94.

Whitehead, T. L. (1992). In Search of Soul Food and Meaning: Culture, Food, and Health (Vol. 25, pp. 94–110). Presented at the Southern Anthropological Proceedings; 25; 94–110, University of Georgia Press.

Williams, E. P., Wyatt, S. B., & Winters, K. (2013). Framing body size among African American women and girls. *Journal of Child Health Care.* doi:10.1177/1367493 512461572

Witherspoon, D., Latta, L., Wang, Y., & Black, M. M. (2013). Do Depression, Self-Esteem, Body-Esteem, and Eating Attitudes Vary by BMI Among African American Adolescents? *Journal of Pediatric Psychology, 38*(10), 1112–1120. doi:10.1093/jpepsy/jst055

Part II

Parenting

Chapter 8

Me, Myself, and I: Biracial Challenges to Mental Health

Mary Harley Gresham

INTRODUCTION

Individuals whose parents are not of the same racial background are eventually forced—either publicly or privately—to confront the question of their own identity. Just some of the questions that might be considered include: Is one part of one's ancestry more important than the other? Is it safe to embrace one's entire heritage when it cannot be seen? Why is your identity the business of other people?

The question of "who" one is is not always contemplated in the solitary quiet of reflective moments, but is shaped dynamically through interactions with others. Moreover, different social contexts that provide the framework for interpersonal interactions exert their own pressures to conform or at least require managing the presumptions of others whose perspectives have been informed by the American paradigm about race—that is, that identity can only be White or non-White. Multiraciality challenges that paradigm (Shih & Sanchez, 2005; Rockquemore & Brunsma, 2008; Rockquemore, Brunsma & Delgado, 2009; Mohan & Chambers, 2009).

Models of monoracial identity development do not completely explain the path to self-acceptance for those of mixed heritage. In the context of the American biopic on race relations, the path to owning "me, myself, and I" for a biracial[1] person may be fraught with confusion, anger and/or frustration. The potential for cognitive and emotional dissonance resulting from the attempt to blend each aspect of one's identity into a cohesive persona is exacerbated by racialized fictions that have supported the American sociopolitical hierarchy for centuries. Although not an attempt to provide an empirical analysis, this chapter will explore some of the ways in which the process of claiming an identity may pose challenges to mental health for persons of mixed heritage.

AMERICA'S RACIAL PARADIGM

In 1994, the American Anthropological Association (AAA) released a *Statement on "Race" and Intelligence* in response to deeply rooted assertions about the intellectual inferiority of people of African descent. The assertion that "intelligence is biologically determined by race" was refuted by the claim that "all human beings are members of one species, *Homo sapiens*," and that "differentiating species into biologically defined 'races' has no scientific basis" (American Anthropological Association, 1994). This claim caused much consternation among the White American population, up to 30% of whom have at least two or three percent African ancestry, a fact that some would attribute to "statistical noise" (Blay, 2013). Moreover, ". . . centuries of sexual coercion account for the fact that most Black Americans today have multiracial ancestry" (Rockquemore & Brunsma, 2008, p. xix).

Despite the AAA declaration, America has been intensely resistant to abandon the use of "race" as a means of classifying individuals in society. As Helms (1992) and others (Frazier, 1969; Goff, 2008; Rockquemore & Brunsma, 2008; Rockquemore, Brunsma & Delgado, 2009; Ramirez, 1994) have noted, White Americans have a vested interest in sociocultural constructions about race and related hierarchies: it allows the power elite to remain White. As recently as March, 2014, Paul Ryan, House Budget Committee chairman, alleged that Blacks were disadvantaged because of their unwillingness to work, and referenced Charles Murray, co-author of *The Bell Curve* (Herrenstein & Murray, 1996), a book that espoused the intellectual inferiority of African Americans (Lowery, 2014).

Reasons for the persistence of racial constructions and their societal ramifications are grounded in the early roots of the American economic system. "There were powerful economic factors such as the demand for

---

[1] "Use of the term biracial denotes individuals with parents from two different races, and may also be termed multiracial or mixed race, consistent with most literature cited. The term 'multiple heritage,' now the accepted terminology, is not as yet widely utilized" (Leong et al., 2014, p. 24).

cheap and permanent labor supply that decided the fate of the Negro. . . . because of the invention of the cotton gin and the rise of the textile industry in England, the slave system became the foundation of the economic life of the South" (Frazier, 1969, p. 22). In the now famous Dred Scott decision of 1857, Chief Justice Taney of the Supreme Court summarized the thinking of that time: "A Negro has no rights which a White man need respect" (Frazier, 1969, p. 43). Such sentiments were taught in schools and universities, justifying the subordination of a people based on myths about their African ancestry which often likened people of color to apes, further rationalizing the exclusion of people of African descent from access to resources and privileges accorded only to White men.

In 1900, W.E. B. DuBois forecasted a continuation of the problem of race at the close of the first Pan African conference in London, England. His remarks referenced phenotypic characteristics of people of African descent: "the problem of the twentieth century is the problem of the color line, the question of how far differences of race—which show themselves chiefly in the color of skin and the texture of the hair—will hereafter be made the basis of denying to over half the world the right of sharing to their utmost ability the opportunities and privileges of modern civilization" (DuBois, 1900).

Even though slavery in Latin American countries, Brazil in particular, accounted for almost 90% of African slaves, the hyperdescent rule—specifying race based on the parent from the so-called dominant race—determined the race of mixed race offspring in those countries. In the United States, however, the "one-drop" or hypodescent rule—specifying race and social status based on the parent from the so-called inferior group—illustrates the extent to which African descent was used to maintain the supremacy of Whites over others in this country. Frazier (1969) suggested that the role of Blacks in the plantation system provided the foundation for race relations that are still seen today in the persistent economic and social inequities in America.

For the multiracial individual in the United States then, the privilege and opportunity of self-identification is made more difficult in the context of America's racial paradigm, that is, the White or non-White bifurcation of both people and social status. Identity for multiracial individuals is further exacerbated by the ambiguity of the "color line."

Developing a Racial Identity

For the most part, theories about identity development describe a progressively clear articulation of a self-concept that may include beliefs about belonging, cultural values, and personal ideals. Identity development has been construed as evolving through stages in a linear fashion while progressing toward a fundamental self-concept (Cross, 1971, 1985; Poston, 1990; Helms, 1990, 1992; Erikson, 1968). In contrast to Freud's psychosexual stages where personality formation was said to be mostly complete by age five, Erikson (1968) believed that ego identity continues to evolve over the course of the entire lifespan and is shaped by social interactions. A healthy ego identity, or sense of self, is the most important task of adolescence, achieved by the successful resolution of conflicts inherent in each of eight psychosocial stages: trust vs. mistrust; autonomy vs. shame; initiative vs. guilt; industry vs. inferiority; identity vs. role confusion; intimacy vs. isolation; generativity vs. stagnation, and ego integrity vs. despair (Erikson, 1968).

Theories of racial identity development build upon Erikson's belief in the importance of contextual influences and also invoke a variation of his notion of "identity crisis"—i.e., a psychosocial conflict at each stage—as the impetus for moving from one level of awareness/acceptance to the next (Cross, 1971, 1985; Helms, 1990, 1992; Poston, 1990). For example, in Cross's (1971) model of developing a Black identity, there are five stages: preencounter; encounter; immersion/emersion; internalization, and internalization-commitment. During the preencounter stage, one has not yet developed an identity that is differentiated by race, but a confrontation with racial bias—for example, being told that "you're pretty smart for someone who is Black"—propels one to the next stage, encounter, where the recognition of racialized experiences pushes one to fully explore or immerse him/herself in Black culture (immersion/emersion). Cross (1971) later reformulated his model to acknowledge the influence of reference group orientation (RGO) (Cross, 1985).

Although Cross's (1985) reformulation allows some room for bicultural identification through orientation to different reference groups, this model is better suited to describe monoracial development than that of mixed race individuals. Since rejection of one culture in favor of another, followed by immersion in the culture of origin at different stages is posited, these models are inherently problematic for those with multiple heritages as "origin" may be elusive.

Early models of mixed race identity were derived from sociological hypotheses about the transition of society from cultural to modern, such that persons moving from one realm to another existed on the fringes of both societies. The marginal individual was described as a

> cultural hybrid, . . . living and sharing intimately in the cultural life and traditions of two distinct peoples; never quite willing to break, even if he were permitted to do so, with his past and his traditions, and not quite accepted, because of racial prejudice, in the new society in which he now sought to find a place. He was a man on the margin of two cultures and two societies. (Goldberg, 2014)

Stonequist's (1937) "marginal man" theory formalized this supposition about people of mixed heritage, describing their existence as uncertain and ambiguous in relation to their parents, peers, and identification with specific groups. Described as a deficit model, the assumption was that the problem with identity and acceptance resided within the individual rather than in social relations of the day.

Poston (1990) offered one of the first positive models of identity development for biracial individuals that rejected the "problem" of being multiracial. In his model, Poston (1990) offered a progression that roughly mirrored that found in monoracial models with the following stages: personal identity; choice of group categorization (monoracial identity or multicultural identity); enmeshment and denial; integration and appreciation of multiple ethnicities and valuing of multicultural identity. Although Poston (1990) notes the influence of personal factors such as phenotype, age, status, social supports, bilingualism, political involvement and individual differences on the choices made in the second stage (p. 183), this model, similar to those for monoracial individuals, results in the integration of multiple characteristics into one biracial identity, a variant of the monoracial resolution.

Root (1998) offered an ecological model that varied in that the progression to an accepted identity was not described as linear, recognizing that the identity of multiracial individuals may shift according to the situational context. According to Root (2003), the final identity might vary by (1) accepting the identity imposed by society, (2) identifying with one (monoracial) or both racial (biracial) groups, or (3) identifying with a new racial group. The introduction of an ecological framework acknowledged the multifaceted influences that affect the psychosocial aspects of multiracial identity development and provided a well-received counterpoint to the monoracial theoretical defaults typically used to understand multiracial identity development. Ecosystems comprised of family dynamics, socioeconomic status, history, politics, culture, ethnicity and age, for example, suggest the variety of factors that affect the expression of identity. The permutations resulting from the intersections of a person with multiple heritages and the environment are infinite. Ecological models also recognized that identity may be fluid, shifting as the situation warrants (Root, 2003; Renn, 2008; Burke & Kao, 2013; Kellogg & Liddell, 2012; Garrod et al., 2014; Ramirez, 1994; Rockquemore, Brunsma & Delgado, 2009).

The only agreement with respect to research on the development of biracial identity is that there *is* no single identity that applies to every mixed race individual (Shih & Sanchez, 2005; Rockquemore & Brunsma, 2008; Rockquemore, Bunsma & Delgado, 2009; Garrod, Kilkenny & Gomez, 2014; Mohan & Chambers, 2009; Borrero et al., 2012). Much of the multiracial research has been conducted on clinical populations, limiting the conclusions that may be drawn (Shih & Sanchez, 2005). Moreover, the results of empirical research about the psychological effects of being multiracial are not definitive, owing in part to the lack of consistency in methodology, theoretical frameworks, and "conceptual definitions of 'biracial,' 'multiracial,' and/or 'mixed-race'" (Rockquemore & Brunsma, 2008, p. 18).

Challenges to Mental Health

So what can be said about the challenges to mental health for biracial individuals? Biracials get more information about who they are not than about who they are; parents, who typically provide the standard against which identity is monitored, may be unable to relate to the experiences of their mixed race children if they themselves are monoracial, and mixed youth may be rejected equally by majority and minority relatives, friends, and communities.

Some research has looked at the impact of the stress of being multiracial in a racialized society. In a study of Hawaiian high school students, who were considered "other" than the norm, Borrera and colleagues (2012) noted that in ". . . Western culture, the notion of a contained, stable, unitary self is prioritized, and valued, whereas, fluid, multiple or ambiguous identities are often interpreted as not having an ethnic identity at all" (p. 2). "Othering" in this study was defined as "(a) cultural and racial ambiguity; (b) categorization and labeling; (c) hierarchical power dynamics and (d) limited access to resources" (Borrero, 2012, p. 3). Hawaiian students who typically self-identify as multiethnic were in the position of having their multiple heritages denied. As the "other" students they were rendered "invisible" in the school setting with a preponderance of monoracial groups.

Root (1998) in her study of biracial siblings, discussed hazing as a form of authenticity testing. In this case "phenotype was a stimulus for hazing. . . . In its traumatic forms it requires a submission or negation of self and the ego, risking emotionally cruel rejection" (p. 243). If one has an ambiguous phenotype, but claims monoracial membership, this may trigger the question, "what are you?" The implied authenticity tests challenge one's identity and may require the display of stereotypic behaviors (i.e., "act" Black or "act" White) that are inconsistent with one's normal behavior in order to fit in and avoid further attacks. Root (1998) describes this form of racial hazing as "cumulative trauma because of their repeated nature, as is the case with emotional abuse . . . they insidiously shape the worldview" (p. 242). Feelings of insecurity, distrustfulness and guilt may result from an accumulation of these personal assaults.

The term "microaggression" (Sue et al., 2007) may be described as "slights that reinforce the power structure" (Borrero et al., 2012, p. 3), yet one wonders at the validity of this term when the effects of constant experience can be so damaging. Most multiracial individuals can offer numerous examples of challenges to their right to defy convenient racial stereotypes. Moreover, ". . . exposure to cumulative experiences of discrimination by multiple groups may produce feelings that one's uniqueness and differences are wrong, leading to further isolation, structural marginality and depression. . ." (Navarette & Jenkins, 2011, p. 792). The term "micro" aggression minimizes, perhaps inadvertently, the substantive injuries that can result from experiencing constant attacks on one's identity. Self-esteem and the quality of interpersonal relationships may develop negatively as a result of challenges to identity that are rooted in oppression or privilege.

Navarette and Jenkins (2011) found that multiracial identity may exacerbate susceptibility to structural marginality: "biracial individuals are more often rejected by both parental groups than bi-ethnic, monoracial individuals. For biracial or multiracial individuals, oppression is linked to racial status" (p. 793). Internal confusion may be a result of this racial ambiguity. Mixed-race individuals often experience opposing cultural demands and experience conflicting cues about appropriate behaviors.

Racial/ethnic identity is an integral component of the self-concept. Mendoza-Denton (2010) considered race-based sensitivity (RS) in African American and Latino college students. He found that the expectation of rejection because of their race caused "anxiety and physiological stress responses . . . (e.g., increases in cortisol)" (p. 2). Anxiety was caused by both direct and vicarious experiences of discrimination due to the expectation that one might be treated in a similar manner in a future where opportunities for rejection might exist. When taking a writing sample, in one condition race was identified, and in the other condition it was not disclosed. In the undisclosed condition, positive feedback resulted in greater self-esteem. However, when race was disclosed, there was no effect for those with high RS, but for students with low RS, positive feedback led to gains in self-esteem (Mendoza-Denton, 2010, p. 3).

Other documented challenges to mental health for biracials include: "identity dissonance," the lack of congruence in how one self-identifies relative to how one is identified by others (Garrod et al., 2014; cf. Seates-Trent, 1995; Rockquemore & Brunsma, 2008), and feeling inauthentic and facing suspicion and antagonism (Root, 1998; Poston, 1990; Kellogg & Liddell 2012; Renn, 2008). An interesting study by Burke and Kao (2013) considered the "burden of whiteness" and considered the negative consequences of having a phenotype that would allow one to "pass" as White in a school setting with other multiracial adolescents. They found that monoracial students who did not look Black had a harder time fitting in than monoracials with a Black phenotype. Acknowledging the importance of situational contexts, Burke and Kao (2013) looked at Black/White and Asian White biracial students and found that in a predominantly White school, they were four times more likely to identify as White than in schools that were up to 66% White. They also found that multiracial students who identified as multiracial were more likely to be misclassified.

The persistence of unconscious bias against African Americans is well documented and is a particularly insidious phenomenon. Law (2011) found that 80–90% of Whites in this study demonstrated unconscious bias even though they saw themselves as open-minded and blind to race. Asked to rapidly match positive and negative words to Black or White faces, participants were faster to attach positive words to White faces and negative words to Black ones. Law (2011) found greater concern about prejudice to be related to lower scores of unconscious bias. Kubota and colleagues (2013) found a willingness to discriminate even at a financial cost by using a game that simulated financial negotiations. In this study, participants "accepted more offers and lower offer amounts from White proposers than from Black proposers and . . . this pattern was accentuated with higher implicit race bias" (Kubota et al., 2013, p. 1). Goff et al. (2008) found that Blacks are implicitly associated with apes and animal relevant language. The authors found that the association with apes influenced both visual identification (faster identification of the animal when first shown a Black face as opposed to a White face) and increased the likelihood of support for violence against Black suspects (Goff, 2008).

On the positive side, some research attests to the advantages of being interpersonally flexible and comfortable across multiple situations with diverse populations. For multiracial individuals, learning to successfully navigate within multiple cultures can lead to greater intellectual, interpersonal, and cultural flexibility (Shih & Sanchez, 2005; Ramirez, 1994; Garrod et al., 2014). Many multiracial individuals develop a healthy resilience that insulates them against negativity, believing that being racist is someone else's problem and refusing to participate in the racial fictions that vie for attention on a daily basis. Multiracial individuals are aided in their ability to cope by strong family and social supports, multicultural pride, and resilience that comes from developing interpersonal flexibility for negotiating their identities in different situations.

CONCLUSION

The issues surrounding the identity of people of multiple heritage are political, social, psychological and intrapersonal. For mixed-raced persons, a phenotype with evidence of "one drop" is still enough to trigger unconscious bias in those who say they are color-blind. In fact the notion of being color-blind is sometimes the "dog whistle" for opposition to affirmative action policies, implying that race no longer matters, which is not yet true for most of America. The mixed-race population is the fastest growing group in this country, and even allowing the selection of more than one race for the 2010 census was controversial: advocates for a multiracial option on the census professed the need to be known by their unique identity rather than being forced to choose one racial category over another. Opponents to the multiracial movement were afraid of losing the ability to monitor inequalities and justify demands for accommodation, believing that the multiracial movement would provide tacit approval for the notion that race was no longer an issue in America.

The biracial individual has occupied a variety of positions in the American social stratum at the boundary of the color line. Given the xenophobic associations of light and White with goodness, and dark and Black with evil, the mixed person was alternately envied and despised by Blacks and Whites at different points in history. Before the Civil War, mulattos, as they were called, served as a bridge between Whites and Blacks. Being of lighter color, and sometimes with hair that was more straight than curly, biracials had greater access to education, skilled occupations, and White culture, resulting in a sense of elitism that was codified by the term "blue vein society," a term that has persisted for generations. After the Civil War, one had to choose sides and, for most of those who could not "pass," the choice was governed by phenotype and the one drop rule, such that most accepted a Black identity. During the Harlem Renaissance, many biracials were members of the talented tenth (DuBois, 1903) and mingled equally among all of the colors in the African American rainbow.

From the 1940s to the late 1960s, affirming a multiracial identity might have been seen as confused, or self-hating. During the Civil Rights era, with its calls for unity and solidarity, such an identity made one appear disloyal to the movement. In 2014, America still has a problem with the color line. Given the persistent negativity attached to dark skin color and/ or evidence of African ancestry, it is not surprising that identity development can be challenging for people of multiple heritages.

> In this country, color reminds one of one's history—how far one has come and how far one has to go. . . . each color we see in our society reminds us of some things we can be proud of as well as some things we would just as soon ignore. However, the shameful things will not disappear simply by pretending that color differences do not exist. Nor will they disappear if color is seen merely as a reminder of ancestral guilt. . . . Moving on should mean that we accept our skin color as an integral part of who we are. . . . If you think about it, the ranges of skin color we have are beautiful and remarkable. It is what we do about them that is unsavory. (Helms, 1992)

The term "multiple heritage" is used to encompass the "multidimensionality of interracial and multiracial individuals" (Leong et al., 2014,

p. 24). This suggests the need to embrace and explore our essential selves; we are shaped, but not defined, by others. Negotiating one's identity occurs daily in multiple situations; the interpersonal experiences that accompany this can stimulate growth and multicultural flexibility. This propensity toward intercultural understanding offers a connection to, and a model for, the global world that we occupy.

Asked about the definition of being multiracial, one person replied:

> I don't think of myself as being multiethnic, I think of myself just as a person. I don't separate myself from everyone else just for that reason; I just think of myself as me. (Mohan & Chambers, 2009, p. 271)

REFERENCES

American Anthropological Association. (1994). Statement on "race" and intelligence. Retrieved from http://www.aaanet.org/stms/race.htm

Blay, Y. (2013, November 20). White supremacist would be Black under America's one-drop rule. Retrieved from http://www.cnn.com/2013/11/20/living/white-supremacist-one-drop-identity/

Borrero, N. E., Yeh, C. J., Cruz, C. I., & Suda, J. F. (2012). School as a context for "othering" youth and promoting cultural assets. *Teachers College Record*, 1–20. Retrieved from http://www.tcrecord.org/PrintContent.asp?ContentID=16246

Burke, R., & Kao, G. (2013). Bearing the burden of whiteness: the implications of racial self-identification for multiracial adolescents' school belonging and academic achievement. *Ethnic and Racial Studies*, 36(5), 747–773. doi: 10.1080/01419870.2011.628998

Cross, W. E., Jr. (1971). The Negro to Black conversion experience: Toward a psychology of Black liberation. *Black World*, 20, 13–27.

Cross, W. E., Jr. (1985). Black identity: Rediscovering the distinction between personal identity and referenced group orientation. In M. B. Spencer, G. K. Brooking & W. R. Allen (eds.), *Beginnings: The social and affective development of Black children*, 155–172. Hillsdale, N.J.: Lawrence Erlbaum.

DuBois, W. E. B. (1900). Address to the nations of the world. Retrieved from http://www.blackpast.org/1900-w-e-b-du-bois-nations-world

DuBois, W. E. B. (1903). "The Talented Tenth." In *The Negro Problem: A Series of Articles by Representative American Negroes of To-Day*, 31–75. Contributions by Booker T. Washington, Principal of Tuskegee Institute, W. E. Burghardt DuBois, Paul Laurence Dunbar, Charles W. Chesnutt, and others. New York, NY: James Pott & Co.

Erikson, E. H. (1968). *Identity: youth and crisis*. New York, NY.: W.W. Norton.

Frazier, E. F. (1969). *The Negro in the United States*. Toronto, ON.: The Macmillan Company.

Garrod, A., Kilkenny, R., & Gomez, C. (eds.) (2014). *Mixed*. Ithaca, N.Y.: Cornell University Press.

Goff, P. A., Eberhardt, J. L., Williams, M., & Jackson, M. C. (2008). Not yet human: implicit knowledge, historical dehumanization and contemporary consequences. *Journal of Personality and Social Psychology*, 94(2), 292–306. doi: 10.1037/0022-3514.94.2.292

Goldberg, C. (2014, August). *Robert Park's marginal man: the career of a concept in American sociology. Laboratorium: Russian Review of Social Research*, North America, 4. Retrieved from http://soclabo.org/index.php/laboratorium/article/view/4/119

Helms, J. E. (ed.) (1990). *Black and White racial identity: theory, research, and practice.* Westport, CT: Greenwood Press.

Helms, J. E. (1992). *A race is a nice thing to have.* Topeka, KS.: Content Communications.

Herrenstein, R. J., & Murray, C. (1996). *The bell curve: intelligence and class structure in American life.* New York, NY: Simon & Schuster.

Kellogg, A. G., & Liddell, D. L. (2012). Not half but double: exploring critical incidents in the racial identity of multiracial college students. *Journal of College Student Development*, 53(4), 524–541.

Kubota, J. T., Li, J., Bar-David, E., Banaji, M. R., & Phelps, E. A. (2013). The price of racial bias: intergroup negotiations in the ultimatum game. *Psychological Science.* doi: 10.1177/0956797613496435

Law, B. M. (2011). Retraining the biased brain. *Monitor on Psychology*, 42(9), 42.

Leong, F. T. L., Comas-Diaz, L., Hall, G. C. N., McLloyd, C., Trimble, J. E. (eds.). (2014). *APA Handbook of Multicultural Psychology.* Washington, D.C.: American Psychological Association.

Lowery, W. (2014). Paul Ryan, poverty, dog whistles, and electoral politics. Retrieved from http://www.washingtonpost.com/blogs/the-fix/wp/2014/03/18/paul-ryan-poverty-dog-whistles-and-racism/

Mendoza-Denton, R. (2010). Relational diversity in higher education: A psychological perspective. Retrieved from http://www.apa.org/science/about/psa/2010/11pelational-diversity.aspx

Mohan, E., & Venzant Chambers, T. T. (2009). Two researchers reflect on navigating multiracial identities in the research situation. *International Journal of Qualitative Studies in Education*, 23 (3), 259–281. doi: 10.1080/09518390903196609.

Navarette, V., & Jenkins, S. R. (2011). Cultural homelessness, multiminority status, ethnic identity development, and self-esteem. *International Journal of Intercultural Relations*, 35 (2011), 791–804.

Poston, W. S. (1990). The biracial identity development model: A needed addition. *Journal of Counseling & Development*, 69, 152–155.

Ramirez, M., III. (1994). *Psychotherapy and counseling with minorities.* Needham Heights, MA.: Allyn and Bacon.

Renn, K. A. (2008). Research on biracial and multiracial identity development: overview and synthesis. *New Directions for Student Services*, 13–21. doi: 10.1002/SS.282

Rockquemore, K. A., & Brunsma, D. L. (2008). *Beyond Black biracial identity in America.* Lanham, MD: Rowman & Littlefield.

Rockquemore, K. A., Brunsma, D. L., & Delgado, D. (2009). Racing to theory or retheorizing Race? Understanding the struggle to build a multiracial identity theory. *Journal of Social Issues*, 65(1), 13–34.

Root, M. P. P. (1998). Experiences and processes affecting racial identity develop-ment: Preliminary results from the biracial sibling project. *Cultural Diversity and Mental Health*, 4(3), 237–247.

Root, M. P. P. (2003). Multiracial families and children: implications for research and practice. In J. A. Banks & C. A. McGee Banks, eds., *Handbook of Research on Multicultural Education*, second edition. San Francisco, CA.: Jossey-Bass, 110–124.

Scales-Trent, J. (1995). *Notes of a White Black woman*. University Park, PA: Pennsylvania State University.

Shih, M., & Sanchez, D. T. (2005). Perspectives and research on the positive and negative implications of having multiple racial identities. *Psychological Bulletin*, 131(4), 569–591.

Stonequist, E.V. (1937). The marginal man: a study in personality and culture con-flict. New York, NY: Russell & Russell.

Sue, D.W., Capodilupo, C., Torino, G., Bucceri, J., Holder, A., Nadal, K., & Equin, M. (2007). Racial microaggressions in everyday life: implications for clinical practice. *The American Psychologist*, 62(4), 271–286.

U.S. Department of Commerce, Economics, and Statistics Administration. (2012). The two or more races population: 2010. Washington, D.C.: U.S. Census Bureau.

Chapter 9

Avoiding Teenage Pregnancy: Too Young to Parent

Kellie Bryant

INTRODUCTION

The United States has one of the highest rates of teenage pregnancy in the world despite the availability of many forms of contraception (Katz, 2011; Mosher et al., 2004; Singh et al., 2004). Fortunately the teenage pregnancy rate has continuously declined since 1990 (except for an increase in 2006); however, the pregnancy rate among Black teenagers remains much higher than White teenagers ("Fast Facts: Teen Pregnancy and Childbearing Among Non-Hispanic black Teens," 2013; Patel & Sen, 2012). The highest rate of unintended teenage pregnancies occurs in Hispanics and Blacks, which is the population that has the greatest potential for the devastating effects of an unplanned pregnancy ("About Teen Pregnancy," 2012). Although Hispanics currently have the highest teenage birthrates, they also have the most significant recent decline in pregnancy rates. Since 2007, the teenage birthrate has declined by 39% for Hispanics, compared to declines of 29% for Blacks and 25% for Whites ("Trends in Teen Pregnancy and Childbearing," 2013).

Teenage pregnancy is a persistent social problem that adversely affects families, children, and society. The impact of teenage pregnancy has detrimental effects such as higher rates of high school dropout, poverty, repeat pregnancies, and becoming a single parent (Brown & Eisenberg, 1995). In addition to the negative impact of teenage pregnancy on the mother and child, the cost of teenage pregnancy is exorbitant. The U.S. spends approximately $11.3 billion a year in public assistance to teenage mothers (Patel & Sen, 2012).

Risk Factors for Teenage Pregnancy

The cause of teenage pregnancy is multifactorial, which includes environmental, biological, and social factors. Teen pregnancy rates are directly influenced by condom use, contraceptive use, and sexual behavior. The recent declines in teenage pregnancy can be attributed to increased contraceptive use and decrease in sexual activity of younger teenagers (Santelli et al., 2009). Additional risk factors for teenage pregnancy are decreased income, depression, poor school performance, early onset of puberty, family history of teenage pregnancy, having an older partner, inadequate sex education, and inadequate access to contraception (Adler, Unibe, & DeVesty, 2012).

Adolescents engage in risky sexual behavior that contributes to the high rate of teenage pregnancy and sexually transmitted infections (STIs). In the United States, 47% of high school students have had sexual intercourse and an astonishing 24% stated they had four or more sexual partners before graduating high school (Goesling et al., 2014). In 2011, an alarming 40% of sexually active high school students did not use a condom during their last sexual encounter (Goesling et al., 2014). These behaviors increase the risks of pregnancy as well as STIs including HIV.

Early puberty has been proven to be a significant factor in the higher rate of pregnancy among Black females (Doswell & Braxter, 2002). Teenagers' impulsivity, inability to contemplate consequences of their behaviors, and inability to delay gratification can be caused by their immature prefrontal cortex (Adler et al., 2012). This immature prefrontal cortex contributes to lack of contraceptive use and unplanned sexual activity. Adolescent females that develop sexual characteristics at an earlier age tend to socialize with an older crowd and attract older males (Doswell & Braxter, 2002). Although their bodies mature at a faster rate, they may lack the social skills and maturity to counteract the sexual advances of these older males. This may lead to Black teenagers being coerced by an older partner to engage in sexual activity before they are ready ("Adolescent Pregnancy—Current Trends and Issues: 1998," 1999). The adolescent craving for love and attention may also lead to the female refraining from using contraceptives due to fear that asking a partner to use contraceptives may jeopardize their relationship (Martyn, Hutchinson & Martin, 2002).

Some teenagers may see motherhood as a legitimate alternative to having a career due to the lack of education and career aspirations (Winters,

2012). Sheeder, Tocce, and Stevens-Simon (2009) found 39% of the teenage participants did not take methods to prevent pregnancy due to ambivalence toward being pregnant, a desire to have a baby, having a partner who wanted a baby, or believing a baby would make their relationship closer (Sheeder, Tocce & Stevens-Simon, 2009).

CONTRACEPTIVE USE AMONG TEENAGERS

Leading causes of unintended teenage pregnancies are lack of contraceptive use and contraceptive failure (Mosher et al., 2004; Rosenberg, Waugh & Burnhill, 1998; Stevens-Simon, Kelly, Singer & Cox, 1996). The highest risk of contraceptive nonuse occurs among women who are most prone to the devastating effects of having an unintended pregnancy, that is, those who are young, poor, and minorities (Sable et al., 2000). The three most commonly cited reasons for lack of contraceptive use among sexually active woman were thinking pregnancy would not occur, difficulty obtaining contraceptives, and fear of the side effects of contraceptives. Other commonly cited reasons for lack of contraceptive use were women not minding becoming pregnant, partner refusal to use contraception, and unplanned intercourse (Singh et al., 2004).

In order to determine causes for contraceptive nonuse, it is important to identify barriers to obtaining contraceptives. Teenagers face additional difficulties due to lack of transportation to facilities, substandard healthcare facilities, and lack of money to pay for the visit and/or contraceptive (Sable, Libbus & Chiu, 2000; Sonfield, Gold, Frost & Darroch, 2004). Cost has been identified as a major obstacle to contraceptive use. Inability to obtain or afford contraceptives is a major barrier faced by 50% of poor adults and teenagers (Gold, 2002). Due to financial restraints, many women from low socioeconomic levels received care from family planning clinics. Clinic settings can be discouraging to women due to the long waiting times, difficulty in obtaining appointments, and substandard medical care. Newer forms of contraceptives are more effective and easier to use; however, these methods may be difficult to obtain due to higher cost (Gold, 2002). Clients with insurance may also face financial obstacles when obtaining contraceptives. Many insurance companies do not cover the cost of contraceptives (Dailard, 2003). Even with insurance coverage of contraceptives, clients may be faced with the cost of co-payments for office visits and testing associated with family planning services (Dailard, 2003).

Public policies can also impact the teenage pregnancy rate. The use of contraceptives among teenagers has also decreased due to federal policies that promoted abstinence-only educational programs (Katz, 2011). Research has consistently shown that abstinence-only programs have not contributed to delaying sexual activity or decreasing teenage pregnancy rates (Katz, 2011). Limited access to emergency contraception in certain states and the lack of abortion services for teenage women can also adversely affect the teenage pregnancy rate (Ely & Dulmus, 2008; Katz, 2011).

One of the most significant factors related to lack of contraceptive use among adolescents is immature sexual behavior. Gunn-Brooks and Furstenberg (1989) found most adolescents' first sexual experience is often unplanned and is not a conscious decision. Since most initial sexual experiences are unplanned, approximately half of adolescents did not use contraception the first time they had sexual intercourse (Gunn-Brooks & Furstenberg, 1989). Unfortunately, the researchers found that most adolescents who did not use contraceptives during their first sexual experience will not use contraceptives during subsequent sexual encounters (Gunn-Brooks & Furstenberg, 1989).

Misconceptions about contraceptives, failure to recognize the risk of pregnancy, and inability to communicate with their partner about contraceptives were commonly cited factors related to contraceptive non-use. Negative attitudes about contraceptives based on cultural beliefs were common factors related to decreased contraception use among minority women (Sable et al., 2000). Women receive inaccurate information about side effects from non-medical professionals such as friends and family members. Since most woman using contraceptives are healthy, they are less willing to take a medication that has side effects. Unfortunately many women are not aware of the many medical and non-medical benefits of contraceptive use such as its ability to decrease the risk of ovarian and uterine cancer, ovarian cysts, acne, and menstrual cramping (Singh et al., 2004). Common concerns about using contraceptives revolved around the side effects of injectables, difficulty taking a pill consistently, fear of condom breakage, unreliability of condom use among partners, and menstrual irregularities from injectables (Sable et al., 2000).

There has been a decrease in condom use among teenagers (Santelli, Orr, Lindberg & Diaz, 2009) that has contributed to the high rate of teenage pregnancy and HIV infection in the U.S. Surprisingly the decreased public health emphasis on HIV prevention may have contributed to the decreased condom use and stagnant changes in teenage sexual activity (Santelli et al., 2009). Unfortunately a large percentage of people infected with the HIV virus acquired the infection during their teenage years. It is estimated that 50% of new HIV infections occur among people younger than 25 years with young heterosexual minority women having an increased risk of acquiring HIV infection (J. S. Santelli et al., 2009).

CONSEQUENCES OF TEENAGE PREGNANCY

Approximately 51% of teenage pregnancies result in a live birth, 35% end in abortion, and 14% are lost pregnancies due to miscarriage or stillbirth (Felice et al., 1999). Teenage abortion rates have remained relatively stable even though there has been a decrease in teenage pregnancy rates. The highest abortion rate occurs among Black teenagers (Kost & Henshaw, 2013). Research has found that teenagers from low socioeconomic backgrounds are less likely to terminate a pregnancy (Hoggart, 2014).

For Black teenagers that decide to continue with their pregnancies, the mothers and their children face many potential adverse medical, social, and financial problems. Pregnant teenagers face a higher incidence of premature birth, poor maternal weight gain, pregnancy-induced hypertension, sexually transmitted infections, and anemia (Klein, 2005). Many social factors have contributed to the higher risk of pregnancy complications such as low socioeconomic status, lack of support from the father of the baby, smoking, drug use, inadequate prenatal care, and low educational levels. Both biological and social factors may contribute to poor outcomes in adolescents. The psychosocial consequences of a teenage pregnancy can include persistent poverty, limited job opportunities, disassociation from the child's father, and subsequent pregnancy (Klein, 2005).

Teenager mothers encounter challenges with childrearing due to their lack of maternal skills. Adverse health problems for the infants born to these teenage mothers include low birth weight infants, poor nutritional status, poor educational attainment, and a higher rate of behavioral and health problems (Health, 2013; Klein, 2005). In addition, teenage mothers have a significantly higher rate of dropping out of high school, which perpetuates the cycle of unemployment or underemployment and a higher rate of their children also not achieving a high school degree ("About Teen Pregnancy," 2012). Long-term effects of a child being the product of a teenage pregnancy can include developmental delay, difficulties in school, behavioral disorders, drug abuse, early sexual activity, depression, and a higher chance of repeating the cycle of teenage pregnancy.

The consequences of teenage pregnancy extend to the economy and society. Teenage pregnancy was estimated to cost the U.S. taxpayers $11 billion in 2008 due to the cost of lost tax revenue from teens, increased incarceration rates among teenage parents, increased health care needs, and cost of foster care associated with these pregnancies ("About Teen Pregnancy," 2012). A lack of education causes a cascade of effects such as increased use of public assistance ("Trends in Teen Pregnancy and Childbearing," 2013).

PREVENTING TEENAGE PREGNANCY

Evidence has shown that effective teenage pregnancy prevention requires effective evidence-based sex education in addition to educating teenagers on cultivating healthy relationships. Simply providing teenagers with education on contraceptive methods or stressing abstinence has not been proven to be effective at reducing teenage pregnancy (Katz, 2011). It will take the support of parents, peers, and the community to significantly decrease the teenage pregnancy rate. Education must be ongoing and should be delivered by trained educators, teaching ways for teenagers to build knowledge and skills in developing healthy and safe relationships. The concept of positive youth development is becoming an increasingly popular approach to combating teenage pregnancy. The concept entails enhancing cognitive, social, and emotional skills with the goal of enhancing decision-making skills that promote better life choices such as avoiding an unplanned pregnancy (Katz, 2011). Positive youth development should build a teenager's self-confidence and character.

In addition to student education, easy access to free contraceptives (including condoms) and family planning services has shown to reduce teenage pregnancy (Santelli et al., 2009). There is a lack of evidence that "abstinence only" programs are effective at reducing rates of teenage pregnancy (Katz, 2011). Fortunately the new Affordable Care Act will have a positive impact on teenage pregnancy. President Obama's plan will improve access to recommended health care services for teenagers and hopefully will increase contraceptive availability for teenagers. The law expands health insurance coverage for preventive services for teenagers, such as contraception, which helps reduce the rate of unintended pregnancies in the United States.

Teenage pregnancy prevention programs are more effective if they include the male counterpart and peer teenager mothers in order to create a bigger impact in reducing teenagers' decisions to engage in risky sexual behaviors. Studies have shown that male teenagers wanting a baby were the strongest predictor of a female teenager's positive attitude toward becoming pregnant (Goesling et al., 2014). Research has also shown that a woman's partner can influence contraceptive use as well. Having an older partner and/or a partner who expresses negative attitudes about contraceptives is associated with decreased contraceptive use. Programs that include teenage mothers discussing their experiences and challenges with being a teenager mother help to reduce barriers to pregnancy prevention messages given by adults (Goesling et al., 2014). Peers play a major role in a teenager's decision-making process; therefore use of teenage parents is an important component in designing and implementing pregnancy prevention programs.

CONCLUSION

Teenage pregnancy has been a social problem that has particularly plagued the Black community for decades. Research has consistently identified age, race, and attitudes about contraceptives, socioeconomic status, future goals, and pregnancy intention as important risk factors for teenage pregnancy (Manlove, Ryan & Franzetta, 2003; Martyn et al., 2002; Stevens-Simon et al., 1996). Despite the availability of safe and reliable contraceptive methods, there are many obstacles to women obtaining contraceptives such as cost and accessibility to contraceptives. Another significant factor in contraceptive use is a woman's attitudes and beliefs about contraception. A negative attitude about contraception can contribute to decreased use and higher levels of unintended pregnancies (Abama et al., 1997; Sable et al., 2000). It is important for women to have accurate information about contraception and to reverse some of the negative myths and fallacies about contraception. If the United States wants to effectively reduce teenage pregnancy rates, there needs to be an increased effort on the state and national level to promote contraceptive use among teenagers through effective sex education and health services and increased funding for contraceptive services (Santelli et al., 2009). Although there has been a steady decline in teenage pregnancy rates in the United States, there is further room for improvement.

REFERENCES

Abama, J., Chandra, A., Mosher, W. D., Peterson, L., & Piccinino, L. (1997). Fertility, family planning, and women's health: New data from the 1995 National Survey of Family growth. In V. a. H. Statistics, (p. 114).

About Teen Pregnancy. (2012, November 21). *Teen Pregnancy*. Retrieved March 3, 2014, from http://www.cdc.gov/teenpregnancy/aboutteen preg.htm

Adler, A. P., Unibe, L. M., & DeVesty, G. (2012). Pregnancy in Adolescence: CINAHL Plus.

Adolescent Pregnancy—Current Trends and Issues: 1998. (1999). *Pediatrics, 103*(2), 516–520.

Brown, S., & Eisenberg, L. (1995). *The Best Intentions: Unintended pregnancy and the well-being of children and families*. Washington, D.C.: National Academy Press.

Dailard, C. (2003). The cost of contraceptive insurance coverage. *Guttmacher Report on Public Policy, 6*(1), 12–13.

Doswell, W. M., & Braxter, B. (2002). Risk-taking behaviors in early adolescent minority women: Implications for research and practice. *J Obstet Gynecol Neonatal Nurs, 31*(4), 454–461.

Ely, G. E., & Dulmus, C. N. (2008). A psychosocial profile of adolescent pregnancy termination patients. *Soc Work Health Care, 46*(3), 69–83. doi:10.1300/J010v46n03_04

Fast Facts: Teen Pregnancy and Childbearing Among Non-Hispanic Black Teens. (2013). *The National Campaign to Prevent Teen and Unplanned Pregnancy*. Washington, DC: The National Campaign.

Felice, M. E., Feinstein, R. A., Fisher, M. M., Kaplan, D. W., Olmedo, L. F., Rome, E. S., & Staggers, B. C. (1999). Adolescent pregnancy—current trends and issues: 1998 American Academy of Pediatrics Committee on Adolescence, 1998–1999. *Pediatrics, 103*(2), 516–520.

Goesling, B., Colman, S., Trenholm, C., Terzian, M., & Moore, K. (2014). Programs to Reduce Teen Pregnancy, Sexually Transmitted Infections, and Associated Sexual Risk Behaviors: A Systematic Review. *J Adolesc Health*. doi:10.1016/j.jadohealth.2013.12.004

Gold, R. B. (2002). Nowhere but uprising cost of title X. *Guttmacher Report on Public Policy, 5*(5), 6–9.

Gunn-Brooks, J., & Furstenberg, F. (1989). Adolescent sexual behavior. *American Psychological Association, 44*(2), 249–257.

Health, O. A. (2013). *Trends in Teen Pregnancy and Childbearing*. www.hhs.gov.

Hoggart, L. (2014). "I'm pregnant . . . what am I going to do?" An examination of value judgements and moral frameworks in teenage pregnancy decision making. *Health, Risk & Society, 14*(6), 533–549.

Katz, A. (2011). Adolescent Pregnancy: The Good, The Bad, The Promise. *Nursing for Women's Health*, 149–152.

Klein, J. D. (2005). Adolescent pregnancy: Current trends and issues. *Pediatrics, 116*(1), 281–286.

Kost, K., & Henshaw, S. (2013). U.S. Teenage Pregnancies, Births and Abortions, 2008: State Trends by Age, Race and Ethnicity (pp. 1–24). New York: Guttmacher Institute.

Manlove, J., Ryan, S., & Franzetta, K. (2003). Patterns of contraceptive use within teenagers' first sexual relationship. *Perspectives on Sexual and Reproductive Health, 35*(6), 246–255.

Martyn, K. K., Hutchinson, S. A., & Martin, J. H. (2002). Luck girls: unintentional avoidance of adolescent pregnancy among low-income African-American females. *Journal for Specialist in Pediatric Nursing, 7*(4), 153–159.

Mosher, W. D., Martinez, G. M., Chandra, A., Abma, J. C., & Willson, S. J. (2004). Use of contraception and use of family planning services in the United States: 1982–2002. In V. a. H. Statistics (Ed.), *Advance Data* (p. 46): Centers for Disease Control.

Patel, P. H., & Sen, B. (2012). Teen motherhood and long-term health consequences. *Matern Child Health J, 16*(5), 1063–1071. doi:10.1007/s10995-011-0829-2

Rosenberg, M. J., Waugh, M. S., & Burnhill, M. S. (1998). Compliance, counseling and satisfaction with oral contraceptives: A prospective evaluation. *Fam Plann Perspect, 30*(2), 89–92, 104.

Sable, M. R., Libbus, M. K., & Chiu, J. E. (2000). Factors affecting contraceptive use in women seeking pregnancy tests: Missouri, 1997. *Family Planning Perspectives, 32*(3), 124–131.

Santelli, J. S., Orr, M., Lindberg, L. D., & Diaz, D. C. (2009). Changing behavioral risk for pregnancy among high school students in the United States, 1991–2007. *J Adolesc Health, 45*(1), 25–32.

Sheeder, J., Tocce, K., & Stevens-Simon, C. (2009). Reasons for ineffective contraceptive use antedating adolescent pregnancies: part 2: a proxy for childbearing intentions. *Matern Child Health J, 13*(3), 306–317. doi:10.1007/s10995-008-0368-7

Singh, S., Darroch, J. E., Vlassoff, M., & Nadeau, J. (2004). Adding it up: Benefits of investing in sexual and reproductive health care. In A. G. Institute (ed.), (p. 40). New York: Alan Guttmacher Institute.

Sonfield, A., Gold, R. B., Frost, J. J., & Darroch, J. E. (2004). U.S. insurance coverage of contraceptives and the impact of contraceptive coverage mandates, 2002. *Perspectives on Sexual and Reproductive Health, 36*(2), 72–79.

Stevens-Simon, C., Kelly, L., Singer, D., & Cox, A. (1996). Why pregnant adolescents say they did not use contraceptives prior to conception. *Journal of Adolescent Health, 19*, 48–53.

Trends in Teen Pregnancy and Childbearing. (2013, December 20). Retrieved March 24, 2014, from http://www.hhs.gov/ash/oah/adolescent-health -topics/reproductive-health/teen-pregnancy/trends.html

Winters, L. I., & Winters, P. C. (2012). Black Teenage Pregnancy: A Dynamic Social Problem. *Sage Open*, 1–14.

Chapter 10

Obesity in Black Girls: The Curse of a Poverty Diet and Fast Foods

Portia Johnson and Yvonne Wesley

INTRODUCTION

The body mass index (BMI) has doubled in the past 30 years for children and adolescents ages 6 to 17 years. Today the numbers continue to rise despite educational efforts to parents and children. Aside from the risk of diabetes, hypertension, and cancer, obesity may lead to behavior problems, poor grades, distorted self-image and potential bullying. According to the 2007–2008 National Health and Nutrition Examination Survey (NHANES), 16.9% of adolescents ages 12–19 years are obese. Among girls, non-Hispanic Black adolescents (29.2%) were significantly more likely to be obese compared with non-Hispanic White adolescents (14.5%).

This chapter explores the reasons why the national average is so high for this particular population. Research has shown the poverty rates are disproportionate in Black communities compared to White communities. A bleak economic picture places Black families at a greater disadvantage. Often the last hired and first fired, Black parents have difficulty providing healthy food choices for their children. Furthermore, one parent households are all too common in the Black community. Within impoverished Black communities there are very few if any major supermarkets to purchase fresh foods, and public transportation is mainly inaccessible. Research has shown that

Black children are exposed to an increased number of processed foods which are high in calories, salt, sugar, fat, and carbohydrates, but have little nutritional value. Fast-food stores are often open 24 hours, cheap, and within walking distance for children after school. Crime rates are also an issue, and many Black communities are deemed unsafe, especially in the major cities, for children to play outside. This leads to lack of exercise and a sedentary lifestyle that contributes to increased weight gain. Aside from the impact of depressed economics, this chapter provides the reader with a look at cultural behaviors that run throughout all socioeconomic groups within the Black community.

OBESITY STATISTICS

Government data show that obesity has increased among adolescents ages 2–19. The prevalence of obesity rose from 11% during the time period 1988–1994 to 15% in the time period 1999–2000 but has not significantly increased since 2000 (National Center for Health Statistics, 2013). There are significant racial disparities in the minority population in terms of obesity and adolescence. Ogden, Carroll, Curtin, Lamb, and Flegal (2010) reported that the 2007–2008 prevalence of BMIs greater than the 85th percentile was greatest for non-Hispanic Black adolescent girls (46.3%) compared to non-Hispanic White adolescent girls (29.9%). However, there was far less difference between Black adolescent boys and girls. For BMIs greater than the 85th percentile, Non-Hispanic Black adolescent girls (46.3%) outnumbered non-Hispanic Black adolescent boys (33.0%).

The statistics indicate a serious obesity problem among Black youth which needs the attention of all health care professionals concerned about the welfare of children. This issue requires immediate attention to prevent the youth from experiencing the most prevalent types of chronic diseases such as hypertension and diabetes. Given the fact that obesity has started trending at an earlier age, it is a strong possibility that many children may not live into the so-called "golden years." Before we explore some of the factors, let's define obesity for this target population.

DEFINITION OF OBESITY

The Centers for Disease Control and Prevention (CDC) (2012) defines obesity as a Body Mass Index (BMI) greater than 30 for an adult. A BMI greater than 30 places an adult at increased health risks. A BMI is calculated as weight in kilograms/height in meters squared (National Heart, Lung, and Blood Institute NHLBI, 1998). In other words, the weight of an adult, in kilograms, divided by the person's height in meters is then squared.

The BMI has been found to correlate with body fat; however BMI varies with age and gender in children. Therefore, the designation of a child or

adolescent (ages 2 to 19 years) as being overweig
comparing their BMI to a gender/age-specific ref
is, CDC's growth chart. Overweight children and/c
who fall between the 85th and 94th percentiles on th
the 95th percentile are considered obese (CDC, 2012)

In the past, Ogden and colleagues (2010) explained
ing BMIs for children and adolescents there are three l
the 85th, 2) at or above the 95th, and 3) at or above th ~ercentiles.
They note that there is not a recommended label for any of the three BMIs-
for-age cut points; therefore they use the term "high BMI" for all three
levels. Although it is most appropriate to refer to obesity and overweight
among adolescents in terms of percentiles, research findings presented in
this chapter use BMIs as the unit of measure.

SOCIOECONOMICS

Approximately 25% of Blacks are at or below the federal poverty line,
compared to 11% of White Americans who are in poverty according to
data from the 2007–2011 American Community Survey (Macartney,
Bishaw & Fontenot, 2013). Poverty has been shown to affect lifestyle patterns and has had an effect on the Black community's culture and lifestyle
which includes fast foods high in salt, fat, and sugar. The literature also
suggests that persons in poverty are more prone to eat processed foods
such as bologna, pork sausage, and hot dogs. Too often in the Black community there is a lack of fresh fruits and vegetables, but increased amounts
of canned foods such as *Spaghetti-Os* and other processed foods.

According to findings from Lucan and colleagues' (2012) qualitative
study of 33 Black participants ages 18–81 from an urban neighborhood,
reasons for eating large amounts of fast foods were the following: fast
foods were more satisfying, tasted better, and were more filling. In addition, the study showed that fruits were not appealing and vegetables were
preferred only if covered with butter, cheese, or fat.

In a longitudinal study of 1,400 Black adult participants, Reitzel and
colleagues (2013) found that many of the sample engaged in behaviors
that were convenient. For example, the use of fast-food restaurants reduced the participants' cost in time, money, and effort. Also, living near a
fast-food restaurant was positively associated with BMI among participants whose incomes were less than $40,000 a year. For participants with
a high density of fast food restaurants in their neighborhood, the relationship with BMI and income was more pronounced. In other words, BMIs
increased as income decreased but mainly in neighborhoods with many
fast-food restaurants.

Similar to Reitzel and colleagues finding restaurant density has an impact, He and colleagues (2012) also found that local food environments

olescents' food purchasing behaviors in London and Canada. If earest fast-food outlet or convenience store was within a .5 mile radius from the adolescent's home there was an increased likelihood ($p <$ .05) of them purchasing fast foods on a weekly basis. Another factor to be considered is portion sizes, according to a writer from Natural News.com (Gomez, 2012). Portion sizes according to this writer have increased at all restaurants, not just fast-food dining establishments. This phenomenon, which has increased over the years, means that people are taking in a lot more calories.

DiSantis et al. (2013) note that Black people are more likely than Whites to be exposed to the promotion of high-calorie, low-nutrient foods and beverages. They also suggest that Blacks are less likely to be exposed to healthier food choices. Findings from their study suggest that food prices influence consumption of low-nutrient/high calorie foods, and Black neighborhoods pose a challenge to achieving healthy eating patterns as there are numerous fast-food restaurants located in Black communities. DiSantis and colleagues indicate that the low cost of "high-calorie/ready-to-eat foods" contributes to a lifestyle of poor health and nutrition.

Home food preparation has been said to promote nutrition in urban populations and it is important to have good cooking skills. According to findings from Kramer and colleagues' (2012) study, family meals appear to be a promising teen obesity prevention strategy. The authors note the healthiness of frequent home-cooked meals as an influence on BMI. In a study of the relationship between home cooking and a teen's BMI in a sample of 240 Black youth ages 10–15 years old, the investigators questioned the influence of psychosocial and demographic factors on home food preparation. Youth participating in a local recreation center from an urban area were invited to complete a questionnaire which focused on the youths' food purchases and consumption for the past seven days. The investigators found that youth of caregivers who used healthier cooking methods had a reduced risk of being overweight or obese. However, it was also discovered that the frequency of caregiver food preparation was associated with the adolescent having a higher BMI. In other words, if the caregiver prepared cooked meals at home the teen had an increased BMI. Certainly this was not what the investigators wanted to find. Therefore, they suggested that the findings may be due in part to how the caregiver prepared the food. Perhaps the study findings would have been different if home-cooked foods were prepared using healthier methods.

Huffman, Kanikireddy, and Patel (2010) compared BMIs of children ages 6–11 in single- and dual-parent households using NHANES data from 1988–1994. They found more obesity among children in single-parent households (41%) compared to children in dual-parent households (31%). In addition, female Black children were found to have the highest incidence of obesity. More startling were their findings that single-parent households reported the highest caloric fat intake, and the consumption of less fruits and vegetables. It was also noted that single-parent households did not eat together as a family, nor did they spend large amounts of time together, and their children were more sedentary. Although this data is not specifically among adolescents, obese children are at increased risk of obesity during their adolescent years. Dating back to the 1990s, researchers (Douthitt & Harvey, 1995) suggested that latch-key children are more prone to obesity. Moreover, the sedentary lifestyle attributed to single-parent households may be due, in part, to the latch-key syndrome.

Aside from parenthood status, the neighborhood environment has been highlighted as a factor adding to adolescent obesity. According to the literature, features of a neighborhood may contribute to the decline in physical activity, thereby creating higher levels of obesity among Blacks. Specifically, Franzini and colleagues (2010) suggest that Black teens are more likely to live in low-income urban areas with barriers such as poor housing, sidewalks, street design, and greater density within these communities. In today's society neighbors experience a lack of trust, there are numerous abandoned buildings with graffiti, and the crime rates are high with increased concentrations of poverty that contribute to instability in the community according to Franzini and colleagues.

Dulin-Keita, Thind, Affuso, and Baskin (2013) obtained data from a cross-sectional study examining sociocultural barriers and facilitators to physical activity among Black teens. These authors found that perceived neighborhood disorder had a significant positive relationship with obesity status. In other words, participants who perceived their neighborhoods as safe also had less obesity. The study also showed that moderate-to-vigorous physical activity was inversely related to obesity status. Simply stated, the more active the participants, the less occurrence of obesity.

Working from a theory of social disorganization which posits that when the prevalence of structural disadvantage increases within a neighborhood, the strength of social institutions' cohesion declines, Nicholson and Browning (2012) claimed that obesity may be the result of a maladaptive response to living in these circumstances. Based on data from more than 5,700 adolescents collected between 1994 and 2002 by The National Longitudinal Study of Adolescent Health, the researchers found that obesity is higher for female adolescents who live in disadvantaged neighborhoods. Furthermore, the study showed that disadvantaged neighborhoods did not have the same impact on males. The researchers attributed these findings to the females' fear of public spaces and lack of security. The findings also suggest that neighborhoods explain racial and gender inequities.

Aside from preferences for high-fat and sugary snacks, limited availability of healthy foods such as low-fat food and appealing fresh fruits and vegetables in school cafeterias and in neighborhood stores, Wang et al.

(2006) found that barriers to students engaging in healthy eating and physical activity included: 1) a lack of organized activities for girls after school hours, and 2) easy access to television and video games. These findings were based on a series of focus groups among 55 students, parents, and food service personnel. Survey results showed that screen time occupied a large portion of the participant's time. Approximately half (42%) spent four hours or more daily watching TV, playing video games, or using the computer, and 29% spent five hours or more daily.

STRONG PARENTAL INFLUENCE

Savage, Fisher, and Birch (2007) noted that eating behaviors begin during the first year of life. They go on to posit that among human infants a genetic predisposition along with repeated exposure to certain foods determines eating behaviors. According to these authors, infants are sensitive to salty, sweet, sour, and bitter flavors, with sweet being most pleasing. They even suggest that a preference for salt develops around the fourth month of life. This may become an important factor for Blacks, given the American Health Association's recommendation that reducing sodium to less than 1,500 mg a day helps lessen disease.

An infant's preference for sweets allows the infant to readily accept foods such as flavored yogurts, fruits, and juices. Conversely, vegetables, which are not sweet, are initially rejected, and must be offered ten to sixteen times before acceptance occurs in childhood according to Savage and colleagues. Savage and colleagues cite research noting that children who drink juices and soda as little as once or twice per day are at increased risk of becoming overweight by sixty percent. Moreover they note that the consumption of sweetened beverages is associated with excessive weight gain among young adolescents ages 11–14.

Parents powerfully shape their offspring's eating patterns which develop in early social interactions (Savage et al., 2007). These authors also explain that scarcity and poverty shape feeding patterns and are passed on from one generation to the next, which then become traditional routines without any question by the parents. In Black communities across the United States clichés are handed down from one generation to another; parents tell their children the following:

- I want you to eat everything on this plate.
- You better not waste one bit of this food.
- Don't you know there are kids starving in other parts of the world who wish they had enough food to eat?
- You look like you are still hungry, eat some more.

The above type statements condition Black children from a very young age to create a distorted type of relationship with food. While it may have been understandable for parents to tell their children to eat up when foods were scarce, today's impoverished communities have an abundance of high-calorie/low-nutrient foods.

In a qualitative study exploring how unique aspects of being raised in a poor Black neighborhood may influence a teen's health behaviors, St. George and Wilson (2012) concluded that future obesity prevention efforts for Black teens should target parenting skills that provide greater support for the adolescent teen girls compared to boys. What this means is that the authors described four parenting styles: 1) authoritative which is high warmth and high control, 2) authoritarian which is low warmth, high control, 3) permissive which is high warmth, low control, and 4) uninvolved which is low warmth and low control. Girls reported receiving and seeking less emotional support than boys for physical activity and eating behaviors. Moreover, peer influence on physical activity and eating behaviors was different for girls compared to boys. Generally, the findings point to the need for increased and refined communication between parent–adolescent and peer interaction regarding physical activity and eating behaviors.

From focus groups that yielded a sample of 45 Black young teens (22 boys and 23 girls) mean age 12.64 years old, St. George and Wilson (2012) asked questions aimed at understanding the teens' family influence, peer influence and their intersection related to the teens' weight, eating habits, and physical activity in boys versus girls. Questions on parental interaction and rules were explored in conjunction with questions regarding parental emotional or tangible support. Results of the study provide implications for interventions as the findings suggest that underserved youth view parenting that is inclusive of both household rules and family interactions, that is, the combination of warmth and discipline, as favorable.

Aside from parenting skills, children are strongly influenced by their parents' actions and behaviors. In a study by Davis, Young, Davis, and Moll (2011) 37% of a child's body mass index (BMI) was predicted by the parental BMI. Eighty-three percent of the parents indicated their child was overweight or very overweight. On a scale from 1–10, parents felt their child being overweight was unacceptable to them. However, these parents were 60.5% obese themselves. The children's siblings were also obese as well as one of the grandparents. The children's average weight was 152 pounds with a BMI of 28.86 and the parents' average weight was 204 pounds with a BMI of 33.9.

Davis and colleagues (2011) report that their sample of 44 Black parent-child dyads, with an average family income of less than $45K from an urban community, perceived themselves as more physically active than most despite the fact that more than half (60%) of the parents were obese.

Describing the most critical component of a child's health, the investigators state that children are more influenced by what happens within the family than what occurs in the community. And yet the children of two families, both with a genetic predisposition for obesity and living in the same neighborhood, may not have the same rate of obesity. Davis and colleagues suggest that childhood obesity is a function of how parents and community interact.

While Davis and colleagues (2011) acknowledge a genetic predisposition to obesity within some families, much of the literature suggests that obesity among poor Black teens is solely based on parenting skills and peer influence which differs by gender. St. George and Wilson's (2012) research also supports the notion that parental influence has an impact on young teens' eating patterns and physical activity. Thompson, Berry, and Hu (2013) highlight the importance of involving families to increase an adolescent's physical activity. They emphasize the value of including parents in designing and implementing interventions with the purpose of increasing physical activity in adolescent Black girls. Moreover, Savage and colleagues' (2007) work theorizes that parents can prevent teen obesity if they change their child's eating behaviors during childhood by offering the same nutritious foods more than ten times.

BODY IMAGE

Merten, Wickrama, and Williams (2008) concluded that obesity during adolescence negatively affects psychosocial well-being. Using a longitudinal design, they found that young adults who were obese during adolescence had less education and career attainment. Moreover, they had more depressive symptoms than their non-obese peers. Looking at gender and race, the authors found that obesity during adolescence for girls was significantly ($p < 0.05$) associated with less attainment. The authors did not find significant racial differences in depressive symptoms among White, Black, and Hispanic adolescent females based on obesity.

At a critical period in which physical development may have long-term psychosocial and health consequences for the adolescent, Merten and colleagues (2008) note a life course effect of obesity. For example, the investigators mentioned that orthopedic, endocrine, and psychological disorders such as depression, plus health risk factors such as diabetes, hypertension, and heart disease are outcomes related to obesity among teens. Additionally, they point to cultural beliefs about physical appearance, and how Blacks' attitudes toward larger body size are more accepting than Whites as a desirable trait. While subscribing to a bigger-is-better attitude, Blacks protest against "anti-fat" mentalities. Merten and colleagues' study also found that the relationship between obesity and attainment was not changed by race. In other words, race did not moderate the effect of obesity on attainment. The investigators attributed this finding to the notion that society accepts, and to some extent expects, Blacks to have a larger body size. Merten and colleagues also make the point that some obese people may have lower incomes as a result of employers feeling that the obese person has fewer job options.

In a secondary analysis of data from predominately (88%) Black and Hispanic participants Martyn-Nemeth and Penckofer (2012) compared levels of self-esteem between normal and overweight/obese minority adolescents. The authors found that the overweight/obese participants reported significantly ($p < 0.05$) lower self-esteem than the normal weight participants. Given the importance of self-esteem during this stage of development which is "role-identity vs. role confusion," it is reasonable to surmise that obesity may be detrimental to body image and the adolescent's "sense of who I am, and what I can become."

Noting that Black teens have been found to have higher levels of self-esteem compared to their White and Hispanic counterparts, Martyn-Nemeth and Penckofer (2012) questioned competing findings that being overweight had a negative impact on a Black teen girl's self-esteem while in other studies it did not. Furthermore, the investigators made the case that obesity within the adolescent population often leads to adulthood obesity, with the threat of chronic illnesses such as cardiovascular disease, diabetes, and cancer. Their study of 101 adolescents utilized a sample of both girls and boys with a mean age of 16.85 years old, and 51% were of normal weight, while 49% were overweight or obese. The investigators also found that self-esteem was a significant ($p < 0.001$) predictor of depression among the overweight/obese teens, but not the normal weight teens. Contrary to their postulate, cultural beliefs about body image among Blacks would shield overweight/obese teen Black girls from low self-esteem. Martyn-Nemeth and Penckofer, explained their findings by mentioning how acceptance of larger body size may be changing.

Reiter-Purtill, Ridel, Jordan, and Zeller (2010) found that obese children with a friend had higher self-perceptions of appearance than those without a friend in a sample of 84 obese (BMI > 95th percentile for age and gender) youth ages 8–16 years old in a pediatric weight management clinic. Moreover, no interaction was identified for global self-worth on obesity status and friendship when comparing 74 non-obese participants to the obese participants. In other words, regardless of friendship and obesity status the children's sense of self-worth was not affected. However, Reiter-Purtill and colleagues' correlational statistics indicated that having more friendships was significantly related to less loneliness and greater global self-worth in obese children, but not their non-overweight peers. The authors attributed this finding to the notion that friendship ties are very beneficial in the classroom and buffer feelings of isolation and loneliness. Perhaps, having friends is particularly important because of social difficulties for obese children such as low peer acceptance. This predominately Black (51.2%) female 58.3% sample had a mean age of 12.44 years old.

Relative to dating, Ali, Rizzo, Amialchuk, and Heiland (2013) found no differences in relationship and sexual behaviors between obese and non-obese Black girls. However, the authors found evidence that obese White teen females were significantly ($p < 0.01$) less likely to have been in a romantic relationship compared to their non-obese counterparts. These findings seem to support the notion that Black males like females with robust figures. Ali and colleagues also noted that delayed sexual initiation is correlated with better educational outcome among female teens. Therefore, overweight females who delay sex may have better educational outcomes and consequently better economic experiences plus stability as they transition into adulthood. Furthermore, the cultural view of ideal body size and obesity stigma may contribute to racial differences in the effect of body size on teen dating and sexual activity.

CONCLUSION

Obesity among Black teen girls is a very serious problem. Efforts that target pre-adolescent children's daily food intake and activity may be the beginning of a solution to eradicate this problem. Replacing processed foods such as bologna and hot dogs with home-cooked meals prepared with more garlic, onions, and bell peppers is just a start. Handing down cooking patterns from generation to generation on how to make delicious healthy food will facilitate the change needed in the Black community.

Simple ways to decrease the amount of sugar intake mainly focused on "less soda is better." Soda for breakfast, lunch, and dinner is a real obstacle. Replacing soda with flavored seltzer water or tap water with a slice of lemon increases hydration and decreases thirst. Sweet snacks such as cookies, cakes, and candy are easily replaced with dried or fresh fruits.

Physical activity is equally as important as eating healthy foods. Black adolescent girls are in most need of support when it comes to exercise. First, the concept of being overweight is not an incentive for this population to exercise. Physical activity must be addressed from a different perspective. The stimulus is to be healthy, not lose weight. For example, mentioning that exercise will help improve grade average as well as concentration for problem solving will motivate this group. Whereas young Black men play basketball and football, teen Black girls need to be reminded to dance with their friends. They should spend at least 150 minutes per week being more active. Window shopping for hours is a great way to stay active. While impoverished Black communities face many obstacles, poverty in and of itself does not need to equate to obesity. Young gifted Black teens can improve their future.

REFERENCES

Ali, M. M., Rizzo, J. A., Amialchuk, A., & Heiland, F. (2013). Racial differences in the influence of female adolescents' body size on dating and sex. *Economics and Human Biology* (In Press). http://dx.doi.org/10.1016/j.ehb.2013.11.001

Centers for Disease Control and Prevention. 2012. *Basics about Childhood Obesity: How Is childhood overweight and obesity measured?* Retrieved October 18, 2013 from http://www.cdc.gov/obesity/childhood/basics.html

Davis, M., Young, L., Davis, S., & Moll, G. (2011). Parental depression, family functioning, and obesity among African American children. *The ABNF Journal, 22*(3) 53–57.

DiSantis, K. I., Grier, S., Odoms-Young, A., Baskin, M. L., Carter-Edwards, L., Young, D. R., Lassiter, V., & Kumanyika, S. K. (2013). What "Price" Means When Buying Food: Insights from a Multisite Qualitative Study with Black Americans. *American Journal of Public Health, (103)*3, 516–522.

Douthitt, V. L., & Harvey, M. L. (1995). Exercise counseling—How physical educators can help. *Journal of Physical Education, Recreation & Dance, 66*(5), 31–35.

Dulin-Keita, A., Thind, H., Affuso, O., & Baskin, M. (2013). The associations of perceived neighborhood disorder and physical activity with obesity among African American adolescents. *BMC Public Health, 13*:440.

Franzini. L., Taylor, W., Elliott, M. N., Cuccaro, P., Tortolero, S. R., Gilliland, J. M., Grunbaum, J., & Schuster, M. A. (2010). Neighborhood characteristics favorable to outdoor physical activity: disparities by socioeconomic and racial/ethnic composition. *Health Place, 16*(2):267–274.

Gomez, G. L. (2012, October 19). When did obesity become an issue? *Natural News.* Retrieved from http://www.naturalnews.com/037596_obesity_statistics_junk_food.html##ixzz2rcA1Wn70

He, M., Tucker, P., Gilliland, J., Irwin, J. D., Larsen, K., & Hess, P. (2012). The influence of local food environments on adolescents' food purchasing behaviors. *International Journal of Environmental Research and Public Health, (9)*4: 1458–71.

Huffman, F. G., Kanikireddy, S., & Patel, M. (2010). Parenthood: A contributing factor to childhood obesity. *International Journal of Environmental Research and Public Health, 7*(7), 2800–2810.

Kramer, R. F., Coutinho, A. J., Vaeth, E., Christiansen, K., Suratkar, S., & Gittelsohn, J. (2012). Healthier home food preparation methods and youth and caregiver psychosocial actors are associated with lower BMI in African American youth. *The Journal of Nutrition. Community and International Nutrition,* 948–954.

Lucan, S. C., Barg, F. K., Karasz, A., Palmer, C. S., & Long, J. A. (2012). Perceived influences on diet among urban, low-income African Americans. *American Journal of Health Behavior, 36*(5), 700–710. doi:10.5993/AJHB.36.5.12

Macartney, S., Bishaw, A., & Fontenot, K., (2013). Poverty rates for selected detailed race and Hispanic groups by state and place: 2007–2011. American Community Survey Briefs. http://www.census.gov/prod/2013pubs/acsbr11-17.pdf

Martyn-Nemeth, P., & Penckofer, S. (2012) Psychological vulnerability among overweight/obese minority adolescents. *The Journal of School Nursing, 28*(4), 291–301.

Merten, M. J., Wickrama, K. A. S., & Williams, A. L. (2008). Adolescent obesity and young adult psychosocial outcomes: Gender and race differences. *Journal of Youth Adolescence, 37*(9), 1111–1122.

National Center for Health Statistics. (2013). Health, United States, 2012: With Special Feature on Emergency Care. Hyattsville, MD.

National Heart, Lung, and Blood Institute (1998, February). Clinical Guidelines on the Identification, Evaluation, and Treatment of Oversight and Obesity in Adults (#98-4083). NIH publication, p. 57.

Nicholson, L. M., & Browning, C. R. (2012). Racial and ethnic disparities in obesity during the transition to adulthood: The contingent and nonlinear impact of neighborhood disadvantage. *Journal of Youth and Adolescence, (41)*1: 53–66.

Ogden, C. L., Carroll, M. D., Curtin, L. R., Lamb, M. M., & Flegal, K. M. (2010). Prevalence of high body mass index in U.S. children and adolescents, 2007–2008. *JAMA, 303*(3):242–49.

Reiter-Purtill, J., Ridel, S., Jordan, R., & Zeller, M. H. (2010). The benefits of reciprocated friendships for treatment-seeking obese youth. *Journal of Pediatric Psychology, 35*(8):905–14. doi:10.1093/jpepsy/jsp140

Reitzel, L., Regan, S., Nguyen, N., Cromley, E., Strong, L., Wetter, D., & McNeill, L. (2013). Density and proximity of fast food restaurants and body mass index among African Americans. *American Journal of Public Health.* doi:10.2105/AJPH.2012.301140

Savage, J. S., Fisher, J. O., & Birch, L. L. (2007). Parental influence on eating behaviors: Conception to adolescence. *The Journal of Law, Medicine and Ethics, 35*(1), 22–34.

St. George, S. M., & Wilson, D. K. (2012). A qualitative study for understanding family and peer influences on obesity-related health behaviors in low-income African-American adolescents. *Childhood Obesity, 8*(5), 466–76.

Thompson, W., Berry, D., & Hu, J. (2013). A church-based intervention to change attitudes about physical activity among Black adolescent girls: A feasibility study. *Public Health Nursing, 30*(3), 221–230. doi:10.1111/phn.1200

Wang, Y., Tussing, L., Odoms-Young, A., Braunschweig, C., Flay, B., Hedeker, D., & Hellison, D. (2006). Obesity prevention in low socioeconomic status urban African-American adolescents: Study design and preliminary findings of the HEALTH-KIDS Study. *European Journal of Clinical Nutrition, (60)*1, 92–103.

Chapter 11

Growth Development and Anticipatory Guidance for African American Girls

Funmi Aiyegbo-Ohadike

Adolescence is a challenging life stage for both the girl undergoing the maturational changes and her parents. Adolescence is a physiologic process, which has psychosocial implications. The parent/child relationship begins a metamorphosis in concert with the physiologic development that takes place within girls. It is a process that ends with the emergence of a woman and a new, young adult/parent relationship. A major source of the stress between parents and their daughters is the development of external sexual characteristics that takes place during adolescence. The development of breasts, the onset of menstruation, and the deposition of fat in the hips and buttocks are a blatant demonstration of the change from child to adult. The basic evolutionary goal of the adolescent years is to produce a functional, young adult female who is capable to reproduce and care for offspring and sustain the species. Beyond the evolutionary requirements of development is the current role of teenage years, which we now look at as a major developmental period, including tasks to be achieved, such as independence from the family of origin, a beginning acceptance of body image, alignment with a peer group, and development of a unique identity (Lemcke, Pattinson, Marshall & Cowley, 1995; Schuster & Ashburn, 1992).

Parents need to be prepared for the teenage years. Parents may seek information from their own experiences, family members, friends, and health care providers for guidance on how to manage teens. Parents may remember their own teenage years with nostalgia, while agonizing about the "new generation" that they are tasked with raising. The data suggest that the teenage years can be fraught with danger for all teens. Teens have been noted to have increased risk-taking behavior (Schuster & Ashburn, 1992). The dangers range from sexual abuse, sexually transmitted diseases (STDs), teen pregnancy, negative body image, and dysfunctional relationships. African American parents may face particular challenges based upon historical factors, current social conditions, class, and economic conditions.

> African-American adolescents 13-19 accounted for 1,919 AIDS cases (55 percent females) and 3,517 HIV infections (62% females); AIDS is the fourth leading cause of death among African Americans ages 25 to 44—a group likely to have contracted HIV as adolescents. (IDPH, 2014)

A recent study found that a perceived negative attitude of parents towards sexual activity and its consequences influenced the behavior of their children, with the authors noting that African American teen boys who lived with parents with this negative perception have fewer sexual partners and less sexual activity (Annang, Lian, Fletcher & Jackson, 2014).

How can parents navigate the deep waters of changes that are occurring during adolescence? The first step is to assess their own level of comfort with issues surrounding sexuality. Human sexuality can be a loaded issue, which many people would prefer to avoid rather than explore. As a society, we are surrounded by sexualized images and messages in the media. The media permeates every aspect of our lives, despite efforts that parents may take to protect their children from inappropriate information. Parents may fail to understand that their children may already have a certain level of sexual awareness before they decide to introduce the topic. Children have a natural sexual curiosity, which may be piqued by the imagery that is readily available on television, social networks, and other electronic and print media. After adults assess their own sexual knowledge and comfort, they must next assess their child's knowledge base.

NORMAL GROWTH AND DEVELOPMENT

There have been discussions surrounding racial differences in the onset of puberty. There are both anecdotal and scientific reports (Simmons &

Blyth, 1987) of an earlier onset of breast development and menarche (onset of menstruation) in Black girls versus that which is noted in White girls. Schuster noted, ". . . hereditary factors and climate show significant correlation with the onset of menarche, which occurs later in colder climates." She also went on to say that the difference in menarche is only earlier in Black females by a few months, versus their White counterparts. She noted a few other factors that influence onset of menarche, including nutritional status, with girls who have more body fat having menarche earlier than girls with leaner body mass, such as female elite athletes (Schuster & Ashburn, 1992).

Normal onset of puberty in girls begins with breast bud development around age 11, then growth of pubic hair, and finally menarche around age 12.5. The process of puberty takes on average 4 years until development is completed. Parents should provide age appropriate timely information as a girl develops. The eleven-year-old girl that starts breast bud development should be aware that breast growth is just the first step in a process that will take a few years to reach completion. She needs to know that her friends may develop at different rates, but that everyone will eventually go through the pubertal changes. Initial reactions by girls to puberty may include embarrassment, with the pre-teen girl wearing layers to cover her growing breasts. She may hunch over or cross her hands over her breasts. Girls who start breast development later may stuff their shirts to appear more developed and start wearing more mature and body-conscious clothing.

Before menstruation begins, girls need to be taught hygiene and self-care; pre-menstruation also provides an opportunity to address sexual activity. Menstruation signals the beginning of the reproductive years. In the initial year following the onset of the menstrual cycle, girls may experience irregular and anovulatory (no egg is released) menses. Parents should advise their daughter to carry menstrual supplies, in case of an unexpected onset of menstrual flow. The irregular periods can be anxiety provoking for a girl who has had some sexual contact and fears being pregnant when she misses a period. There can also be irrational fears of pregnancy still floating around, based on poor understanding of the mechanics of reproduction, with myths such as becoming pregnant from kissing, or sitting on a toilet seat. Providing girls with a book on menstruation and having them read it and then come with their own questions is a non-threatening, self-paced way of giving girls reliable information on development. Many schools have health classes where they review this information, but some districts have been prevented from talking about reproduction and sexual activity because there has been community sentiment against it.

In addition to breast development, growth of pubic hair, the onset of menses, and increase in height, girls will also experience a change in body mass. Girls may begin to wrestle with their self-image and comfort with their changing self. A girl who was previously thin will develop mass in the hips and breasts, which may lead to attention from boys and girls who now find her burgeoning form attractive. Girls may try to manipulate this changing frame by dieting or increasing exercise. It is important that parents guide girls through this change with positive feedback, acknowledging that the change is taking place, but reassuring girls that the change is expected and normal. Some traditional cultures have rites of initiation that celebrate the changes that occur in adolescence, giving a communal stamp of approval to the changes taking place. The celebrations usually involve older women who welcome the girl into womanhood.

DEVELOPMENTAL ISSUES AND HIGH RISK CONDITIONS

Pregnancy and Sexually Transmitted Infections

Pregnancy is the leading cause for girls to not complete school. Before the onset of menstruation, parents need to be discussing their values and beliefs about sexuality. Parents may idealize their daughters and not see them as sexual beings. Parents may not accept that part of normal growth and development involves sexual play and sexual fantasies. Parents need to be aware that sexual learning takes place during adolescence and that if parents do not engage in open communication with their children, behaviors may be hidden and become a source of shame and anxiety for their daughters (Lemcke, Pattinson, Marshall & Cowley, 1995; Ross, Channon-Little & Rosser, 2000).

The CDC reports lower use of birth control among African American and Hispanic teen girls, leading to a birthrate that is 2–3 times higher than their White counterparts. Girls who are born to teenage moms have a significantly increased risk of becoming teenage moms themselves in later life. Recalling a discussion with one mother who had her daughter at 16: The mom asks: Do you think I should allow my 18-year-old daughter to go on the pill? She's getting ready to go away to college and I once found condoms in her backpack, and she does have a boyfriend. The nurse practitioner informed her that her daughter might already be having sex, since 46% of high school students report having had intercourse. African American and Hispanic girls are 2–3 times more likely to give birth during the teenage years than their White counterparts. Although teen pregnancy has been on a decline over the past two decades, it still remains a significant risk for teens. There are over 400,000 teen births per year and you do not want your daughter to fall into that demographic. Unfortunately many parents, even when confronted with evidence to the contrary, find it difficult to accept their children's sexual activity, even though many parents were sexually active at the same age. The nurse practitioner advised the mother to seek contraceptive counseling for her daughter, with the expectation that if the daughter was not already sexually active, she may become so in the future (CDC Vital Signs April 2011, 2011).

Based upon the parental belief system, they may want abstinence to be the central message in discussions of sexuality. Parents may decide to place sexual activity strictly within the context of marriage, putting aside other committed relationships and casual sex. Having abstinence as a goal doesn't preclude a discussion of contraception and safe sex. Parents may aspire to a set standard, but a hormonal teen, who is still establishing a sense of a separate self, may find herself in compromising situations. Parents need to take into account the impact of peer pressure, the development of an individual identity, and natural curiosity. The teen girls who become pregnant or contract sexually transmitted infections (STIs) are cautionary tales, but they do not reflect the full range of teen sexual activity. Many teens safely explore their sexuality with age-appropriate partners and survive the experience without permanent scars. Parents must be cognizant of their own emotional baggage, biases, and fears when it comes to teen sexual activity. Educating girls about contraception is not the same as permitting the activity. Many parents feel that a discussion of contraceptive methods is equivalent to sanctioning the activity. Parents should provide the information on contraception and disease prevention and continue to provide a structured environment, where their values and beliefs are on display.

St. Hill reports that African Americans are generally not discussing sexual issues with their teens, and the Centers for Disease Control and Prevention (CDC) found that youth aged 13–24 accounted for an estimated 26% of all new HIV infections in the United States in 2010. As reported in this report, African American females ages 13–24 were the largest female population group to be diagnosed with HIV, in addition to pregnancy and STIs. HIV infection is of significant concern, because those who contract the disease will have lifelong infection and will need to manage all of the chronic manifestations of the condition. Other STIs, such as hepatitis, human papilloma virus (HPV), and herpes also cause chronic conditions and have long impacts. Bacterial infections of the female genitourinary tract can cause acute infections that are treatable with antibiotics if identified, but they also can cause more severe conditions including pelvic inflammatory disease and sterility if they are not diagnosed or treated in a timely fashion (Centers for Disease Control and Prevention, 2012).

During the teen years, girls are developing their ability to set long-term goals. One of the challenges of the teen and early adult years is delaying gratification in order to achieve future goals. A teen that contracts an STI may be more concerned about the consequences of telling her parents about her sexual activity, and less concerned with the long-term consequences of the symptoms that she is experiencing. Independent access to health care is a barrier to teens seeking information and reproductive exams. Teens may be dependent on their parents for payment, insurance, and in some states actual appointment setting for reproductive health. Teens may find it difficult to navigate the world of health care, unless there is a clinic on the school campus. Even when there are clinics nearby, teens may be intimidated about approaching adults to discuss reproductive issues. They need to be assured that their confidentiality and privacy will be protected.

Parents who bring their daughters in for sexual health counseling, initial or follow-up exams, can be divided into two camps. The first group consists of parents who are proactive, engaged, and resigned to the fact that teens are sexual beings who may act on their feelings and desires. The second group consists of parents who are shocked into submission, discovering to their chagrin that their teens are currently engaged or have been engaged in sexual activity. Regardless of which group the parents belong to, the teens have the same need to be treated with dignity and respect and to establish a habit of sexual health.

The initial gynecologic exam will consist of history taking, including onset of puberty and assessment of where the girl is in the process of development, followed by a general health history and questions about sexual activity. The appointment can take place with a parent present if both the teen and the parent are comfortable with that arrangement. If either party is not at ease, then it is better to have the parent wait outside. If the parent asks if they can be privy to what is discussed by the health care provider and the teen, they have to be aware that the laws and statutes of the state they reside in may govern the right to full disclosure. The health care provider should also advise both parent and child their relationship is evolving, and the sharing of information by the teen needs to be consensual.

The voluntary sharing of general information about their sexual activities helps teens to develop trust and establish boundaries. Girls need to be able to decide whom to trust with the intimate details of their lives, and how much to disclose about their activities. This a very difficult area for parents to relinquish control to their teens. Anger and disappointment may drive the parents' reactions. The health care provider needs to reassure them that they have done a good job with raising their daughter and have brought her to the best place to address her health care needs. They need to be informed that they are not alone in facing sexual health issues with their teen.

If a teen discloses to the health care provider that she is contemplating sexual activity, or currently having sex, the provider will proceed with an initial pelvic exam pap smear and cultures. The initial exam will establish a baseline, from which the provider will provide education and treatment. The provider should stress consistent condom use with intercourse to prevent pregnancy and STIs. Adults should not assume that just because a teen is sexually active, she is knowledgeable about condom storage and use. The provider can either review the use of condoms or refer the teen to an outside agency or teen group for more education. Depending on the age, insurance coverage, and parental preference, a teen may also be placed on oral contraceptives. Any provider prescribing oral contraceptives to teens should be aware that the young women should be established in their menstrual cycle for two years and capable of following the regimen. Oral contraceptive pills can be prescribed to teens for other noncontraceptive indications ranging from acne, to heavy menses, to irregular menstrual periods. The provider should also give a stern warning that oral contraceptive pills do not prevent STIs.

Other contraceptive devices that are available to teens include implantable devices, vaginal ring, vaginal sponge, diaphragm, and spermicides. In the United States, women who have not given birth are not typically offered intrauterine devices (IUDs). IUDs are 99% effective, but because of controversies with previous devices and initial cost of insertion, they are underutilized in the United States. A parent may need to be involved in their teen's contraceptive use because of issues surrounding medication administration, coverage of cost, as well as the necessity for medication or treatment consent and state regulations regarding treatment of minors.

When it comes to deciding if a teen should start using contraceptives, or if condoms should be made available to teens, the deciding factor is based on the answer to this question: "Is this teen going to have sex with or without contraception?" Based on statistics the answer is yes. More than half of the pregnancies among all women are unplanned, which would mean more than 200,000 of the 400,000 teen births per year are unplanned. The take-home message on teen contraception is that more than 200,000 girls each year find themselves in situations where they are having sex without contraception, or with inadequate contraception.

Teenagers are also at risk for being involved in dysfunctional relationships. In a CDC study, 1 in 5 women reported having some sort of intimate partner violence between ages 11 and 17. An early experience of intimate partner violence sets expectations for girls in terms of future relationships. Intimate partner violence can be defined as verbal abuse, physical attacks, or sexual coercion. Only 30% of teens who are involved in violent intimate situations report the violence. The relationship between the teen and the parent is very important to early identification and prevention of intimate partner violence. If a teen girl is involved in an abusive relationship, a parent may be the person she turns to. A parent may also notice changes in their child, who can become isolated, anxious and/or depressed about her situation. A teen who has grown up in a home where there was physical or verbal abuse may expect relationships to be about controlling and abusing the other partner. A savvy healthcare provider may pick up clues that a girl is being coerced, forced, or trafficked into sexual activity. Parents should be alert to the possibility of sexual abuse and exploitation in children of every age. Steps must be taken to separate the girl from her abuser, and assure her safety. In some states health care providers are mandated to report abuse or suspected abuse.

The teen years are an important time for a girl to start to recognize her value and develop her sense of self. An abusive relationship can cause an emotional disturbance that affects a girl in school, in extracurricular activities, and in her peer group. Teen girls are often labeled as hormonal and prone to mood swings. It's important that parents recognize when a girl is experiencing emotions that are outside of the expected spectrum. A teen that withdraws from her usual activities, social circle, and declines in schoolwork may be going through a challenging situation. The teen may seek out a trusted adult to share with. Mothers who have been through abusive relationships may have ambivalent feelings about seeing their daughters going through the same thing. Counseling may help to resolve these issues, if the family is open to considering it. The most important issue is assuring the girls' mental and physical health and safety.

Teen girls role-play adult situations such as dating, modeling what they see at home, in their peer group, and in the media. Girls also feel pressure to be in a "couple" and "date" when other girls in their peer group are doing "it." The peer pressure may lead a girl who has no experience of healthy relationships to tolerate abusive behaviors. Most teen girls are struggling with establishing self-esteem in a world full of images. Girls are in transition during the teen years, and their bodies are still growing and developing. A girl may see herself and value herself based on the perception of others. If she has been labeled as a "pretty girl," "fat girl," "tomboy," "slut," "fast," "mean," or "ghetto," the labeling will have implications on her social status, and she may want to maintain that status. Dating a partner who is violent may be part of the projected image that a girl has been led into. Girls need to be empowered to understand that their roles are not permanent, and their true selves are not defined by any one experience. They need to be coached and mentored by adults who can guide them through negative circumstances. Girls who play sports or partake in other extracurricular activities have the added benefit of receiving praise and being valued for skills beyond their burgeoning sexual selves.

SUMMARY

The teen years are formative in the development of the adult female. Girls are faced with multiple challenges as they go through the maturational process. It is the role of both parents to shepherd a girl through the perilous parts of growth and development. The issues covered in this chapter foster the greatest challenges for every generation. The current times are punctuated by the power and ubiquity of media. We cannot underestimate the lure of images and the impact that they have on the adolescent girl. Parents will always harken back to their teenage years, and there are some commonalities, but there are always unique dynamics such as media and technology that highlight the differences between generations.

Communication is the key to remaining engaged with a teen girl. Parents should give girls the opportunity to express themselves without fear of disappointing the parents with their choices. When it comes to the choice to become sexually active, parents need to remain ahead of their teens by acknowledging that young people may feel urges to have sex. An appropriate discussion defines the parents' expectations but takes into account the pressures that child may be facing to behave otherwise. The ideal may be abstinence, but societal pressures, social norms, and individual preferences may propel a girl towards early sexual activity. Because the responsibility for an unplanned pregnancy often falls to the parents of a pregnant girl, parents may feel compelled to be very strict and set unrealistic expectations.

A visit to a health care provider can help to educate both parents and teen girls about what to expect during adolescence. Regular visits as a girl grows and develops will provide a forum for families to express their concerns in a nonjudgmental environment. Questions about the physical and psychological changes can be addressed. Reliable information on STIs and contraception can be reviewed, and treatment can be provided. Although sexual education should begin at home, if there are issues or barriers to such discussions in the home, a visit to a health professional can facilitate the dialogue.

REFERENCES

Annang, L., Lian, B., Fletcher, F. E., & Jackson, D. (2014). Parental attitudes of teenage pregnancy: Impact on sexual risk behavior of African-American youth. *Sex Education: Sexuality, Society & Learning,* 14(2), 225–237.

APA Task Force on the Sexualization of Girls. (2007, June 1). *Report of the APA Task Force on the Sexualization of Girls.* (E. L. Zurbriggen, ed.) Retrieved January 5, 2014, from www.apa.org/pi/wpo/sexualization.html

CDC. (2013, August 26). Retrieved March 18, 2014, from CDC: http://www.cdc .gov/HealthyYouth/sexualbehaviors/

CDC Vital Signs April 2011. (2011, April 1). Retrieved from CDC Vital Signs April 2011 Preventing Teen Pregnancy in the U.S.: https://www.cdc.gov/ vitalsigns

Centers for Disease Control and Prevention. Estimated HIV incidence in the United States, 2007–2010. (2012, December 1). *HIV Surveillance Supplemental Report.* Retrieved March 1, 2014, from CDC: http://www.cdc.gov/hiv/ yopics/surveillance/resources/reports#supplemental

Davis, S., & Tucker-Brown, A. (2013). Effects of Black Sexual Stereotypes on Sexual Decision Making Among African American Women. *The Journal of Pan African Studies, 5*(9), 111–128.

The Heinz Endowment. *Gender Norms: A Key to Improving Health and Wellness Among Black Women & Girls.* Howard Heinz Endowment, Vera I. Heinz Endowment. Pittsburgh.

IDPH. (2014, March 18). Retrieved March 18, 2014, from www.idph.stat.il.us/us/public/respect/african_american.htm

Jarrah, S. S., & Kamel, A. A. (2012). Attitudes and practices of school-aged girls towards menstruation. *International Journal of Nursing Practice, 18*, 308–315.

Lemcke, D. P., Pattinson, J., Marshall, L. A., & Cowley, D. S. (1995). *Primary Care of Women.* East Norwalk, CT: Appleton & Lange.

Ross, M. W., Channon-Little, L. D., & Rosser, S. B. (2000). *Sexual Health Concerns* (2nd ed.). Philadelphia, PA: F. A. Davis.

Schuster, C. S., & Ashburn, S. S. (1992). *The Process of Human Development: A Holistic Life-Span Approach* (3rd ed.). New York, NY: Lippincott.

Simmons, R., & Blyth, D. A. (1987). *Moving into Adolescence: The impact of pubertal change and school context.* Aldine De Gruyter.

St. Hill, P., Lipson, J. G., & Meleis, A. I. (2003). *Caring for Women Cross-Culturally.* Philadelphia, PA: F. A. Davis.

Chapter 12

African American Girls' Spirituality and Resilience

Hope E. Ferguson

In early spring of 2014, Karyn Washington, a young Black woman known for her blog addressing colorism, "For Brown Girls," committed suicide. By all accounts, Washington was a positive, church-going young woman who had dedicated her young life to helping "brown girls" overcome self-hatred and celebrate their own unique beauty (Workneh, 2014). In the online eulogies that followed her unexpected death, friends and commentators noted how, historically, Black women are expected to be strong, resilient, and able to hold things together in the toughest circumstances: single parenthood, bad or abusive relationships, poverty, and discrimination. It is the Black woman who is historically looked to as the backbone, or matriarch, of the Black family (LiaLia, 2014).

Washington's untimely death, which followed the loss of her own mother, was seen as illustrative of the limits of a young woman's resilience. In the face of loss, the re-emergence of cruder forms of racism following the election of the first Black president, and the lack of a sense of self-value that many young African American women have internalized from the wider culture (and that Washington sought to combat), it was thought that the young woman, a shining role model for so many, was in fact, not able to save her own life from depression and despair (LiaLia, 2014).

How do young African American women persevere in the face of racism, colorism, discrimination, peer pressure, a hypersexualized culture, and their divergence from the greater culture's norms of beauty and behavior? How do young Black women develop the perseverance to handle loss at an early age and to prepare for a life of wholeness, goodness, healthy self-regard, and productivity, where their personal, professional, and family lives are characterized by strength and vitality?

Young Black women must resist the images that they see in the media that tell them they must look a certain way or behave a certain way to be accepted. They need to resist internalizing the values of the culture that combine the worship of celebrity and wealth and where girls who don't feel beautiful, beloved, or materially blessed, can feel that society's demands are impossible to meet.

In the second decade of the twenty-first century, it can be argued that the image of the Black woman has again taken a downturn. Historically, the Black woman was seen as the strong matriarch, the mammy, the siren, or loose woman. In the 1970s, following the civil rights movement, the Black woman in the media was portrayed as sassy, fierce, and independent, à la Foxy Brown, an afroed crime-fighter portrayed by the beautiful actress Pam Grier. Or on the other hand, there were the saintly Black women, such as Rebecca Morgan in the film *Sounder*, or Jane Pittman, of *The Autobiography of Miss Jane Pittman*, portrayed by the dark-hued "serious" actress Cicely Tyson (Bogle, 2001).

Now, when young women turn on their flat-screen television sets, instead of Pam Grier or Cicely Tyson, they are confronted with *The Real Housewives of Atlanta* or *Basketball Wives*. With long weaves, false eyelashes, heavily made-up faces, and "bodacious" bodies, these women are sassy, finger-pointing, head-rolling, and quick to settle their differences through verbal or even physical altercations. They have totally embraced a Eurocentric model of beauty, while at the same time embracing some of the worst stereotypes about African American women as hypersexualized, bossy, and difficult; displaying "ratchet" behavior, they are constantly used and misused by the rappers, ballers, tattoo artists, and other men they consort with. Daytime talk shows such as British media personality Trisha Goddard's focus on extreme dysfunction on the part of Black women and all of their relationships—with parents, siblings, and men.

Many young Black women similarly look to successful Black women like Beyoncé and Rihanna as role models. Both singers present themselves in a Eurocentric and highly sexualized manner. Yet they also seek to portray themselves as "fierce" young women whom nobody will mess with, such as Beyoncé's alter ago Sasha Fierce, and song "Run the World (Girls)."

In the meantime, although Black women have long accounted for the majority of college and higher degrees in the Black community (*Journal of Blacks in Higher Education*, 2009), the Yale study found that highly educated Black women were twice as likely to have never married by age 45, compared to their White counterparts, and twice as likely to be divorced, widowed, or separated (Nitsche & Brueckner, 2011). Although there has been debate over how the statistics were arrived at, experience and data show a lower rate of marriage among Blacks than Whites (*New York Times*, 2011), Blacks have been called the "least coupled people" on the planet. So, in spite of their accomplishments, many Black women, primarily the college-educated and higher socioeconomic women, find themselves alone for a large portion of their lifetime, without the natural comfort that a partner can bring (Butler, 2009).

Given such ills, how does the church address the needs of young Black women between the ages of 13 and 18 today? How can a sense of belovedness (by God) and self-worth prevent young Black women from harmful behaviors, such as gang membership (for a sense of belonging), drug use, or sexual promiscuity? How can such young women develop a healthy and whole sense of self and belonging that will allow them to grow into contributing members of the community, and not be embittered, engaged in self-harm, or determined to try to eradicate that which makes them unique: hair, skin color, African features, and ways of interacting and being in the world?

In her book, *Trouble Don't Last Always*, Evelyn Parker, assistant professor of Christian Education at the Perkins School of Theology, Southern Methodist University, recalls her own upbringing in the segregated Black community in Mississippi in the early 1960s. She recalls the segregated theaters and water fountains: the water fountain designated for Whites, sparkly and clean; for Blacks, gray and dingy. She remembers sitting in the balcony of the segregated theater, but thinking she had the "best seat in the house."

She also remembers having to go to the side of an establishment to order ice cream on a hot day. Yet, because of the strength and self-assurance of people she knew in the Black community, she grew up with a secure sense of self-regard and identity. According to Parker (2003):

> Walking downtown was like moving through thick air. There was always the feeling of pushing against a strong, invisible force. You could not see it. You only felt the tiredness of your muscles and the frustration of your mind after being downtown. This tiredness was relieved only when you returned across the tracks to the African American neighborhood. It sheltered us from the onerous atmosphere of downtown.

On the other hand, the Black community, somewhat self-contained, offered an atmosphere of light and hope. "In contrast to downtown, in my neighborhood the air was light, electric, and pulsating with possibility" (p. 2).

Parker attended church at the St. James Christian Methodist Episcopal (CME) Church, where she describes the spirituality, as it was in so many Black churches of the era, as focusing more on social justice than personal piety. Rather than evangelical, charismatic, Afrocentric or Holiness spirituality, the church fit firmly in the social justice tradition that produced the Rev. Martin Luther King Jr., Medgar Evers, and others.

She was also buoyed by role models such as her grandmother, "Miss Vergie," who always walked with her head up, looked Whites in the eye, and who commanded respect as she went about her daily business, and seemed to thrive in spite of living in the Jim Crow South (Parker, 2003).

In my own family, my great-grandfather and grandfather were African Methodist Episcopal ministers. My grandfather, whom I never met, was an overseer of the churches in the Baltimore area. I remember my father and aunts recalling being present at basement meetings of the NAACP at the church. My father taught us, as he had been taught, the Negro national anthem, "Lift Ev'ry Voice and Sing." We would gather round the piano on occasion and sing the song as a family. The African American church, indeed, has been a womb to the civil rights movement and also a place of refuge for those in the African American community.

Contrast that to the environment that young people find today. Parker writes in *Trouble Don't Last Always* that

> African-American communities are no longer considered as bastions against the evils of racism. Predominantly Black schools, churches, and families forming our neighborhoods are no longer assumed as the respite ecology for Black children. The Black church is not connected with a viable movement comparable in purpose, youth involvement, and media visibility to the civil rights movement. (p. 5)

In his article, "The Inconceivable Start of African-American Christianity," Mark Galli writes about the beginnings of the Black church. Although the more pious slaveholders would arrange services for the slaves, the "real" church took place at a distance from the plantation, in the swamps or woods, where the slaves felt free to worship a God with whom they felt connected and truly loved by.

Quoting an observer, Peter Randolph, a slave in Prince Georges County, Virginia, until he was freed in 1847, Galli writes,

> They have an understanding among themselves as to the time and place. . . . This is often done by the first one arriving breaking boughs from the trees and bending them in the direction of the selected spot. After arriving and greeting one another, men and women sat in groups together. Then there was preaching . . . by the brethren, then praying and singing all around until they generally feel quite happy.

The speaker arises and talks very slowly, until feeling the spirit, he grows excited, and in a short time there fall to the ground 20 or 30 men and women under its influence. The slave forgets all of his sufferings, except to remind others of the trials during the past week, exclaiming, 'Thank God, I shall not live here always!"

Galli observes, "It is a remarkable event not merely because of the risks incurred (200 lashes of the whip often awaited those caught at such a meeting), but because of the hurdles overcome merely to arrive at this moment. For decades all manner of people and circumstances conspired against African Americans even hearing the gospel, let alone responding to it in freedom and joy."

The authenticity of the conversion of the slaves was noted by observers, including Jonathan Edwards, according to Galli. "In 1733, during a local revival instigated by his preaching, Jonathan Edwards noted, 'There are several Negroes who . . . appear to have been truly born again in the late remarkable season.'" Galli writes that when the Great Awakening arrived in full—with shouts and groans of spiritual ecstasy—Blacks began to swell the crowds coming to hear revival preachers. He writes,

It is amazing that under these circumstances [oppression by White "masters" who quoted scriptures like "slaves obey your masters"] that any slaves found the Christian message convincing. And yet Blacks clearly saw the difference—a difference White owners were utterly blind to—between the message of the Bible and the slave-holding culture in which it was taking root.

It is well known that slaves identified with the bondage of the children of Israel in Egypt, and that many spirituals have a double meaning. "Go Down Moses," "Swing Low, Sweet Chariot," and others spoke of a dual hope: the hope of freedom and the hope of ultimate release from earthly troubles at the time of death (Parker, 2003). Parker calls this hope "emancipatory hope."

"To possess emancipatory hope is to expect transformation of hegemonic relations and to act as God's agent ushering in God's vision of equality for humankind," she writes. "Emancipatory means freedom from domination. Verbs such as 'challenge,' 'examine,' 'confront,' 'free,' and 'transform' are commonly used in association with the term 'emancipatory.'"

How can this history be applied to the plight of young Black women today?

During a telephone interview, Karen Dace, vice chancellor for diversity, equity, and inclusion at Indiana University–Purdue University, Indianapolis, notes the importance of giving girls a model to look up to whether Biblical or in her day-to-day life (April 2014).

Dace, originally from Chicago, and active in her African Methodist Episcopal church there, wrote a paper about the disturbing trends she observed during Vacation Bible School one summer. The children spanned elementary age to young teens and were predominantly African American. However, a few girls were Caucasian as they were foster children of one of the parents. Throughout most of the program, Dace observed that the Black girls, while often mistreating one another, and name-calling and denigrating other girls (for dark skin and "nappy" hair) were determined to get near the White girls and to impress and compete for the attention of the Black boys. Dace realized that by focusing on heroes of the Bible such as David and Moses, and ignoring examples of females in the Bible, the girls were taking in the unspoken notion that their lives were not as valuable, integral, and used of God, as were the boys'.

In her paper, "Bright Eyes, Dim Eyes: The Masculinization of African-American Spirituality," she writes:

"We had only told the girls stories of men in the Bible. We hadn't told the girls about the great women of the Bible: about Deborah or Yael. While the girls needed to know about these women, the boys needed to know it too." Dace continues,

> . . . unwittingly we had taught a Black boy's song. . . . Acutely aware of the challenges facing young African American men, we designed a program that would uplift them. Consequently, we paid very little attention to uplifting the young women. After all, as one African-American pastor noted, "I'm not worried about Black women, they've already got it together." Although this pastor was not affiliated with this particular program or this church, the sentiment that African-American women "have it all together" is common among many within and without the community. . . . Instead of legitimizing the girls, we designed a program that further diminished their significance in God's plan by excluding any meaningful discussion of women in the Bible. Their readings and activities asserted the invaluable role men played in God's plan with little mention of women. . . . Of course our female children's eyes were dim. Why should they have been able to recall the simplest of facts? They came to us with low self-esteem, full of self loathing, and we failed to offer them any reason to alter those destructive feelings. (Dace, 1997)

Dace, a single woman, realized the importance of female models when she overheard a girlfriend's daughter telling her mother that she wanted to be like Miss Karen when she grew up. In the same telephone interview, she said, "I didn't realize the impact of my lived life on this young girl."

Why did the young girl admire "Miss Karen"? Because Miss Karen owned a home, had a nice car, a fur coat, "and didn't no man give it to her."

Both Dace and Parker note the importance in the African American community of women: mothers, aunts, godmothers, grandmothers, othermothers, in the spiritual formation of young girls. Older women, as the Bible states (Titus 2:4), are to disciple, or mentor the younger women; model appropriate behavior and encourage them. Dace continues in the interview: "Older women are supposed to teach the younger women. Older women are not doing what they're supposed to be doing for the younger women. Don't pretend like you've always been so holy." Be honest about mistakes you've made. It's not do as I say, not as I do. Don't sell them cheap. Don't let them think value is tied up with who they are in a relationship with."

The importance of mothers and fathers in establishing spiritual resilience in young girls cannot be emphasized enough. The family ideally should act as a sheltering cocoon for the development of young girls, where they pick up cues that their lives are significant and worthy to be cherished.

I go back again to my own family. In fifth grade, my African American teacher was teaching about slavery in our social studies class, and told us that slaves had, in fact, been well cared for and happy. After informing my mother of this, she immediately went to the school to confront the teacher with the historical reality of slavery. My mother held up to us as heroes people like Nat Turner, who led a slave rebellion in Virginia in 1831, the White abolitionist John Brown, Malcolm X, and the Rev. Martin Luther King Jr. As children, although we were allowed to play with any dolls we wanted, only dolls of color could accompany us off family premises. Through these things, my sisters and I picked up as if by osmosis, that Black people were valuable, and that Black girls (and dolls) were worthy of pride.

I recall my father, who had promised my mother to see us all through college, saying that he wanted us to always be able to take care of ourselves . . . with or without a man. The family ought to be the bedrock of a girl's self-esteem and sense of worth.

Black girls, however, often pick up messages, such as that they are nobody without a man. In the interview, Dace recalls the zealousness with which older women in her church would try to pair her and advise her on any single man who came to the church, regardless of whether or not he was a good or realistic prospect. She was dating a promising young man at the same time as she was accepted for tenure on her job; yet the excitement and congratulations all centered on the relationship and not the accomplishment, Dace recalls.

In her book, *The Sacred Selves of Adolescent Girls: Hard Stories of Race, Class, and Gender*, Parker presents a taxonomy of response for the African American girl, which she describes as Realization, Resistance, Resilience, and Ritual. She uses Miriam, Moses's sister, as an illustration of a woman who did all four. According to Parker,

A girl should be empowered to sense when she is being treated unjustly due to her race/ethnicity, gender, class, or sexual orientation . . . Girls should realize when something has gone awry and be able to name the wrongdoing on the basis of an understanding of systems and powers rather than merely personalizing the wrongdoing.

She believes that "critical consciousness" is an aspect of healthy spirituality.

A healthy spirituality for a girl is one that resists those powers that seek to dehumanize her. Resistance is spiritual opposition to all that hinders the complete flowering of a girl. An oppositional spirit rejects the academic mediocrity of lazy school counselors and teachers and chooses academic excellence instead. . . . But resisters also recognize the evil existing in social structures and political systems. . . .

According to Parker, resilience is the result of the "spiritual practices of realization and resistance among girls. . . . This is spiritual fortitude by which a girl's strength of mind empowers here to refocus, re-gather, re-connect, and re-center courageously amid dehumanizing adversity." This could take the form of a song, a prayer, a moment of silence.

Finally, ritual is a way of bringing the sacred into the everyday. "It is also an organic way of refueling the cycle of movements from realization to resistance and then resilience," Parker writes. "Rituals are a natural expression of acknowledging and experiencing something greater than ourselves. Rituals complete our spirituality."

She uses Miriam, the sister of Moses, as an example of a woman who experienced realization, resistance, resilience, and who used ritual.

She goes on to reference Phyllis Trible's "Bring Miriam Out of the Shadows," writing,

Miriam, the big sister of Moses, was smart, watchful, and wise. In silence she stood near the river's bank and watched her baby brother floating in a waterproofed papyrus basket. It was the plan of Miriam and her mother, Jochebed, that his clandestine voyage would not be noticed.

His sister stood at a distance, to see what would happen to him (Exod. 2:4). With an eagle's eye, she watches intensely. Does she know she will shape the destiny of her brother and the history of her people? Pharaoh's daughter discovers the baby boy among the reeds. Miriam's questioning eye and critical mind empower her to speak. "Shall I go and get you a nurse from the Hebrew women to nurse the child for you?" (Exod. 2:7).

When Pharaoh's daughter agrees, Miriam goes and gets her and Moses's mother and therefore, not only is Moses's life spared, but he spends his infant and toddler years with his biological mother.

Parker goes on to conclude that Miriam resisted the exclusivity of Moses's priestly power later when she confronted the prophet with: "Has the Lord spoken only through Moses? Has he not spoken through us also?" (Num. 12:2).

Parker also posits Fannie Lou Hamer, a civil rights activist from Mississippi and a founder of the Mississippi Freedom Democratic Party, as a model of resilience for young African American women. "Hamer showed a tenacity, determination, and perseverance few thought possible, given the powers of apartheid in the segregated South. Her fortitude was grounded in a deep piety and Christian faith. She embodied courage, determination, and a capacity to re-center amid oppressive chaos," she writes.

Hamer is known for her saying, "I got sick and tired of being sick and tired." However, Parker writes that Hamer's life "illustrates her spiritual fortitude." Jailed and beaten, along with Annelle Ponder and 16-year-old June Johnson in the Winona, Mississippi jail (17-year-old Euvester Simpson was with the women, but had not been beaten; she nonetheless witnessed the assault), she points to the "communal nature of resilience, and "the importance of relational practices of resilience."

Concluding the telephone interview, Dace said she is encouraged by young women such as her nieces, who are 17 and 18, and who are part of the movement of embracing their African looks and hair.

She emphasized the importance of girls getting their worth from their belovedness to God.

"If we use that as a guidepost for every decision we make: Since I am a child of the King, how do I carry myself; how do I walk? What comes out of my mouth? When do I get up and change the channel? When do I walk away from some of these friendships?

"Teach girls not only who they are, but whose they are. That you are a child of the Most High God and He will not have you to settle for anything less."

REFERENCES

Bogle, D. (Oct 24, 2001). *Toms, Coons, Mulattoes, Mammies, and Bucks: An Interpretive History of Blacks in American Films*, Fourth Edition, Bloomsbury Academic.

Butler, A., & Kamau. (May 8, 2009). *The Love Ethic: The Reason Why You Can't Find and Keep Beautiful Black Love*, Twinlineal Institute.

Dace, K. L. (1997). "Bright Eyes and Dim Eyes: The Masculinization of African-American Spirituality."

Galli, M. (February, 2014). "The inconceivable start of African-American Christianity," Christianity Today.com. Retrieved from the Christianitytoday

.com website: february-web-only/inconceivable-start-of-african-american -christianity.html

More Than 4.5 Million African Americans Now Hold a Four-Year College Degree. (2009). *The Journal of Blacks in Higher Education.*

lialiaallinmyhead.wordpress.com LiaLia. (2014). Words to my sister, my beloved brown girl extraordinaire, Karyn Washington.

New York Times. (2011, Dec. 20). Room for Debate: "black Men for black Women?" Retrieved from the *New York Times* website: http://www.nytimes.com/ roomfordebate/2011/12/20/black-men-for-black-women

Nitsche, N., & Brueckner, H. (2011). "Outcomes and Marriage Behavior of Highly Educated Women over Time." *Journal of Women's Health* 20(3): 474–475.

Parker, E. (2003). *Trouble Don't Last Always.* Pilgrim Press.

Parker, E. (2010). *The Sacred Selves of African-American Girls: Hard Stories of Race, Class, and Gender.* Wipf and Stock Publishers.

Workneh, L. (2014). "Karyn Washington, creator of 'For Brown Girls' website, reportedly commits suicide at age 22," *The Grio.*

Part III

Education

Chapter 13

"Oral Sex Is Not Sex"

Jamesetta A. Newland

INTRODUCTION

Expressions of human sexuality are common during adolescence and are a part of normal development and growth. Pre-pubertal and pubescent adolescents are interested in sex whether or not they act on that interest. Sexual behaviors expose adolescents to the potential for acute and chronic physical and mental health related conditions. Health education programs have traditionally targeted the prevention of pregnancy and sexually transmitted infections, by focusing on vaginal sexual intercourse and the initiation, age of initiation, frequency, number of partners, and condom or other contraceptive use (Bersamin et al., 2007; Remez, 2000). Noncoital sexual activity in adolescents has not been well studied and might not be adequately addressed by professionals who regularly interact with youth. This chapter will review sexual behaviors in adolescents in general but focus on oral sex and the implications for sexually transmitted infection (STI), specifically oropharyngeal cancer (OPC) attributed to infection with the human papillomavirus (HPV). Current efforts toward prevention of OPC will be discussed. The sexual behaviors of African American (AA) adolescent females will be presented within the context of sexual behavior, based on current research evidence.

The Centers for Disease Control and Prevention (CDC) conducts a biennial survey to identify health-risk behaviors that contribute to the leading causes of death and disability among youth and adults. One area in which teens are questioned is sexual behaviors that contribute to unintended pregnancy and STIs. The Youth Risk Behavior Surveillance System (YRBSS) is a psychometrically sound instrument that has been used since 1991 to collect data from high school students. Data from this national school-based survey for 2011 were supplemented with data from 47 school-based state, 6 territorial, 2 tribal, and 22 large urban school district surveys conducted by local educational and health agencies and tribal governments. Methodological strategies ensured that the sample was representative of students in grades 9 through 12 (CDC, 2013a). Data from the 2011 YRBSS survey indicate that 47.4% youth had ever had sexual intercourse; 33.7% had had sexual intercourse in the 3 months prior to the survey; and 15.3% had had 4 or more partners during their lifetime. Only 60.2% had used condoms with their last sexual intercourse (CDC, 2012a). When looking at data for Black youth compared to Hispanic and White youth, percentages for the Black youth were higher for "ever had sexual intercourse" (60.0% versus 48.6% and 44.3%, respectively), "had sexual intercourse for the first time before age 13 years" (13.9% versus 7.1% and 3.9%), and "had sexual intercourse with four or more persons [during their life]" (24.8% versus 14.8% and 13.1%) (CDC, 2012b). One challenge with questioning youth about sexual intercourse, however, is that the term is not always defined in explicit terms, and therefore leads to possibly inaccurate or incomplete information. Sexual intercourse has different meanings for different individuals.

DEFINING ADOLESCENT SEXUAL BEHAVIORS

Researchers have demonstrated the necessity for individuals working with adolescents to know how these adolescents define sexual behaviors. Proxy terms might include sexual intercourse, virginity, abstinence, and other forms of noncoital sexual activity, such as oral sex (Bersamin et al., 2007; Childs et al., 2012; Remez, 2000; Sanders & Reinisch, 1999). Many authors, however, do specifically ask about vaginal, oral, and anal sex. In a qualitative study with AA girls ages 12–14 years, one participant stated,

> Because a lot of the girls they probably don't even know what it [oral sex] is. And they talk about it. And when you say like, finger [sex], they probably don't think it's something. 'Cause it [oral and finger sex] ain't sex until like his penis put in her. (Childs et al., p. 5)

Bersamin and colleagues (2007) were very specific in asking girls and boys ages 12–16 years whether they had ever engaged in sexual activity: genital touching; oral sex—"a girl/boy puts her/his mouth or tongue on your genitals or you put your mouth or tongue on a girl's/boy's genitals";

vaginal intercourse—"when a boy puts his penis into a girl's vagina"; and anal sex—"when a boy puts his penis into another person's anus, rectum, or butt" (p. 184). Results revealed that 70.6% considered a boy or girl still a virgin if they participated in oral sex, 16.1% for anal sex, and only 5.8% for vaginal intercourse. Alternately, these same youth considered a boy or a girl abstinent if they had engaged in oral sex (33.4%), anal sex (14.3%), or vaginal intercourse (11.9%). The researchers surmised that this lack of agreement on definitions might be a reflection of the beliefs about sexual behavior expounded by the larger society.

The public is exposed to conflicting media messages all the time, and confusion results. The most famous case surrounded oral sex when headline news in 1998 broke during the impeachment proceedings of President Bill Clinton over an inappropriate relationship with Washington intern Monica Lewinsky. President Clinton proclaimed emphatically, "I did not have sexual relations with that woman." He defended himself against a charge of perjury by stating that technically his statement about sexual relations was "legally accurate." The definition of sexual relations approved by the U.S. District Judge was "a person engages in 'sexual relations' when the person knowingly engages in or causes contact with the genitalia, anus, groin, breast, inner thigh, or buttocks of any person with an intent to arouse or gratify the sexual desire of any person" (Baker & Harris, 1998). Legal advisors determined that this definition did not cover oral sex performed on the president. Politicians involved in similar sex scandals had previously disclaimed extramarital oral sex as adulterous, and therefore, not sex (Nelson, 2013). Impeachment proceedings were unsuccessful and the country was divided over what constituted their right to know about the public and/or private behaviors of prominent individuals.

Noncoital Sexual Behaviors

Remez (2000) focused on the explosion in media coverage about adolescent noncoital sexual behaviors of mutual masturbation, oral sex, and anal intercourse. These behaviors were often considered precursors to vaginal intercourse. Adolescents believed health risks were nonexistent or lower because these behaviors were not linked to pregnancy and they thought did not involve a risk of STI transmission. Middle school–aged girls viewed oral sex as a "bargain" because of the aforementioned; they were positive toward noncoital sexual behaviors because they still believed they were virgins and had control over the situation in oral sex; boys had control in acts involving vaginal intercourse. Adolescents distinguished between oral sex as having no emotional ties while vaginal sex was associated with relationships, making it easier to participate in oral sex. Similar beliefs about relationships and sexual behaviors were expressed by respondents in other studies (Childs et al., 2012; Fava

& Bay-Cheng, 2012). Partnered noncoital behaviors were reported for a sample of women in the United States (U.S.) aged 14–94 years. Narrowing data to 14–19-year-olds revealed consistent participation in oral sex. For the 14–15, 16–17, and 18–19-year-olds; they had received oral sex from a male partner in the previous year by 10%, 23.5%, and 58%, respectively. They had given oral sex to a male partner by 11.8%, 22.4%, and 58%, respectively. Percentages were lower for either receiving or giving oral sex with a female partner, with the highest percentage in the 18–19-year-olds giving oral sex to a woman (Herbenick et al., 2010).

Looking at pre-adolescents and younger adolescents, three research teams had similar findings (Anderson et al., 2011; Dancy & Crittenden, 2010; De Rosa et al., 2010) related to parental influence. Anderson et al. (2011) studied gender differences in a group of AA fifth grade pre-adolescents aged 10–11 years. In girls, the association with virginity fostered a favorable attitude towards refusing sex; a favorable attitude towards abstinence was associated with less anticipation of sexual activity. Surprisingly, however, 18% of the boys and 5% of the girls had already had sex, and 56% and 22%, respectively, anticipated engaging in sexual activity in the next 12 months. Parental influence through talking about sex increased girls' anticipation but decreased boys' anticipation. Dancy and Crittenden (2010) discovered that low income AA females 11–14 years old were at risk for initiating sexual activity beginning at age 12 and risk increased with age. Sexual activity was clearly defined by "Vaginal sex is the boy's private part enters the girl's private part; anal sex is the boy's private part enters the girl's butt; and oral sex is the girl's mouth touches the boy's private part or butt or the boy's mouth touches the girl's private part or butt" (p. 150). Intentions to refuse sex and perception of maternal monitoring had positive implications for the adolescent girl to delay sexual activity. In the third study by DeRosa et al. (2010), 9% of the almost 5000 youths in the study had ever had sexual intercourse, and 8% had had oral sex—7% of sixth graders, 8% of seventh graders, and 18% of eighth graders. Intercourse and oral sex were highly correlated. Black and Latino youth reported somewhat lower rates of oral sex than sexual intercourse. The first intercourse usually happened in a romantic relationship, also noted by Remez (2000) and Childs et al. (2012). The majority of these young adolescents felt that their parents would not approve of them having sex if they knew (De Rosa et al., 2010).

Predictors of male and female adolescents' transitions to intimate sexual behavior were investigated to gather information for developing health interventions (Ronis & O'Sullivan, 2011). The researchers were interested in transitions from abstinence to oral sex to sexual intercourse, and abstinence to sexual intercourse. Predictors of transition to more intimate sexual behavior over a 6-month period included lower religiosity for both genders, but lower self-esteem for boys and higher lifetime alcohol use for girls. The adolescents in this study were 13–16 years old and only 1.3% were Black. More research to explain gender differences was recommended by the authors. Drugs and alcohol use were also found to place many adolescent females at greater potential for high-risk sexual behaviors (Morrison-Beedy, 2010); 70% of the sample identified as Black/AA and 11% were Mixed/Multiracial. Of the total sample, 32% reported recent sexual experiences that involved oral sex and 70% of the Black/AA group reported having multiple partners, which increases the risk of STI transmission. Likewise, in a sample of young sexual minority women (YSMW) aged 16-24 years—who identified as gay/lesbian (50%), bisexual (46%), or questioning/unsure (4%)—older age, alcohol abuse, and having an older sexual partner were significant predictors of sexual risk. Fifty-seven percent of respondents were non-White with 18% AA. Oral sex was queried as part of several items combining vaginal, oral, and anal sex. AA identity versus non-AA identity increased STI risk (Herrick et al., 2013).

One study looked at oral sex during adolescence within the perspective of normal sexual development and distinctions between cunnilingus (male to female) and fellatio (female to male) (Fava & Bay-Cheng, 2012). Using undergraduate women (30% were women of color) from higher socioeconomic strata at a private college, researchers found that oral sex as a first sexual experience was higher than sexual intercourse (through recall) and fellatio usually preceded cunnilingus. No association was found between initiation of cunnilingus and psychological functions or sexual coercion. The authors mentioned that other published studies have suggested that adolescent females likely perceived more sexual coercion when initiating fellatio, and adolescents from lower socioeconomic strata reported a higher percentage who initiated sexual intercourse before oral sex. The authors encouraged researchers and others who work with adolescents to approach adolescent sexuality and sexual behaviors from a more normative and positive developmental perspective (Fava & Bay-Cheng, 2012).

All these studies have inherent limitations. Self-report measures that rely on recall are not the most reliable source of information, and adolescents might be inclined to give socially acceptable responses in a face-to-face interview versus the anonymity in completing an online survey. Certain barriers to finding out about adolescent sexuality include the need for parental consent even when adolescent assent is obtained. Conservative attitudes from the community and voices of resistance to sex education programs can impact implementation of these programs. Legislators who control funding for health education and service programs can stall intervention efforts. The fear that talking about sex with adolescents will lead them to engage in sexual behaviors is a continuing misconception to overcome. And the question of who is responsible for instructing adolescents about sex—the school or public agency or adults in the home, remains controversial in some communities. Inaccurate information provided by the media strongly influences adolescent perceptions. But the bottom line is that adults must work to-gether to learn how adolescents define sexual behaviors, what risky sexual behaviors they engaged in, what information they need, the best way to deliver the information, and strategies to reduce risky sexual behaviors. Human sexuality is an undeniable part of an adolescent's development to adulthood. Unfortunately, this development might be influenced by race and ethnicity. Researchers have tried to identify factors that might be differ-ent for AA adolescents in this development.

AA Adolescent Females

AA adolescent females are vulnerable to participation in high-risk sex-ual behaviors. Several studies looked at the girls' ability to negotiate safer sex behaviors (Auslander et al., 2014; Crosby et al., 2013; Teitelman et al., 2011; Voisin et al., 2012). One third of AA girls aged 15–21 years who were recruited for a study to identify markers of knowledge about STI preven-tion did not know that females were more susceptible to contracting STIs than males. One third also did not understand that having an STI increased human immunodeficiency virus (HIV) acceptance risk. One third had in-correct information about the use of condoms and engaged in practices that actually reduced the efficacy of condoms when they were used. No questions were asked about sexual behaviors. Predictors of high STI knowl-edge were being older, having greater self-mastery, and being employed (Voisin et al., 2012). Mother-daughter communication was found to be a protective factor in STI prevention among AA young women (Paxton, Hall & Bogarin (2014). For two-thirds of the young women, mothers had pro-vided information about sex during childhood or adolescence.

Similarly, communication about sexual behaviors and the use of con-doms was dependent on the AA girl's knowledge, confidence to introduce the topic (Auslander et al., 2014; Crosby et al., 2013), and anticipated re-sponse from her male partner (Teitelman et al., 2011). Adolescents with low sexual communication self-efficacy were more likely to report unpro-tected oral sex and vaginal intercourse. In a study to determine the feasi-bility of women using a microbicide (topical agent that kills HIV and herpes simplex type 2 viruses [in development]) during receptive oral sex, being older, being AA, and having discussed the microbicide surrogate (an over-the-counter lubricant) with their partner were associated with having used the microbicide surrogate during a sexual episode (Auslander et al., 2014). Researchers stressed that discussions about oral sex must be considered in the design of clinical trials. Fear of physical, verbal, or part-ner threats prevented some AA girls from suggesting condom use to a male partner (Teitelman et al., 2011). One in 3 AA adolescent females expe-rienced all three types of abuse while 1 of 3 experienced at least 1 of the 3 types of abuse. Consequently, they engaged in unprotected sexual behaviors, some having been forced. Researchers recommended that interventions were needed geared to helping AA girls negotiate condom use.

The Teen's Popular Perspective

So what are teenagers saying about oral sex outside of research studies? What is shared on social media? In 2009 on ABC's *Good Morning America*, Ameila McDonell-Parry shared a story about the Teen Sex Trend: Blow jobs are the new goodnight kiss! Watch the video at http://www.thefrisky .com/2009-05-29/teen-sex-trend-blow-jobs-are-the-new-goodnight-kiss/.

Another reporter filmed a documentary titled Oral Sex Is the New Goodnight Kiss, which can be viewed on YouTube at http://www.you-tube .com/watch?v=CL-yZKLb59Q. The teenagers, although videotaped, were open about practices involving oral sex. They confirmed what researchers had found. Oral sex was not sex to most teenagers; it was no big deal. You were still a virgin. Oral sex was a win-win and girls traded blow jobs for drugs, clothes and jewelry, homework, or anything else they wanted. But they did not view this as prostitution because they did not receive money directly for services. Rainbow parties are popular in which girls wear different shades of lipstick and the boy at the end of the night with the most different color rings around his penis is the winner. In viewing comments on several teen sites, it appears that oral sex is not always reciprocal; girls are more willing to perform fellatio than boys are willing to perform cunnilingus. Girls even look at giving oral sex as homework, a skill in which they strive to become expert. You must learn how to do it; you must do it; you must practice it until you are good at it; and then you must receive recognitions for being good (http://jezebel.com/5877183/education-minded-teen-girls-say-blow-jobs-are-like-homework). Teenage girls more likely to engage in oral sex are educated and from higher socioeconomic classes. As research has demonstrated, AA teenage girls are more likely to engage in vaginal intercourse before accepting oral sexual practices. There is an abundance of websites targeting adolescents and discussions about sex; avoiding those which are pornographic is the challenge. Teens are also exposed to images and behaviors in popular movies which might have some influence on their own sexual behaviors.

SUMMARY

In summary, adolescents are sexual beings and do engage in risky sexual behaviors. AA girls are at higher risk for early initiation of sexual intercourse, having multiple sexual partners over the lifetime, and a greater prevalence of STIs related to unprotected sexual activity. AA girls are also more likely to participate in vaginal intercourse rather than oral sex, and they more often will give rather than receive oral sex. AA girls have poor access to culturally appropriate sex education and lack adequate knowledge about sexual behaviors and proper condom use and transmission of STIs. Herrick et al. (2013) identify disparities in STI prevalence in AA adolescents that can be attributed to factors that go beyond sexual risk behaviors. These factors include lower socioeconomic status of racial/ethnic minorities leading to poverty, lack of access to adequate health care, a dearth of culturally appropriate sexual health education, adolescent perceptions of low personal risk, and stigma and discrimination based not only on racial minority status but also sexual minority status. Other inequalities include differences in educational opportunities, lack of employment or adequate health insurance, and historical mistrust of the U.S. health care system. Regardless of these barriers, AA adolescent females must be included in efforts to educate youth about safe sex behaviors, including oral sex.

STIs ASSOCIATED WITH ORAL SEX

The dictionary definition of oral sex is "sexual activity in which the genitals of one partner are stimulated by the mouth of the other; fellatio or cunnilingus" (Oxford Dictionary, 2014). Sexually transmitted infections are spread through saliva, blood, vaginal secretions, semen, fecal material, and skin-to-skin contact. The oral mucosa in the mouth is easily injured and epithelial tissue that is compromised from open sores, abrasions, or inflammation is more susceptible to infection. Another entry point for infection is unhealthy or injured gums. Swollen or bleeding gums might have open areas at the base of the teeth for entry of microorganisms. The mouth to the genital or anal area is like a circle; infection in one area can be transmitted to infection in the other area. Adolescents perceive noncoital sexual behaviors are safe compared to vaginal intercourse and are unlikely to use barrier protection. Therefore, oral sex is not without risk of transmission of STIs.

Infections that can be transmitted through noncoital sexual behavior such as oral sex include viruses (HIV, herpes simplex virus [HSV] 1 and 2, HPV, and hepatitis A, B, C) and bacteria (gonorrhea, chlamydia, syphilis, chancroid, shigella, salmonella, and other enteric infections associated with anal sex but linked by oral-genital or oral-anal sex [American College of Obstetricians and Gynecologists (ACOG), 2013]. Although saliva has components that inactivate HIV and the risk of transmission is low, there is still a risk. Herpes (HSV) infection can be transmitted through kissing; fever blisters are a common culprit. Oral HSV (type 1) can be transmitted from the mouth to the genitals through oral sex just as genital HSV (type 2) can be transmitted from the genitals to the oral cavity. Hepatitis A is transmitted through fecal contamination of the oral cavity. Hepatitis B can also be transmitted through feces as well as semen, saliva, and blood (bleeding from gums or vagina). Sexual transmission of Hepatitis C is rare but can occur. Females often are not symptomatic and might not be aware they have a vaginal or cervical STI. There are no guidelines for testing oral or anal sex in women who are asymptomatic. Males, however, are more likely to be symptomatic with certain bacterial STIs. Bacterial infections can be treated with antibiotics and cured. Viral infections remain with the infected person for life but symptoms and progression of disease can be managed with medication to maintain quality of life. Of all the STIs, HPV poses the greatest risk for long-term morbidity and mortality associated with oral sex behaviors.

Oral Sex and the Human Papilloma Virus (HPV)

Reports have documented the association of the practice of oral sex and the incidence of oropharyngeal squamous cell carcinoma (OPC) or cancer (CDC, n.d.-a; Chaturvedi et al., 2011; Gillison et al., 2012; Goberville, 2010). HPV causes normal cells in infected skin to turn abnormal. Most of the time, the body fights off the infection over 1–2 years and the infected cells revert to normal. In cases where this reversal does not occur, precancer or cancer develops in the back of the mouth at the base of the tongue and tonsils. It takes a long period of growth, usually years before OPC might cause symptoms like persistent sore throat, earaches, hoarseness, enlarged lymph nodes in the neck, pain when swallowing, and unexplained weight loss. And some people have no symptoms (CDC, n.d.-a). HPV positive OPC is associated with sexual behavior while HPV negative OPC is associated with chronic tobacco and alcohol use.

The prevalence of oral HPV infection in 2009–2010 among men and women aged 14 to 69 years was 6.9% with the highest prevalence among 30- to 34-year-olds. There was a strong association between lifetime as well as the recent number of vaginal or oral sexual partners and oral HPV prevalence. Smokers also had higher rates of infection. Prevalence was higher among individuals who first performed oral sex at 18 years or younger. Adolescents 14–17 years had a prevalence rate of 1.7% and those 18–24 years had a rate of 5.6% (Gillison et al., 2012). HPV positive OPC was more likely to be found in younger persons versus HPV negative tumors on the anterior tongue, floor of the mouth, and mucosa inside the cheeks found in older persons 40 to 60 years old (Goberville, 2010). Rates of OPC in men were much higher than in women, approximately threefold. One theory to explain the wide gender differences proposes that women's higher rates of genital HPV infection confer greater protection against subsequent oral infection (Gillison et al., 2012). The prevalence among Black participants was higher than among White participants (10.5% vs. 6.5%) but was not statistically significant (Gillison et al., 2012). The exponential increase of 225% in HPV positive cases of OPC between 1988 and 2004 and decline of 50% in HPV negative cases during the same period might represent an increase in oral sexual activity and oral HPV exposure over time (Chaturvedi et al., 2011; Gillison et al., 2012).

Throat cancer and oral sex made the headlines in non-medical publications when actor Michael Douglas announced in 2013 that the type of oral cancer he had was caused by HPV contracted from cunnilingus (Brooks, 2013; Kotz, 2013). This increased awareness about the longevity of the virus and how sexual behaviors decades before could cause cancer when one was older. Medicine has been working to counter the upward trend in HPV related OPC by promoting vaccination against the virus.

HPV Vaccine

There are over 100 strains of HPV, most of which are harmless. Infection with HPV type 16 has most often been discovered in cases of OPC (Chaturvedi et al., 2011; Gillison, 2008; Gillison et al., 2012). One strategy to stall the increase in HPV cancer related to oral sex is vaccination against HPV. The quadrivalent vaccine Gardasil® was approved by the Food and Drug Administration in 2006 for administration to girls aged 9 to 26 years. The vaccine protects against HPV types 16 and 18 that cause 70% of cervical cancers and the majority of other HPV associated cancers and HPV types 6 and 11 that cause 90% of genital warts. A bivalent HPV vaccine Cervarix® was introduced in 2009 that provides protection against cervical cancer, HPV types 16 and 18. Both vaccines include three injections over a 6-month period. Gardasil® is also approved for administration to boys aged 9 through 26 years (CDC, 2013b; Gillison, 2008). Ideally, the vaccine is administered prior to the adolescent's sexual debut. Its efficacy in preventing oral cancers is unknown (Chaturvedi et al., 2011; Daly, 2011; Gillison, 2008). Data at the CDC indicate that vaccination coverage in 2012 was only 53.8% and well below the target set of 92.6% (CDC, 2013b). Part of the reason was missed appointments during which a health care provider could have taken advantage of an opportunity to administer the vaccine. When parents were asked why they did not intend to vaccinate their daughters within the next 12 months, the top five reasons were "the vaccine not needed (19.1%), vaccine not recommended (14.2%), vaccine safety concerns (13.1%), lack of knowledge about the vaccine or the disease (12.6%), and daughter is not sexually active (10.1%)" (CDC, 2013b, p. 592). No vaccine is without side effects but the safety profile of these two HPV is acceptable.

Studies with AA girls and their parents or caregivers about the acceptability of the HPV vaccine and intentions to take the vaccine demonstrated that AA race decreased the likelihood of vaccination compared to reports in the White race (40% less). The initiation of sexually intimate behavior, however, increased the likelihood of vaccination (Keenan, Hipwell & Stepp, 2012; Read, Joseph, Polishchuk & Suss, 2010). Information about preventing cervical cancer through vaccination was of interest to the teens and parents. Yet they lacked knowledge about available public financing for the costly vaccine and the recommended timing of vaccination before sexual initiation. Daly (2011) also found that lack of knowledge about HPV and the vaccine among health care providers was also a barrier to meeting CDC immunization goals. Public health prevention of cervical cancer is screening for secondary prevention and HPV vaccination for primary prevention.

Role of the Helping Professional

The first step in reducing high risk noncoital sexual behaviors among adolescent girls is taking a thorough sexual history. ACOG (2010) recommends that the first reproductive health visit for developmental assessment be scheduled between 13 and 15 years. The scope of the visit will depend on the needs of the teen. This does not preclude a pediatric provider from discussing sexual behaviors with a younger girl if circumstances dictate the need or the girl asks for information. The health care provider should allocate some time alone with the teen without the parent in the room and assure the teen that the discussion will be kept confidential unless she discloses information that suggests potential danger to self or harm to others. That type of information must be shared with appropriate persons to keep her safe. A comprehensive age-appropriate history is taken (Carcio & Brooks, 2010; CDC, n.d.-b; Damas, Hein, Powell & Dundon, 2012; Dunn, 2009). As recommended by researchers, questions about sex need to be very specific and not targeted at only vaginal intercourse and prevention of pregnancy and STIs. Questions must also explore actual sexual behaviors that include noncoital sexual behaviors, such as self and mutual masturbation, anal and oral sex, and the use of sex toys and other sexual stimulants. The CDC (n.d.-b) offers a comprehensive guide for taking a sexual history that follows the 5 P's: Partners, Practices, Protection from STIs, Past history of STIs, and Protection of pregnancy. Providers are encouraged to adapt and supplement this guide with questions that fit their population; it can be found at http://www.cdc.gov/std/treatment/SexualHistory.pdf.

Likewise, other professionals who interact with teens should take advantage of opportunities that present to discuss sexual behaviors and the inherent risks associated with engaging in oral sex and other noncoital sexual behaviors. Do not concentrate just on vaginal intercourse. Gaining trust is a key component to establishing open and honest communication. According to all reports, AA teenage girls initiate sexual behaviors earlier than their White counterparts, are more likely to engage in vaginal intercourse first and then other noncoital behaviors, are more susceptible to acquiring a sexually transmitted disease, and less likely to receive the HPV vaccine that protects against cervical cancer and possibly oral cancer. Advocate in communities for sex education to keep our teenagers safer and healthier.

REFERENCES

American College of Obstetricians and Gynecologists (ACOG), Committee on Adolescent Health. (2010). The initial reproductive health visit. *Obstetrics & Gynecology, 116*(1), 240–243.

American College of Obstetricians and Gynecologists (ACOG), Committee on adolescent health & committee on gynecologic practice. (2013). Addressing health risks of noncoital sexual activity. *Obstetrics & Gynecology, 122*(6), 1378–1383.

Anderson, K. M., Koo, H. P., Jenkins, R. R., Walker, L. R., Davis, M., Yao, Z., & Nabil El-Khorazaty, M. (2011). Attitudes, experience, and anticipation of sex among 5th graders in an urban setting: Does gender matter? *Maternal and Child Health Journal, 15*(Suppl 1), S54–S64. doi:10.1007/s10995-011-0879-5

Auslander, B. A., Catallozzi, M., Davis, G., Succop, P. A., Stanberry, L. R., & Rosental, S. L. (2014). Adolescents' and young women's use of a microbicide surrogate product when receiving oral sex. *Journal of Pediatric and Adolescent Gynecology, 27*(1), 37–40.

Baker, P., & Harris, J. F. (1998, August 18). *Clinton admits to Lewinsky relationship, challenges Starr to end personal "prying."* Retrieved on March 3, 2014 from http://www.washingtonpost.com/wp-srv/politics/special/clinton/stories/clinton081898.htm

Bersamin, M. M., Fisher, D. A., Walker, S., Hill, D. L., & Grube, J. W. (2007). Defining virginity and abstinence: Adolescents' interpretations of sexual behaviors. *Journal of Adolescent Health, 41*(2), 182–188. doi:10.1016/j.jadohealth.2007.03.011

Brooks, J. (2013, June 2). *Michael Douglas on Liberace, Cannes, cancer and cunnilingus.* Retrieved March 17, 2014 from http://www.theguardian.com/film/2013/jun/02/michael-douglas-liberace-cancer-cunnilingus

Carcio, H. A., & Brooks, P. (eds.). (2010). The health history. In H. A. Carcio & M. C. Secor, *Advanced health assessment of women: Clinical skills and procedures* (2nd ed.) (pp. 27–58). New York: Springer Publishing Company.

Centers for Disease Control and Prevention (CDC). (n.d.-a). *Human papillomavirus (HPV) and oropharyngeal cancer-CDC.* Accessed on 11/10/2013 at www.cdc.gov/std/HPV/HPV-oral-factsheet-nov-2013.pdf

CDC. (n.d.-b). *A guide to taking a sexual history.* [CDC Publication 99-8445]. Accessed on 3/10/2014 at http://www.cdc.gov/std/treatment/SexualHistory.pdf

CDC. (2012a). Youth risk behavior surveillance—United States, 2011 [Surveillance Summaries]. *Morbidity and Mortality Weekly Report, 61*(4).

CDC. (2012b). *Youth risk behavior surveillance system: Selected 2011 national health risk behaviors and health outcomes by race/ethnicity.* Accessed on 11/10/2013 at http://www.cdc.gov/healthyyouth/yrbs/pdf/us_disparityrace_yrbs.pdf

CDC. (2012c). Human papillomavirus-associated cancers—United States, 2004–2008. *Morbidity and Mortality Weekly Report, 61*(15), 258–261. Accessed on 11/10/2013 at www.cdc.gov/mmwr/pdf/wk/mm6115.pdf

CDC. (2013a). Adolescent and School Health: Youth Risk Behavior Surveillance System (YRBSS). Accessed 3/03/2014 at www.cdc.gov/healthyyouth/yrbs/brief.htm

CDC. (2013b). Human papillomavirus vaccination coverage among adolescent girls, 2007–2012, and postlicensure vaccine safety monitoring, 2006–2013—United States. *Morbidity and Mortality Weekly Report, 62*(29), 591–595. Accessed on 11/10/2013 at www.cdc.gov/mmwr/pdf/wk/mm6229.pdf

Chaturvedi, A. K., Engels, E. A., Pfeiffer, R. M., Hernandez, B. Y., Xiao, W., Kim, E., . . . & Gillison, M. L. Human papillomavirus and rising oropharyngeal cancer incidence in the United States. *Journal of Clinical Oncology, 29*, 4294–4301. doi:10.1200/JCO.2011.36.4596

Childs, G. D., White, R., Hataway, C., Moneyham, L., & Gaioso, V. (2012). Early adolescent African American girls' perceptions of virginity and romantic relationships. *Nursing (Auckl), 2012* [NIH Public Access online], 1–16. doi: 10.2147/NRR.S37084

Crosby, R. A., Voisin, D. R., Diclemente, R. J., Wingood, G. M., Salazar, L. F., Head, S., . . . McDermott-Sales, J. (2013). Relational correlates of unprotected oral and vaginal sex and among African-American adolescent females [Abstract]. *Sexual Health, 10*(3), 284–286. doi:10.1071/SH12086

Daly, A. M. (2011). Providing adolescent-friendly HPV education. *The Nurse Practitioner, 36*(11), 35–40.

Damas, T., Hein, L. C., Powell, L. C., & Dundon, E. (2012). Child and adolescent sexual development and sexual identity issues. In E. L. Yearwood, G. S. Pearson & J. A. Newland (eds.), *Child and adolescent behavioral health: A resource for advanced practice psychiatric and primary care practitioners in nursing* (pp. 89-1-9). West Sussex, UK: Wiley-Blackwell.

Dancy, B. L., Crittenden, K. S., & Ning, H. (2010). African-American adolescent girls' initiation of sexual activity: Survival analysis. *Women's Health Issues, 20*(2), 146–155. doi:10.1016/j.whi.2009.11.015

De Rosa, C. J., Eghier, K. A., Kim, D. H., Cumberland, W. G., Afifi, A. A., Kotlerman, J., . . . & Kerndt, P. R. (2010). Sexual intercourse and oral sex among public middle school students: Prevalence and correlates. *Perspectives on Sexual and Reproductive Health, 42*(3), 197–205. doi:10.1363/4219710

Dunn, A. M. (2009). Developmental management of adolescents. In C. E. Burns, A. M. Dunn, M. A. Brady, N. B. Starr & C. G. Blosser (eds.), *Pediatric primary care* (pp. 132–149). St. Louis, MO: Saunders Elsevier.

Fava, N. M., & Bay-Cheng, L. Y. (2012). Young women's adolescent experiences of oral sex: Relation of age of initiation to sexual motivation, sexual coercion, and psychological functioning. *Journal of Adolescence, 35*(5), 1191–1201. doi: 10.1016/j.adolescence.2012.03.010

Gillison, M. L. (2008). Human papillomavirus-related diseases: Oropharnyx cancers and potential implications for adolescent HPV vaccination. *Journal of Adolescent Health, 43*(Suppl 4), S52–S60. doi:10.1016/j.jadohealth.2008.07.002

Gillison, M. L., Broutian, T., Pickard, R. K. L., Tong, Z., Xiao, W., Kahle, L., Graubard, B. I., & Chaturvedi, A. K. (2012). Prevalence of oral HPV infection in the United States, 2009–2010. *JAMA, 307*(7), 693–703. doi:10.1001/jama.2012.101

Goberville, S. (2010). Oral sex: HPV-positive oral cancer. [Abstract of Can oral sex be as dangerous as smoking?]. *Dental Abstracts, 55*(4), 216–217.

Herbenick, D., Reece, M., Schick, V., Sanders, S. A., Dodge, B., & Fortenberry, J. D. (2010). Sexual behavior in the United States: Results from a national probability sample of men and women 19–94. *The Journal of Sexual Medicine,* 7(Suppl s5), 255–265. doi:10.1111/j.1743-6109.2010.0212.x

Herrick, A., Kuhns, L., Kinsky, S., Johnson, A., & Garofalo, R. (2013). Demographic, psychosocial, and contextual factors associated with sexual risk behaviors among young sexual minority women. *Journal of the American Psychiatric Nurses Association, 19*(6), 345–355. doi:10.1177/1078390313511328

Keenan, K., Hipwell, A., & Stepp, S. (2012). Race and sexual behavior predict uptake of the human papilloma vaccine. *Health Psychology, 31*(1), 31–34. doi:10.1037/a0026812

Kotz, D. (2013, June 10). *Throat cancer and oral sex.* Retrieved on March 3, 2014 from http://www.bostonglobe.com/lifestyle/health-wellness/2013/06/09/michael-douglas-blames-throat-cancer-oral-sex-what-are-risks/Akb38cr5CCvj2HUKXJ5SCP/story.html

Morrison-Beedy, D. (2010). Risk behaviors among adolescent girls in an HIV prevention trial. *Western Journal of Nursing Research, 33*(5), 690–711. doi:10.1177/0193945910379220

Nelson, S. (2013, January 25). *Bill Clinton 15 years ago: "I did not have sexual relations with that woman."* Retrieved on March 3, 2014 from http://www.usnews.com/news/blogs/press-past/2013/01/25/bill-clinton-15-years-ago-i-did-not-have-sexual-relations-with-that-woman

Oxford University Press. (2014). Oral sex—definition. *Oxford dictionary.* Accessed on 3/3/2014 at http://www.oxforddictionaries.com/us/definition/american_english/oral-sex

Paxton, K. C., Hall, N. M., & Bogarin, E. (2014). Family influences during childhood on African American women's sexual behavior during young adulthood. *Universal Journal of Psychology, 2*(3), 113–116.

Read, D. S., Joseph, M. A., Polishchuk, V., & Suss, A. L. (2010). Attitudes and perceptions of the HPV vaccine in Caribbean and African-American adolescent girls and their parents. *Journal of Pediatric and Adolescent Gynecology, 23*(4), 242–245. doi:10.1016/j.jpag.2010.02.002

Remez, L. (2000). Oral sex among adolescents: Is it sex or is it abstinence? *Family Planning Perspectives, 32*(6), 298–304.

Ronis, S. T., & O'Sullivan, L. F. (2011). A longitudinal analysis of predictors of male and female adolescents' transitions to intimate sexual behavior. *Journal of Adolescent Health, 49*(3), 321–323. doi:10.1016/j.jadohealth.2010.12.010

Sanders, S. A., & Reinisch, J. M. (1999). Would you say you "had sex" if . . .? *JAMA, 281*(9), 275–277.

Teitelman, A. M., Tennille, J., Bohinski, J. M., Jemmott, L. S., & Jemmott, J. B. (2011). Unwanted unprotected sex: Condom coercion by male partners and self-silencing of condom negotiation among adolescent girls. *Advances in Nursing Science, 34*(3), 243–259. doi:10.1097/ANS.0b013e31822723a3

Voisin, D. R., Tan, K., Salazar, L. F., Crosby, R., & DiClemente, R. J. (2012). Correlates of sexually transmitted infection prevention knowledge among African American girls. *Journal of Adolescent Health, 51*(2), 197–199. doi:10.1016/j.jadohealth.2011.12.022

Chapter 14

Barriers to Mental Health Services and African American Girls

Ursuline R. Bankhead

Writing this chapter sent me to another place and time. I was transported back to the Pacific Northwest and the early 1990s, where I was fortunate enough to find a job working with teen parents (many African American and Latina) as a substance abuse prevention counselor. I worked in their homes and schools, co-facilitated groups, and did individual counseling. I gained work experience no books or classes could prepare me for. Since then, I have worked with families and individuals in various settings (e.g., courts, homes, schools, clinics, and community agencies).

What does all of that have to do with counseling barriers for African American girls? Nearly always, regardless of age, there was a palpable hesitancy among ethnic minority clients about entering into a therapeutic relationship—something I understood well on a visceral level.

Throughout this chapter, I will refer to people of African descent residing in the United States alternately as Black and African American. This is with the understanding that not all Black people residing in the United States define themselves as African American.

HISTORIC ISSUES

Let's begin with some basics about the relationship between mental health treatment and African Americans. Holliday's (2009) exploration of the history of Black psychology reveals that Black psychologists have had to fight to become visible within the profession, while simultaneously fighting to have issues important to African Americans recognized as real societal and mental health issues. Simply, when we examine most mental health research we find a Eurocentric, male perspective, even when comparisons are made to ethnic minority groups. Consider *The Bell Curve*'s authors Hernnstein and Murray (1994), citing correlational statistics to back up the assertion that Blacks are genetically inferior to Whites and Asians. The underperformance (particularly, we're speaking of intelligence testing) is viewed as representing intrinsically deficient traits in Blacks that cannot be overcome, as opposed to an ongoing history of oppression for racial and ethnic minorities and, in other research, sexism towards women. History shows us that mental health treatment has often viewed Blacks from a deficiency perspective (Guthrie, 2004). So where does that leave Black girls in the realm of mental health?

STATISTICS

It is important to consider how the following statistics influence the experiences of Black girls, possibly providing a framework for understanding some of the social issues many African American children are facing. These statistics show how these issues may preclude African American families and their daughters seeking or utilizing mental health services. I have included statistics to show trends, not predictions, for Black families and children in America.

As per the United States Census (2013) African Americans comprise approximately 14.2% of the U.S. population; this is inclusive of anyone, adult or child, who solely or partially identifies—or is identified—as being of sub-Saharan African descent. And, approximately 12.5 million—or nearly 17%—of all American children are Black; of those children 72% of African American children were born to unwed parents. At the time of the Census, nearly 67% of Black children lived in single-parent households (KidsCount, 2013). However, a non-custodial parent may be a significant and active part of the child's life (Jones & Mosher, 2013). Unfortunately, more than one-third (38.2%) of Black families with children live in poverty (U.S. Census, 2013), which causes many family stressors for adults and children, and suicide is the third leading cause of death for African American youth, following accidents and homicide (American Association of Suicidology, 2012; Suicide Prevention Resource Center, 2013).

Additional statistics regarding children's mental health are alarming. Consider the following: According to the National Center for Children in Poverty (2010), up to 80% of children in need of mental health services never access them, and approximately 20% of all children have a long-term diagnosable mental disorder, and many mental health disorders present between the ages of 7 and 11, while often life-long mental disorders usually reveal themselves during the teenage years. Additionally, Black children, who make up nearly half of all children in foster care, and those in urban areas, are less likely to receive mental health care than their White counterparts, even though they are more likely to have experienced trauma, family disruption, or school problems, in addition to poverty (National Center for Children in Poverty, 2010). In other words, mental health services are not being utilized for those who may benefit the most from that support. Those statistics speak to potential everyday barriers to counseling.

BEING A BLACK AMERICAN GIRL/TEEN

This chapter gives an overview of some specific barriers to counseling for Black girls as gender, race, socialization, and developmental tasks come together. This intersection impacts mental health access and utilization.

Throughout this chapter, we're going to follow a fictitious 12-year-old girl named Kelly who lives with her mother. Kelly's mother works a full-time clerical job and manages the household. Her mother is both loving and supportive. Her parents divorced when she was a toddler; however, she sees her father several times a week and speaks with him nearly daily. Kelly is a good student and is described as pleasant by her teachers. However, on occasion she hears her teachers make joking references to "baby's mamas" and statements like "You know most of these kids don't have fathers." Also, although she dresses nicely, she was recently asked if her family needed assistance from the school's food pantry. These instances make her uncomfortable, although she is unsure of exactly why.

Identity

To understand some of the barriers facing Black girls and teens, we must begin with the caregivers, as they are the source of socialization. Socialization is defined as the messages transmitted across generations about norms, expectations, beliefs, and values from within the culture (Hughes et al., 2006). Shorter-Gooden and Washington's (1996) work realized the importance of racial identity for Black adolescent girls. Their research found that Black girls received the message that they had to defeat the stereotypes about being Black, and that they felt driven to overcome race-based obstacles. This perhaps made them more sensitive to racial messages than some males regarding overcoming and recognizing racial barriers (Fuller, 2001). The researchers also noted that the mother-daughter relationship was important to these teens, and was the primary source of socialization about Black womanhood.

Black girls are inundated with messages about their identity. Carolyn West's (2008) exploration of the archetypes of African American women and the concerns about the internalization of those roles is important to review. West reports three primary roles:

1) Mammy, who is considered unattractive, overweight, self-sacrificing, nurturing, and asexual (e.g., Aunt Jemima). In more modern terms, West and others (e.g., Harrington, Crowther & Shepherd, 2010) would refer to her as the Superwoman or Strong Black Woman.

2) Sapphire is the "angry black woman" who pushes away her family, and cannot maintain close relationships. She is the one "no one can tell anything to."

3) Jezebel, who is sexually promiscuous, or liberated; we may see her role in videos or reality television.

We are able to see all of these roles, often overlapping, in their most stereotypic fashions when we tune into talk shows (e.g., *Maury*), reality shows (e.g., *The Real Housewives of Atlanta)*, commercials of Black women serving others (e.g., Pine-Sol commercial) (Fuller, 2001), or in music videos. The common theme between these roles is strength and independence from relying on others, all precluding the ability to ask for help.

Let's consider Kelly again and how these roles play out for her. Kelly's mother is known as "the rock" within the family, taking care of problems and rarely "losing her cool." Kelly routinely hears her mother say, "I don't need anybody to help me. I do it ALL on my own." And, "Don't you *ever* depend on anyone for anything . . . you're a Black girl and people will doubt you . . . don't ever show weakness, people will walk all over you . . . you're strong." Kelly admires and respects her mother's strength—and rightfully so. However, Kelly's aunt is in a physically abusive relationship and Kelly hears references to her aunt as being "weak," and expressions of disdain and frustration with the situation. What Kelly doesn't hear is how the cycle of violence occurs and the difficulties of leaving such a relationship, and not that her aunt isn't necessarily "weak," but is "trapped" and scared. So the initial barrier is set for many Black girls. They don't ask for help out of fears of being viewed as weak and unable to handle themselves. Like their mothers, they are strong.

In revisiting Kelly, we find that she is being bullied at school and online. Her teachers notice she is becoming withdrawn, but assume it is related to an issue at home or her entry into adolescence. Kelly is becoming increasingly depressed, and is often irritable—which creates conflict with her parents—but feels she should be able to handle it herself. She has told no one what is going on.

A few issues arise in the above scenario. One is the recognition of distress in African American girls prior to a crisis. While Kelly may not want to kill herself, she may eventually have suicidal ideations. Also, as she continues to be in distress, she would benefit from support. A significant barrier is not recognizing signs of distress in Black girls. How do we know, before it's too late, that they need help? Look for increased moodiness, withdrawal, poor grades, and aggressiveness. We're looking for changes in behaviors and affect that are detrimental. Then, we need to intervene if problems are persistent.

CULTURAL BARRIERS TO COUNSELING

Why Would I Want to Send My Girl to Them?

To better understand the intracultural barriers to treatment we need to begin with the adults and take a retrospective approach. We must begin with their caregivers. Given poor medical outcomes and ongoing health disparities, research finds that adult African American women continue to have some mistrust of mental health and medical facilities (Thompson, Bazile & Akbar, 2004). It then only makes sense that young African American girls would be socialized to have similar beliefs. And given the history of Blacks and mental health, it makes sense that some parents would be hesitant to turn over the welfare of their children to mental health providers, resulting in Black girls being hesitant to open up in treatment.

Beliefs about Mental Health/Mental Illness

I mentioned the socialization of Black girls as influencing counseling barriers. So what do Black women believe about mental illness, mental health, and mental health treatment? What beliefs may be passed on to their daughters? Interestingly, Ward, Clark, and Heidrich (2009) interviewed African American women about perceptions of mental health and treatment and found that they generally understood mental illness to be limited to symptoms such as detachment from reality, confusion, and feeling/being out of control of their actions. In other words, they did not associate mental illness with the less dramatic concepts of generalized anxiety or chronic depression. Additionally, when asked about the causes of mental illness, the women cited racism, poor health, and family history as factors, but did not view mental illness as a medical concern. However, mental illness was viewed as a lifetime struggle sometimes resulting in incarceration or institutionalization. Lastly, they reported medication as the treatment, but not cure, and often as a detriment to mental health clients. Another theme the researchers found, which is consistent in the literature, is that Black women believed they are supposed to always be strong even to the point of diminished health (Matthews, Nelesen & Dimsdale, 2005). Mental illness was seen as a long-term, incurable condition brought on by some social ills, resulting in possible institutionalization of some sort, which will then result in the individual being medicated, but never getting better. Given this perspective, why would a parent want to acknowledge mental illness? And why would they—given those beliefs—want to get treatment for their children under these circumstances?

Role of the Black Church

The African American church can be viewed as an appropriate and realistic alternative to support African American communities (Boyd-Franklin, 2010). Black children and adolescents involved in church tend to have higher grades and feel more connected to their communities (Christian & Barbarin, 2001). The Black church has served as a place that goes beyond the teaching of religious doctrine. For the African American community, it has served as a community hub where children are raised and taught about cultural expectations and norms. For many, church is a safe place to get emotional support and to form community connections. However, sometimes families or individuals do not/cannot share their struggles with the church, or their needs are beyond the scope of the church, such as with psychosis, PTSD, and so on.

Unfortunately, some African American congregations discourage families from going outside the church for support, instead feeling that seeking outside support is a sign of lacking faith, while simultaneously airing their dirty laundry outside of the community. An older child may be told "pray on it" and "God will handle it if you just trust Him." For young children and adolescents who may be questioning their own beliefs about faith and religion, this advice may not be developmentally or personally useful.

PRACTICAL BARRIERS TO COUNSELING

Black children miss and cancel counseling and therapy appointments with some regularity, making it easy for clinicians to assume these families and children are obstructing treatment, which sometimes is true. However, other issues bear consideration, such as the practical issues making access to care difficult for many families.

Transportation

In the late 1990s, I lived in the rural South, working with families in both home and clinic settings. Often, those families seen in the clinic relied on others for rides to the grocery store, the child's school, medical appointments, and so on. On some occasions the car broke down or there was a flat tire. With no bus lines in many rural areas, a broken car or a ride that falls through means the mental health appointment may have to be cancelled or rescheduled. It becomes less of a priority than getting a ride to the grocery store or work. Likewise, in some urban areas, families are referred to clinics/clinicians in suburban areas where bus schedules can be non-existent, scarce, and/or unpredictable. While clinicians become understandably frustrated about missed appointments, late appointments, or repeatedly rescheduled appointments, we must consider if the very act of coming to the clinic is a barrier for many families.

So what can be done about this? How do we improve access? Consider contingency planning with the client and family if there are many missed appointments. Is it possible to plan for tele-counseling (e.g., telephone, Skype, or FaceTime)? Unlike any other time in history, we have options to access clients outside of the physical clinic setting. Perhaps alternating tele-therapy with face-to-face visits, to lessen the burdens on an already stressed family, will lessen this barrier to receiving mental health treatment.

Finances

Another practical consideration is paying for services (National Alliance on Mental Illness, 2009). Consider a parent working full-time, earning a low wage to middle-class income. Given household expenses and bills, even with a sliding fee scale or copay, attending counseling weekly or bi-weekly can strain the family's financial resources, resulting in mental health services becoming limited and/or inaccessible to the child. Additionally, if the referral is to a mental health provider who is not within the network of the family's insurance provider, the costs can be prohibitive. Lastly, some caregivers work variable shifts, and cannot afford to take much time off from work to get the child to multiple appointments, or they risk income or even their employment status. These are things we should keep in mind prior to assuming a family is obstructing mental health access for their child, or that they "don't care," which is the rejoinder of sometimes frustrated clinicians who have lost that block of time.

Let's consider how transportation and finances may play out for Kelly. Kelly's mother wanted Kelly tested for a gifted and talented program for a new school. The psychologist's office is several miles away in the suburbs. Unfortunately, as they were leaving for the appointment, the car battery died. While her mother called around to get a ride to the appointment and contacted the auto club, time passed. They made it thirty minutes late and could not be seen. Kelly's mother tried to explain the situation and reschedule, but the next appointment would not be for over three months, too late to get into the school next year. Her mother is angry, frustrated, and disappointed at the delay. She is upset that the clinician did not understand that situations occur outside of one's control.

CULTURAL COMPETENCE ISSUES

Information and Communication

Some research has found that often African Americans are concerned that counseling will lead to the use of medications (Ward, Clark & Heidrich, 2009), which is aversive for many parents. Sadly, many families and children are unsure of what counseling entails or how it can help resolve problems, even without medications. Richardson and colleagues (2003) found that Blacks are less likely than Whites to undergo mental health counseling or psychotherapy, and are more likely than Whites to receive pharmacotherapy. Providers may assume that Blacks don't want counseling and may not make referrals for counseling or psychotherapy, or may offer services in an offhand manner as opposed to sharing how non-pharmacological treatments can actually be effective.

As we return to Kelly, we notice her grades are slipping even further, and her parents begin to worry about her level of irritability and note she is increasingly withdrawn. Initially, they ground her to encourage improved grades and discourage disrespect, but there is no improvement. Her teachers also begin to notice significant changes and refer her to the school counselor. Her parents agree to a mental health referral to a community mental health clinic, where she meets with a pediatric psychiatrist and a licensed mental health provider. During the intake, there is very little conversation with Kelly and instead a focus is placed on what is going on in the home and the conflict between Kelly and her parents. Additionally, the busy clinic staff does not thoroughly explain the intake process to Kelly and her parents, nor is the therapeutic process explained. No treatment goals are explored, and Kelly is encouraged to behave at home and school. She next sees the psychiatrist, who restates the need for better behavior and then puts her on an antidepressant. This surprises her parents and makes Kelly feel guilty and ashamed for needing medication. She is worried that she might be "crazy" and not strong like the women in her family. After the three weeks on medication, her parents notice increased withdrawal and irritability. Her parents cease the medication and terminate treatment, due to fears the medication makes her worse and dissatisfaction with the intake appointment.

The above scenario is not uncommon, leading some clinicians to assume that families are not invested in their children. This may lead to additional barriers to treatment and a lack of trust in mental health providers. It would not be surprising if Kelly's parents return to their own supports—family, community, and church—which is usually the manner in which Black families manage distress (Boyd-Franklin, 2010), and see mental health treatment as ineffective and damaging to Black children.

Where Are the Black Psychologists?

Many ethnic minorities considering or entering into treatment wonder "Will they understand me?" "Will I be stereotyped and judged?" and "Will I have to explain everything to them?" It is because of these reasons that ethnic minorities seek out clinicians of similar backgrounds for themselves (Thompson, Bazile & Akbar, 2004) and their children. Given the limited numbers of African American clinicians, this is problematic. The numbers are striking: Blacks comprise approximately only 2–6% of all psychologists (American Psychological Association, 2004; National Alliance on Mental Illness, 2009), 4–7% of all licensed social workers (Morris-Compton, 2007; National Alliance on Mental Illness), and 2% of psychiatrists (National Alliance on Mental Illness). Further complicating the numbers is that these individuals do not represent only clinicians; they may be in research, academia, consultants, administrators, etc. And even of those who are clinicians, not all work with children and adolescents. Essentially, there is a problem of supply and demand with African American clinicians. The inability to have someone they feel "safe" with is a barrier that can feel insurmountable for Black girls.

"But I'm Colorblind"

While I was teaching a multicultural counseling course several years ago, a student repeatedly assured me she was "colorblind," not a racist, and was without a "biased bone in my body." While my former student's intentions may have been good, a young Black female does not live in a "colorblind" world. Given the statistics, we know that mental health clinicians are overwhelmingly White and female. What has been found is that "colorblindness" sets up a system of ignoring possible covert and overt issues of race and culture which may arise (Apfelbaum, Sommers & Norton, 2008; Neville et al., 2013). Also, research has shown that being colorblind does not work clinically and fails to acknowledge the role and impact of culture, potentially creating distance between a clinician and client (Apfelbaum, Sommers & Norton, 2008). Additionally, Burkard and Knox (2003) found that the higher a clinician rated him or herself on scales of colorblindness, the less their empathy for the client.

This does not mean all, or even any, clinical issues are about race or culture, but that the clinician must be open to discussions of race and bias. However, the lack of empathy shows a possible unconscious bias against African Americans. How might this impact Kelly?

Kelly's mood and grades still are not improving, so her parents agree to try another therapist and are clear they will use medication only as a last resort. After a few sessions, Kelly opens up to the therapist about the bullying. The bullying is related to her looks and is now hurting her self-esteem. Kelly is a thin, attractive, dark-skinned girl who decided to wear her hair in an Afro. She loves her new look and she wants to "look like myself." Some of the girls at her middle school began making racial slurs and commenting on her "Blackness" and "ugliness." She shares this with her White counselor, who responds with obvious discomfort and suggests that perhaps Kelly should consider changing her hair to make herself feel better. Additionally, the counselor assures her that the other girls "probably didn't really say that, maybe you misunderstood them?" Kelly then shuts down emotionally for the rest of the session. She tells her parents that she will not return to counseling, but won't tell them why.

In this case, the counselor is well-meaning, but has engaged in microaggression (biased comments and/or behaviors that aren't meant to be insulting). Her statement, a microinvalidation (Capodilupo & Sue, 2013), invalidated Kelly's experience as an African American girl experiencing racism, as well as suggesting Kelly holds some responsibility for her bullying by suggesting she change her hair. It is likely that this counselor sees herself as colorblind. Given Kelly's developmental stage, it may be difficult for Kelly to articulate what happened and why she does not want to return to counseling. Such interactions with clinicians inadvertently impose barriers with cultural incompetence, based on bias or their discomfort.

SUMMATION

While the focus of this chapter is barriers to mental health treatment for Black females, we have to consider a couple of issues. First, the research focusing on this topic is scarce in the literature. In actuality, there was more literature focusing on young African American males and treatment barriers than young women. This may be in part due to young Black females having better academic and ultimately financial outcomes than Black males—even though rates of incarceration are increasing (Morris, 2013).

However, I want to stress a few key issues: 1) parents and clinicians need to do a better job of recognizing emotional issues with young Black women, and understand the roles of the Strong Black Woman and Sapphire from a cultural perspective; 2) additionally, Black girls deal with microaggressions, such as assumptions (e.g., living in poverty, absent father, sexually active, etc.) and the associated comments about their lives; 3) and the combination of exposure to racist vitriol on the Internet and negative portrayals of Black females in various media impacts their sense of self-worth and beauty.

Many of the barriers to counseling are simply practical in nature: transportation, cost, location, and scheduling. Also, the parents and children are often assumed to be disinterested or resistant to treatment, which is not always the case. Clinicians should work with families to discuss possible solutions to these practical issues. Additionally, some research is showing that there is efficacy with texting adolescents to remind them about their clinic appointments (Branson, Clemmey & Mukherjee, 2013) and this should be considered as a tool.

Clinicians would benefit not only from being aware of the cultural issues that act as barriers to treatment, including the reasons for mistrust, but from also genuinely addressing their own biases and gaps in cultural knowledge related to race. All multicultural research points to clinicians considering the appropriate use of community resources, such as churches and community groups, to provide additional support. Educating clinicians to increase cultural competence and empathy would decrease those particular treatment barriers. Educating the Black community about how counseling and psychotherapy can benefit Black girls, while providing basic information about the counseling process, will give families a sense of understanding and allow them to be partners in the therapeutic process.

Let us conclude this chapter with Kelly. Her most recent clinician sought consultation from a more experienced and culturally competent therapist, who explains that Kelly's experiences were invalidated. They explored the clinician's biases and the cultural and developmental struggles that many Black girls face. After the consultations, Kelly and her family were contacted with the goal of reinitiating services. Kelly reluctantly agreed, and soon found the clinician to be open to her experiences as a Black female. Kelly then learned how to manage conflict, utilize her supports and strengths, while validating her identity as a healthy Black female.

Important aspects to consider are that the clinician sought consultation and was open to addressing her own gaps in knowledge, while making herself receptive to Kelly's experiences. She also modeled how to re-establish relationships and move from mistrust to trust. She helped lower a barrier to counseling by being open to learning and changing her clinical style.

REFERENCES

American Association of Suicidology. (2012). *African American suicide fact sheet.* Retrieved from http://www.suicidology.org/c/document_library/get _file?folderId=262&name=DLFE-528.pdf

Apfelbaum, E. P., Sommers, S. R., & Norton, M. I. (2008). Seeing race and seeming racist? Evaluating strategic colorblindness in social interaction. *Journal of Personality and Social Psychology, 95*(4), 918–932.

Bailey, D. S. (2004). Number of Psychology PhDs Declining. *Monitor, 35,* 18.

Branson, C. E., Clemmey, P., & Mukherjee, P. (2013). Text message reminders to improve outpatient therapy attendance among adolescents: A pilot study. *Psychological Services, 10,* 298–303.

Boyd-Franklin, N. (2010). Incorporating Spirituality and Religion into the Treatment of African American Clients. *Counseling Psychologist, 38,* 976–1000.

Burkard, A. W., & Knox, S. (2003). Effect of therapist color-blindness on empathy and attributions in cross-cultural counseling. *Journal of Counseling Psychology, 52,* 387–397.

Capodilupo, C. C., & Sue, D. W. (2013). Microaggressions in counseling and psychotherapy. In D. W. Sue & D. Sue, *Counseling the culturally diverse: Theory and practice* (6th ed., pp. 147–173). Hoboken, NJ: Wiley.

Christian, M. D., & Barbarin, O.A. (2001). Cultural resources and psychological adjustment of African American children: Effects of spirituality and racial attribution. *Journal of Black Psychology, 27,* 43–63.

Fuller, L. (2001). Are we seeing things? The Pine-Sol lady and the ghost of Aunt Jemima. *Journal of Black Studies, 32,* 120–131.

Gan, S., Zillman, D., & Mitrook, M. (1997). Stereotyping effects of Black women's sexual rap on White audience. *Basic and Applied Social Psychology, 19,* 381–399.

Guthrie, R. V. (2004). *Even the rat was White: A historical view of psychology* (2nd ed.). Boston: Pearson.

Harrington, E. F., Crowther, J. H., & Shepherd, J. C. (2010). Trauma, binge eating, and the "Strong black Woman." *Journal of Consulting and Clinical Psychology, 78,* 469–479.

Hernnstein, R., & Murray, C. A. (1994). *The Bell Curve: Intelligence and class structure in American life.* New York: The Free Press.

Holliday, B. G. (2009). The history and visions of African American psychology: Multiple pathways to place, space, and authority. *Cultural Diversity and Ethnic Minority Psychology, 15,* 317–337.

Hughes, D., Rodriguez, J., Smith, E. P., Johnson, D. J., Stevenson, H. C., & Spicer, P. (2006). Parents' racial/ethnic socialization practices: A review of research and agenda for future study. *Developmental Psychology, 42,* 747–770.

Jones, J., & Mosher, W. D. (2013). *Fathers' involvement with their children: United States, 2006–2010. National health statistics reports.* Retrieved from http://www.cdc.gov/nchs/data/nhsr/nhsr071.pdf

KidsCount (2013). KidsCount Data Center. Retrieved from http://datacenter.kidscount.org/data/tables/107-children-in-single-parent-families-by#detailed/1/any/false/867,133,38,35,18/10,168,9,12,1,13,185/432,431

Matthews, S. C., Nelesen, R. A., & Dimsdale, J. E. (2005). Depressive symptoms are associated with increased systemic vascular resistance to stress. *Psychosomatic Medicine 67,* 509–513.

Morris, M. W. (2013, March 18). National Council on Crime and Delinquency: Searching for Black Girls in the School to Prison Pipeline. Retrieved from http://www.nccdglobal.org/blog/searching-for-black-girls-in-the-school-to-prison-pipeline

Morris-Compton, D. (2007). Wanted: African American Men in Social Work. *Social Work Today, 7,* 24.

National Alliance on Mental Illness (2009). *African American community fact sheet.* Retrieved from http://www.nami.org/Template.cfm?Section=Fact _Sheets1&Template=/ContentManagement/ContentDisplay.cfm&Content ID =53812

National Center for Children in Poverty (2010). *Children's mental health: What every policymaker should know.* Retrieved from http://www.nccp.org/publicati ons/pub_929.html

Neville, H. A., Awad, G. H., Brooks, J. E., Flores, M. P., & Bluemel (2013). Colorblind racial ideology: Theory, training, and measurement implications in psychology. *American Psychologist, 68,* 455–466.

Richardson, J., Anderson, T., Flaherty, J., & Bell, C. (2003). The Quality of Mental Health Care for African Americans. *Culture, Medicine and Psychiatry, 27,* 487–498.

Suicide Prevention Resource Center (2013). Retrieved from http://www.sprc.org/ sites/sprc.org/files/library/Blacks%20Sheet%20August%2028%202013 %20Final.pdf

Thompson, V. L. S., Bazile, A., & Akbar, M. (2004). African Americans' perceptions of psychotherapy and psychotherapists. *Professional Psychology, Research and Practice, 35,* 19–26.

U.S. Census Bureau. (2013). *U.S. Bureau of the Census, Income, Poverty, and Health Insurance Coverage in the United States: 2012.* Retrieved from http://www .census.gov/prod/2013pubs/p60-245.pdf

Ward, E. C., Clark, L. O., & Heidrich, S. (2009). African American women's beliefs, coping behaviors, and barriers to seeking mental health services. *Qualitative Health Research, 19,* 1589–1601.

West, C. (2008). Mammy, Jezebel, Sapphire, and their homegirls: Developing an oppositional gaze toward the image of Black women. In J. Chrisler, C. Golden & P. Rozee (eds.), *Lectures on the psychology of women* (4th ed., pp. 286–299). New York: McGraw Hill.

Chapter 15

Black Adolescent Girls in Foster Care

Betty Boyle-Duke

Foster care is commonly referred to in many states as Child Protective Service (CPS) and has been in existence for many years. A formal system for out-of-home placement began in the United States in the late 1800s as agencies began monitoring poor, orphaned, or immigrant children who boarded with wealthy families often as indentured servants. By the turn of the century, the emergence of child welfare and labor laws gave rise to organizations with the goal of providing a more formalized approach to monitoring children not living with their natural families (Children's Aids Society, n.d.). These organizations, some state-run or faith-based, oversaw either the placement, financial responsibility, or enforced safety regulations for the protection of these children (Askeland, 2006).

Today, the U.S. child welfare system is comprised of interconnected programs, with direct delivery of services through county, local, state, or private nonprofit agency providers. The government establishes policies, regulations, mandates, and often the state health departments provide direct oversight that guides funding for foster care provisions. Child placement may include a variety of settings that not only include young children, but also adolescents and in some jurisdictions young adults up to the age of 21 (see Table 15.1). Unfortunately, youth in foster care make up some of the nation's most troubling social, health, and economic related statistics. All aspects of the foster care system are developed to

Table 15.1.
Types of Foster Care* Placement

Boarding Foster Family
Emergency or Satellite Placement
Kinship Care
Residential Group Home/Congregate Care
Medically Fragile
Supervised Independent Living Program (SILP)
Therapeutic Long-term
Trial Home Visit for Youth

* Foster care terminated at age 18 but extended up to age 21 in 16 states.

protect endangered minors and aim to provide a temporary respite for at-risk youth, but may not always align with children returning home whenever possible.

BACKGROUND AND PURPOSE

This chapter will discuss Black adolescents, particularly girls in foster care. Girls are vulnerable to sexual abuse, violence, exploitation, as well as a host of other pressures (Chamberlain, Leve & Smith, 2006; Dowdell, Cavanaugh, Burgess & Prentky, 2009). Furthermore, adolescents in foster care are at particular risk as they are mostly likely to exit care by ageing out to independent living and are less likely to be adopted or reunited with birth families as compared to infants, toddlers, or school age children. Black children presently make up approximately 15% of the U.S. population yet comprise about one-third of the children residing in foster care facilities (U.S. Department of Health and Human Services, 2012; Casey Family Programs, 2011; Knott & Donovan, 2010). The reasons for these disparities, which point to a number of socioeconomic factors and societal irregularities, are important to highlight if reduction in these statistics are to occur.

There are multifactorial reasons for foster care placement, but often children are removed from their homes as a result of reported abuse or neglect. Children of color are not, however, victims of these offensives more than any other racial or ethnic group, yet they are involved with child welfare at far greater numbers as more cases of abuse or neglect are substantiated (Font, Berger & Slack, 2012; U.S. Department of Health and Human Services [USDHHS], 2012). This is of great importance since youth in foster care are at greater risk than those living at home for poor outcomes. These youth typically have higher rates of teen parenting, homelessness, drug use, mental illness, and school failure at increased numbers when compared to teenagers not involved with foster care (Courtney & Heuring, 2005).

Social Issues

Regardless of its mission, the current foster care system has room for tremendous improvement as children are underserved (sometimes over-served or overrepresented in the mental health services), traumatized (SAMHSA, 2011; Walsh & Mattingly, 2011), and often endure a lifetime of difficulties while in care (Center for the Future of Education and Learning, 2010). For many, foster care is far from temporary, with the average length of stay in 2011 lasting two or more years (USDHHS, 2012). There have been advances in decreasing the average length of stay for youth in out-of-home care in some states by focusing on accelerating permanency goals with guidance and support from federal mandates such as the Adoption and Safe Families Act (renamed Promoting Safe and Stable Families Program). Yet despite these efforts, there are still too many teenagers re-maining in the child welfare system who leave unprepared for what lies ahead.

Although Black children remain a minority of the U.S. population, they are maintained in foster care longer and in disproportionate numbers as compared to children from other races (U.S. GAO, 2007). This disparity ex-ists due largely in part to the inequities existing throughout the various stages of the child welfare process, including more allegations made and founded among African American families, increased rates of entry into fos-ter care, and differences in the amount of family preservation services avail-able in certain settings (Hill, 2005; Wulczyn & Lery, 2007). Disproportionality varies widely by state, and in some areas Black youth are twice as likely to enter care than White youth (Hill, 2007) even though they comprise a mi-nority of the demographics (such as North Carolina or Texas).

Involvement with many of the public systems these families encounter further perpetuates the placement of Black children into foster care. Social constructs have led to disproportionality in not only child welfare, but in the legal and judicial systems as well. Blacks are overrepresented in the U.S. penal system, which contributes to many Black children being fos-tered. Blacks are imprisoned six times the rate of Whites with 1 in 100 women residing in American prisons (Pew Charitable Trust, 2008). Blacks and Hispanics make up nearly 60% of prisoners yet represent just over a third the U.S. population. With parents imprisoned at greater rates, chil-dren of color are left exposed to removal from their homes at greater rates than Whites, since some estimate 60% of female prisoners, who are often the main caregiver, have minor children (Glaze & Morushak, 2010). Existing policies and laws are often applied to Blacks differently than Whites and keep these arrest-related statistics disproportionate. This country's long history of racial inequality and oppression has resulted in today's continued struggles with institutional racism within the criminal justice system for Blacks in the way of racial profiling and draconian drug laws, leaving prisons overpopulated with minorities at alarmingly higher rates. Reports indicate Whites' drug use has been greater, but Blacks often receive for more severe drug-related sentences than do Whites (Fellner, 2009; National Association for the Advancement of Colored People [NAACP], n.d.). One obvious example includes the practice of mandated, longer prison terms for possession of crack cocaine, its use more commonly found in lower economic, minority communities versus powder cocaine which is more prevalent in other affluent, predominantly White areas (Fryer, Heaton, Levitt & Murphy, 2013). Stiff prison sentences keep the Black family fragmented with children being removed from their natural families in near similar instances where children from other backgrounds would remain in their homes.

Imprisonment of caregivers is not the only reason for child removal, as mental illness, child abuse, and neglect are also common reasons. Again these issues do not appear solely in one community over another but may often be exacerbated when coupled with stressors related to poverty, low socioeconomic status, or joblessness, making child rearing more challenging. Child welfare workers' responses to parents experiencing these conditions are quite different depending on race. This is an area for further exploration for schools of social work and professional social work organizations to work on enhancing the perceptions, reactions, and actions leading to workers' decisions and recommendations for placement of Black children into foster care.

Relatedly, the unemployment rate for Blacks still remains twice the rate of Whites (U.S. Department of Labor, 2012), which also adds to an increase in impoverished living conditions. Poverty is a known source for many of today's societal ills with its effects deeply rooted in the removal of thousands of children annually. It has been shown children from low-income households experience social and health conditions that, given few financial resources, place them at greater risk for future academic, employment, criminal, or behavioral problems (Griggs & Walker, 2008; Williams Shanks, Kim, Loke & Destin, 2010). Although intended to provide assistance and support, foster care has not been shown to improve the conditions of youth who may already be struggling; many in care remain on a steady pathway to continued poverty.

A review of work funded by the Annie E. Casey Foundation, Data on Children in Foster Care indicated trends among households entrusted with caring for fostered youth (O'Hare, 2008). Results drawn from key census data concluded the following in regards to the social, economic and demographic backgrounds of foster home households as compared to households where no foster children were housed:

- More likely to be low-income, depend on public assistance, and spend >30% of income on rent

- More likely to depend on public assistance as main financial resource
- Less likely to have a household member graduate high school or head of house graduate college
- Less likely to have a head of house or spouse who worked in the previous year or held full-time employment
- Larger households compared to other households with non-fostered children
- A larger ratio of children to adults living in the household
- Less likely to be married-couple households and more likely to be cohabitating couple
- More likely to be single-parent households

Given the low education attainment and the stress of overcrowded, disadvantaged living conditions they are leaving, many girls ageing out face adversity and problematic transition periods. Moreover, adults who were formerly in foster care reported similar demographics once they aged out: early parenting, high school drop-out, fewer marriages, inadequate housing, low wage earnings, and poverty (Courtney et al., 2011; Leigh, Huff, Jones & Marshall, 2007).

There are a multitude of opportunities for governmental entities and advocacy groups to ameliorate conditions leading to entry in foster care. Yet in the absence of such efforts the focus must lie in meeting the needs of those in foster care for improved outcomes as well as addressing the needs of youth exiting social service custody.

ADDRESSING NEEDS OF BLACK GIRLS IN "CARE"

Behavioral Health Concerns

Foster care placement negatively impacts girls on many fronts with length in care and frequent moves known as "foster care drift" being reliable indicators. Multiple moves throughout the system deny girls the stability and the capability to learn life skills they desperately need. These girls experience interrupted socialization and are not fully forming social norms. They have difficulties in securing lasting relationships and exploring their heritage, leading to a deficit in their sense of belonging.

According to Erik Erikson's theory of psychosocial development, adolescents and young adults typically receive signals that help form traditions, self-identity, and intimacy during this time (Erikson, 1968). Removal from birth parents or relatives interferes with this process, affecting a youth's ability to form or maintain close intimate relationships. As per Erikson "a feeling of being home in one's body, a sense of knowing where one is going and an inner assuredness of anticipated recognition from those who count" are key for successful outcome at this stage (Smith, 2011, p. 71). It is easily recognizable that foster care placement interferes with this stage of healthy development, leaving the youth unable to maintain connections with loved ones, and affects their own sense of self. In place of healthy development, behaviors like defiance, mistrust, anger, or conduct disorders may be displayed.

Youth in foster care also exhibit signs of grief, which may often be overlooked. Separation from family, even for a short term, leaves many with a tremendous sense of loss. This is a particularly difficult type of grief to face as the loss is often ambiguous, unlike the finality associated with death of a parent. In contrast to separation due to death, fostered children are aware their families exist, but may not understand why they can't live with them and feel unwanted. This is an important aspect to monitor and integrate in any counseling sessions as this grief can further impede a girl's ability to maintain lasting relationships. Without closure, many avoid building close relationships since they fear these relationships won't last or they fear all relationships will end in loss or separation (Hasenecz, 2009).

Sexual Health

Girls in foster care are extremely vulnerable and more likely to have been victims of sex abuse, violence, and maltreatment (Worthington-Dunn & Baynes, 2013). Foster care is comprised of nearly half (48%) females (Child Welfare Information Gateway, 2013) and girls of color may report racial discrimination, and some experience sexism as well (Smith, 2013). In addition, by the age of 19 females in foster care are twice as likely as non-foster care teens to become pregnant with many of these teenage mothers having subsequent pregnancies (Boonstra, 2011). Adolescence already proves to be a challenging time for any girl with rapid pubertal physical changes, yet combined with the instability that accompanies foster care placement adds further stress and strain on her development.

Females in foster care reportedly engage in sexual activity at an earlier age and have higher pregnancy and birthrates than same-age youth not in foster care. In 2006, the Midwest study offered findings that adolescent girls in foster care were more likely to have engaged in sexual activity than their same-aged peers. They were also less likely to have used contraceptives in the previous year. In addition, nearly one-third of the young women in foster care reported a history of pregnancy, compared with 19% of their same-aged non-foster-care peers. In the last decade there has been a steady decline in the number of teen pregnancies in this country but Black adolescents continue to have double the birthrate of their White peers (Courtney et al., 2011).

Pregnant girls living in foster care often lack the necessary community safety nets that serve as protective factors in delaying sexual activity and encourage contraceptive use. Effective pregnancy prevention programs report that youth who have close family ties, a sense of community connection, and school involvement maintain lower pregnancy rates. Parental monitoring, "connectedness" to family, and school involvement provided the best evidence for improved outcomes pertaining to teen sexual behavior (Markham, 2010). These conditions were most successful in delaying coitarche and produced consistent contraceptive use. These strategies have not been found as effective in youth in foster care as these vital relationships mentioned are the very ones that are often absent or unavailable to many living in foster care. This may contribute to the difficulty in reducing pregnancy among this particular subgroup of adolescents. As noted by the National Conference of State Legislatures' brief on teen pregnancy: "Teen pregnancy prevention programs tend to emphasize parental involvement and improve family dynamics, but at least one high-risk teen population . . . foster care does not benefit from this type of intervention" (National Conference on State Legislatures, 2009, p. 2). Additionally, of those who become pregnant, many will endure subsequent pregnancies in the absence of these supports.

Moreover, teenage girls in foster care may be ambivalent regarding preventing pregnancy as becoming a parent they believe would compensate for their perceived failed experiences with their own parents. It may also serve as a way to experience unconditional love. Without necessary tools to succeed or the ability to resolve issues from their own experiences, having a child for many seems logical. These tools are typically ones acquired at home from families of which these teens are deprived while being in foster care. Furthermore, without examples or independent life (IL) skills on effective parenting and child rearing while in care, teen mothers face a greater chance of their offspring being placed into foster care (National Campaign to Prevent Teen and Unplanned Pregnancy, 2012), feeding a vicious cycle.

For girls in foster care, coercive relationships where contraceptive sabotage may occur, uncertainty on whose responsibility in the child welfare organization it is to provide reproductive health counseling, and instability due to frequent placement relocations are other reasons associated with risk of pregnancy among this population. As stated previously, frequent placement leads to interruptions in a child's life, and in addition medical care coverage, counseling, and education may be severely affected by these placement changes (Boonstra, 2011). Frequent moves result in disruption of care and exposure to multiple, uncoordinated health care delivery sites with every move. In the realm of sexual health, these resulting gaps in care are concerning, causing unnecessary delays in birth control counseling and access, which for many youth needs to occur in a timely manner. Furthermore, the Midwest Evaluation revealed most of the girls in foster care (66%) had unwanted pregnancies compared with 50% of teens in the general population. This suggests that foster care youth may be experiencing more barriers to pregnancy prevention services and sex education than teens not in care. This notion reinforces the idea that access to readily available family planning counseling and sexual health education is crucial for this population.

Supports for Girls Ageing Out

Children in foster care often suffer from exposure to multiple traumatic events including the act of being removed from their home. In response, many agencies have moved towards a trauma-focused approach in care delivery. However, this shift in treatment must consider trauma affects females differently than males. Girls and boys are at risk for different kinds of trauma and the effects may not be observed similarly between the two. Girls are often victimized at higher rates than boys, specifically for sexually related assaults (Worthington-Dunn & Baynes, 2013). They often internalize their response to trauma, engaging in self-harm activities (i.e., cutting), substance abuse, or are more likely to suffer from post-traumatic stress disorder (PTSD) or depression (Pecora et al., 2009). Noting the relationship between girls' trauma and the resulting effects sets up a new approach for stakeholders to design programs that can positively impact girls in improving school completion, negotiating relationships, juvenile justice involvement, teen pregnancy, and mental health concerns.

Acknowledging and understanding the unique set of needs girls have are the first steps a successful program must take in an effort to avert these outcomes and address the complex, varied needs of girls in foster care. Agencies can offer gender-specific approaches to the trauma-informed services currently being implemented for best outcomes (HCH Clinician's Network, 2010). Some existing trauma-focused programs and frameworks like the Sanctuary Model®, Seeking Safety, or the Sidran Institute's approach to trauma care can be adopted and tailored to ensure the needs of females in foster care are being adequately met.

Girls ageing out of foster care also need specific support in order to become productive and well-adjusted community members. In addition to trauma, a myriad of additional issues plague these girls as they transition to living independently. Most states discharge adolescents at age 18, with a dozen or so states emancipating young adults from care at 21. Many in traditional family settings do not leave home by this age, remaining home until they've gained the skills to transition successfully to independence, continuing to rely on familial supports until they are ready (Furstenberg, 2010; Walsh & Mattingly, 2011). Without these supports in place those who age out face many difficulties to live independently. In planning for discharge, issues addressing insufficient housing options, weak educational plans, and income security must be considered. Planning for life after care should include access to programs that improve school completion and job readiness skills which work best to help combat the economic and social challenges often encountered upon leaving foster care. Funding streams financing job-training programs for youth, especially programs that combine receipt of high school or equivalency diplomas, including any special educational needs or other academic support must be prioritized. Housing continues to remain a challenge as well, since many are discharged to live in supportive housing, public housing, low-income housing or short-term, unstable living arrangements, which ultimately results in homelessness for many. A medical home model that encompasses interdisciplinary, collaborative efforts between social work, mental health, medical, and educators would work best to address the physical and emotional health care needs, including sexual health education during the time the teen spends in care as well as a model to follow upon discharge.

Breaking the Cycle

Fortunately, there has been a tremendous decline nationwide in the total number of youth residing in foster care over the last decade with over half a million children in care ten years ago, but closer to 400,000 youth remain in care today (Child Welfare Information Gateway, 2013; USDHHS, 2013). This decline is attributed to the enforcement of stronger permanency goals especially for young children moving on to more permanent living arrangements such as reunification or adoption. The creation of the Adoption and Safe Families Act, the Fostering Connections to Success and Increasing Adoptions Act of 2008, has allowed states the latitude to implement policies that reduce the duration of out-of-home placements in many states' foster care programs. Despite these advances, Black adolescents continue to have the longest stays in care and only 10 states represent 90% of these improved permanency conditions (USDHHS, 2013). Foster care will likely always remain in existence as long as families and children are in need, but these recent advances indicate that changes in the current system are possible nationwide. Yet as custodial guardians, or "in loco parentis" as the legal term is coined, foster care has to go beyond just satisfying youths' basic needs for food, shelter, and at worse beyond being a depository for minority children. Most importantly, foster care reform must embody principles that enforce fair treatment and just entry of all children regardless of race into CPS custody.

Shifting the focus and resources to preventative programs or safe alternatives that work to strengthen families once trouble is identified would better serve those involved in the child welfare system. This would help minimize the number of child removal cases given the dismal outcomes for these youth once they enter, and even more alarming age out of foster care. In the event placement cannot be avoided, ensuring permanent placement should be paramount in all states with as few placement changes as possible or kinship care when feasible. The stability of few or secure placements has demonstrated better educational, physical, and mental health outcomes (Rubin, Oreilly, Luan & Lucalio, 2007). Youth who have minimal school interruptions have improved school attendance and school performance. Most importantly, few placement disruptions allow for the development of strong, positive relationships with caring adults to occur, which should be emphasized given the proven efficacy of these approaches (USDHHS, 2005). Kinship care should always be prioritized when possible as children residing with relatives often fare better than those in congregate or non-kinship settings (Avery, 2010; Metzger, 2008; Shaw & Goode, 2008); it also promotes healthier adult connections than other foster care settings.

Increasing the age of emancipation or financial support until age 21 is also advisable in more localities across the United States as the additional years for discharge planning has shown tremendous promise for youth to learn necessary life skills (Human Rights Watch, 2010). Cost savings would also occur as multiple reports note that the costs associated with poorer outcomes far outweigh expenditures associated with improving education, housing, health care, and work programs for these ageing youth. This shift would lessen costs states spend for juvenile detention, homeless services, or public assistance benefits, which are systems many youth rely upon when services fail them when they age out. This investment in improving youth would also help society given their potential future contributions as workers, taxpayers, and service consumers (Courtney & Heuring, 2005). Investment in programs that assist in improved mental health management and community-based family supports (Casey Family, 2011) would also aid in this endeavor and should be made more readily available in the community being served.

Foster care in its current form provides basic needs for youth with small gains in the area of supporting its alumni. Federal funds like John H. Chafee funds are set aside for independent life skills training, yet many youth are at a great loss in this area once they age out. Enhancing independent life skills training as real life training to better accommodate what youth are truly facing once they leave care should be implemented early in the child welfare process.

This chapter has focused on known risk factors for foster care placement, especially for African American girls, and also areas of focus needed for child welfare reform prior, during and after foster care for these youth. Once in care, youth ageing out will need a tremendous amount of support in order to obtain optimal results, which currently is not being met for many. Funding for programs that support aftercare to ensure that adequate housing, education, medical coverage, and sufficient financial needs are met would help to improve the bleak statistics so many of these youth face upon discharge. The government's acknowledgment of the need for improvements is an important first step in bringing together key child welfare proponents and policy makers to further improve services for the nation's foster care youth. Knowing that time spent in foster care often adversely affects youth makes it imperative that legislators and their administration maintain a commitment to expanding their focus and funding to include programs and services that divert children and families from long-term foster care involvement. Ironically, states spend significantly more to cover costs related to foster care as compared to preventative services aimed at keeping families together, which have shown better outcomes for youth.

In general, teens in care are less likely to reach permanency goals of reuniting with birth parents as compared to younger children. Black teens are least likely to be adopted as compared to children of other races, and the older they become the lower the likelihood they will be adopted. This often leads to children 12 and older remaining in care for longer spans of time, with nearly half ageing out of care at an age of emancipation that varies by state. Given the dismal statistics associated with removal from biological families and the many difficulties teens face upon emancipation, a shift towards working at reducing the unnecessary, sometimes biased foster care placement for Black youth would seem like an obvious, necessary step for child welfare reform.

The federal government in their oversight of state policies should identify and enforce the use of best evidence-based programs, which appear to be making advances in the field of child welfare. These programs should be highlighted, evaluated, and replicated in areas still needing transformation. Additionally, charitable organizations like the Annie E. Casey Foundation, which are committed to providing resources or financing research that uncovers and fulfills unmet needs of vulnerable youth, can also be used to inform policy changes to the current foster care system.

Known risk factors leading to poorer outcomes for girls in care have been identified as well as protective factors for those who persevere despite their life circumstances. Delivery of services to youth in foster care involves many professionals including lawyers, judges, social workers, and educators as well as health care providers. Improving care of youth while residing in foster care must include an inter-professional approach. Joint communication among those planning and overseeing the placement of these children is of the utmost importance if smooth transitions and best outcomes are to be achieved. This improved communication between providers would help reduce the instability so many of these youth face while in care. The use of medical homes where concerted, centralized care is provided will deter the inconsistency in care so many girls face while in care and also help counter some of the ill effects noted when only sporadic, disrupted custodial, physical, and mental health care is received.

Suggested improvements offered in this chapter will only scratch the surface until major changes in the fabric of America occurs, such as eliminating the racial biases existing in the nation's family and criminal court systems as well as the challenges of the existing economic class structure. Until reconciliation and widespread acknowledgment that these conditions continue to exist across the nation there will be no true far-reaching impact to the foster care system.

The U.S. foster care system, although long-term in existence, lacks longitudinal evidence concluding whether placement has a positive or negative effect on the overall lives of young people as compared to youth raised at home (Doyle, 2007). Conducting research to retrieve longitudinal data remains a challenge for child welfare but what is known has been summarized in this chapter. Several areas for improvement in foster care around policy and practice changes have been identified. The association of poor life outcomes with foster care, particularly for Blacks who are continually overrepresented in this system, continues to be an area of grave concern but needs additional awareness from public officials for true amelioration. Removing conditions that place Black youth in care disproportionately as well as countering problems that youth face upon discharge also warrant a closer look. Enforcing policies on a more formalized system of transition has to be established to meet the needs of adolescents and should take place prior to discharge (not upon discharge) in a timely, effective manner. These are areas where professionals working in the area of child welfare and policy makers involved in foster care can focus restructuring efforts.

REFERENCES

Askeland, L. (ed.). (2006). *Children and youth in adoption, orphanages and foster care: A historical handbook and guide*. Westport, CT: Greenwood Press.

Avery, R. J. (2010). An examination of theory and promising practice for achieving permanency for teens before they age out of foster care. *Children and Youth Services Review, 32*, 399–408. doi:10.1016/j.childyouth.2009.10.011

Boonstra, H.D. (2011). Teen pregnancy among young women: A Primer. *Guttmacher Policy Review*, 14(2).

Casey Family Programs. (2011). *Child welfare fact sheet* [Fact Sheet]. Retrieved from http://www.casey.org/Newsroom/MediaKit/pdf/CWFactSheet.pdf

Center for Mental Health Services and Center for Substance Abuse Treatment. Diagnoses and Health Care Utilization of Children Who Are in Foster Care and Covered by Medicaid. HHS Publication No. (SMA) 13-4804. Rockville, MD: Center for Mental Health Services and Center for Substance Abuse Treatment, Substance Abuse and Mental Health Services Administration, 2013.

Center for the Future of Education and Learning. (2010). *Grappling with the gaps: Toward a research agenda to meet the educational needs of children and youth in foster care.* Santa Cruz, CA. Retrieved from http://www.cftl.org/documents/2010/ResearchGaps.pdf

Chamberlain, P., Leve, L., & Smith, D. K. (2006). Preventing behavior problems and health risking behaviors in girls in foster care. *International Journal in Behavioral Consultation and Therapy,* 2(4), 518–530.

Child Trends. (2012). *Foster care.* Retrieved: http://www.childtrends.org/?indicators=foster-care§hash.WU4kMbuo.dpuf

Child Welfare Information Gateway. (2011). *Addressing racial disproportionality in child welfare.* Washington, DC: U.S. Department of Health and Human Services, Children's Bureau. Retrieved from www.childwelfare.gov/pubs/issue_briefs/racial_disproportionality/racial_disproportionality.pdf

Child Welfare Information Gateway. (2013). *Foster care statistics, 2012.* Washington, DC: U.S. Department of Health and Human Services, Children's Bureau. Retrieved from: https://www.childwelfare.gov/pubs/factsheets/foster.pdf

Children's Aid Society. (n.d.). *History.* Retrieved from http://www.childrensaidsociety.org/about/history

Courtney, M. E., & Heuring, D. H. (2005). The transition to adulthood for youth "aging out" of the foster care system. In D. W. Osgood, E. M. Foster, C. Flanagan & G. R. Ruth (eds.), *On your own without a net: The transition to adulthood for vulnerable populations* (pp. 27–67). Chicago: The University of Chicago Press.

Courtney, M., Dworsky, A., Brown, A., Cary, C., Love, K., & Vorhies, V. (2011). *Midwest evaluation of the adult functioning of former foster youth: Outcomes at age 26.* Chicago, IL: Chapin Hall at the University of Chicago.

Dowdell, C. B., Cavanaugh, D. J., Burgess, A. W., & Prentky, R. A. (2009). Girls in foster care: A vulnerable and high-risk group. *American Journal of Maternal Child Health,* 34, 172–178. doi:10.1097/01.NMC.0000351705.43384.2a

Doyle, J. (2007). Child protection and child outcomes: Measuring the effects of foster care. *The American Economic Review,* 97(5), 1583–1609.

Erikson, E. (1968). *Identity: Youth and crisis.* New York/London: W.W Norton & Company.

Fellner, J. (2009). Race, drugs and law enforcement in the United States. *Stanford Law and Policy Review,* 20, 257–292.

Font, S. A., Berger, L. M., & Slack, K. S. (2012). Examining racial disproportionality in child protective services case decisions. *Children & Youth Services Review,* 34(11), 2188–2200.

Fryer, R. G., Heaton, P. S., Levitt, S. D., & Murphy, K. M. (2013). Measuring crack cocaine and its impact. *Economic Inquiry,* 51(3), 1651–1681.

Furstenberg, F. (2010). On a new schedule: Transitions to adulthood and family change. *The Future of Children: Transition to Adulthood,* 20(1), 63–87.

Glaze, L. E. & Marushak, L. M. (2010). Parents in prison and their minor children. Bureau of Justice Statistics. Retrieved from http://bjs.ojp.usdoj.gov/index.cfm?ty=pbdetail&iid=823

Griggs, J., & Walker, R. (2008). The costs of child poverty for individuals and society: A literature review, Joseph Roundtree Foundation.

Hasenecz, N. (2009). Fixing Foster Care—5 Strategies for Change. *Social Work Today,* 9, 3.

HCH Clinician's Network. (2010). Delivering trauma informed services. *Healing Hands*, 14(6),1–8. Retrieved from: http://www.nhchc.org/wpcontent /uploads/2011/09/DecHealingHandsWeb.pdf

Hill, R. B. (2005). *Synthesis of research on disproportionality in child welfare: An update.* Casey/CSSP Alliance for Racial Equity in the Child Welfare System.

Hill, R. B. (2007). *An analysis of racial/ethnic disproportionality and disparity at the national, state, and county levels.* Casey/CSSP Alliance for Racial Equity in the Child Welfare System. Retrieved from http://www.cssp.org/publications /child-welfare/alliance/an-analysis-of-racial-ethnic-disproportionality -and-disparity-at-the-national-state-and-county-levels.pdf

Human Rights Watch. (2010). *My so-called emancipation: From foster care to homelessness for California youth*, U.S.

Knott, T., & Donovan, K. (2010). Disproportionate representation of African-American children in foster care: Secondary analysis of the National Child Abuse and Neglect Data System, 2005. *Children and Youth Services Review*, 32(5), 679–684.

Leigh, W. A., Huff, D., Jones, E. F., & Marshall, A. (2007). *Aging Out of the Foster Care System to Adulthood: Findings, Challenges, and Recommendations*, Joint Center for Political and Economic Studies, Washington DC.

Markham, C. M., Lormand, D., Gloppen, K. M., Perskin, M. F., Flores, B., Low, B., & House, L. D. (2010). Connectedness as a predictor of sexual and reproductive health outcomes for youth. *Journal of Adolescent Health*, 46, S23–S41.

Metzger, J. (2008). Resiliency in children and youth in kinship care and family foster care. *Child Welfare*, 87, 115–140.

National Association for the Advancement of Colored People (NAACP). [n.d.]. *Criminal Justice Fact Sheet, 2009–2014* [Fact Sheet]. Retrieved from http:// www.naacp.org/pages/criminal-justice-fact-sheet

National Campaign to Prevent Teen and Unplanned Pregnancy. (2012). *Preventing teen pregnancy through outreach and engagement: Tips for working with Foster Care and Juvenile Justice.* Washington, DC: retrieved from http://www .thenationalcampaign.org/resources/pdf/CDC-foster-care.pdf

National Conference on State Legislatures. (2009). *Making a difference for at-risk population: Teen Pregnancy Prevention*, Washington DC. Retrieved from http://www.ncsl.org/documents/health/teenpregnancy09.pdf

O'Hare, W. (2008). *Data on Children in Foster Care from the Census Bureau.* Baltimore, MD: Annie E. Casey Foundation. Retrieved from http://www.aecf.org/~ /media/PublicationFiles/FosterChildrenJuly2508.pdf

Pecora, P. J., Jensen, P. J., Romanelli, L. H., Jackson, L. J., & Ortiz, A. (2009). Mental health services for children placed in Foster Care: An overview of current challenges. *Child Welfare*, 88, 5–26.

Pew Charitable Trust. (2008). *One in 100: Behind bars in America 2008*, Washington DC. Retrieved from http://www.pewstates.org/uploadedFiles/PCS _Assets/2008/one%20in%20100.pdf

Rubin, D. M., Oreilly, A., Luan, X., & Lucalio, A. R. (2007). Impact of placement stability on behavioral well being for children in foster care. *Pediatrics*, 119, 336–344.

Shaw, E., & Goode, S. (2008). *Fact Sheet: Vulnerable Young Children* [Fact Sheet]. Retrieved from The University of North Carolina, Chapel Hill, FPG Child

Development Institute. http://ectacenter.org/~pdfs/pubs/factsheet_vuln erable.pdf

Smith, S. (2013). Black feminism and intersectionality. *International Socialist Review*, Issue 91.

Smith, W. (2011). *Youth Leaving Foster Care: A Developmental, Relationship-Based Approach to Practice*. Oxford University Press: New York.

Substance Abuse and Mental Health Services Administration. (2011). *Addressing the Needs of Women and Girls: Developing Core Competencies for Mental Health and Substance Abuse Service Professionals*. HHS Pub. No. (SMA) 11-4657. Rockville, MD: Substance Abuse and Mental Health Services Administration.

U.S. Department of Health and Human Services. Administration for Children, Youth and Families, Children's Bureau. (2005). A report to Congress on adoption and other permanency outcomes for children in foster care: Focus on older children. Washington, DC.

U.S. Department of Health and Human Services, Administration for Children, Youth and Families, Children's Bureau. (2012). Child Maltreatment. Retrieved from http://www.acf.hhs.gov/programs/cb/research-data -technology/statistics-research/child-maltreatment

U.S. Department of Health and Human Services, Administration for Children, Youth and Families, Children's Bureau. (2012). The Adoption and Foster Care Analysis and Reporting System (AFCAR). Retrieved from www.acf .hhs.gov

U.S. Department of Health and Human Services, Administration for Children, Youth and Families, Children's Bureau. (2013). Trends in foster care and adoption (FFY 2002–FFY 2012). Retrieved from http://www.acf.hhs.gov/ sites/default/files/cb/trends_fostercare_adoption2012.pdf

U.S. Department of Labor. (2012). African American Labor Force in the Recovery. Retrieved from: http://www.dol.gov/_sec/media/reports/blacklabor force/

U.S. Government Accountability Office (GAO). (2007). African American children in foster care: Report to the Chairman, Committee on Ways and Means, House of Representatives. Retrieved from http://www.gao.gov/new.items /d07816.pdf

Walsh, W. A., & Mattingly, M. J. (2011). Long-term foster care: different needs, different outcomes. *The Carsey Institute at the Scholars' Repository*. Paper 139. Retrieved from http://scholars.unh.edu/carsey/139

Williams Shanks, T. R., Kim, Y., Loke, V., & Destin, M. (2010). Assets and child well-being in developed countries. *Children and Youth Services Review*, 32, 1488–1496. doi:10.1016/j.childyouth.2010.03.011

Worthington-Dunn, K., & Baynes, K. (2013). Responding to the needs of adolescent girls in foster care. *Georgetown Journal on Poverty Law and Policy*, 20, 321–349.

Wulczyn, F., & Lery, B. (2007). *Racial disparity in foster care admission*. Chapin Hall Center for Children at University of Chicago, IL.

Chapter 16

Education vs. Schooling: Black Adolescent Females Fight for an Education in the 21st Century

Gloria A. Gibson

INTRODUCTION

The United States is a nation where students of all cultural ethnicities are supposed to be able to rise above their race, class, and gender status and receive a quality education. However for some racial and gendered groups the above notion does not apply to them. Specifically, Black adolescent females who attend urban high schools do not receive the same quality of education as their White female counterparts attending suburban public high schools. It has been well documented that educational institutions have not been neutral sites when it comes to the gender and racial socialization of students (Ballantine, 1993; Bennett deMarrais & LeCompte, 1995; Bowles & Ginitis, 1976; Parsons, 1959; Solomon, 1992). In addition, Kozol (1991) states the "Denial of 'means of competition' is perhaps the single most consistent outcome of the education offered to poor children in the schools of our large cities . . ." (p. 83). Woodson (1990) also found that schools have been racially biased when it comes to Black students. He states, "The so-called modern education with all its defects, however, does others [Whites] so much more good than it does the Negro, because it has been worked out in conformity to the needs of those who enslaved and oppressed weaker peoples" (xii). The educational system was set up by White oppressors to benefit their children while at the same time it has convoluted Black people's cognitive abilities to the point they accept being oppressed. Specifically, Woodson (1990) postulates Blacks who are educated in White-dominant schools where the interest of those who are in power are maintained (Bowles & Ginitis, 1976; & West, 2001) start to believe in the inferiority of the Black race in relation to their White counterparts.

REVIEW OF THE LITERATURE

This notion of quality education for White students as well as their Black counterparts has been negated by research in urban school districts, which has found Black students are not receiving the same quality of education as White students (see Kozol, 1991; Ladson-Billings, 1994; Fordham, 1996 for discussion). Therefore, the "Mis-education of Black girls learning in a white educational system" continues to school them academically instead of educating them (Shujaa, 1994; Kozol, 1991; Powell, 1997). Black girls attending urban school districts understand that there are rules and regulations they need to follow in order to conform to school norms, such as how to behave in class, submit all class assignments on time, and graduate in four years from high school, to name a few. However, there are Black adolescent females who are aware they are not receiving the same quality of education as their White female counterparts attending suburban public high schools. For generations there has been a saying which pertains to females in Black households, "girls should be seen and not heard."

Therefore, for some Black adolescent females attending urban public high schools this "saying" continues to permeate their academic lives because they accept the dominant ideology that they are academically inferior to their White female counterparts, which continues to silence and marginalize them. However, for Black feminist writer bell hooks (1989), coming to voice from silence is revolutionary act. "As a metaphor for self-transformation, it has been especially relevant for groups of women who have previously never had a public voice, women who are speaking and writing for the first time, including many women of color" (p. 12). The "revolutionary act" of conducting research in urban and suburban public high schools gives voice to Black adolescent females who have been marginalized. Therefore, this study explores the thoughts and lived experiences of two groups of Black adolescent females as they create and enact their class, race, and gender identities at Thomas Fisher High School which is located in a predominantly White suburb of Williamsburg, and Benjamin Franklin High School located in the inner city of Williamsburg, New York.

There is limited research that solely focuses on Black teenage girls' gender and racial identity construction within the context of educational institutions. When Black females have been included in research studies it has been in relation to their Black male and White female counterparts and often from a White scholar's viewpoint. Conducting research on Black adolescent females in the spaces of their urban and suburban high schools allowed them to move from being silenced to giving voice to their lived realities of what it means to be Black and female in their educational institutions. Moving from silence to voice is a way to allow Black adolescent females to turn from object to subject.

As objects their voices remain muted, but as subjects they can speak and be heard. Researchers (hooks, 1989; Jones and Gooden, 2003; Collins Hill, 2000; Mullings, 1997) have found that for marginalized women, coming to voice is an act of resistance which allows them to transform from object to subject. As a subject, marginalized women can now "speak" about their lived experiences of being Black and female compared to White women. In addition, this research on Black adolescent females moving from silence to voice, then from object to subject, gives way for more research on this particular gender group to be conducted.

BLACK WOMEN'S RACIAL IDENTITY

The historical conflict between Black and White women started with how Black people were originally perceived by White males. "Whiteness" was seen as beautiful and pure, in contrast to the "Negro" who was ugly because their skin color was dark. Black people's racial identity was formed by White male supremacist views of what constituted "beauty" (Jordan, 1968). In 1550, the first English voyagers came to West Africa to trade goods with the native people. The Englishmen considered West Africans as a different kind of people from themselves, and noticed their customs, language, lack of clothing, and being un-Christian was the opposite of them. The Englishmen not only observed the cultural differences, but also the physical ones, including skin color.

The Englishmen described West African people as being "black," which at that time had a negative connotation. According to Jordan (1968), the British people had clear notions of what the colors Black and White meant to them: "[W]hite and black connoted purity and filthiness, virginity and sin, virtue and baseness, beauty and ugliness, beneficence and evil, God and the devil" (p. 7). The White British women exemplified what was considered feminine: "Whiteness, moreover, carried a special significance for Elizabethan Englishmen: it was, particularly when complemented by red, the color of perfect human beauty, especially female beauty" (Jordan, 1968, p. 8). Englishmen perceived West African women as Black, with large breasts, thick lips, and a broad nose, which they considered unattractive, specifically "ugly."

This negative perception about the Black females still continues in the 21st century. Collins Hill (2000), Fordham (1997), hooks (1984, 1989), Jones and Gooden (2003), and Mullings (1997) all write about the marginalization of Black women compared to their White counterparts. According to Fordham (1997):

> In America, White womanhood is often defined as a cultural universal. Yet the moral superiority of White womanhood is rarely explicitly verbalized in the academy. Indeed it is most often labeled "femaleness" minus the White referent. Nonetheless, White and middle class is the "hidden transcript[s]" . . . of femaleness, the womanhood invariably and historically celebrated in academe. In striking contrast, Black womanhood is often presented as the antithesis of White women's lives, the slur or the "nothingness" . . . that men and other women use to perpetuate and control the image of the "good girl" and by extension the good woman. (p. 82)

Specifically, Black women compared to their White female counterparts are considered the "dark nothingness" of the female gender, according to the White-dominant lenses of what it means to be female. Therefore, Black women are the "dark objects" of White women, which has dehumanized them as "female" since the first Englishmen in West Africa in 1550 defined what constitutes beauty. This negative image of Black women still continues today through the "hidden transcripts" of the media, fashion, and the music industry. Jones and Gooden (2003) also found that Black women shift their identity in order to learn how to deal with America's racist and sexist misconceptions of them as females. Jones and Gooden found "black women in America have many reasons to feel this deep sense of dissatisfaction. As painful as it may be to acknowledge, their lives are still widely governed by a set of old oppressive myths circulating in the White-dominated world" (2003, p. 2). There are 19 million Black women who make up 7% of the United States population, and Jones and Gooden (2003) have found that little information is known about the psychology of them.

For instance, "the way they experience the workplace, the complexities of their romantic lives, the challenges they face as mothers . . . their spiritual and religious practices, these and so many other aspects of their lives are largely unknown to the wider community" (Jones and Gooden, 2003, p. 2). Furthermore, for Black women (hooks, 1984; Collins Hill, 2000; Baszile, 2006) being invisible is what places them on the margin of the dominant White society. Black women are the "objectified other" of their White female counterparts, whereas White women are "subjects" that are visible in society and against which standards of womanhood are measured.

Schools not only educate and prepare students for occupational roles in society (Bowles and Ginitis, 1976; Proweller, 1998), but they also aid in gender and racial socialization. Feminist scholars (Rassiguier, 1994; McRobbie, 1978; Valli, 1988) have found the various ways that schools, whether in the United States, England, or France, contribute in some ways to girls' racial and gender identity formation.

METHODOLOGY

In this chapter I discuss my interviews with twenty-nine Black adolescent females who attended urban and suburban public high schools in Williamsburg, New York. The names of the school districts, city, and participants' names have been changed to maintain confidentiality. I did not change the interview excerpts from the participants in order to maintain the integrity of the discourses between them and myself. I entered Thomas Fisher High School, which is in a suburb of Williamsburg, New York, on September 13, 2000, to collect data from fifteen participants and exited the site on December 14, 2000. I collected data five days a week observing students in their English, Math, Photography, Public Speaking, Creative Writing, and Social Studies classes. I entered Benjamin Franklin High School, which is located in the inner city of Williamsburg, New York, to collect data five days a week from January 4, 2001, through June 15, 2001. I observed all fourteen of my participants in their English classes because most of them attended them on a consistent basis unlike other classes such as Earth Science and Math which they did not attend on a regular basis; specifically, they would cut these classes.

This study used qualitative methods grounded in a critical cultural framework to gain knowledge of how Black adolescent female students create and enact their gender and racial identities in the context of an urban and a suburban high school. Qualitative research is an umbrella term used to refer to several research strategies that share certain characteristics. Bogdan and Biklen (1982) describe qualitative research as ". . . soft; [data] that is, rich in description of people, places, and conversations, and not easily handled by statistical procedures" (p. 2). Therefore, this chapter is grounded in two assumptions: first, Black female students attending urban and suburban public high schools are experts on how their identities are constructed and deconstructed in their respective high schools; second, Black female students are the only ones who can voice the lived reality of what it means to be adolescent Black, and female, and attend an urban or suburban public high school. As Way (1996) notes, "studies of human development need to investigate how the individuals themselves perceive their environment" (p. 175). Specifically, despite the negative gender and racial notions society has assigned to Black females, there is a critical need to implore adolescent Black teenage girls to share stories of how their gender and racial identities are developed in educational institutions which sometimes negate them as feminine.

EDUCATION VS. SCHOOLING: BLACK GIRLS FIGHT FOR AN EDUCATION

Shujaa (1994) noted that it is generally thought that education will be an outcome of schooling; however, there are differences between the two constructs for students attending large urban school districts. "Too many of our children are trapped in urban school systems that have been 'programmed' for failure" (Madhububuti, 1994, p. 1). The groundbreaking court case *Plessy v. Ferguson* (1896) stipulated that "racial segregation" in educational institutions for White and Black students was legal under the "separate but equal" laws of the Constitution of the United States of America. However, academic researchers (Kozol, 1991; Bowles and Ginitis, 1976; Woodson, 1990; Davidson, 1996) have found that for Black students and other minority groups attending public schools in large urban school districts their educational experiences have been "separate," but not "equal" compared to their White counterparts attending suburban public schools. In addition, Shujaa states, "In African-American folk language the phrase 'going to school' and 'getting an education' are typically used in ways that imply that 'schooling' and 'education' are an overlapping process" (1994, p. 13). Specifically, sometimes education and schooling overlap, but African Americans receive more schooling than education, which continues to marginalize them compared to their White counterparts who are educated versus schooled.

Furthermore, Shujaa (1994) has found "The failure to take into account differing cultural orientations and unequal power relations among groups that share membership in society is a major problem in conceptualizations that equate schooling and education" (p. 14). Some of the participants at Benjamin Franklin realized that they were being schooled and not educated and they wanted to see certain changes in their high school in order to get a good quality education.

Moreover, students at Thomas Fisher and Benjamin Franklin high schools know the value of getting a quality education which allows them to be academically prepared to attend college and get a good-paying job. In addition, the participants expect that the teachers teaching them are qualified in their disciplines. Marci, Pam, Diane, and Wendy expected the teachers teaching them to be certified in their subject area. Therefore, students have certain expectations that the teacher teaching them will have "acceptable moral character, and proficiency in the subjects to be taught" (Lortie, 1975, p. 17). However, some of the participants at Thomas Fisher and Benjamin Franklin felt their school districts needed to replace some of the teaching staff because they are incompetent as teachers.

When I asked the participants what is one thing you would change about the teaching staff at their high schools, Marci, Pam, Lisa, Diane, and Wendy revealed their negative experiences with teachers at their high schools. Marci, a junior at Benjamin Franklin, gives her viewpoint on the changes that need to take place with the teaching staff at her high school.

> I'd have teachers that [are] teaching classes [they are certified to teach]. If a teacher is supposed to be teaching science and he is teaching Spanish he should be teaching science. . . . Like these freshmen have teachers that are not [sup]posed to be teaching them. I'm glad I passed Algebra B, last year. [Be]cause the teacher is gone now, so whoever [students] in Algebra B they not getting the right teaching; because that teacher is not a math teacher. That teacher is whatever else or a sub [substitute] teacher.

Marci acknowledges she has observed there are teachers at Benjamin Franklin High School who are teaching classes they are not qualified to teach, and as a result the students suffer the consequences of not being academically prepared. Pam, a junior at Thomas Fisher, narrates that she would change some of the teachers at her high school because they are racist; she would like to see a more diverse teaching population.

> Because they [White teachers] don't know what they doing. Some of them are racist. Mixed like Black anything this is just I don't know this school is full of White people, and it's only one Black Teacher [Mr. Brunner] so I would mix it up with teachers and students.

At the time of this study there was only one Black teacher at Thomas Fisher High School, which has not gone unnoticed by Pam and the other Black students. In addition, Pam would also like to see Thomas Fisher have a more diverse population of students at the high school.

Diane, a senior at Benjamin Franklin, would also like to change some of the teaching staff at her high school because she feels they do not care about the students.

> I would change some of the teachers' attitude(s) [be]cause some of them act like they don't care. They [teachers] just here for a paycheck. They [teachers] just don't care and some care. I would change some of the teachers.

This theme of teachers not caring about their students succeeding academically also continues with Wendy's interview, who is a senior at Benjamin Franklin and also agrees with Diane that some teachers only care about their paycheck and not the students.

I feel some of my teachers they're cool, but ah, some of them aren't. I think some teachers they just here just for the money. Some teachers are here for the pay. Like, when they [teachers] did that strike back in September. Some of these teachers shouldn't be striking because they really don't be teaching anything in the first place. So what's the sense of going on a strike if you don't teach nothing [anything]? Why you [teachers] striking? Don't give them no higher pay if they not going to teach you.

According to Diane's and Wendy's interviews they are aware there are some teachers at Benjamin Franklin High School who do not care if the students are learning, but are only working there for a paycheck. Wendy's interview continues with her narrating how the teachers at Benjamin Franklin are incompetent:

I feel I think that's I think that's a disappointment to like the school and the community and for us 'cause that makes us look bad for not know-ing stuff. We [students] go somewhere else [a different school] and we don't know what they're talking about, but we think we know what they're talking about because we were told this way and it's wrong.

Because of the lack of quality teachers at Benjamin Franklin, if Wendy and her classmate were to go to a different high school or to college they would not be prepared academically. Wendy explains why she is ashamed of being a student at Benjamin Franklin:

I think that's a big disappointment for the school and for us to be ranked in a lower class of the Regents. Like there's nobody basically pass Regents in the newspaper and on the news in the newspaper that were low. [We] we're the low[est] I think were the last school on the list to be ranked as low Regents [scores].

Wendy's interview is referring to her high school which was on the three major news networks for having the lowest Regents scores for the Williamsburg School District. She believes that if Benjamin Franklin had a better quality of teaching staff that cared about the students' education, then maybe the high school would not have been ranked low for their Regents scores. This notion also ties into Diane's interview about having teachers who really care about their students and are not just teaching for a paycheck. During my interview with Wendy I also asked her to define what a good teacher is. Wendy states:

Definition of a teacher that teaches takes time out [to] teach the, the kids the lesson and to help them step-by-step. And the definition of a teacher that doesn't teach, teacher that just throws work at you go over it just say they think they going over one time. Not giving no explanation just reading off of something from a piece of paper. Then [the teacher] tell you do it and when you ask a question they don't know their selves and they just tell you, you know leave it alone. Just try your best to do it to the best of your abilities [and] you can't do it if you don't know it.

For Wendy, a good teacher is one who cares about his or her students and makes sure that the students not only can do the lesson, but comprehend what is being taught. A teacher who cannot teach, according to Wendy, is a person who gives the students work, but does not take time to go over the lesson with them. In addition, some of the participants have noted that some teachers are not able to answer students' questions about a lesson, telling them to "just try your best to do it to the best of your abilities [and] you can't do it [the work] if you don't know it." I interpreted this statement to mean that some of the teachers who are not able to explain the lesson to the students encourage them to leave it blank instead of working with them to find out how to complete the work.

Marci and Pam state some of their teachers are not knowledgeable in the subjects that they are teaching, which results in students being schooled and not educated. Wendy's lived reality at Benjamin Franklin is that there are teachers who should not be teaching because students are not learning, which results in failure on the Regents Exams and being on the news as a low achieving high school.

According to Wendy, a good teacher is one that makes sure students comprehend the lessons. However, Wendy has noted that there are some teachers who themselves do not understand the lessons they are teaching and even encourage students to not attempt parts of the assignments they cannot do, to basically leave it blank. Marci, Pam, Diane, and Wendy's narratives clearly show that these Black females are not content with the quality of education that they are receiving from teachers in their high schools, whether attending an urban or suburban high school. Not all of the participants in the study had a negative experience with the teaching staff at their high schools.

However, some of the participants had opposite experiences with their teachers at Thomas Fisher and Benjamin Franklin high schools. Tyra's interview validates she's had good learning experiences with some of her teachers.

GG: Teachers you have now, what is the relationship like with them?
TH: They're, they're okay, I like them. They're like they actually care. They actually make sure you do [the] their work. Make sure you get it done. Don't understand it, explain it, and stuff like that.

GG: What about Mr. Morton? You like his class?
TH: Yeah his class is okay . . . I don't do nothing [anything] in there.
      You just go there to read and write that's it.

Both Tyra and Diane attend Benjamin Franklin, yet each had different experiences with teachers at their high school. According to Tyra, the teachers make sure the students understand what they are learning, and Mr. Morton, Tyra's English teacher, is one example of a good teacher. However, according to Tyra, she does not do any "real work" in his class. Mr. Morton's class is structured in that the vocabulary words for the week are on the board and the students know that at the end of the week they have a test. In addition, the literature assignments are given to the students with the readings required for each marking period. Furthermore, from my observations Mr. Morton does not go over the literature assignments with the students as a class; instead if they have questions about the reading assignments, students meet with Mr. Morton on an individual basis and he helps them with the assignments.

In Mr. Morton's and Mr. Felder's English classes I observed two teachers who really cared about their students getting an education and doing well academically. However, in both of these English classes I observed the students were not being taught learning or knowledge for its own sake, but were being prepared how to specifically take the English Regents Exams in June. In both Mr. Felder's and Mr. Morton's English classes the students were told which books and poems they could use to help with the writing section of the English Regents Exams. Shujaa (1994) states, "Many believed that if we had first-rate facilities/buildings, supplies, environment, teachers and support personnel, a quality education would follow. This is obviously not true. We now understand that there is a profound difference between going to school and being educated" (p. 3). Somewhere during the high school experience students stopped being educated and are now being specifically prepared to take Regents Exams in the major subject areas. This particularly affects mostly Black students in inner city schools.

CONCLUSION

This study examined how Black adolescent females, who are juniors and seniors at Thomas Fisher and Benjamin Franklin high schools, construct their gender and racial identities in an urban and suburban public educational institution. Specifically, the study attempted to understand the culture of Black adolescent females who are attending public high school in the twenty-first century and ascertain how school life affects their gender and racial construction. It has been well documented by feminist scholars (Collins Hill, 2000; Fordham, 1996; hooks, 1984, 1989; Jones &

Gooden, 2003; Proweller, 1998) that Black women are considered the objectified other in comparison to their White female counterparts. Black women have not been attributed the same level of beauty as White females. This negative perception of Black women and adolescents is still apparent in the narrative of the participants of this research.

REFERENCES

Ballantine, J. (1993). *The sociology of education: A systematic analysis.* Englewood Cliffs, New Jersey: Prentice Hall.

Baszile, T. B. (2006). In this place where I don't quite belong: Claiming the Ontoepistemological in-between. In T. R. Berry & N. D. Mizelle (eds.), *From oppression to grace* (pp. 196–208). Sterling, Virginia: Stylus.

Bennett deMarrais, K., & LeCompte, M. (1995). *The way schools work: A sociological analysis of education.* New York: Longman Publishers.

Bogdan, R., & Biklen, S. A. (1982). *Qualitative research for education: An introduction to theory and methods.* Boston: Allyn & Bacon.

Bowles, S., & Ginitis, H. (1976). *Schooling in capitalist America.* New York: Basic Books.

Collins Hill, P. (2000). *Black feminist thought: Knowledge, consciousness, and the politics of empowerment* (2nd ed.). New York: Routledge.

Davidson, A. (1996). *Making and molding identities in schools: Student narratives on race, gender, and academic engagement.* New York: State University of New York Press.

Fordham, S. (1996). *Blacked out: Dilemmas of race, identity, and success at capital high.* Chicago: University of Chicago Press.

Fordham, S. (1997). Those loud Black girls: (Black) women, silence and gender passing in the academy. In M. Seller & L. Weis (eds.), *Beyond Black and White: New faces and voices in U.S. schools* (pp. 81–111). New York: State University of New York Press.

hooks, b. (1984). *Feminist theory: From margin to center.* Boston: South End Press.

hooks, b. (1989). *Talking back: Thinking feminist, thinking Black.* Boston, MA: South End Press.

Jones, C., & Gooden, K. (2003). *Shifting: The double lives of Black women in America.* New York: Harper Collins Publishers.

Jordan, W. D. (1968). *White over Black: American attitudes toward the Negro 1550–1812.* New York: W.W. Norton and Company.

Kozol, J. (1991). *Savage inequalities: Children in America's schools.* New York, NY: Crown Publishers.

Ladson-Billings, G. (1994). *The dreamkeepers: Successful teachers of African American children.* San Francisco: Jossey-Bass Publishers.

Lortie, D. C. (1975). *Schoolteacher: A sociological study.* Chicago: The University of Chicago Press.

Madhububuti, H. R. (1994). Cultural work: Planting new trees with new seeds. In M. Shujaa (ed.), *Too much schooling too little education: A paradox of Black life in White societies* (pp. 1–6). Trenton, New Jersey: Africa World Press Inc.

McRobbie, A. (1978). Working class girls and the culture of femininity. In *Women take issue.* Women's Studies Group. (pp. 96–108). London: Hutchinson.

Mullings, L. (1997). *On our own terms. Race, class, and gender in the lives of African American women.* New York. Routledge.

Parsons, T. (1959). The school class as a social system: Some of its functions in American society. Harvard Educational Review, 29(4), 297–318.

Powell, L. (1997). The achievement (k)not: Whiteness and "black underachievement." In M. Fine, L. Weis, L. Powell, L. Mun Wong (eds.). *Off White: Readings on race, power, and society* (pp. 1–12). New York: Routledge.

Proweller, A. (1998). *Constructing female identities: Meaning making in an upper middle class youth culture.* Albany: State University of New York Press.

Rassiguier, C. (1994). *Becoming women, becoming workers: Identity formation in a French vocational school.* Albany: State University of New York Press.

Shujaa, M. (1994). Education and schooling: You can have one without the other. In M. Shujaa (ed.), *Too much schooling too little education: A paradox of Black life in White societies* (pp. 221–244). Trenton, New Jersey: Africa World Press Inc.

Solomon, P. (1992). *Black resistance in high school: Forging a separatist culture.* Albany: State University of New York Press.

Valli, L. (1988). Gender identity and the technology of office education. In L. Weis (ed.), *Class, race, and gender in American education* (pp. 87–105). New York: State University of New York Press.

Way, N. (1996). Between experiences of betrayal and desire: Close friendships among urban adolescents. In B. J. Leadbeater & N. Way (eds.), *Urban girls: Resisting stereotypes, creating identities* (pp. 173–192). New York: New York University Press.

West, C. (2001). *Race matters.* New York: Vintage Books.

Woodson, C. G. (1990). *The mis-education of the Negro.* Washington, DC: Africa World Press, Inc.

Chapter 17

Suicidality among Gifted African American Females Attending Elite Schools: Impact of Diminished Community Support

Aquilla Frederick

I saw Emma, a tall, slim, and attractive 17-year-old African American girl at our mental health center for a psychiatric evaluation, because of depression and suicidality. Her mother accompanied her. Emma was a senior in high school and was attending a top boarding school. She had a history of chronic sadness, low self-esteem and a preoccupation with thoughts of death since early adolescence. Her mother reported becoming aware of her daughter's depression recently and expressed concerns about Emma's increased emotional distress.

This concern was precipitated by Emma's last suicide gesture two weeks prior to coming for therapy in which her brother witnessed her holding a knife toward her throat. Emma reported that at times the pain became so unbearable that she started keeping a knife under her pillow in case she needed to finally end the pain. Emma also admitted to putting chairs in front of her bedroom door to prevent access two days prior to the first therapy session. Emma's brother acknowledged having awareness of his sister's suicidality to the therapist and their mother for the first time, and shared that he blocked the thoughts because it was painful. Moreover, his decision not to tell their parents earlier was because he did not believe Emma would hurt herself, but he did think she needed help for the depression. Emma's feelings of emptiness on a daily basis caused her to wonder if death was preferable. Emma reported that her first suicidal thought occurred in 7th grade when she considered stabbing herself, and the second one was in 8th grade when she contemplated ingesting household chemicals. She also spoke of feeling unloved (especially by her father) and believed killing herself would not affect her parents. Despite these frequent thoughts of self-destruction over the years, she never shared this with her family, but believed they should have known. This left Emma feeling that she did not matter to anyone. However, Emma's unwillingness to share this information did not negate the fact that she recognized the seriousness of the situation and on her own did obtain limited, intermittent psychotherapy and medication for depression at the boarding school she attended. That being said, Emma expressed having an extremely close bond with her brother.

Allison, a 22-year-old African American female, was referred to our mental health center for follow-up treatment after a serious suicidal attempt resulted in her hospitalization. She attended the initial session alone and I saw her with the staff psychiatrist. Allison was a recent graduate from an elite university and had relocated to New York City for a job. Her daily activities were limited to work and graduate school. She enjoyed writing and spent most of her free time writing about profound despair and loneliness. In addition to feeling unattractive she was having doubts about her ability to establish meaningful relationships with others which precipitated the suicidal gesture in which she took an overdose of sleep medication. Although her depressed mood was known to others, it was treated casually and basically went unnoticed.

Allison grew up with a single parent and had a very strong bond with a maternal aunt. She was identified as intellectually gifted at an early age. The absence of family and community support along with increased job dissatisfaction made her situation extremely high risk. This continuous battle to prove her competency in a nonsupportive work environment led to another serious suicidal attempt. I saw Allison for four months intermittently before this last gesture, and once more the resulting hospitalization and treatment with medication and psychotherapy provided limited improvement.

The similarity in these and other stories of young adolescent females of African descent who made attempts to end their psychological pain by suicide was remarkable to me. These girls were exceptional, extremely intelligent, and attended some of the country's most prestigious private schools and universities. Additionally, many of the families were middle-class, two-parent households with graduate degrees. Another salient factor was that the girls left their communities at early ages to attend predominantly White educational institutions.

Drawing on my work with the above case examples, the focus of this chapter is to explore how factors such as loss of community support, racism and parental challenges can contribute to the depression and suicidal behavior of African-American females attending elite schools.

Thus, my working hypothesis was that leaving home created a sense of disconnection from family and community, and without these systems to offer validation the girl's sense of self eroded over time resulting in feeling inauthentic and doubt about the legitimacy of her intelligence. In addition, certain stresses also interfered with the ability to relax and enjoy the freedom of not always having to strive for perfection.

THE RELEVANCE OF DIMINISHED COMMUNITY SUPPORT

I thought about the relevance of this loss in these two young women's everyday lives and how it might contribute to their profound sense of despair. By looking for similar behavior patterns with these clients and reviewing research, I hoped it would provide answers to other nagging questions I have such as: why would such accomplished and gifted women want to end their lives, and was this a new epidemic among this population?

Moreover, I felt overwhelmed by the number of cases in such a short period of time and its implications, so I reached out to other colleagues about my concerns. At times I was so astounded while listening to these stories that I agonized about what could be causing this level of pain in their lives. I reflected on my own journey leaving my family and community in Georgia to attend school in New York City where I experienced feelings of estrangement and isolation. When I think about the meaning of community, I wonder what influences were present at that time which may have provided me with a sense of psychological protection that may not be present in these girls' lives. My decision to live with my uncle during my freshman year rather than on campus helped me remain connected with supportive family, thus enabling me to diminish the impact of loss of community. Additionally, it enhanced my sense of belonging and personal value, which helped to mitigate my feeling of isolation. My interest in the idea of community as protective and life-sustaining stems from the stories I heard about how my great-grandparents survived slavery as children after their parents were sold to other slave owners. My great-grandparents survived as children because of a caring community that included blood relatives and functional role kinship that offered comfort in times of tremendous loss. I believe that a nurturing community for African Americans has always been very important for one's collective psychological health and well-being.

With respect to these young African American girls, I wondered whether they were emotionally or psychologically equipped to survive in these predominantly White institutions without a constant infusion of community support. If not, I question what they need to prepare themselves for such endeavors other than being intellectually gifted.

SUICIDALITY AMONG AFRICAN AMERICAN FEMALES

The literature review revealed that there is a lack of or very limited writing about suicidal ideation among African American adolescent females. Poussaint and Alexander (2000) argue that there is a greater evidence of reported suicidal attempts among African American females today than in the past. Their study indicates that prior to the 1980s the assumption was that African American teenagers made suicidal attempts at a much lower rate than Whites. However, today it is estimated that 25–40% of college students experience suicidal thinking. Accordingly, Hardy and Laszloffy (2005) report that during the last decade the suicide rate for youth between the ages of 10 and 14 has tripled, college-age self-inflicted harm is the third leading cause of death, and girls make attempts four to eight times more often than boys.

Black Americans downplay outward signs of depression or suicidal thinking and the topic is rarely discussed. Williams (2000) notes that the prevailing attitude is, the less said about suicide publicly, the better for African Americans. Family members can sometimes fail to acknowledge the seriousness of the psychological distress. They have been socialized to disregard depression and self-harming thoughts because of their desire to appear strong and competent. Thus, there is this tendency toward suffering in silence.

It is difficult to know whether the rise in the rate of reported self-harm among African American females in the past 20 years represents a higher incidence of this behavior, or the increased use of mental health services by African American females in recent years.

IMPACT OF RACISM IN THE LIVES OF AFRICAN AMERICAN STUDENTS

Matsuda comments (as cited in Poussaint & Alexander, 2000) that the long-term negative effect of White skepticism about Black performance is viewed as a key detriment to the achievement of many Black students. The belief is that Black students often think there is something wrong with them if they are having difficulties acclimating to life in elite schools. According to Poussaint and Alexander (2000), the psychological residuals of trauma from years of institutional racism and discrimination continue to be evidenced within the lives of the Black privileged class. The psychologist Joy Leary (2005) notes that a lack of confidence in one's own efficacy can hinder the achievement of Black individuals.

hooks (2003) asserts the view that while Black children educated in predominantly White settings are more likely to have a diverse group of friends, they also have greater self-doubt about their self-worth and value. They often enter these settings with fragile self-esteem and the feeling or perception that "you really don't belong." These negative projections on one's self, such as giving up, anger, isolation, and even fear of failure serve to complicate their career aspirations. Tatum (1999) identifies this as the "syndrome of not belonging," stating that the pressures of trying to fit in, conform, or communicate in the acceptable form of the majority culture results in anxiety and interferes with one's natural abilities and modes of expression. hooks (2003) discusses her experience as a professor at some of the nation's top schools where students continue to be viewed as academically inferior. Indirect messages were conveyed by faculty members aimed at humiliating and shaming students, breaking one's spirit. Their self-esteem plummets when they must face the reality that so-called caring White people still harbor racist attitudes regarding Blacks.

NAVIGATING THE RACIAL TERRAIN

According to Cose (1993) Black parents face difficult challenges of attempting to teach their children how to navigate the racial landscape for which they have limited understanding. How can Black parents prepare children for life's reality regarding racism while also preparing them for greater possibilities? He challenges the notion that the children of parents who grew up needing an enormous amount of psychological armor may only require a fraction. Cose refers to middle-class families whose day-to-day experience is residual racism that can be subtle, yet pervasive. Cose's talk of armor here is part of the burden Blacks carry to protect themselves against racial stresses. He posits that for millions of Blacks who won educational victories during the civil rights movement there is diminished optimism, in that traditional coping strategies have become less effective as a source of support. That is, we are no longer able to rely on the larger community of African Americans as a means of softening life's struggles, especially those arising from racism and discrimination. Hence, rather than a sense of shared community and common purpose, which once characterized Black neighborhoods, it is now growing Black isolation.

Blacks endured centuries of cruelties during slavery and the Jim Crow era and managed to avoid self-destructive behavior. Moreover, hooks (1993) writes that when Blacks lived in the Jim Crow years, within their own neighborhoods, schools, churches, and larger communities, they were much more vigilant in the midst of racism. She also raises the question as to whether an element within forced segregation encouraged Blacks to withstand psychological, emotional, and physical hardships to defy any suicidal impulses they may have experienced. Unfortunately, very little has been done to address this question in mainstream media.

INTEGRATING COMMUNITY AS TREATMENT STRATEGY

Emma's family agreed to meet for individual and family sessions on a weekly basis. During this initial process I inquired about the family history. In each case I was curious about their experiences as it related to their loss of a supportive community, the impact on their sense of self-worth in the school environment, and how this contributed to suicidal thinking. My first step in creating a sense of community was to elicit the family's support in establishing a safety plan to ensure Emma's protection. They agreed to monitor her behavior, making sure that all weapons were removed from the home immediately. Additionally, the family would call 911 if she exhibited any imminent danger to self.

Shortly after starting therapy Emma was accepted to a top Ivy League university on a full academic scholarship. After relocating she continued to be plagued by recurring depressive episodes with intermittent suicidal thoughts and chronic insomnia, despite her academic success. As I continued to expand my thoughts with this case, I wondered whether because her sense of self was that of an intellectually gifted person, this became her primary sense of identity. Although Emma could no longer attend sessions I agreed to continue with telephone contact. During a telephone conversation with Emma she shared an incident that triggered another depressive episode. During her second semester she was accepted into an honors class with all White male students. Her White male professor asked why she had taken the class and questioned her qualifications. This occurred in the presence of peers and she was shamed and humiliated. This contributed to Emma feeling tremendous self-doubt regarding her intellectual competency in the class.

I believe a continuous onslaught of psychological devaluation can cause erosion to one's sense of self. The hostile nature of this type of environment is one in which both verbal and nonverbal assumptions are made about how students enter the university. The racial climate was described as tense inside and outside classrooms. There is also this feeling of invisibility, the sense of being viewed as qualified only by affirmative action, devoid of one's intellectual merit. Also, the ongoing negative interaction with faculty instilled a sense of self-doubt. Anderson (2012, October 21) describes how students attending private schools in New York City described a type of racism that materializes itself not in insults, but in polite indifference, silence, and segregation. One of the students reported that "You can do a lot of psychological damage to people by ignoring them for an extended period." Another student at a different high school was told that it was "the result of affirmative action" that she could attend the school. Today this student still experiences similar negative sentiments toward herself regarding the perception.

Emma's sense of self became so fragile that, although dropping out of school was not a viable option, it became a brief consideration. Moreover, her unwillingness to share these struggles with her immediate family contributed to heightened feelings of lack of support. Despite this new crisis she was not in any imminent risk of self-harm, which was a hopeful sign. At this juncture I felt an urgency to try to encourage her to get some other support system in place on campus. I inquired about other friends of color, organizations that may provide supportive space, and counseling services where she could talk about her concerns, and she said that students did not talk to each other about these types of problems.

When I asked about talking to her immediate family she refused to burden her family because they would view her as being weak. Anson (1987) in his work *Best Intentions: The Education and Killing of Edmund Perry* indicates that at these elite boarding schools students are caught in a system where everyone thinks you should be happy, including parents. Instead they find there are tears because you are not happy. Moreover, Anson (1987) states that the idea is that you are not supposed to have problems; if so, you don't talk about them. In fact there is a double message: I want you to talk to me about what is going on, while the other is, don't tell me anything that will freak me out. Your feeling is that every nuisance is viewed by a Black student as hostile, so you have the sense of constantly being examined.

In this case my hope was that my remaining accessible to Emma as a resource during this period would lend an element of support. Hence, she agreed to re-engage in psychotherapy treatment and resume medication management on campus, along with engaging in more social activities with students of color. She excelled in her studies and the following semester was accepted as a special scholar to participate in developing new infrastructures in an underdeveloped country.

I recognized that working with these young women without the eyes and ears and emotional connection of a supportive community rendered the therapist somewhat impotent. This was especially true in Allison's case. Despite my efforts to establish a safety plan, her ability to engage in self-regulating behavior during crisis moments without the involvement of others was ineffective. I concluded that trying to work with Allison and keep her safe was impossible to do alone. So after this latest incident my goal was to find a way to reconnect Allison with family support.

After her discharge from the hospital I discussed these thoughts with her, and suggested that the best course of treatment would be for her to return home to her family and continue with psychotherapy and medication. We also talked about what I could disclose to her family at this time. She agreed that I could contact them, but she would share with them later about the details. Allison's family was contacted in her presence and I discussed my thinking about the importance of her reconnecting with a supportive family and community to regain her strength and help reduce symptoms. The family agreed to the plan, and discharge arrangements were made for Allison to return home. Later follow-up revealed that Allison continued with psychotherapy and had not made any further suicidal attempts. After a year of being back home Allison reported that she had entered a PhD program with a total remission of symptoms.

In these cases the idea of reconnecting one to family and community or providing accessibility as a source of support for healing is, however, in the rudimentary stage, but I would cautiously conclude that there is evidence to suggest here that returning to a nurturing and supportive community helps to reduce symptomology and provides a protective mechanism against suicidality. This may affirm that strong enough positive influences can moderate negative effects. hooks (2001) points out that racism could have made life for African Americans intolerable but our communities sustained us. By talking to one another about the pain, Blacks created a shared community of care and support. One remedy for healing offered by hooks (2003) is that if you wake up and find yourself living someplace where there is no one you love and trust, no community, it is time to leave town—to pack up and go immediately—to a place where there are arms that will hold you and not let go.

SUMMARY

In conclusion, the aforementioned anecdotes introduce a unique way to think about family therapy treatment for suicidal African American females attending elite schools and the impact of diminished community support. I am incorporating ideas from a social justice lens by integrating the intergenerational legacy of slavery and coping strategies with that of family and community support systems. My conclusion is that African American communities that help decrease individual loneliness and isolation allow one to tolerate, survive in, and manage the alienation of non-supportive, racist environments and serve as a protection against suicide. In regard to continued racism in predominantly White institutions, the experience of "not belonging" for African American students is subtle but pervasive. Thus, in considering these challenges it may require parents to be more diligent in preparing their children with necessary armor to navigate these racist terrains. First, parents must recognize signs of psychological distress with these adolescents, and seek mental health support. Second, parents should maintain frequent communication to enhance their sense of connectedness and belonging even if this might be viewed as invasive, and encourage the formation of supportive spaces with others. Third, parents need to willingly engage in regular, open discussion regarding experiences of racism and discrimination in these White educational institutions. Fourth, it is important that parents and students have an awareness of race-related stressors at these schools, so I recommend reading *Best Intentions: The Education and Killing of Edmund Perry* by Robert Anson. There is a strong need for more insightful information that would help in understanding suicidality among this population.

REFERENCES

Anderson, J. (2012, October 21). Admitted, but Left Out: Minority students at New York City's top private schools say they are confronted by a racial and economic divide that manifests itself as indifference and social segregation. *New York Times* (Metropolitan: pp. 1, 6).

Anson, R. S. *Best Intentions: The Education and Killing of Edmund Perry.* New York: Random House, 1987.

Cose, E. (1993). *Rage of a Privileged Class: Why are middle-class Blacks angry? Why should America care?* New York, NY: Harper Perennial.

Hardy, K.V., & Laszloffy, T. A. (2005). *Teens Who Hurt: Clinical Interventions to Break the Cycle of Adolescent Violence.* New York, NY: The Guilford Press.

hooks, b. (1993). *Sisters of the Yam: Black Women and Self-Recovery.* Boston, MA: South End Press.

hooks, b. (2001). *Salvation: Black People and Love.* New York, NY: HarperCollins.

hooks, b. (2003). *Rock My Soul: Black People and Self-Esteem.* New York, NY: Atria Books.

Leary, J. (2005). *Post Traumatic Slavery Syndrome: America's Legacy of Enduring Injury and Healing.* Milwaukie, OR: Uptone Press.

Matsuda, M. Remarks made at the TransAfrican Forum, January 11, 2000, Washington, D.C. (the long-term negative influence of White skepticism about Black performance was cited as being a key detriment to the achievement of many Black students).

Poussaint, A. F., & Alexander, A. (2000). *Lay My Burden Down: Understanding Suicide and the Mental Health Crisis among African Americans.* Boston, MA: Beacon Press.

Tatum, B. D. (1999). *Assimilation Blues: Black Families in White Communities: Who Succeeds and Why.* New York, NY: Basic Books.

Williams, T. M. (2000). *Black Pain: It Just Looks Like We're Not Hurting.* New York, NY: Scribner.

Chapter 18

Sex Trafficking and Black Girls: Breaking the Code of Silence in Schools and in Our Community

Virginia A. Batchelor and Illana R. Lane

INTRODUCTION

The story of a very courageous young woman appeared on the front page of *USA Today*. She revealed to the world that at the age of sixteen she was homeless and that a sex trafficker in America had violated her human rights. Her story should outrage all who read it. She, like so many others, found herself victimized over and over by the traffickers. This young girl's life was transformed into one of despair. Her dreams were deferred for someone else's economic gain, because human commodities are more valuable than a snort of coke or a shot of heroin.

The judicial system, educational systems, family, and faith-based institutions are not as aware or knowledgeable as they should be of the underpinnings that support the growth of sex trafficking as a viable industry. To make matters worse, victims and survivors have experienced exploitation by family and alienation by faith-based communities, relationships that are supposed to provide solace and acceptance.

Sex trafficking is an ideal business for opportunistic predators because it has proven to be a safe avenue for them to dodge stiff sentencing or punishment at all (Batchelor & Lane, 2013; Kortla, 2010; Brewer, 2008). The sale of a woman or a girl is less likely to get the seller in trouble than the sale of guns. Sex traffickers profit in all ways because, unlike drugs, people are a "renewable commodity" and low maintenance. For victims, however, it can be a life sentence because most often, they are criminalized rather than rescued and they are stigmatized by derogatory terms that reference them as prostitutes and sexually indiscriminate. Although their human rights were stolen, more often than not, the justice system seals their criminalization with a list of offenses (i.e., a criminal record) that keeps them from being able to start their lives over in a manner which they deserve (e.g., legitimate employment or as a college student). All in all, victims are punished for unlawful acts committed as a result of fraud, and/or being forced and coerced by human sex traffickers.

Domestic children who are trafficked usually end up in juvenile detention facilities rather than protective services. Therefore, it is reasonable to conclude that children, not properly identified as victims, are failed by a system that should protect them and thus are subjected to violent and exploitive situations (U.S. Department of State: Diplomacy in Action, 2013).

The principal purpose of this chapter is to build educational awareness of domestic minor sex trafficking that occurs among African American girls. This is an issue that is not addressed in schools and among circles that might aid in education, advocacy, and intervention for victims of domestic minor sex trafficking.

THE TRUTH ABOUT HUMAN SEX TRAFFICKING

General Overview

The face of human sex trafficking is perceived to be individuals who are not citizens of the United States or migrant workers (U.S. Department of State, 2013). The truth about human sex trafficking is that it is a global issue and the number of cases that occur in the United States is staggering. In North America, 15 hubs of sex trafficking were identified (Girls for Sale Map, 2011) (see Table 18.1).

According to Chuang (2006), eighty percent of all trafficked persons are female. Up to 50% are minors, and the majority is trafficked into commercial sexual exploitation or slave labor (Zdrojewski, 2008). Although sex trafficking is not limited to women, reportedly, mostly women are coerced into the commercial sex industry. Additionally, it is important to note that minor children are greatly targeted by opportunistic predators.

Sex trafficking victims are more likely to be African American. According to Emery, Heffron, and Moore (2012), 26% of the victims of sex trafficking are Whites, while 40% are most likely to be African Americans,

Table 18.1.

North American City	Statistics/facts as to why these cities are susceptible hubs
Phoenix, Arizona	Average age of girls trafficked: 14.8 136 children arrested in 2010 for prostitution
Los Angeles, California	One of the top three trafficking entry points 80% of victims are women and girls 10,000 women sexually exploited
San Francisco, California	Commercial center and industrial port Over 80% of victims women and girls 27% of victims under 18 and 67% of victims under 24
Portland, Oregon	Ranks second in child sex trafficking Large number of homeless teen runaways—high risk exploitation and near major highway
Chicago, Illinois	5th in trafficked women in U.S. 62% of the women were in sex trade prior to 18 Connects to east coast and midwest and has a large airport
Toledo, Ohio	Top city for recruiting children for sex trafficking Near several major national highways and growth of immigrant population 300 girls between 10–17 identified as sex trafficking victims
New York, New York	3,500 underage girls in the sex trade 12 years is average age of entry to prostitution JFK International Airport top hub for international human trafficking Adult ads and community newspapers Ads generate 35% of community newspaper revenue
Atlanta, Georgia	Over 500 underage girls sexually trafficked each month 100–150 girls raped for profit each weekend 14 years is average age of sexually exploited teen Within 7 years young girls die of STDs or are murdered
Miami, Florida	10,000 prostitutes and underage girls in city for Super Bowl Super Bowl special ad on Craigslist advertised sex with 14-year-old-girl
Vancouver, Canada	Lax immigration laws and close proximity to the U.S. border Large sporting events lead to short-term increase in prostitution & traffickers
Las Vegas, Nevada	Girls 10 years old are forced into prostitution and the younger the child, the more profitable the trade 5,122 victims of domestic minor sex trafficking between 1994 and 2007 400 victims discovered in May 2007

(continued)

Table 18.1. (continued)

North American City	Statistics/facts as to why these cities are susceptible hubs
New Orleans, Louisiana	100 underage sex trafficking victims in Baton Rouge in 2006 57% of shelter visitors were victims of sexual abuse 35 cases of parents directly prostituting their own children
Mexico City, Mexico	2nd busiest airport in Latin America, and organ trafficking Pick up homeless children, take to hospital, traffic organs, and leave them for dead
Tijuana, Mexico	Close proximity to U.S. border High number of sex industry business owners
Houston, Texas	Leading trafficking site in the U.S. Tolerate commercial sex industry and near major highways and large international airport In 2006 had more sex-oriented businesses than any other U.S. city ¼ of all trafficking victims end up in Texas

Girls for Sale Map (2011). Retrieved from https://maps.google.co.nz/maps/ms?ie=UTF8&hl=en&msa=0&msid=200273141589609424876.0004938160154f2e4a0c8&ll=34.322967,-98.571396&spn=29.774906,49.12674&source=embed

and more than half (62%) of confirmed sex trafficking suspects are African American. Estimations of women and children that are trafficked into the United States for sexual exploitation range between 45,000 and 50,000 a year (Rieger, 2007). More recent data report that 100,000 and 300,000 children are trafficked in the United States (Emery, Heffron & Moore, 2012).

According to Finklea, Fernandes-Alcantara, and Siskin (2011), a number of sex trafficking crimes in the United States have been identified; however, the number of unidentified crimes and the nature of the occurrences of human sex trafficking are not available. Ninety-four percent of victims are female and 13% of the "confirmed" sex trafficking victims are 25 or older (Emery, Heffron & Moore, 2012). Eighty-one percent of sex trafficking suspects are male while 19% of confirmed sex trafficking suspects are female. The statistics are representative of the government's best estimate (Larsen, 2011).

As of late, the severity of sex trafficking crimes against U.S. citizens has been at the center of discussion in the media. Billboards and news stories alert the community at large that human sex trafficking is an epidemic that is spreading. Domestic minor sex trafficking on average affects children as early as 12 years of age (U.S. Department of Education office of Safe and Drug-Free Schools in Washington, DC, 2007). However, according to the information obtained by interviewing individuals from different professional paths, law enforcement, and social work, there is no average age. Victims are as young as two years; the oldest, age 62 (Batchelor & Lane, 2013).

Instances of domestic minor sex trafficking (DMST) of children world-wide and in the United States are on the rise (Batchelor & Lane, 2013; Hodge, 2008). Reportedly, 800,000 minor children are unaccounted for; and of a great urgency is that 33% of that number in 2008 were African American, and 60 percent of those missing Black children were female and between 13 and 15 years of age (Gordon, 2006; Tillet, 2010). The statistics are alarmingly high and yet unawareness of this issue is even higher. In one respect, individuals who are 18 years of age are not considered to be minors (Laczko & Danailova-Trainor, 2009). Therefore, women whose trafficking experiences began as minors, but were not identified until they became adults, are often perceived as prostitutes rather than victims.

Sex trafficking as defined by the United Nations (2000) Protocol to Prevent, Suppress and Punish Trafficking in Persons, Especially Women and Children, Supplementing the UN Convention against Transnational Organized Crime is:

> The recruitment, transportation, transfer, harboring or receipt of persons, by means of threat or use of force or other forms of coercion, of abduction, of fraud, of deception, of the abuse of power or of a position of vulnerability, or of the giving of payments or benefits to achieve the consent of a person having control over another person, for the purpose of exploitation. This definition of trafficking consists of three core elements: 1) the action of trafficking which means the recruitment, transportation, transfer, harboring or receipt of persons; 2) the means of trafficking which includes the threat of or use of force, deception, coercion, abuse of power or position of vulnerability; and 3) the purpose of trafficking which is always exploitation. In the words of the Trafficking Protocol, article 3, exploitation shall include, at a minimum, the exploitation of the prostitution of others or other forms of sexual exploitation, forced labor or services, slavery or practices similar to slavery, servitude or removal of organs. (United Nations Office on Drugs and Crimes [UNODC], 2004, p. 42; United Nations Global Initiative to Fight Human Trafficking [UNGIFT], 2008, n.p.)

It is important to understand that human sex trafficking is not prostitution. However, as noted by Kortla (2010), sex trafficking is also inclusive of prostitution because some individuals are forced into participating in survival sex (e.g., pornography, stripping, and escort services).

BLACK GIRLS AND COMMERCIALISM

The African American community is no stranger to the history of slavery in America. Harriet Ross Tubman shepherded many enslaved people of African descent north to Canada to reclaim their lives. However, our communities are blinded to the fact that human sex trafficking, also referred to as modern slavery, is disrupting the lives of Black girls.

According to the State Department 2013 Trafficking in Persons Report, approximately 47,000 victims were brought to light in the last year, compared to up to 27 million people living in slavery. This massive gap represents millions who toil unseen and beyond the reach of law (U.S. Department of State, 2013). Additionally, this gap represents unidentified victims who stand before the law but are placed right back into the way of opportunistic predators. Finally, it shows how far we have to go in this effort to mitigate modern-day slavery in the United States.

In the wake of the growing numbers of missing children, little attention is focused upon the increasing numbers of young Black girls being kidnapped and sold into sexual slavery. Black girls are prime targets of sex trafficking. The unprecedented number of African American girls who disappear from their classrooms, communities, and churches, only to end up exploited, remains uncounted because Black children are seldom considered high-profile cases (Gordon, 2006; Tillet, 2010). They are often presumed to be just a "runaway" rather than missing due to misperceptions that paint negative images of them. Naomi, a former victim and now prevention educator, spoke to this concern regarding African American girls. The Amber Alert has been reported to be reserved for White girls whereas Black girls are presumed to be runaways. Most cases involving Black children are not newsworthy. As for those rare exceptions, the Rowan Towers incident and the Shaniya Davis case are examples that have made high-profile status. In the case of Rowan Towers, the defendant pleaded guilty to child endangerment for the rape of a 15-year-old girl. He was sentenced to probation and the charges for aggravated sexual assault and statutory rape were dropped (Coryell, 2011). Shaniya Davis who was trafficked by her mother to settle a drug debt died at age five (Tillet, 2010; Netter, 2009; Saar, 2009).

Five-year-old Shaniya Davis's violent death sparked awareness of sex trafficking crimes that plague the Black community (Desmond-Harris, 2013). Malika Saada Saar states, "People sold for sex in this country are American children who are disproportionately black and brown. They are between the ages of 12 and 13—middle school aged" (as cited in Desmond-Harris, 2013, n.p.). Malika Saada Saar, one of the founders of the Rebecca Project for Justice, an agency that raises awareness of and opposes human rights violations in Africa and the United States, spearheaded an initiative that resulted in shutting down Craigslist ads that market children (Desmond-Harris, 2013). Since this only shut down some of the ads, the fight against the business enterprise of sex trafficking continues.

Herbert (2006) informed his readership that Atlanta, Georgia (a city with a large Black population) had become a place that provided lucrative opportunities for sex traffickers to grow their business. The misidentification of Black girls by, for example, the judicial system supports an underlying structure that is an aggressive business enterprise and like pandemic flu continues to enslave them. Thus, the people who are supposed to protect them are partnering with the people persecuting them. Some girls have reported they are bailed out by their pimps and forced back into the streets.

Moreover, since human sex trafficking is regarded as a criminal offense, victims are prosecuted, rather than provided an avenue for escape. They are forced to endure it and forced to observe people whom they befriended on the track endure violence. To be abandoned by people who can make a difference strengthens the stronghold of the traffickers, pimps, sellers, and buyer. Non-supported victims continue their silence, the cycle of violence is maintained, and recruitment continues. Said best by Zdrojewski (2008), "The invisibility of the crime is easily maintained since victims rarely denounce their traffickers out of fear, and furthermore lack the power to pressure public authorities to take action" (p. 19).

Moreover, victims are controlled by drugs and emotional and physical violence. As previously stated, the lack of awareness as well as the severity of human sex trafficking in the United States, and especially as it relates to the state of affairs centering on children, only supports the stability of the commercial sex industry. Throughout the literature, the numbers of sex trafficking cases change dramatically because this crime is not easily tracked and the victims, in most cases, are considered the criminal. Therefore it is important to understand what sex trafficking is because of the number of mistrials concerning cases of human sex trafficking and/or cases that never make it to court because victims are afraid to come forward. For these reasons this problem is not as transparent as some people would like to believe.

METHODOLOGY AND INTRODUCTION OF THE PARTICIPANTS

According to Biernacki and Waldorf (1981), a snowball sampling method or chain referral sampling proves best suited when the focus of the study is a sensitive matter. This research method is designed with the sole purpose of acquiring an insider perspective while ensuring the safety of the respondents. In-depth interviews were made possible by the assistance of people who were considered by survivors to be insiders and trustworthy. In this respect, the insider provided prospective respondents with information regarding the study. The prospective respondent then made initial contact to set up a date and time to meet based upon the established level of comfort. As with all studies, participants may choose not to participate at any time. Six women participated in the study providing a personal account as social workers, law enforcement professionals, and other professionals who were once victims, and thus providing a deeper understanding of human sex trafficking. Further, these survivors are now working as anti–human trafficking professionals and are providing services to rescue and support other victims.

Faith, an African American social worker, has been an active participant in building awareness of human sex trafficking by profession. She works at a child advocacy center (CAC), is a forensic interviewer, and assists with policies and procedures. She operates in a managerial role. She also works with legislating bodies to pass the asset forfeiture bill.

Hope is Latina and bilingual. She has over 30 years of experience in law enforcement. As a deputy sheriff, she serves as the Director of the Human Trafficking Task Force and Alliance. She provides training for law enforcement professionals as well as communities, educational entities, and service providers. She also collects data for the entire task force. As a researcher, she works in partnership with Northwestern University, which provides all of the tabulations of trafficking scores for task forces throughout the nation.

Keturah, an African American woman, has been working informally in the area of anti–human trafficking since 1998 and formally since March of 2008. She has performed extensive work with at-risk populations. Keturah also holds a degree in Urban Ministry. She is with the Department of Homeland Security. Most of her work has been on the policy or programmatic level. In both areas, she is involved in training and development and issues of policy and programs.

Keturah is involved at a governmental level with the advisory council on faith-based and neighborhood partnerships. She has supported recommendations put forth by the advisory council and partnerships regarding any specific need as it relates to human trafficking and also to those working in the field. Keturah is actively leading, organizing, and developing curriculum for clergy across faith traditions and in particular for those who are disproportionately being victimized that include both ethnic and cultural communities and also religious minority communities.

Ruth is an outreach director of an internationally known organization located in the southeastern part of the United States. Like Faith, she is also a social worker. Ruth's work as a graduate student involved outreach and awareness pieces to educate the community on gender-based violence issues. She writes prevention education programs and provides educational services for at-risk populations. Ruth's outward appearance serves to broaden the perspectives of the members of the community regarding human sex trafficking because she is young, White, and very aware and knowledgeable of the issues centering on human sex trafficking.

Esther is an African American who as a young girl was groomed and coerced into the sex industry at age 12 by her military father. Her immediate family consisted of a mother, father, and two sisters. She lived with her two sisters for the first 12 years of her life. Her mother endured abuse by her father because Esther was believed not to be his child. The truth of her birth was revealed to her by her maternal aunt. Her aunt explained that her uncle was her biological father and that her cousins were her siblings. Her mother did not protect her but rather became a co-conspirator in the abuse directed toward her. Her sisters, like her birth mother, entered into the cycle of abuse and carried out the cruelty. She is no longer in contact with them because the situation was life-threatening.

Esther, once survivor, now victor, soldier, and modern-day abolitionist, has since founded her own organization. She is humble, and while she is the president of her organization, she refers to herself as a "sister in the cycle." The cycle of which she speaks is her work which involves rescuing young women, girls, and young boys. She and her team first rescued about 68 girls and 6 boys. She explained that raising money to take care of those she's rescued and for those she has yet to rescue is central to survivors' restoration. She considers herself a chief fundraiser and advocate rather than a president and CEO.

Naomi, abused by sex traffickers and society, now helps to save the innocence of other children, young women, girls, and boys as a Prevention Education Coordinator for an organization in the southeastern part of the United States. She is also a Correction Education Coordinator. As a survivor advocate, she: 1) handles the media relations work; 2) educates the community about human sex trafficking; 3) attends meetings at the White House; and 4) meets with members of Congress and large major interest groups such as state delegates to make sure that legislation gets passed to help victims.

These women fight against human sex trafficking from different vantage points. Furthermore, they provide more insight about this widespread issue from different vantage points. As stated by Naomi, it is difficult to eradicate the problem if the problem is not understood to be a problem. Together, these women provide information that is not readily available in books. All of these women are involved in writing curriculum, outreach, policy, and programming. Since the first examination of domestic minor sex trafficking, the prevalence of services has improved, however not nearly as much as it is needed.

DECONSTRUCTING THE "FAST TAILED GIRL" AND THE HAPPY HOOKER

Stereotypes of Black girls such as the "fast tailed girl" or the "happy hooker" have led some people to believe that Black girls are promiscuous and hypersexual. This myth is not only mentally and emotionally abusive, it gives predators a pass to prey upon and victimize Black women, girls, and children for their economic gain. Meanwhile, according to Kendall and Golden (2013), Black girls are referred to as "fast tailed" by people who are close and influential in their lives. Some of these circles of oppression are governed by their own mothers and the mothers of the churches within the Black community, abusive Black men and by some Black male leaders who dare not address it; and through societal influences (i.e., schools, media). In other words, negative notions of Black womanhood place Black girls and women at risk to be mistreated and harmed while abusers receive support and protection for their wrongdoing.

Frundt (n.d.) cautions us not to judge and turn away from the young girl on the corner who is covering up a baby face with makeup so thick that one cannot see the physical and mental abuse, and the power of the pimp who has her so scared for her life and others that she feels compelled to protect. With respect to attitudes about Black girls, Esther (Founding President & Victor) described how her "fast tailed" image was shaped by members in her household. She responded:

> My pimp was my father in that household. It wasn't someone living outside that lured me away. He was doing that. He had systematically broke down all of my barriers that would tell me what was right and wrong and made me feel as if I was nothing, not even worthy of being thrown away. He did that systematically every day of my life. My mother supported that behavior, became his bottom: calling me a whore and a bitch.

Frundt (n.d.) is an African American who wrote about her experience as a victim of sex trafficking. She lived in approximately 20 foster homes before she was adopted at age 12 by individuals she described as loving parents. Frundt does not allude to any abuse; defying them and finding her own identity was her top priority. She explained that she was insecure and vulnerable and thus ran away from home to be with an older man (grooming her with attention and gifts), ten years her senior. (Grooming is a long process used to draw victims to gain their trust and dependency.) At 14 she was forced into the sex trade by a "nice" guy who drove her to school and forced her to service 18 men a day (Free the Slaves, 2010).

Although Esther (Founding President & Victor) lived in places around the world, it did not free her from the stereotypes that shape Black womanhood; nor did it free her from the violence of sex trafficking. She expressed:

> I don't know how many junior high and high schools I was in because at twelve years old, my mother put me out and I became homeless and abandoned. I had just been beaten very badly by my mother's

husband. He beat me like he was beating a man. That last punch to my face had me go down about 13 steps. After the last slurs, you're a bitch, and you're a whore, and you're not my daughter anyway, get out my house . . . I was able to get to a neighbor's home. She let me in because there's a screaming 12-year-old at your door banging. We called the military police and they came and took me to the hospital. I remembered being examined and the discussion about my injuries. They asked my mother if she would like to press charges against the man who had just beaten me, her husband, and she replied no.

The "fast tailed" stereotype generates a negative attitude that leads people who may be able to intervene to take a position that Black girls, as minors, are asking for sexual advances or choose to be sex workers. It is important to deconstruct the "fast tailed" stereotype because it silences Black girls, which further empowers predators. Their silence is controlled by both predators and by people who might be of assistance to them because they do not want to be blamed for what predators should be made accountable. From the experience of the victim, it is as though it is legal for predators to steal the human rights of their victims.

BLACK GIRLS AND SCHOOLING EXPERIENCES

Negative images consistently haunt Black women and girls and as well shape their experiences in every aspect of their lives. That is, "the fast tailed girl asks for trouble and deserves the trouble that follows the asking." As an illustration, Esther (Founding President & Victor) spoke to us regarding her schooling experiences. She explained that she did not receive any help from anyone at school even though the bruises were visible.

My school was predominately White. They just looked at me as "just" another brown girl or Black girl, and could really care less. So they ignored all of the signs; and even when I just went to them and said look at me . . . this is happening, they turned and went away.

Naomi (Prevention Educator & Victor) reported having attended schools in about 6 different states and dropping out in her sophomore year because she was trafficked. In the end she received a GED. She spoke mostly of the girls she met as a high school student and while being trafficked. Naomi had this to say:

I learned that the majority of the young girls that I worked with were in my high school. One out of every 3 in my high school were trafficked. One out of 3 girls are either approached by a trafficker or trafficked; that's a large number. With all my friends, going to the track it was like going to a high school reunion. I had 2 cousins who were already involved in the lifestyle.

Further, Naomi spoke of the large numbers of girls who are and were trafficked out of high school. Her experiences indicate that principals, teachers, and other school personnel are either unaware or turn a blind eye to girls who are victims and potential recruits of sex trafficking. Dressed for work in attire that did not resemble what one wears for legitimate work or for a job interview, Naomi explained:

I eventually just stopped going because I was too tired because I worked 'til 7:30 a.m. and then I had to leave school by noon because of afternoon lunch rush (to service men).

IDENTIFICATION AND ADVOCACY

Innocent Black girls are disappearing from school sites, from other children's homes, and sometimes from their own homes, ending up in the sexual economy, never to be found. For effective advocacy, it is important to educate school administrators, teachers, students, parents, the community, and the faith-based community.

Identifying Victims at School

Victim identification is critical and is the first step in stopping human sex trafficking. The U.S. Department of Education Office of Safe and Drug-Free Schools (2007) provides a list of signs and behaviors that are exhibited by victims. Although the list is not comprehensive and not all young girls are victims based upon what is listed, it is especially important to use as a guide. For suspected victims, it is important to seek professionals such as counselors or social workers who can make determinations and devise an appropriate plan of action. A victim:

- Has unexplained absences from school for a period of time, and is therefore a truant
- Demonstrates an inability to attend school on a regular basis
- Chronically runs away from home (Not all minors who run away are abused. However, in some cases minors run away to protect themselves because they view living on the streets as safer than staying at home (Hyde, 2005; Martinez, 2006))
- Makes references to frequent travel to other cities
- Exhibits bruises or other physical trauma, withdrawn behavior, depression, or fear

- Lacks control over her or his schedule or identification documents
- Is hungry, malnourished, or inappropriately dressed (based on weather conditions or surroundings)
- Shows signs of drug addiction

Additional signs that may indicate sex-related trafficking include:

- Demonstrates a sudden change in attire, behavior, or material possessions (e.g., has expensive items)
- Makes references to sexual situations that are beyond age-specific norms
- Has a "boyfriend" who is noticeably older (10+ years)
- Makes references to terminology of the commercial sex industry that is beyond age-specific norms; engages in promiscuous behavior and may be labeled "fast" by peers (U.S. Department of Education Office of Safe and Drug-Free Schools, 2007, n.p.)

Prevention

Education and safety measures to prevent and intervene in issues of sex trafficking can prove costly for buyers and sellers. At risk for sellers is the potential to lose a tremendous amount of capital gains and the means to continue to grow their businesses. At risk for buyers is the ability to purchase sex. The ultimate concern is the threat of compromising the freedom of survivors and the stigma of their being associated with sex crimes.

Minors do not choose prostitution. However, U.S. culture supports the victimization of minors. The entertainment industry is notorious for normalizing false images of Black womanhood. Offensive language that refers to Black women and girls as bitches and hoes breeds brutality. Putting an end to human sex trafficking involves understanding the grooming process that leads to misperceptions of victims. Trafficking victims are viewed by society as perpetuators and contributors to their own demise. The cycle of violence which they endure is part of their grooming to become recruiters. The victims of sex trafficking are forced to recruit others by necessity (i.e., for survival). Therefore it is important to understand the mental state of victims. Naomi (Prevention Educator & Victor) explained that the "bottom girl" is directly below the pimp and has to recruit. If she doesn't, she is in danger of being killed.

Education Is Instrumental: Knowledge Is Power

Providing education to the community, schools, and faith-based communities about a serious issue that has grave consequences for Black girls is an important step toward saving our girls. In consultation with Keturah regarding her work with human trafficking cases, she reported that African American, African, Latino, and Asian communities are highly impacted by human sex traffickers. Keturah (Anti–Human Trafficking Worker) explained that in her work, she targets and develops curriculum to talk to faith-based communities. These persons may or may not attend a congregation or house of worship. Within the African American, African, Latino, and Asian communities some have said approximately 77% who are victimized in the United States are of ethnic and cultural minority groups, but oftentimes they are not in the forefront of dealing with these issues.

Education and training provided by government agencies, educational institutions, and churches is essential. Keturah is involved with curriculum development and training that is taking place within the faith-based community. Hope (Deputy Sheriff) is very active in promoting education for judges who try cases for domestic minor sex trafficking. The decisions they make can either help to mitigate the problem or to stabilize the commercial sex industry. She states that it's a felony to sell a person, but rarely do judges charge accordingly. It's important that judges receive the same amount of training as law enforcement.

All of the women are involved in education and training. Faith (Social Worker) trains personnel of the Department of Juvenile Services. Naomi (Prevention Educator & Victor) is involved in training pre-service teachers. Ruth (Social Worker) teaches a four-part curriculum that was developed in 2007. She covers what human trafficking is and the glorification of pimp culture; and finally Esther (Founding President & Victor) conducts training for classroom teachers. Although more people are involved in the fight for human rights for victims of human sex trafficking, the occurrences are not lessening. Predators are getting smarter and engaging in new and innovative ways to protect this enterprise.

CONCLUSION

Human sex trafficking is a domestic issue and should be addressed as such. Additionally, this issue must be addressed in schools and the Black community at large. There is momentum to save women and girls around the world; however for Black girls in the United States, it is not to the same degree. The impact upon Black girls is immeasurable. In order to effectively advocate for victims, education and training on governmental levels, state and communitywide, is the best defense toward eradicating growing networks of predators.

According to Zdrojewski (2008) human sex trafficking is only just beginning to be looked at through a human rights framework rather than as an industry that individuals enter into voluntarily. She argues that it is essential that states first address the trafficking problem as an internal human rights issue that affects its political, social, and economic systems. There must be a concerted effort to save Black girls who are U.S. citizens. In 2008, Zdrojewski argued the urgency for states to recognize the domestic manifestations of human sex trafficking. Although there are policies in place that address human sex trafficking, the U.S. government must bear down more heavily upon this issue because still today "the cost is high, encouraging corruption and compromising key relationships with other states" (Zdrojewski, 2008, p. 19). The scope of human sex trafficking is immeasurable; identification of victims is essential for their survival and ours.

REFERENCES

Alcindor, Y. (2012). Sex Trafficking in the USA—"That's Slavery": Children's advocates are battling the nation's plague in plain sight. In *USA Today,* Thursday, September 27, 2012.

Batchelor, V., & Lane, I. (2013). Breaking the Code: Domestic Minor Sex Trafficking and School Children. In J. Hall (ed.), *Children's Human Rights and Public Schooling in the United States.* Rotterdam: Sense Publishers.

Biernacki, P., & Waldorf, D. (1981). Sampling: Problems and Techniques of Chain Referral Sampling. *Sociological Methods and Research*, 10(2), 141–163.

Brewer, D. (2008). Globalization and Human Trafficking in Topical Research Digest: Human Rights and Human Trafficking. Retrieved from http://www.du.edu/korbel/hrhw/researchdigest/trafficking/Globalization.pdf

Chuang, J. (2006). Beyond a Snapshot: Preventing Human Trafficking in the Global Economy. *Indiana Journal of Global Legal Studies:* Vol. 13: Iss. 1, Article 5. Retrieved from http://www.repository.law.indiana.edu/ijgls/vol13/iss1/5

Coryell, L. (2011). Trenton man accused in Rowan Towers rape case admits child endangerment. For the *Times.* Retrieved from http://www.nj.com/mercer/index.ssf/2011/03/trenton_man_accused_in_rowan_t.html

Desmond-Harris, J. (2013). Sex Trafficking's Black and Brown Victims: Young girls of color are forced into sex slavery with no way out. Posted: September 23, 2013 at 12:53 AM. Retrieved from http://www.theroot.com/views/sex-traffickings-victims-young-black-and-brown

Emery, A., Heffron, L., & Moore, D. (2012). Human Trafficking: Black Girls Are Still Enslaved. Central Texas African American Family Support Conference. Retrieved from http://www.ctaafsc.org/ama/orig/2012_Conference/PPT/pdf/Human_Trafficking_Final__2-11-12.pdf

Finklea, K. M., Fernandes-Alcantara, A. L., & Siskin, A. (2011). Sex Trafficking of Children in the United States: Overview and Issues for Congress. Congressional Research Service, June, 21, 2011. Retrieved from http://www.fas.org/sgp/crs/misc/R41878.pdf

Free the Slaves. (2010). Frederick Douglass 2010 Award Winner: Tina Frundt, USA. Retrieved from http://www.freetheslaves.net/Page.aspx?pid=558

Frundt, T. (n.d.). Enslaved in America: Sex Trafficking in the United States. Retrieved from http://www.womensfundingnetwork.org/resource/past-articles/enslaved-in-america-sex-trafficking-in-the-united-states

Girls for Sale Map. (2011). Retrieved from https://maps.google.co.nz/maps/ms
?ie=UTF8&hl=en&msa=0&msid=200273141589609424876.0004938160154f
2e4a0c8&ll=34.322967,-98.571396&spn=29.774906,49.12674&source=em
bed

Gordon, E. (2006). Black Children Missing in Alarming Numbers, for NPR
Copyright © 2006. May 09, 2006 9:00 AM. Retrieved from http://www.npr
.org/templates/story/story.php?storyId=5393141

Herbert, B. (2006). Young, cold and for sale. *New York Times:* The Opinion Pages,
October 19, 2006. Retrieved from http://www.nytimes.com/2006/
10/19/opinion/19herbert.html

Hodge, D. (2008). Sexual trafficking in the United States: A domestic problem with
transnational dimensions. *Social Work,* 53(2), 143–152.

Hyde, J. (2005). From home to street: Understanding young people's transitions
into homelessness. *Journal of Adolescence, 28,* 171–83.

Kendall, M., & Golden, J. N. (2013). Fast Tailed Girls: Examining the stereotypes
and abuse that Black girls face in gradient: Black women+ art, media, social
media, socio-politics and culture. December 1, 2013. Retrieved from http://
www.gradientlair.com/post/68646097154/fast-tailed-girls-stereotyped
-abused-black-girls

Kortla, K. (2010). Domestic minor sex trafficking in the United States. *Social Work*
55(2), 181–187.

Laczko, F., & Danailova-Trainor, G. (2009). Trafficking in Persons and Human
Development: Towards a More Integrated Policy Response. Online at
http://mpra.ub.uni-muenchen.de/19234/MPRA Paper No. 19234, posted
13. December 2009 07:13 UTC.

Larsen, R. (2011). U.S. Human Trafficking Incidents, 2008-2010. *Journalist's Resource:
A research portal and curated database.* Retrieved from http://journalistsresou
rce.org/studies/government/criminal-justice/human-trafficking

Martinez, R. J. (2006). Understanding runaway teens. *Journal of Child and Adolescent
Psychiatric Nursing, 19*(2), 77–88.

Netter, S. (November, 2009). Dad: Shaniya's Mom Trafficked Her to Settle Drug
Debt. Retrieved from http://abcnews.go.com/WN/accused-shaniya-davis
-kidnapper-charged-murder-rape/story?id=9136407

Rieger, A. (2007). Missing the mark: Why the Trafficking Victims Protection Act
fails to protect sex trafficking victims in the United States. *Harvard Journal of
Law & Gender, 30.*

Saar, M. S. (2009). Shaniya's Shame. (Posted November 19, 2009 at 2:46PM.)
Retrieved from http://www.theroot.com/views/shaniyas-shame

Tillet, S. (2010). Black Girls Are Still Enslaved: The sexual trafficking of our young
females is happening at an alarming rate. Who will free them? Posted: April
10, 2010 at 7:52 AM. Retrieved from http://www.theroot.com/views/
black-girls-are-still-enslaved

UNGIFT. (2008). Global Initiative to Fight Trafficking. UNODC, Vienna.

United Nations. (2000). *Protocol to prevent, suppress and punish trafficking in persons,
especially women and children, supplementing the United Nations convention
against transnational organized crime.* General Assembly resolution 55/25.
New York, NY: United Nations General Assembly.

United Nations Office on Drugs and Crime (UNODC). (2004). *United Nations Convention Against Transnational Organized Crime and the Protocols Thereto,* UNODC, Vienna.

U.S. Department of Education Office of Safe and Drug-Free Schools in Washington, DC. (2007). *Human Trafficking of Children in the United States: A Fact Sheet for Schools.* Retrieved from http://www2.ed.gov/about/offices/list/osdfs /factsheet.pdf

U.S. Department of State. (2013). The State Department 2013 Trafficking in Persons Report. Retrieved from http://www.state.gov/j/tip/rls/rm/2013/211833.htm

U.S. Department of State: Diplomacy in Action. (2013). Misperceptions Lead to Missed Opportunities to Identify Victims. June 1, 2013. Retrieved from http://www.state.gov/j/tip/rls/fs/2013/211627.htm

World Health Organization. (2012). Understanding and addressing violence against women: Human Trafficking (edited by Sarah Ramsay). Retrieved from http://apps.who.int/iris/bitstream/10665/77394/1/WHO_RHR_12.42 _ eng.pdf

Zdrojewski, K. (2008). The Development of Sex Trafficking in Central America. In *Topical Research Digest: Human Rights and Human Trafficking.* Retrieved from http://www.du.edu/korbel/hrhw/researchdigest/trafficking/Central America.pdf

Chapter 19

Critical Conversations Using Poetry to Empower Adolescent Girls of African Descent to Effectively Address Their Sexual Health and Well-Being

Lindamichelle Baron

WHAT'S AT STAKE?

There are myriad issues with profound implications for young women and their sexual health. A range of factors influence the health choices and behaviors of all adolescents. The Centers for Disease Control and Prevention (CDC) documents the relationship between poverty and early, unplanned pregnancy as well as sexually transmitted infections. The statistics further indicate that having sexually transmitted diseases and infections (STIs) increases the probability of contracting HIV/AIDS. Research connecting poverty to sexual risks may have implications as to why, according to statistics, girls of African American descent are at greater risk for unintended pregnancy, sexually transmitted infections (STIs), and HIV infection. STDs can complicate pregnancy and may have serious effects on both a woman and her developing baby. Recently, parents of girls as young as 12 and 13 are being urged to have their daughters vaccinated to prevent the human papillomavirus (HPV), a cause of most cervical cancers. Lives are at stake.

At the same time, there has been a highly charged political and emotional debate regarding the outcomes and underlying messages inherent in teaching teenagers about sexuality and the ways they can protect themselves from negative outcomes. Those on one side of the debate insist that teaching teens how to protect themselves against sexually transmitted diseases and unplanned pregnancy is giving tacit permission to have sex. Accordingly, they believe, abstinence should be the only option offered young people. Supporters of Comprehensive Sexuality Education (CSE), on the other hand, contend that programs sponsored by "abstinence only" organizations withhold information from young people, thus "promoting questionable and inaccurate opinions," thereby "threatening fundamental rights to health, information, and life" (Duberstein et al., 2006, 72).

Adolescents receive messages about their sexual self from the media, social networks, and through interactions with others. How they interpret these messages can have a profound impact on the decisions they ultimately make. Exposure to personal health-related information and reading about health-related issues and concerns are not enough to save young people from possibly severe consequences based on the lack of a deep understanding. They need health literacy. The World Health Organization (WHO) defines health literacy as the "personal, cognitive and social skills which determine the ability of individuals to gain access to, understand, and use information to promote and maintain good health (Nutbeam, 2000, p. 263).

TEACHERS AS LEARNERS, LEARNERS AS TEACHERS

When I began teaching in Bedford Stuyvesant, Brooklyn, my mentor Adelaide Sanford, the principal of Crispus Attucks School, shared with me her life trajectory, which went from being a graduate of one of the "Seven Sisters" Ivy League colleges to becoming an inner-city educator and administrator. Her first assignment was a small class of twelve or so 6th grade special education students, mostly African American males. The only priority, the principal insisted, was for Ms. Sanford to keep the class quiet and out of trouble.

Ms. Sanford decided, in spite of her instructions, to teach the young people to read. As she engaged them in conversations regarding their previous lack of progress, the students gave what seemed to her to be a cogent rationale for their lack of reading success. It was, according to the students, the irrelevant textbook series, *Dick and Jane*, that they were given to read, which made no reference to their lives nor related to their individual or community experiences.

The students volunteered the title of a book that would relate to them, *Dick and Pussy*. Ms. Sanford determined to reach the students with the materials they requested. She went to the principal insisting on funds to purchase those books. The principal's face turned red as he explained that she had been "played." The title they gave her was actually the colloquial terms for male and female sexual organs. Instead of taking their actions personally, and punishing them, Ms. Sanford returned to the class more motivated to help them reach their unrecognized potential. In fact, she used their preoccupation with sex to begin their instruction. If they were going to discuss sexual terms in her class, then she required that they use the academic vocabulary: "penis" and "vagina."

Even today, generations after the sexual revolution, sexual terms are seldom embraced, mentioned, or even referred to except in health education classes. Students are usually silenced when these topics are broached, and even traditional or nontraditional terms are not used in content area classrooms. Yet this inexperienced, naïve teacher decided to reach her students by incorporating the provocative topic into her teaching. She recognized the truth embedded in their off-color joke. The textbooks did not relate to their lived experiences.

Ms. Sanford led them toward developing their own texts, using a nontraditional approach, Experience Charts, considered best practice for early childhood reading instruction but not for use with early adolescents. She wrote their stories, unabridged and unedited, on large chart paper. The stories were sometimes explicit and graphic, yet she was committed to documenting the actual content as told, as long as the sexual references used the "official" vocabulary. Those stories eventually veered away from stories made to shock her, and amuse peers, to stories of their lives. The large White charts became their text. They began connecting their stories to the more conventional literature sixth graders were expected to read. The students evolved into readers. They also discovered their voices. By the end of the school year, the young people whose highest expected achievement for the year was not to disrupt, passed the standardized reading exams with higher grades than other 6th grade classes in the school.

Aspects of the practices shared in this anecdote could be called progressive in that progressive educators, as John Dewey (2007) suggests, attend to the whole child, not just academic instruction. The motivation to learn is intrinsic, not guided by grades but by the desire to read, think, and question. A community is created in the classroom in which students learn with and from each other. The learning is active, such that students are involved in constructing ideas rather than passively absorbing or practicing skills. The pedagogies that are consistent with these belief systems are critical pedagogies, influenced by the works of Paulo Freire (1970), focused on the abilities of students to rethink and reassess power and ultimately to prepare to take action.

This chapter will explore the proposition that adolescent girls of African descent can discover their voice, self-empowerment, and social justice, creating a positive impact on their sexual health through engagement with poetry and critical discourse in school settings. I will refer to aspects of two programs that have the promise of being effective in critical areas of literacy and health, aligned with the tenets of critical pedagogy. I also will reflect on my use of poetry as pedagogy and implications for critical conversations in content area classrooms.

Catherina Ashcraft (2012) contends, in "But How Do We Talk About It?: Critical Literacy Practices for Addressing Sexuality with Youth," that conversations in which adolescents are encouraged to explore issues of sexuality should be brought into the content area classrooms because they are powerfully relevant to youth who are often mentally and physically consumed with related issues. She, in fact, suggests that these conversations not be held exclusively out of concerns about students' sexual health, but because of the two tenets of critical literacy pedagogy: "1) its emphasis on helping youth examine the discourses, narratives, and texts that shape their identities and lived experiences, and 2) insistence that such critical examinations begin with the texts most relevant for youth" (p. 598). Ashcraft calls these conversations "daring." Indeed, they are. Parents often are asked to sign off on their child's participation in workshops, sessions, and courses in which sexual issues are discussed. If these discourses are intermittently brought into the content area classrooms, what are the consequences for those administrators and educators who are engaged with these critical conversations? Would teachers have to ask parents to give permission, a priori, to discussions that may emerge in the context of evoking life issues and connecting them to content?

As much as I support daring conversations in class for the sake of empowering students to make sense of their lives, sexualities, and sexual identity through critical literacy, disastrous consequences related to health issues cited earlier make an even more powerful imperative. As Fine and McClelland (2006) indicate, "young people are dying for good conversation about sexuality and they are dying without it" (p. 328)

The phrase "dying for good conversation" is not hyperbole. There are sexual health consequences that are impacting the African American community at significantly higher rates than other communities (CDC). I contend that educators must prepare to seize the time and consider the validity of allowing provocative, sexually explicit conversations and contemporary texts into the classroom to reach students as they connect to traditional texts, in order to engage in authentic conversations in an age when access to knowledge and application of that knowledge are essential.

DARING CONVERSATIONS

I enter this conversation as an educator, teacher of teachers, and a poet who has been invited to hundreds of school systems throughout the east coast and the other areas throughout the country. The poetry I share with young people in auditoriums and classrooms is filled with messages of self-empowerment, and love of self and others. Yet, I have also been asked to use my presentations to address issues of sexual health. As such, I am compelled to examine the possible pedagogies of adult-led discourse that could offer adolescents perspectives that provide an opportunity to inform their decision-making around sexuality and the resulting issues. I have long considered my style of poetry, written from the oral tradition, "poetry as pedagogy." Where does my pedagogy of poetry take me, and where does it take those who experience such pedagogy?

I'm writing this chapter as an opportunity to reflect on my practices as a performing educator/poet who is committed to being a teacher, and teacher of teachers, who seeks to support individuals, positively transforming their lives. As bell hooks writes,

> My hope emerges from those places of struggle where I witness individuals positively transforming their lives and the world around them. Educating is always a vocation rooted in hopefulness. As teachers we believe that learning is possible, that nothing can keep an open mind from seeking after knowledge and finding a way to know. (hooks, 2003, p. xiv)

One question I ask myself is simply, "What can I discern from some of the research on programs embracing critical literacy and critical health literacy?" The other question is, "What can I learn as I explore the impact of my 30 years of engagement with young people through poetry-driven presentations?" I reflect over numerous anecdotes (stories) that suggest that for some students a one-time literacy-based interaction with an adult regarding poetic references and conversations considered difficult to discuss and daring, can have short-term and long-term impact. My goal is to embed best practices into the classroom instruction that will support transformational, progressive, critical conversations with adolescent girls, with a focus on those of African descent. Of course, I propose using contemporary poetry as a tool of the trade.

UNLEARNING, LEARNING, RELEARNING, REFLECTION, AND EVALUATION

I reflect on my practice by considering the cycle of critical pedagogy. I'm revisiting my practices and experiences, willing to unlearn in order to relearn and evaluate. One such reflective cycle took place months after I had spoken at a local high school. It was near the end of summer. Students had been on summer break for several months. A young man seemed to recognize me and asked, "Aren't you that lady that came to Springfield Gardens High School?"

When I acknowledged that I was, he seemed less than impressed and added, "You know, that poem you did messed us up. The girls weren't giving up anything for about two weeks after you left." Based on his reaction, blaming me and my poem for the young ladies "abstaining" for two weeks, I mentally replayed the 45-minute visit in an auditorium that held several hundred teenagers. The response to my recitation of the rhyming verse of a poem called "Righteous Rap" with a clichéd repeated line, "say no," turned into a "teachable moment."

A cacophony of male voices from the audience "booed" me. I actually loved it. It was proof positive that they heard me. How often does that happen to a poet in an audience of high schoolers? I chuckled aloud and turned my attention to the young ladies in the audience, saying, "Listen to the fellas out there. They don't want you to hear me. What do you think that's about? Remember what Aretha Franklyn sang, *'you better think, think, think about what you trying to do to me.'* After listening to them, ladies, I think *you* better think! Think about what they are trying to do to you!" And then I continued reciting my poem.

When he says how much he loves you,
Wants you to love him too,
Says let's get physical. . . physical,
When physical is not what you know you should do
Don't do it!!!
Look him right in the eye,
You don't have to be shy,
True love is more, you'll find,
Than what he has in mind;
Say "no."

What was it about that interaction that, according to one young man's perception, impacted the high school females' action for several weeks? The poem itself is rather cliché. In fact the "say no" initiative was geared to drug use rather than sexual relations. I doubt it was the poem that made the impact, but perhaps my unexpected engagement with the young audience. Maybe the young women heard me, in that moment in time, because in spite of the male critics in the audience, I would not allow myself to be silenced. In fact, their lack of affirmation empowered me. Was it my response to the young men's negative response to the poem that was more powerful? Was it that I presented myself to the young ladies less as an adult figure and more as one who was with them? There is only room for conjecture. So, I reflect. I think. I have not yet determined from whence cometh the impact: Thus, this self-reflective chapter.

I have been asked to use my poetry and motivational talk to bring real conversations to adolescent girls and at the same time encourage them to consider making informed, thoughtful choices regarding their sexual interactions. The bringing of "real conversations" may be the issue. My life experience is from a different time and place. My willingness to share that place as honestly as I can, and yet not judge those to whom I am speaking may be as important, if not more important, than the actual poet. I am from the "old school" with a twist. "A Shout Out About a Way Out" refers to my "backinthedayness":

We used to encourage monogamy;
We cited issues of morality.
And mostly females were told what to expect.
Girls had their dignity to protect.
Playing house with the boys got you no respect.

If females didn't practice what they were taught,
The males used stuff so they wouldn't get caught.
They knew that if their lady's belly spread,
Like it or not, they'd have to get wed,
Or they'd meet her daddy and get dead.

Some of my poetry is considered didactic, and accessible. But it is imbued with elements of the spirit of Harlem Renaissance, particularly Langston Hughes, empowered by the traditions of poets of the Black Arts Movement of the 1960s and 1970s. The Black Arts movement, as described by Kaluma ya Salaam, in *The Oxford Companion to African American Literature*, not only advocated political engagement and independent publishing, but much like the poetry I write and present, was "innovative in its use of language":

Speech (particularly, but not exclusively, Black English), music, and performance were major elements of Black Arts literature. Black Arts aesthetics emphasized orality, which includes the ritual use of call and response both within the body of the work itself as well as between artist and audience. This same orientation is apparent in rap music and 1990s "performance poetry" (e.g., Nuyorican Poets and poetry slams).

In many ways my pedagogy as a poet is from the revolutionary tradition of that movement in that much of it is written to encourage critical thought, and to encourage the exploration of unvoiced interpersonal and sociopolitical issues.

One of my earliest invitations to make daring conversation through poetry was in a Brooklyn high school, Benjamin Banneker, in the late 1990s. I was asked to conduct a session with young women, all of whom were of

African descent. I was to discuss issues regarding sexual encounters. This experience happened years before I began consciously researching approaches to enter daring, sexual conversation with young women. I had no idea why the school's principal had selected me for this task. I was a much older adult, although obviously of the same gender and race as the students. I was not an expert. I had not prepared a script or researched approaches to conduct such sessions. I knew I was a poet, an educator, a professional developer and even a motivational speaker, but not a sex education guru.

A male poet of my same generation was meeting with the male students on that same day and time. This was Abiodun Oyewole, a member of The Last Poets poetry troupe, from the Black Arts Movement–era group that is widely considered a foundational influence on rap. I imagine the high school administrator recognized the possibility of the two of us using poetry as a catalyst to open gender-specific discussions. I had in my repertoire several poems that explicitly or implicitly referenced sexual interactions and self-empowerment. I went to the school, poetry in hand, and a prayer that I could be relevant to the 60 or so young women I was to address on that day.

I remember the day vividly, although the session took place ten or more years ago. My first imperative was to get the young women's attention. After briefly introducing myself, I had an epiphany. I remember saying, "I'm a guest and I don't know any of you in the audience. But I believe that some of you treat your sneakers better than you treat your own body." One of the young ladies called out, "What you mean?" "Well," I continued, "how many of you wear name brand sneakers?" Most in the audience acknowledged they did. I then asked, "Which are the best sneakers?" Two or three name brands were mentioned from the group. "How many of you would let somebody put their feet in your sneakers?" One of the students shouted out, "I wouldn't let nobody put their feet in my sneakers, they might have athlete's foot." I continued, "Then what do you think can happen if you let somebody put a part of their body in you?" The same student who had previously shouted out then almost inaudibly uttered an expletive. "I never thought about it like that," she said. The power of metaphor!

Thus started the conversation. My prayers answered, I was able to be relevant to the young women before me. I don't remember the specifics of the rest of the session, only that we discussed sexual and relational issues honestly, and that I used my poetry as a prompt. Following a later session with parents, in which I recalled that experience, I was asked to write a poem using the same metaphor. It is now part of a repertoire I use to encourage young people, particularly adolescent girls of African descent, to reflect on their current and future sexual choices. The poem encourages abstaining from sexual encounters while at the same time providing another option to protecting self from the murderous possibilities of sexually transmitted diseases.

Metaphor for Our Times

This is the "Don't let everybody
put their naked feet in your shoes"
. . . blues.
Not only do their feet sweat,
but a fungus is not all you get.

This is the "Don't let everybody
put their naked feet in your shoes"
. . . blues.

This is also the "Don't put your naked feet
in everybody's shoes"
. . . blues.

You don't have to run to the door
every time opportunity knocks.
And if you decide to open the door,
don't forget to wear your socks.

I often reflect on and try to unpack what may have taken place at such moments that seem to resonate with adolescent audiences. Sometimes they love the rhythm and the rhyme. I realize there are other points in the presentation where students seem most engaged when they have to "figure it out." *"You don't have to run to the door every time opportunity knocks, and if you decide to open the door, don't forget to wear your socks"* is the point at which I experience signals that they "get it." They love when they "get it."

What I must continue to work toward and use the research to inform, is how to engage in the conversations that don't take the traditional route of preaching at them, and instead work through a process of getting information, inspecting the information, and making connections to their lives. This reflection helps inform my evolving practice and hopefully has implications for other practitioners. Aspects of poetic craft, such as metaphor, similes, personification, rhyme, rhythm, and repetition invite young ladies into conversations with their peers and an adult with whom they have decided to connect. Poetry seems to lend itself to enhanced communication. My experiences have led me to believe adolescents find contemporary poetry written from the oral tradition compelling.

Piotr Gwiazda, in a 2007 review published in Jacket online magazine of *Poetry and Pedagogy: The Challenge of the Contemporary*, a collection of essays edited by Joan Retallack and Juliana Spahr, shows how one of the book's contributors, Maria Damon, offers readers suggestions about the use of poetry in the classroom that illustrates some of the points I'm attempting to make in this essay. Gwiazda writes:

> Maria Damon . . . imagines teaching poetry as "empowering citizenry," especially in conjunction with materials that don't normally get studied in the classroom. As part of her critique of established pedagogical stances, she urges teachers to close the gap between traditional and contemporary poetry by taking more interest, in and out of the classroom, in "counterperformance" (her examples include Bob Kaufman's life and work, poetry slam artists, hip-hop and rap) and "micropoetics" (graffiti, prison poetry, vernacular poetries). Damon's intervention is particularly remarkable for its appreciation of marginalized poetries and her respectful attention to previously unexamined forms of orality. As she claims, it is primarily when we pay attention to "post-literate" forms that we become better attuned to the social practice of language. Texts themselves become sites of collective meaning-making rather than hierarchical instruction as both teachers and students learn "new ways of hearing, reading, seeing, experiencing, making the transparent opaque and the opaque transparent."

Two other experiences I reflect on suggest a long-term impact on adolescent behavior. In one case, a woman who seemed to be in her thirties or forties recognized me as I was entering her deceased brother's wake. She stopped me after I introduced myself and called over her twin teenage daughters. She referred to me as she told them that it was this lady's poem that she heard when she was a teenager that made her decide to wait until she met their father to have the both of them. The poem was "When I Do My Thing." Again, the question, what was it about the poem, presentation, presenter, or combination that constructed the perceived impact?

A recently retired middle school principal shared a second incident, involving the same poem. He had the opportunity to see one of the students who graduated years before, working in a department store. During their brief conversation he asked if she was married. She was not. He then asked if she had any children. He reports that she looked at him incredulously, and responded. "No, I don't have any children. I told you I'm not married." To which he responded, "I'm sorry to have offended you, but there are quite a few young women who have children and are not married." She responded, "But don't you remember that lady you had come to the school and did that poem 'I'll do my thing when I get my ring'?" I was that lady. The poem was the one I wrote as a teenager. I don't and didn't perceive the poem itself to be transformational. It shares characteristics of cultural relevance such as the use of non-standard dialect, play on words, rhythm, rhyme, repetition, and other elements of poetic expression that may invite students to appreciate the poem and the message. In fact, recently the same message exploded on the scene with Beyoncé's rendition of "All the Single Ladies," a song that exalts commitments. Maybe it was the combination of openness to hearing the voices of the young people in the rooms that I entered, reading the unspoken thoughts of the young people and connecting my realities to theirs. Here is an excerpt from my poem, "When I Do My Thing," found in *Rhythm & Dues Poetry and Idea Book,*

"I'll do my thing when I get my ring,"
I said to muscular, mobile,
arms-hands around besides/upon me.
"But baby," he said,
"a ring ain't no fun in bed."
"N-O!" I replied
as I moved his hands and body aside.
"There ain't gonna be no thing
'til I get my ring."

"Wow!" he said kinda slow.
"like that's really a blow.
You supposed to be a loving woman,
how you think you're gonna show?
We've been huggin and lovin,
sharin and kissin.
If you can't think of me,
try to dig what you're missin."
"Uh, uh, uh," he went on, his voice nearly gone,
"I look at my woman all ready to squeeze her,
and instead of a woman, I encounter a freezer."

I often share the background of that poem with young people. I let them know it was written for an actual person in my life, the boy who took me to my prom. I tell how he was tall, dark, and handsome . . . and played basketball. Yet I made the decision that the money for the prom tickets, the corsage, and the limousine was not enough to make me believe I should do something I didn't feel I was ready for. I also share that I ultimately did marry him . . . years later.

Someone always asks, "Did you do your thing before you got married?" To which I reply, with a smile, "I don't know if that is any of your business." I wonder if it is the poetry in connection with honest, authentic conversations that makes an impact that can last two weeks and beyond twenty years.

Other strategies seem to impact students, such as in my "flipping the script." I place them in charge of making the class engaging. They have been known to present my poems better than I do. The meanings and their connections are evident in their presentations. In coed sessions, many of the messages of my poems are designed to reach adolescent girls. The style of the poetry is contemporary and rhythmic. They are invited to go beyond making it their own, to creating their own.

"I'm the Man" . . . Turning around what was a common phrase in the early 2000s to refer to young women "being self-empowered, such that they are 'the man.'":

I don't have to live large to know I'm in charge
I know where I stand
I live with a _____ and a plan
So I say, hey, I'm the man.

I don't mean I like women
Or I like to act tough
I like to get pretty
And strut my stuff.

On some occasions I invite students to dramatize the poems, through Reader's Theater or other creative engagement. What is important in the process of students taking parts of the poems and making them their own is the freedom to manipulate the text. In sessions, students may decide to change the words that don't resonate with them. For instance, instead of using "uh, uh, uh," or "dig" when preparing to present "When I Do My Thing," some groups changed the wording to make it more relevant to them. I asked them to decide how to present the work. Once the students used a poem that referenced violence and combined part one and part two into a call and response. The presentation was more powerful than it was originally conceptualized. After they manipulate the text and perform it, sometimes during the process we discuss the poem's connection to them. Is it real? How can they make it real to them? What are your real issues? The process initiates some daring conversations.

Did you think? Did you plan?
Or did all you do was want that man?
Did you ask him to commit?
Did he pretend a little bit?
Or did you listen to the words he said and let words, not actions,
Take you to bed?
What did you use your body for?
Did you really think he'd love you more?

Critical Health Literacy

According to Don Nutbeam's (2000) model of health literacy skills, there is a wide range of social determinants that impact health such as income, early life experience, health care services, political empowerment, and gender equity. Health literacy reaches beyond health education designed to impact individual health and lifestyles by encouraging individuals and communities to take action. There are three levels to Nutbeam's definition of health literacy: the first level is *functional* literacy, which communicates factual knowledge about health risks; the second level is *interactive* health literacy, based on development of skills such as problem solving, communication and decision making; the third level is *critical* health literacy, in which individuals use awareness of social determinants of health for independent or community action. The third component also includes the capacity to critically analyze and wield greater power over individual and community life events and situations.

Health literacy and critical literacy pedagogy can provide young women the opportunity and power to assess the messages they are receiving from a variety of texts. Critical literacy instruction in conjunction with critical health literacy education may address sexual risk taking and health disparities in youth. Even as data and statistics are presented as documented "truths" used to highlight the health imperative, I'm exhorted, by the philosophy and theory of Paulo Freire, to look through a critical lens, as I teach others to do the same. There is a broader context considered in this text as it relates to critical pedagogy. Freire's (1970) conceptualization of critical pedagogy, although he never used that term, is beyond gender, race, and social class to issues of social justice. According to the precepts of critical pedagogy even the research cited in the introduction of this chapter could be suspect and must be reconsidered through the lens of injustice and power. Burbules and Berk (1999) explain the difference between critical thinking and critical pedagogy. Critical pedagogy goes beyond assessing propositions to be assessed for their truth but as "part of a system of belief and action that have aggregate effects within the power structures of society." The example they provide uses the contention regarding African Americans' lower scores on IQ tests:

> Indeed, a crucial dimension of this approach is that certain claims, even if they might be "true" or substantiated within particular confines and assumptions, might nevertheless be partisan in their effects. Assertions that African-Americans score lower on IQ tests, for example, even if it is a "fact" that this particular population does on average score lower on this particular set of tests, leave significant

larger questions unaddressed, not the least of which is what effect such assertions have on a general population that is not aware of the important limits of these tests or the tenuous relation, at best, between "what IQ tests measure" and "intelligence." Other important questions, from this standpoint, include: Who is making these assertions? Why are they being made at this point in time? Who funds such research? Who promulgates these "findings"? Are they being raised to question African-American intelligence or to demonstrate the bias of IQ tests? Such questions, from the Critical Pedagogy perspective, are not external to, or separable from, the import of also weighing the evidentiary base for such claims.

Today's adolescents must be prepared to dig beneath the surface of traditional narratives to uncover issues of social injustice that directly and indirectly impact their personal and community well-being, potential wealth, and their sense of themselves and others.

There are in-school and after-school programs throughout the country that are designed to persuade adolescents to resist early sexual intercourse and drug use. Health classes in schools help students in functional literacy, learning about their developing bodies and gaining information about prevention of pregnancy and sexually transmitted diseases. The Centers for Disease Control and Prevention (CDC) provides research that suggests commonalities of effective HIV and STD prevention programs for youth. Effective health programs assist young people to develop behaviors and attitudes that promote overall health and well-being which also leads to reduction of risky sexual behaviors. Effective programs are those that are taught by trained instructors, are age-appropriate, and support healthy behaviors. Well-designed and well-implemented programs have been shown to reduce risk by delaying first sexual contact, reducing the number of sexual partners, decreasing sex without condoms, and increasing condom use.

The Office of Adolescent Health (OAH) website provides evidence-based programs that list program models of the Department of Health and Human Services (HHS). This searchable database of the program models on the Department of Health and Human Services' (HHS) List of Evidence-Based Teen Pregnancy Prevention Program Models indicates programs with impacts on teen pregnancies or births, sexually transmitted infections (STIs), or sexual activity. One of the more promising approaches indicated by research provided on the site is Youth Asset-Development programs.

Youth asset-development programs, including those conducted in schools, teach youth how to solve problems, communicate with others, and plan for the future. They also help youth develop positive connections with their parents, schools, and communities.

Youth asset-development programs typically address multiple health risk behaviors and are commonly provided to children and adolescents over a number of years. Evidence indicates that these programs can be associated with long-term reductions in sexual risk behaviors. (Gavin, et al.)

One program that seems to combine properties of youth asset-development programs and also includes practices that empower young people by embedding critical pedagogies that Nutbeam (2000) calls Critical health literacy is ESPERANZA. The community-based educational program located in the west side of a large western city was studied by Catherine Ashcraft in order to explore a process of facilitating critical discussions about sexuality in classrooms. In her article, "But How Do We Talk About It?: Critical Literacy Practices for Addressing Sexuality with Youth," Ashcraft uses her study to describe how a program can invite "daring conversations" with young people.

The program, designed to "advance self-sufficiency for low-income urban youth," included trained adult project specialists and teenage peer educators who were selected through a series of interviews that ensured that they had the willingness and capacity to entertain other points of view. The peer educators were extensively trained in sexual health issues and provided opportunities to give presentations in schools and community organizations. They were required to participate in weekly meetings, trainings, and "rehearsals."

Ashcraft described classroom discussions that challenged the "traditional power balances" between teacher and students, citing an initial activity "name that part" that invited students to brainstorm all the slang words for reproductive organs they could think of. The adult specialist then provided insight as to how the inexhaustible number of "unofficial" terms actually suggested society's discomfort in discussing sex. The program employed critical literacy strategies that gave voice to adolescents' issues and concerns surrounding sex that are most often silenced in classrooms. The specialists and peer educators used discussions of various narratives to engage students in the exploration of the complexities in the messages surrounding issues of sex. Implicit in the discussions were the "important connections between language and power—the way that language positions people differently and shapes one's ability to advocate for oneself" (Ashcraft, 2012, p. 609).

RECOMMENDATIONS

Elizabeth Inglesias and Sherry Cormier (2002) in "The Transformation of Girls to Women: Finding Voice and Developing Strategies for Liberation" encourage us to consider the "losses that occur for adolescent girls across cultural groups and social class and to examine the implications that those losses present for practitioners" (p. 259). They emphasize the loss of "voice" by revealing data and research that indicate differences based on ethnic and racial identity. One example, the research of Peplau and colleagues (1999), suggested Latina and White American girls were more repressed with expressing anger, while African American girls "seemed to be able to give voice to their anger." Yet they had a more difficult time expressing sadness and pain. Educators must develop strategies that help empower young women by helping to give them voice in all circumstances. Inglesias and Cormier reframe the term resistance such that it is consistent with critical pedagogies. They cite Robinson and Ward (1991), who believed that young African American women can and should be prepared to resist racial, gender and economic oppression by using tools of critical literacy to "think critically about oneself, about the world, and about one's place in it" (p. 266).

- A good point of entry may be using poetry to begin the conversation. We must create habits of mind that we communicate to our young women so that they question assumptions and actions that have injurious implications for them, as they work toward positive change. Although I referenced several of my own poems in this chapter, as a way to enter the conversation, I end with an excerpt from Margaret Walker's poem "For My People" to implore educators to explore every avenue to reach our young people. Certainly, in this article the focus is on the sexual health and well-being of female African American adolescents.

    For the cramped bewildered years we went to school to learn
    to know the reasons why and the answers to and the
    people who and the places where and the days when, in
    memory of the bitter hours when we discovered we
    were Black and poor and small and different and nobody
    cared and nobody wondered and nobody understood.

- As we revisit the research and statistics on adolescent girls of African descent, educators must be the ones to care, to wonder, and to understand. We must use programs and practices already available to us to support our young people's sexual health and self-empowerment. Use programs that research indicates are successful youth asset-development programs, and personal experiences that work . . . let's use those.

- And we must continue to develop new forms of engagement. The philosophy and practice of critical pedagogy, critical literacy, and critical health literacy exhorts us to use any means necessary to teach for self-empowerment and social justice in support of our children's mind, body and spirit.

REFERENCES

Ashcraft, C. (2012). But how do we talk about it?: Critical literacy practices for addressing sexuality with youth. *Curriculum Inquiry, 42*(5), 599–624.

Baron, L. (2007). *Rhythm & dues: Poetry and ideas.* Garden City, NY: Harlin Jacque Publications.

Baron, L. (2007). *For the love of life: Life lyrics from an oral tradition* (3rd ed.). Garden City, NY: Harlin Jacque Publications.

Burbules, N., & Berk, R. (1999). Critical thinking and critical pedagogy: Relations, differences, and limits. In T. Popkewitz & L. Fendler (eds.), *Critical theories in education.* New York: Routledge.

Centers for Disease Control and Prevention (CDC). http://www.cdc.gov/ Changes in Formal Sex Education: 1995–2002: 182–189.

Delpit, L., & Dowdy, J. K. (2002). *The skin that we speak: Thoughts on language and culture in the classroom.* New York: New Press.

Dewey, J. (2007). *Experience and education.* New York: Simon & Schuster.

Duberstein L., Santelli, J. S., & Singh, S. (2006). Changes in formal sex education. *Perspectives on Sexual and Reproductive Health, 38*(4): 182–189.

Fine, M. (1992). Sexuality, schooling and adolescent females: The missing discourse of desire. In M. Fine (ed.), *Disruptive voices: The possibilities of feminist research.* Ann Arbor: University of Michigan Press, pp. 31–60.

Fine, M., & McClelland, S. (2006) Sexuality, education and desire: Still missing after all these years. *Harvard Educational Review, 76*(3), 297–338.

Freire, P. (1970). *Pedagogy of the oppressed.* New York: Continuum.

Gavin, L., Catalano, C., David-Ferdon, K., & Markham, C. A review of positive youth development programs that promote adolescent sexual and reproductive health. *Journal of Adolescent Health, 46,* S75–S91.

Gee, J. P. (1996). *Social linguistics and literacies: Ideology in discourse* (2nd ed.). London: Falmer.

Gwiazda, P. (2007). Rev. of Retallack, J., and Spahr, J., Poetry and Pedagogy: The challenge of the contemporary. *Jacket 34-October-2007.*

hooks, b. (2003). *Teaching Community. A pedagogy of hope.* New York: Routledge.

Inglesias, E., & Cormier, S. (2002). The transformation of girls to women: Finding voice and developing strategies for liberation. *Journal of Multicultural Counseling and Development, 30,* 261.

Irvine, J. (2002). *Talk about sex.* Berkeley: University of California Press.

Kaluma ya Salaam. (1997). *The Oxford Companion to African American Literature.* New York: Oxford University Press.

Norton, N. E. L. (2011). Cutting like a razor: Female children address sexism and sexuality through poetry. *Curriculum Inquiry, 41*(4), 433–455.

Nutbeam, D. (2000) Health literacy as a public health goal: A challenge for contemporary health education and communication strategies into the 21st century. *Health Promotion International, 15*(3): 259–267.

Ohye, B., & Daniel, J. (1999). The "other" adolescent girls: Who are they? In N. Johnson, M. Robers, & J. Worell (eds.), Beyond appearance: a new look at adolescent girls. Washington, DC: American Psychological Association, pp. 115–128.

Peplau, L. A., DeBro, S. C., Veniegas, R. C., & Taylor, P. L. (eds). (1999). *Gender, culture, and ethnicity*. Mountain View, CA: Mayfield.

Robinson, T., & Ward, J. V. (1991). A belief in self far greater than anyone's disbelief: Cultivating resistance among African American female adolescents. In C. Gilligan, A. Rogers, & D. Tolman (eds), *Women, girls and psychotherapy: Reframing resistance*. New York: Haworth Press, 87–103.

Walker, M. (1942). *For my people*. New Haven: Yale University Press.

Chapter 20

Finding Nem[a]: Modeling and Mentoring for Adolescent African American Females' Development of Self-Identity

Sheila Marie Aird

Finding Nemo (2003), the Pixar animated movie production, sets the stage for an interesting departure on the topic of African American young women and self-identification. Although it may seem odd on the surface to compare this particular animated film to real life, the film contains many messages underneath the seemingly child-like animation. In fact, one can connect the life of the one-fin fish raised by a single sometimes overbearing/overprotective parent to an adolescent's quest to find one's self.

Removing the fact that Nemo is presented as a male fish, the film offers a look at an age-old problem of the parent-child dichotomy and the switch from child to pre-adult in that relationship. Anxieties and loss of control escalate as the child asserts one's independence, the parent is unwilling to let go, and the child is not heeding the parent's advice; followed at times by loss and failure to finally finding one's self. Additionally, feelings of fear for the child and of the outside world, as well as the parent(s) negotiating how to teach and model positive behavior when they may have demonstrated the same type of rebellious behavior, present challenges. How do parents negotiate this precarious position of adolescent development while still learning about themselves and without sounding as though their experience is the child's? What if the child does not want or see the value of the parents' advice? How does one protect and at the same time let them grow and through life's journey find themselves? These questions and many more are vital to negotiating with and understanding the important adolescent period. In fact, *Finding Nemo* offers many messages and one of the most important is, *it takes a village* to help raise a child. The village may consist of familial ties as well as strangers who offer at times the sweat of their brow to help in the raising of a child.

Therefore, the objective of this chapter is to posit the effects of mentoring African American young women using informal conversations and written evaluations to demonstrate how these opportunities and relationships positively impact the development of their self-identity. Utilizing the *it takes a village approach,* I will reflect on an organization that I am involved with that is run by African American and Latina women. It is my hope that it will demonstrate the importance of the contribution to self-development and identity through the eyes of the young women involved. Through their voices the efficacy and the importance of this type of mentoring demonstrates how powerful this relationship can be for young women as they gain both social and cultural capital and in the process change the way they see themselves and others.

Adolescence is normally considered the period beginning at approximately 12 years of age and ending around 18–21 years of age. This marker as a defining age is malleable and dependent on the country, author, and/or research that may adjust the entry into adolescence by one or more years while referring to the earlier range as "tweens." In short, adolescence is the beginning of preparation for adulthood. Regardless of the cultural age definer, it is the ready-or-not point in which the child is moved physiologically and socially from one level to the next.

One can agree that the organic transformation from child to adolescent is difficult at best for both the parent and the child. However, today's young African American women face some of the hardest challenges of any generation. Although there are similarities in the growing-up process regardless of the generation—which include but are not limited to alienation from parent(s), rebellion, possible sexual experimentation, and other changes in behavior—it is nonetheless painstakingly obvious that today's adolescent African American females are embroiled in a coming of age indoctrination that can be likened to hazing with consent. I use that term loosely as a metaphor in which to situate the conversation. It appears (if one listens to the media and statistics) that our sisters, daughters, and future leaders, without any idea or concern about consequences and whether through choice or pressure, have their agency often called into question.

Much has been written about young adults and peer pressure (friends without benefits), media portrayals, and music all presenting differing degrees of imagery and sound that contribute to some of our youth's behavior and perceptions of self. Some of these concerns are not new and are re-enacted in differing forms as each generation looks to find themselves. In the case of African American young women and their development of self, there are additional components that also contribute to the "who am I" self that includes the normal adolescent experience and the racial and stereotypical identity of being an African American in America. The messages transmitted *writ large* and through subtle overt and covert messaging can help reinforce or negate negative influences that contribute to young female's identity development.

However, unquestionably one of the greatest influences on this generation, referred to as the Millennials or Generation Z, is social media. This group is defined as those born between 1995 and 2012. This platform and the audience/participant act of engaged virtual participation can and do influence the process of fitting in, finding self, and feelings of empowerment, whether real or imagined. Today's adolescents in some cases are modeling behavior based on media portrayals, reality shows, peer scrutiny, and the perceived freedom of the wild wild west (internet and social media). The uncareful engagement in these can have devastating and long-lasting effects.

While conducting preliminary research for the topic, I determined that there is a plethora of information on adolescents from a psychological, social, physiological, and socioeconomic standpoint. One can also find studies on adolescents in general. However, there is much less research on African American adolescents and the construction of self-identity. What does exist, although rewarding, is minimal at best and/or includes African American female adolescents within the context of others. Yet, although there is not an abundance of information, more scholars are researching and writing on the African American adolescent experience and contributing to the body of literature (Ianni, 1996; Tatum, 1997; Stevens, 1997).

Consequently, I was prompted to think about how my experience and the work of other African American women giving of their time, expertise, and guidance translated to African American adolescents' identity formation. In addition, I was also keenly aware of a growing number of community-based African American women who are utilizing various approaches to inform, empower, and engage young African American women. These women introduce African American adolescents to infinite possibilities and offer them the keys to authoring their own lives. It was at that time the idea for this reflection took place.

Mentor is defined as one who "advises, guides, encourages, and inspires another person during an extended period of time" (Webster's

Dictionary). However, there is another piece that is important to the development of self-identity in young African American girls. It has been referred to as the natural mentor. Not only relegated to the African American community, it is thought of as a mentoring experience with members or extended members of the family, teachers, and others.

During adolescence it takes a combination of approaches and different types of conversations and experiences to encourage young African American girls to deeply reflect on who they are, who they would like to become, and their value. This is where modeling is important for this purpose; it is defined as "an example for imitation or emulation" (Webster's Dictionary). The modeling behavior can be viewed as a role model for the person or group in question. In this case, an important additive for these young women is that "they look like me."

MENTORING AFRICAN AMERICAN ADOLESCENTS

The acronym for The Image Initiative Inc. is *Imagine Me Achieving Great Expectations*. It stands as a fundamental call to action, a directive, a question and answer all in one that seeks to offer young women of color an invitation to success. The vision to help young disenfranchised African American women began as a class project by a young inspiring African American female student. The idea behind the project came to fruition when The Image Initiative Inc., a community-based 501(C) non-profit organization located in Syracuse, N.Y., was officially formed. The mission is to mentor at-risk African American and Latina young women enrolled in the Syracuse city school district. Embedded within the organization is the CHOICES (Creating Heightened Opportunities in Community, Environment, and Self) program that is geared towards introducing the young ladies to skill building and life choices as well as the understanding and belief that they can achieve infinite possibilities. This organization is comprised of a collection of professional women of color that hold positions in education, social services, non-profit, business, communications, and the entertainment field. "We believe that cultivating a strong self-image and sense of self-worth is key to success" (http://www.imageinit iative.org/). Through their continued service they aim to enlighten, engage, and empower young women of color and provide them with the tools and resources to be productive, responsible citizens. For the past ten years this organization has worked with the young women of Syracuse, holding workshops and an annual conference to introduce young women to their potential and to act as a support system.

Over the years, attendance at the annual conference has grown from the initial thirty students to over 125 students. One of the keys of success continues to be the engagement and presentation of women that "look like them." How does the mentoring of African American young women by African American women impact their identity, self-worth and development?

Yani, a 16-year-old, speaks about her thoughts and experiences in regard to mentoring and the Sisters Empowering Sisters Conference.

Attending the conferences for over 7 years really gives you a closer look at what African American females go through. The workshops and presentations are very informative. We are given positive feedback and advice. It makes you feel self-confident, empowered, and happy and thankful that you are able to participate. What is so incredible for me and my friends is that the women all look like us. They keep it real and prove to us that we are important. (Personal Conversation, 2014)

Jasmine notes,

It is exciting listening to powerful, beautiful, intelligent women that tell us we can do anything. This year they called us Epic super heroes. They came from all over the place and shared stuff with us on their career, their troubles as a teenager, and how they overcame the problems. Some came from bad homes, had trouble in their life, and still succeeded. They actually said they would help us. I thought they were just saying that . . . but they weren't.

SELF-IDENTITY AND THE LOOKING-GLASS SELF

What is self-identity and how is it created? Self-identity simply can be thought of as the quality or qualities that make one person different than another. It is how we define ourselves and does not include how others perceive us. However, Cooley argues that the looking-glass self is how a person sees oneself as a result of interpersonal interactions and the perceptions of others (Cooley, 1998, p. 189). In other words, the looking-glass self is based not only on how we see ourselves but also how we think others see us.

Beverly Daniel Tatum writes,

The concept of identity is a complex one, shaped by individual characteristics, family dynamics, historical factors, and social and political contexts. Who am I? The answer depends in large part on who the world around me says I am. Who do my parents say I am? Who do my peers say I am? What message is reflected back to me in the faces and voices of my teachers, my neighbors, store clerks? What do I learn from the media about myself? How am I represented in the cultural images around me? Or am I missing from the picture altogether? (1997, p. 52)

Anderson in his work *Code of the Street* situates the social environment and its contribution to self-identity. According to Anderson, "Children from even the most decent homes must come to terms with the various influences of the street." He further notes that there is a connection between the environment and self-identity (Anderson, 1999, pp. 67–68).

Renee, a 16-year-old rising star, offers her perspective on self-identity.

To me, self-identity is the things you know about yourself. A person can ask another person, "what do you think about yourself?" and a person can say "well, I'm kindhearted, pretty, do not like depending on people, I fear the unknown, etc. . ." Self-identity is supposed to be what you think and are confident in and about yourself. Over time, I think the meaning has changed. I feel like people, including myself, are influenced by what seems to be cooler or better, and then that sort of becomes their identity. Many things I see on TV do not serve a purpose for real self-identity. Reality TV (what is supposed to be real life TV/honest) does not serve that purpose. Being yourself should be accepted in any profession or event in life. How you speak, listen, love, dress, eat, sleep, work, laugh, and so on, is YOU. It all defines you as a person. Also, I think about when I see many small White women with long, beautiful flowing hair being shown all the time in advertisements on television. On the other hand, there are commercials that try to persuade us to be "natural." Yet there are more White women with flowing hair and extensions than there are women wearing natural hair. As a young lady, it is kind of difficult to just say yes I am beautiful with my natural hair and my full lips and my body that is different than theirs. It is very confusing but I am working hard to love me. I would define myself as an observer. I sit and watch how people do things and react. I used to think I had something to prove to my so-called "friends." I wanted to act like them. Now I am finding me.

Renee also notes,

When I look at TV, I think the producers and planners make you put on pounds of makeup and push you outside your comfort zone. But we don't always think or care about that. We look at the life, clothes and the things, and think if we are like them we will be good. I sometimes think I can't be me or whatever I am supposed to be . . . because I don't know what that is. I get good advice at home but I am someone else outside. I want to feel comfortable in my skin.

Marissa expressed her feelings as follows,

I am light-skinned and let everyone know I am Black. I think sometimes I do it when I don't have to just so I can feel who I am. I don't think I am pretty but I don't let anyone know. Plus, before the conference and the CHOICES program I didn't think about who I wanted to be and how much people cared.

One young lady recently wrote a letter to the mentors and organization.

I became involved in the Image Initiative in 2005 when I was a sophomore in high school. I had just finished a very rough freshman year where I passed only half of my classes for the entire year. Upon coming to the conference, I was involved in a lot of trouble with young girls who I thought were my friends. I came to the conference knowing that some of the girls that I did not like would attend. This along with the fact that I got a chance to get out of school for a day became my only motive for going to the conference. When I got there, it was rough hearing the women talk about different diseases, higher education, and bullying. Out of all the topics discussed that Friday, bullying stood out the most. I was a product of bullying and in return, I became a bully.

That Friday changed my life. At the end of the day, we had to participate in a motivating and empowering activity. This activity gave me the opportunity to tell others who I really wanted to be. I realized while participating that I needed to get myself together because I wanted to make my goals come true. That activity taught me the importance of saying no to certain activities and people. What I heard in that session were things that my mother also told me, but I never listened to. Hearing other young people talk about what was going on in their lives gave me the reassurance I needed to push through my pain. That Friday I learned that many people had it worse than me.

This conference is needed because it gives young women the chance to change and make something out of themselves. Here I am a graduate of William Nottingham High School and a graduate of Syracuse University where I completed a double major. I am currently a graduate student at Syracuse University and through it all, the Image Initiative has been with me every step of the way. This program helped me find my voice and to embrace who I am. This conference also challenged me to accept the things that I cannot change and taught me how to work towards the ones that I could change. This conference needs your support simply because it saves lives, one young girl at a time.

IMAGE INITIATIVE ALUM

Diamond wrote on her experience as follows:

I've been going to the Image Initiative's Sisters Empowering Sisters Conference for many years. This two-day event is very influential on me and the girls who go and take in the information. This conference shows young girls of color that they are worth something to this world. It is not easy to believe this when the girls sometimes come from homes that don't support their dreams. Even sometimes it is hard to believe in yourself with the support from home but sometimes it takes people whom you don't know to make girls believe in themselves. Although I have the best support system at home, it sometimes is still great to hear from women that look like myself that are not related to me, that I can do anything that I put my mind to. It's very exciting and exhilarating to know that there is a community of women that care about my future, and that I can do great things and follow my heart.

Another young lady noted:

I don't really see me outside of my house and friends and their family. When I look at magazines and television shows, except for Black shows, we are not really there and if we are we look and dress like White people. I like to see shows where we are doing positive stuff and dress nice. I think people look at us sometimes because of the way we dress and talk like we are nothing. It makes me mad and sad at the same time. Sometimes I just act a certain way because I think that is what people think anyway.

Lisa states:

I don't know who I am. I act different ways if I am around different people. I am learning that I can be me. The conference and the ladies that talk to us make me think I can do anything I want. I just have to work hard. I want to go to college and leave my neighborhood. I want to be somebody. I am tired of people looking at me like I am invisible. The African American women that talk to us make me feel I am beautiful.

Cari noted:

Before being involved in the organization, I didn't think anyone cared. No one listened. When the lady asked me what I would do if I could do anything . . . I said nothing because no one cares. She asked how and what would I like to change . . . I told her it didn't matter because no one listens. She took the time to talk to me and told me I was powerful. I could do anything I wanted to do and be good at it. She asked me if I could change something . . . what would that be? I told her I hated my neighborhood and the people who were destroying everything. She told me if I wanted change like in my neighborhood I could begin by writing my representatives and I could get others involved. She said she would help me. I now think maybe I can . . . maybe I can . . . I'll see if anyone listens.

The question of self-identity and the looking-glass self is embedded in the responses of these young women. However, their comments simply scratch the surface on what they are experiencing. There are additional challenges they face that are unlike others and on the surface young African American females' attitudes and thoughts of self may not adequately reflect their true self.

Returning to the proverb *it takes a village*, recently mentors within the organization were asked to answer the following question. Why is mentoring these young women so important? Following are their responses.

Nicole Watkins, founder of The Image Initiative Inc., reflected, "As a woman, mentoring young women is as natural and necessary to me as breathing. To whom much is given much is required. I have excelled and been successful in areas of my life due to those women who have taken the care to impart wisdom, experience, and most importantly time. They gave of themselves and as such I give of myself . . . as natural and necessary as breathing."

Cheryl Dixon Hills, a twenty-five-year guidance counselor, stated, "Mentoring these young women teaches me that I can see my youth through their eyes, that I have control over the present, while looking at them as my future. I can teach them the value of a Sense of Self and an appreciation for the Road that they have yet to travel. 'You only Live Once: Make it Count.'"

Afua Boeheme, PhD student and member of the board of the Image Initiative Inc., replied, "Here's my thoughts. When you mentor a young person you make an investment in the future. There's no better way to communicate to someone their value and their worth than that."

Griselda Rodriquez, PhD and member of the Image Initiative Inc. board, stated, "Mentoring teaches me compassion. It helps me remember what I needed as a teenager and, in turn, provide these things to younger sisters."

CONCLUSION

The benefits of natural mentoring for both the mentee and the mentor are boundless and should not be thought of as a replacement for a parent(s). Instead the natural mentor should be viewed as a part of a network (village) that is involved in the development of the adolescent. However, some of the challenges that face young African American women and those that work to inspire them have changed and taken on a new persona. Examples such as negative media portrayals, ideas and portrayals of what constitutes beauty, peer pressure, social media, cyberbullying, designer drugs, socioeconomic disenfranchisement, covert racism, and lack of equal educational pursuits are just a few of the issues that African American female adolescents face on a daily basis. However, although this work focused on one organization, there are many organizations and groups both secular and religious based throughout the United States that work to uplift young African American women (see Delta Academy, Diamond in the Rough, Girls Who Rule The World, Black Girls Rock as examples). Regardless of their geographical location, their mission/vision is the same. They mentor, support and empower young African American girls.

Although there is a great deal that needs to still be done as we continue to elevate these young African American women, the role of the mentor provides an extraordinary opportunity that allows for a give-and-take relationship. It is reciprocity at its best, and not unlike Nemo, through the help and guidance of dedicated mentors, adolescent females can and will continue to benefit from the positive influences in their community.

REFERENCES

Anderson, E. (1999). *Code of the street*. New York: W.W. Norton & Co.

Banks, I. (2000). *Hair Matters: Beauty, Power and Black Woman's Consciousness*. New York: New York University Press.

Belgrave, F. Z. *Sisters of Nia: A Cultural Enrichment Program to Empower African American Girls*. Champaign, IL: Research Press.

Brown, J. D., & Stern, S. R. (2002). Mass media and adolescent female sexuality. In G. M. Wingood and R. J. DiClemente, eds. *Handbook of Women's Sexual and Reproductive Health*. New York, NY: Plenum Kluwer Press, 93–112.

Collins, P. (2009). *Black feminist thought: knowledge, consciousness, and the politics of empowerment*. New York: Routledge.

Cooley, C. H. (1998). *On Self and Social Organization*. 1st ed. Chicago: University of Chicago Press.

Hall, R. (1995). The bleaching syndrome: African Americans' response to cultural domination vis-a-vis skin color. *Journal of Black Studies, 26*, 172–184.

Hill Collins, P. (2000). *Black Feminist Thought: Knowledge, Consciousness and the Politics of Empowerment*. New York: Routledge.

Ianni, F. A. (1996). The caring community as a context for joining youth needs and program services. *Journal of Negro Education, 65*(1), 71–91.

Jackson, A. J. 2008. "Self-Identity Among African American Women." *The Eagle Feather* 5. doi:10.12794/tef.2008.107

Stanton, A., Unkrich, L., Walters, G., Lasseter, J., Peterson, B., Reynolds, D., Brooks, A., et al. (2003). Buena Vista Home Entertainment (Firm). *Finding Nemo.* Burbank, Calif: Buena Vista Home Entertainment.

Stevens, J. W. (1997). African American female adolescent identity development: A three-dimensional perspective. *Child Welfare League of America*, 76(1), 145–172.

Tatum, B. D. (1997). The complexity of identity. In *Why Are All the Black Kids Sitting Together in the Cafeteria? and Other Conversations about Race.* New York: Basic Books, 52–74.

Chapter 21

The Mis-Education of Black Girls: Learning in a White System

Jessica J. Jones

> So much of America's tragic and costly failure to care for all its children stems from our tendency to distinguish between our own children and other people's children—as if justice were divisible. —Marian Wright Edelman

As an advocate for all of the children America has left behind and labeled "the impossibles," Marian Wright Edelman motivates all to self-reflect and evaluate the meaning of social justice. In postmodern educational experiences, defining justice and the nature of those social experiences remains relevant for leaders. As providing access to the masses becomes less of an obstacle for education leaders, lack of sustainment continues to impede true progress, especially for Black girls in the educational system. Edelman's viewpoints are reminiscent of Greek philosopher Plato and his protestations about social justice and individuals navigating through life as copies and false representations of reality, existence, and success (Reeve, 1992). Congruent to educational practices in America, in his parable "Allegory of the Cave" Plato demonstrates society's disconnect—justice divided according to false pretenses and experiences pervading the human condition. This parable of the conflict of the human psyche and its relation to ascertaining true knowledge and sensory experience incepted an idealism that permeates even in contemporary thought (Reeve, 1992). Defining the complete educational experience of Black girls is an ambitious venture. Nonetheless, the exploration of definitions and pluralities tends to point towards certain power relationships or ideologies in existence (Robbins, 2000). Similar to Plato's quest, education leaders are faced with the task of addressing the meaning of education for a Black girl in the 21st century and the nature of such in a White, patriarchal system of education. Arguably, the same cave experience exists for the Black female, one whose education has been filtered through a series of misses—a misunderstood, misinformed, and misdirected shadow of the real. All of these inadequacies have led to her mis-education.

Synonymous to the prisoners in Plato's cave, the Black female sees "nothing of herself or of those [educated] alongside her, except the shadows thrown by the fire-light on the walls [of her mind by the puppets, which do not look like her or empathize with her culture]" (Reeve, 1992, p. 189). Many of her White *and Black* counterparts have convinced her that she is classified as the "other" (Hull, Scott & Smith, 1982), and the shadows she sees function as the reality she conceived in her mind, which was created by them. The parapet hides the light that causes the shadows of the educators or educational system. All she has to do is "stand up, turn [her] head, and walk with [her] eyes lifted to the light" (Reeve, 1992, p. 191) and she would enter the realm of reality, thus leaving the world of shadows and learning what she perceived as reality has been an illusion. However, she does not. In fact, she cannot—not yet.

Her reflection is not an included representation in the shadows. Her history and her culture are not reflected there. The White system defines the Black girl's body image, culture, belief systems, perception of self, and various meanings of success for her. She has been taught to let her passions guide her since society has indeed gendered her into thinking so. Because she is imprisoned in her socially constructed body, her psyche does not recall the "once-perfect knowledge of the Forms" (Reeve, 1992, p. 189). The White educational system subversively dissipated the reality of the Black educational experience. Because of this relative ignorance, she does not know that those who existed before her and those in front of her have been incapacitated by the same system. From the lack of encouragement of pursuing a degree in the STEM field to the virtual absence of racial dialogue in school curriculum, the Black girl has been taught to find comfort in assimilation.

Every shadow she sees has been cast through the male gaze or the White gaze (hooks, 1982). The constant media displays of Black female caricatures, who falsely emulate success, strength, and education, confirm the comforting assimilation the White system teaches. Becoming a faux housewife based on location or an athletic connection and finding love in the hip-hop music industry are the shadows she views in the caves of her mind. Ironically, these television shows are dubbed reality TV, when like the prisoners in Plato's cave, they, too, are mere shadows of the White system's illusive definition of success.

The Black girl has been taught to feel guilty. She wears the condemning "A" on her chest, but unlike Pearl in Hawthorne's *The Scarlet Letter,* the Black girl's shame is not adultery; her "A" stands for apologetic (Hawthorne, 2009). This socially constructed guilt teaches her to feel guilty or sorry for speaking out or having an opinion, for choosing a career over a man or bearing children, for desperately trying to attain independence, for setting standards that are just too high, and for seeking truth. She receives this teaching in the early years, and the earlier and the longer she receives it, the more she will believe the shadows. As a result, she acquiesces, self-internalizes, and is well on her way on a path that has predetermined her to be ineffective and mediocre, because the myth of becoming a strong and highly educated Black woman includes a series of apologetics and compromise as a young woman navigating her way through the system.

The purpose of this chapter is to explain the meaning of the nature of education for Black girls in the twenty-first century. If Black girls are to become successful and forge though the system, Black representations in the church, community, and school systems must focus on "the need for service rather than leadership" (Woodson, 1990, p. 111). Many have "made it" and many have arrived at what the social elites deem successful. However, Black girls view these images of success from a distance. As these young girls constantly "window shop," searching for an image that emulates their reflection, they see none or at least none that is in reach. Ultimately, some become lost in the shadows of their hidden caves, while others prove to be resilient and transport themselves through the world of shadows (hooks, 1994). Yet, even in that transport, the reality remains an illusion of what it means to be an educated Black girl growing up in a system that facilitates invisibility and subversion, thus producing more disillusioned, outspoken, but conditioned leaders, who rarely see service as the vehicle towards a reality that intersects Black experiences of girls rather than essentializing them.

In their article about Black girls and the plight in education, Evans-Winters and Esposito (2010) called for more research by scholars of color with Black girls at the forefront of discussion. Making the claim that the educational concerns of Black girls are no longer on scholars' agendas, Evans-Winters and Esposito (2010) assert, "the gratuitous neglect of Black girls' educational development may be a result of agendas that overlook or ignore the significance of multiple identities, oppressions, and consciousness" (p. 22). Extrapolating from Regina Austin's 1995 article, "Sapphire Bound," they further claim that the Black female educational experience is overshadowed by the stereotyped misnomer often attributed to Black women. The angry Black woman label exists in many social and political circles. Unfortunately, this misnomer infiltrated school systems, where Black girls' assertion becomes mistaken for aggression, fortitude replaced with androgyny, and voiced autonomy interpreted as unnecessary loudness (Fordham, 1993; Evans-Winters & Esposito, 2010).

For this reason, Evans-Winters and Esposito (2010) iterate critical race feminism best encapsulates the complex experience of Black girls. Exploring the various structural and ideological barriers impeding Black girls' education remains an imperative endeavor for scholars. In 2009, Black students trailed Whites (83%) and Hispanics (71%) with a 66% on-time graduation rate among all public high schools (U.S. Department of Education, 2012). Even though Black girls tend to fare better than their male counterparts in matriculation rates, the dropout rate in 2009 for Black girls (8.1%) still proved higher than White female students (4.1%) (U.S. Department of Education, 2012). Undeniably, Black boys have their own challenges in the educational system; however, Black girls encounter various forms of marginalization; distorted body image, gendered and racial stereotypes, and punitive disciplinary actions in school, which all contribute to the identity crisis many of them face (Townsend et al., 2010).

According to Morris (2007), intersectional theory best suits the exploration of inequality and the racial, gender, and class factors that often occur together and alter meanings and life experiences of individuals. Because none of these occurs in seclusion or absent of the other, the theory of intersectionality frames "a complex view of social inequality and reality" (Morris, 2007, p. 291). This complex reality and world of pluralities prove to exist for Black girls in education, which can also elucidate why Black girls often remain mis-educated. In order to encourage social and scholastic policies and transform instructional practices in the classroom (Evans-Winters & Esposito, 2010), resiliency must be encouraged and demonstrated by mentors, to whom Black girls can relate and break away from an education that has taught them that it is best to stay in their place (Woodson, 1990). However, if the chains are to be broken off the mind of the Black girl, leaders in the educational field must first engage in discourse that allows them to dispel the stereotypes and adequately understand, inform, and redirect the Black girl.

THE MISUNDERSTOOD BLACK GIRL

In postmodern education, many teachers and administrators perceive Black girls as loud, improper, and androgynous individuals, who pose a constant threat to authority and lack the femininity required to "behave well" in school (Morris, 2007). This type of behavior disparages educational success and helps to solidify or add value to the stereotypes that exist, which define Black girls as having too much attitude and challenging authority through loud or highly dramatized verbal exchanges (Fordham, 1993). Most feminist literature contends Black girls' voices have been silenced in classrooms, where autonomy is lost and self-esteem deflated (Grant, 1984). Contrastingly, recent research suggests Black girls are actually vocal leaders in class discussion and tend to participate more than their male counterparts (Morris, 2007). Even though this increase in participation and vocal expression would prove a positive aspect for Black girls, unfortunately, many teachers welcome their voice, but iterate that Black girls' voices tend to be coupled with loudness and assertive attitude (Morris, 2007). This perceived loudness is another form of misunderstanding that occurs in the educational exchange between teachers, administrators, and Black girls. Although expression is encouraged, because it is not the "proper" form of expression expected by those in authority, the Black girl's voice leads to her demise in the eyes of her teachers and administrators.

In a personal interview, an elementary school principal with over 30 years of experience in the system, described what she has observed: iterating Black girls are often misunderstood by teachers and administrators (including those who share their race and/or gender) because they are constantly seeking recognition and being heard due to lack of affirmation from home and forced early parental roles (Anonymous, personal interview, September 23, 2013). Many of these girls are not being affirmed at home and in turn, their resoluteness and strength that they exhibit are often misunderstood as "wanting to be seen, when instead they just want to be heard" (Anonymous, personal interview, September 23, 2013). The breakdown of the family unit has contributed to the displayed over-aggression, and teachers perceive these girls as discipline problems, failing to recognize that many Black girls are indeed in authoritative roles at home, which makes it difficult for them to shift authority back over to the teacher. Many of these girls have to care for younger siblings at home in a motherly role and this forced responsibility causes Black girls to view themselves as being on the same level with their teacher, the authority figure in the classroom (Anonymous, personal interview, September 23, 2013). Therefore, the perceived obnoxious attitude, loudness, and aggression teachers attribute to Black girls are direct results of external disparaging economic or social situations (Harris, 2009).

Interestingly, a recent high school graduate and first generational college student recalls her primary and high school years in a personal interview, contending Black girls are not necessarily misunderstood, but are distracted by boys, home environment, and social media (Anonymous, personal interview, October 5, 2013). She asserts that teachers actually perceive Black girls more positively than they perceive Black boys and the expectations teachers have are realistic and encourage Black girls to improve themselves (Anonymous, personal interview, October 5, 2013). She goes on to explain that being outspoken is a necessity in order to "survive" in school amongst peers, but Black girls have to perform with teachers and administrators in order to avoid stereotypes and fulfill teachers' and administrators' expectations and perceptions. Even though the student believes Black girls are not stereotyped, she believes that performance plays a big role in ensuring their success, even if that performance is indeed an "act" or loss of self:

> To avoid being "called out" by teachers, I and all Black girls had to play the role. Playing the role made sure I wasn't bothered—wasn't labeled by teachers. I am outspoken, but only when a teacher is not around. I maintained a 3.5 G.P.A., did my school work and they thought I was a good girl for doing so. (Anonymous, personal interview, October 5, 2013)

The performance factor and passivity or docility connected to the good girl stereotype tends to permeate as a reoccurring theme in the intersection of race, gender, and class (Delpit, 1995; Dillabough, 2003).

Although the student believes teachers do not misunderstand Black girls, her performing or fulfilling the teachers' point of view of what constitutes a "good girl" demonstrates this disconnect or misunderstanding. From her educational experiences, she learned that assimilation ensures longevity and success in the White system, and instead of a liberating educational experience, a binding and conforming one paints the facade of educational acceptance and accomplishment (Freire, 1970/2005). She does not realize that her acquiescence, though willingly, is a subversive form of oppression (Freire, 1970/2005). Many Black girls perpetuate a myriad of factors that keep them fulfilling a "safe" educative experience, and their education makes it essential to do so (Woodson, 1990). The concern with keeping up the good girl appearance for teachers proves indoctrination. According to Freire (1970/2005), indoctrination is most successful when self-depreciation becomes an internalized characteristic. The aforementioned student identifies as having high self-esteem, being studious, and socially and emotionally centered; however, her anxiety involving school never stemmed from the opinions of her peers—she instead consumed herself with not becoming what most teachers perceive Black girls to be. Although she would not be characterized by most definitions as having low self-esteem, she does self-deprecate in some ways in order to pass in academia. When asked why she thought this existed, she replied, "Once you've been labeled by a teacher [or administrator], there's no coming back from that. If 'passing' got me through, then I'd rather pass for the rest of my life" (Anonymous, personal interview, October 5, 2013).

THE MISIDENTIFIED BLACK GIRL

Black girls often encounter gendered racial socialization where family members, school experiences, and media shape individuals' identity. Because Black girls are a part of two disvalued or marginalized groups (female and Black), escaping from the negative effects of this "double jeopardy" depends upon the inclusiveness of their learning and support systems (Jones Thomas, Hoxha & Hacker, 2012). Traditional displays of female stereotypes, such as Jezebel and Sapphire images, portray Black girls as controlling, loud, seductive, and argumentative (Townsend et al., 2010). Postmodern depictions of Black female stereotypes involve video vixens in music videos, over the top reality television housewives, and glorified teen pregnancy shows (Townsend et al., 2010).

Even though there has been a recent embracing of the natural hair movement, there are few favorable portrayals of Black women as being beautiful, strong, and independent absent of a Eurocentric viewpoint (Jones Thomas et al., 2012). Because of the pervasiveness of misidentified media images of Black girls and a lack of local positive representations, many Black girls encounter barriers in education because of their own misidentified perceptions of self (Chavous et al., 2003). Therefore, having a connection to or significantly identifying with an ethnic group encourages positive viewpoints of academic achievement (Townsend et al., 2010). However, if no or few positive representations exist in the home environment or if media images counter strong ethnic identity, then Black girls have a higher chance of succumbing to racial stereotypes (Chavous et al., 2003). When interviewed about Black girls and their loss of identity, the elementary school principal proclaims there is a misconception about identity issues and Black girls because many a time individuals view this as a lower-class problem only, when in reality, Black girls from all classes experience identity crisis (Anonymous, personal interview, September 23, 2013). This belief proves accurate as the first-generational college student asserts she was raised in a middle-class household, but still possessed apprehension from time to time concerning her image:

I'm a full-figured girl and I never really obsessed over my weight, because my shape was liked by the boys. I wasn't sexually active or anything; I just kinda inherited those "big body" genes. So, my body image wasn't really a concern. But, there was a time when I cut my hair a lil' short as a beginning thought of "going natural" and surprisingly, some of my *teachers* [male and female] freaked out! One of the female Black teachers told me she couldn't believe I was going all Black on her and one of the male White teachers told me while laughing it off, "boys 'round here won't like you, now . . . better grow you some hair back" I forgot about going natural then . . . I figured it was best to wait to "go black" once I entered college. There were a few girls who actually did it [went natural]. But, they were unpopular already, so it didn't matter anyway what teachers thought of them. (L. Taylor, personal communication, October 5, 2013)

Interestingly, much of the research suggests peers have the largest influence on adolescents' identity development, and there is less focus on teachers' impact on students' perception of Blackness (Jones Thomas et al., 2012). As this student's experience denotes, for Black girls, who may have conquered pressure from their peers, authority figures, especially those who are in the role of educating, play a pivotal part in Black girls' identity development by either helping to affirm or to discourage a strong connection to one's ethnicity (Jones Thomas et al., 2012). Even though Lakeisha has not received any negative comments from her peers and was encouraged to "go natural" by her parental support system, her teachers' words influenced her decision most. More research needs to be done in order to address this area of identity development and classroom interactions.

THE MISINFORMED BLACK GIRL

Black girls remain misinformed due to the lack of resources available where they have an opportunity to learn and to succeed. Because of the lack of or minimal resources, Black girls are often unequipped to compete with their White counterparts. This disadvantage exists because of the misinformation school systems delve out (Anonymous, personal interview, September 23, 2013). Not receiving student-centered learning and lacking support programs for academic expansion renders Black girls vulnerable to a system that fails to prepare them to meet basic standards (Townsend et al., 2010). A Black English and Language Arts teacher in a rural southern high school describes the new danger Black girls face that is being drilled into them daily:

In addition to external issues or other gendered or racial plights, Black girls now have to deal with receiving messages about being standardized. They are classified as unsatisfactory, approaching basic, basic, etc., academically and yet, the system has not ensured that they have everything they need to succeed. Teachers teach tests and administrators push paper and are forced to enforce egregious policies. Gone are the days of "real" teaching. Unfortunately, it's [the system] set up for them to either fail or hope and settle for mediocrity. I once heard a colleague tell a Black female student to learn to be satisfied with her C. "After all, a C is passing." Can you believe that? She needs to *learn* to be satisfied with it! And, that's just what most of my Black female students do—pass through instead of excel. It's not totally their fault, though [Black girls]; they're receiving mixed signals. One signal says you need to do over and above according to standardized testing and the other signal says a C is okay, and it's okay because you don't "see" anyway. They're expected to meet minimal requirements from the get-go and participation in school-related after-school activities is viewed as a waste of time. (Anonymous, personal interview, June 8, 2013)

Research has shown that student involvement in extracurricular activities and support programs is linked to student success and reduces negative behavior (Frederick & Eccles, 2006). However, Blacks are less likely to participate in after-school activities or support programs because of economic reasons (Simpkins, Vest & Becnel, 2010). Also, the decrease in funding for music and the arts in schools plays a major role in the recent increased behavior issues and dropout rates for Black girls (Simpkins et al., 2010). In 2000, girls participated most in music and performing arts extracurricular activities with a 32% rating, contrasted to the 2% decrease in 2009 (Aud, Kewal Raman & Frohlich, 2011). Even though the aforementioned statistics do not categorize according to race, other research shows Black males typically have the highest participation in athletic-related activities and Black girls are involved in the arts (Simpkins et al., 2010).

Moreover, a decline in funding and lack of appreciation for the arts compromise Black girls' educational dexterity. As a result, many of them undertake other unfavorable activities or lack the inspiration and encouragement often provided through participation in extracurricular activities to gain leadership and interpersonal skills and to improve self-esteem (Frederick & Eccles, 2006). Empirical research postulates students involved in the arts or athletic-related activities tend to have better self-knowledge concerning ability and value (Simpkins et al., 2010). When Black girls participate in these types of activities, they not only become better informed about themselves, but they also develop motivation and succeed in school and beyond (Frederick & Eccles, 2006). According to Wigfield et al., 2006, when students fail to participate and remain committed to extracurricular activities, they have a higher chance of not being committed or motivated to develop a positive identity, to remain in school, to matriculate, and to pursue post-secondary education opportunities.

THE MISDIRECTED BLACK GIRL

Black girls are being misdirected by school systems' approach to discipline. The inception of zero-tolerance policies in school coupled with racial and gender stereotypes has led to more Black students overly epitomizing school discipline problems and suspension rates (Winn & Behizadeh, 2011). As more schools seek police presence in schools, harsh punitive discipline action takes precedence over preemptive approaches and policies such as conflict interventions, student counseling, parent-teacher conferences, and even in-school suspension (Kupchik, 2009). Zero-tolerance policies exist as the remedy for all discipline issues. In the past, teachers, administrators, and education leaders collaborated to improve conditions; however, currently, they acquiesce into misdirected thinking (Winn & Behizadeh, 2011). In-school suspension and after school detention have been replaced with juvenile detention centers and group homes. Black women and girls are the leading growing population in detention centers (Simkins, Hirsch, Horvat & Moss, 2004) and Black girls are often disciplined more harshly for less serious offenses in school (Kupchik, 2009).

According to Simkins et al. (2004), when school systems adopt a misdirected approach to discipline, such as zero-tolerance and police presence only policies, students, particularly minority students, are being groomed for the school to prison pathway. The majority of Black girls who are suspended, expelled, or fail grade levels with no interventions or alternative positive reinforcements typically have a higher chance of becoming incarcerated, dropping out, becoming pregnant and dependent on government assistance programs (Simkins et al., 2004). If Black girls are to avoid the school to prison pipeline snare, teachers, administrators, and other educational leaders must develop strategies that redirect discipline issues. One interviewee recalls her first year as an elementary school principal at an academically unacceptable school:

My first year as principal was indeed a challenging, but fruitful one. I had to devise strategies and get teachers to "buy" into the vision I had for the school. Academic performance was extremely low. Funding was depleted. Teacher and student apathy were high, and student discipline was an issue. The previous administrator had a zero-tolerance policy and students were suspended for fighting (serious offense) all the way down to not having last night's homework (not so serious). Teachers were used to dumping students in the office and classroom management seemed like a curse word to them. I knew redirection was the best option for improving discipline issues—otherwise if I followed the previous administration's approach, the school would be empty. (Anonymous, personal communication, September 23, 2013)

If Black girls are to function in an educational space that ensures a school to post-secondary education path and not a school to prison path, out of school suspensions need to be replaced with in-school nurturing alternatives, where student aggression becomes displaced by positivity. As demonstrated by the aforementioned administrative experiences, redirection offers the best long-term benefits:

> My first year I had a sixth grader who was a behavior problem. She was very aggressive and bullied a few of her peers. Ironically, she was an honor student, with a 3.4 G.P.A., but she gave her teachers hell regularly. Instead of suspension, her punishment involved serving as a school buddy for the lower grades. She had to help the kindergarten teachers clean up, prepare activities, and conduct story time. All of this took place during her morning and afternoon recess and during P.E. She couldn't attend any after-school functions until her buddying time was complete. She also couldn't purchase any items from the concession and her parent had to sign off on her daily buddying logs. This form of *punishment,* one that forces her into acts of service, allowed her to redirect her anger and she became passionate about helping and developed responsibility and a sense of agency. This young girl, who averaged three suspensions a year under previous administration, finished the year with no suspensions and no more behavior referrals. She's not the only one, but she was the first in the school buddy program, and her redirected behavior let us know we strategized correctly. (Anonymous, personal interview, September 23, 2013)

When education leaders replace misdirected discipline approaches with redirected ones such as the aforementioned example, service can become the impetus for change where discipline problems can become disciplined leaders.

MENTORING—THE VEHICLE FOR RESILIENCY

In his profound and provoking text, *The Mis-education of the Negro,* Carter G. Woodson (1933) provides constructive insight into the many issues plaguing Blacks post-slavery and beyond. Over eight decades later, his postulations remain palpable and necessitate change in the Black community, especially in regards to education. Woodson (1933) calls for more individuals who are willing to serve, and he iterates many leaders help to bind instead of lead and liberate the race. Similarly, Black girls need fewer leaders in name only and more individuals who are willing to mentor and demonstrate resiliency and strength. Black girls need fewer spokespersons and more servant-leaders, those who model leadership and rising above by working in the trenches. What good is a program, youth summit, or dialogic roundtable if at the close of the event, all proceed back to their homes only to plan the next movement, revolution, or event?

According to Freire (1970/2005), leaders who resemble the aforementioned spokespersons do not liberate and are indeed non-liberated themselves; they do not take dialogic action and as a result, focus on promoting a selected few (more leaders) and leave the community in shambles. As Woodson iterates,

> If the [Black person] could abandon the idea of leadership and instead stimulate a larger number of the race to take up definite tasks and sacrifice their time and energy in doing these things efficiently, the race might accomplish something. . . . Workers will solve the problems which race leaders talk about and raise money to enable them to talk more about. Oratory and resolutions do not avail much. (1933, pp. 118–119)

Mentoring has been considered the form of service that facilitates cognitive, emotional, and social growth in adolescents (Spencer & Liang, 2009). Although mentoring has been introduced in school systems and embraced in certain areas more than others, Black girls need more gender- and race-specific prevention programs to enrich their lives academically and to develop a positive ethnic identity (Evans-Winters & Esposito, 2010). This author realizes that individuals of a different race are quite capable of nurturing a positive mentoring experience and there are documented examples noting this success. However, the theory of critical race feminism best suits the need for more mentoring by women of color; this intersection of race and gender (and class) helps leaders take an anti-essentialist approach and enact educational practices that will war against gender and racial oppression (Evans-Winters & Esposito, 2010).

The majority of literature involving mentoring lacks examining ways mentoring directly affects educational policies that more inclusively intersect class, gender, and race (Evans-Winters & Esposito, 2010). Historically, community-based mentoring and school-based mentoring programs function opposite of one another having divergent foci (Anastasia, Skinner & Mundhenk, 2012). Community-based programs tend to develop identity and social-emotional skills, while school-based programs concentrate more on academic success (Anastasia et al., 2012). Even though both of these settings prove effective, school systems need to promote school-based mentoring that not only focuses on improving academic success of Black girls, but also combines academic improvement with cognitive, emotional, and social stability (Anastasia et al., 2012; Hirsch, Mickus, & Boerger, 2002).

Putting Service to Work: Implications for Practice

Holistically speaking, Black girls are championed for graduating and pursuing post-secondary education at higher rates than their male counterparts

(U.S. Department of Education, 2012). Despite that noted achievement and other documented success stories of Black girls beating the odds within the Black community, Black girls lag behind White girls academically (U.S. Department of Education, 2012). If leaders in the educational system truly aspire to shape more resilient Black girls, a call to action needs to take place at every ground level. The following suggestions are recommended based on observations, interviews, and review of recent research:

Teachers need to establish and voice higher expectations for students in the classrooms. Many Black girls no longer view their teachers as authority figures that care about student learning and success beyond the girls who fit the mold of what it means to be a *proper* Black girl (Jones Thomas et al., 2012). As the young college student iterated, students recognize early on when teachers appear apathetic towards their learning and apathy tends to set the tone for the academic year. Setting clear goals and high expectations at the beginning of the school year will improve Black girls' perception concerning ability and cause them to regain trust in their teachers again (Morris, 2007). Voicing these expectations motivates students and fosters growth.

School systems need to solicit help from education and other professional retirees as volunteer mentors. Even though many school systems may not have funds allocated for support programs that advance diversity and academic efforts, there are many retirees who are looking for ways to remain active and can volunteer and mentor students. These retirees are success stories within themselves, as they have either obtained a degree or adopted a trade and successfully navigated through the workforce. Targeting these retirees and facilitating collaboration improves community relationships with area schools and models local success stories and positive representations of achievement for Black girls (DuBois & Karcher, 2005). Black women who have retired as educators, business professionals, entrepreneurs, and leaders in technical and trade fields are an untapped wealth of resources needed in school systems.

Peer mentoring groups need to be included as school-based clubs or extracurricular activities. Much of the literature focuses on adult-youth mentoring. However, positive peer mentoring can effect change and help Black girls feel more connected to and develop a sense of belonging in the school and social environment by increasing self-esteem (DuBois & Karcher, 2005). To see Black girls, who are slightly older, succeed at the middle and high school or college level enhances their development. Many higher education faculty members develop service-learning courses in their education or inter-disciplinary curriculum. If school systems would initiate contact with professors, many of their mentoring programs could benefit from local universities' service learning courses and curricula.

Target parents by offering school-based services and support centers for parents. Other than parent-teacher conferences, schools need to increase the awareness and visibility of parents in school activities and programs. Parent-teacher associations can add mentoring to their agendas, and adopting a Parent Resource Center, much like the elementary school principal interviewed referenced having at her school, bridges the gap between parent-school relationships and communication and provides a place where parents receive support for ensuring Black girls' success.

Lastly, churches could do more to support mentoring efforts. Even though faith-based organizations have little connection with the majority of public school systems, leaders from local area churches often have individuals within the church who can mentor. Some states have governor-led initiatives that support this form of mentoring (Sherman, 2003). Church leaders can formulate mentoring groups within the church as one of their community service undertakings and increase awareness about the alarming plight of Black girls. In 2009, roughly 29% of high school seniors mentioned religion as a significant factor in their life that affects their success in school (U.S. Department of Education, 2012). Faith-based partnerships or school adoption can improve community relations and provide guidance, encouragement, and academic support to schools in need, especially at low socioeconomic and low performing schools. Ethnic groups have always stated a strong sense of religion and faith helped to eradicate various social and economic ills occurring in their lives (Jones, 1993). Faith-based mentoring is a hands-on approach for significantly improving opportunities for Black girls in the community.

CONCLUSION

The multifaceted educational experiences of Black girls need to be understood and examined more in-depth at the pedagogical level. As determinations to lessen high school dropout rates for Black boys continue, scholars in the field must not neglect the essentials of the Black girl. More gender- and intersecting race-based research is needed with documented success stories of individuals demonstrating resiliency and programs effecting change. Researchers and education policymakers cannot afford to ignore Black girls' plight and silence efforts that foster fortitude. All leaders must embrace a service mindset and ensure that this debilitating educational cycle ceases to perpetuate.

REFERENCES

Anastasia, T., Skinner, R., & Mundhenk, S. (2012, Spring). Youth mentoring: Program and mentor best practices. *Journal of Family and Consumer Sciences, 104*(2), 38–44. Retrieved from http://search.proquest.com

Anonymous. (2013, June 5). Personal interview.

Anonymous. (2013, September 23). Telephone interview.

Anonymous. (2013, October 5). Personal interview.

Aud, S., Kewal Raman, A., & Frohlich, L. (2011). *America's youth: Transitions to adulthood* (NCES 2012-026). Washington, DC: Government Printing Office.

Chavous, T. M., Bernat, D. H., Schmeelk-Cone, K., Caldwell, C. H., Kohn-Wood, L., & Zimmerman, M. A. (2003). Racial identity and academic attainment among African American adolescents. *Child Development, 74,* 1076–1090. Retrieved from http://search.proquest.com

Delpit, L. (1995). *Other people's children: Cultural conflict in the classroom.* New York: The Free Press.

Dillabough, J. (2003). Gender, education, and society: The limits and possibilities of feminist reproduction theory. *Sociology of Education, 76,* 376–379. Retrieved from http://search.proquest.com

DuBois, D. L., & Karcher, M. J. (eds.). (2005). *Handbook of youth mentoring.* Thousand Oaks, CA: Sage Publications.

Edelman, M. W. (2008). *The sea is so wide and my boat is so small: Charting a course for the next generation.* New York, NY: Hyperion.

Evans-Winters, V., & Esposito, J. (2010). Other people's daughters: Critical race feminism and Black girls' education. *Journal of Educational Foundations, 24*(1), 11–24. Retrieved from www.proquest.com

Fordham, S. (1993). Those loud Black girls: (Black) women, silence, and passing in the academy. *Anthropology and Education Quarterly, 30*(3), 272–293. Retrieved from www.proquest.com

Frederick, J., & Eccles, J. (2006). Is extra-curricular participation associated with beneficial outcomes? Concurrent and longitudinal relations. *Developmental Psychology, 42*(4), 698–713. Retrieved from http://search.proquest.com

Freire, P. (2005). *Pedagogy of the oppressed* (30th Anniversary ed.). (M. Bergman Ramos, trans.). New York, NY: The Continuum International Publishing Group. (Original work published 1970).

Grant, L. (1984). Black females' "place" in desegregated classrooms. *Sociology of Education, 57,* 98-111. Retrieved from www.proquest.com

Harris, P. (2009). Economies of color. In E. N. Glenn, *Shades of difference: Why skin color matters* (pp. 1-6). Palo Alto, CA: Stanford University Press.

Hawthorne, N. (2009). *The scarlet letter.* New York: Penguin Books.

Hirsch, B. J., Mickus, M., & Boerger, R. (2002). Ties to influential adults among Black and White adolescents: Culture, social class, and family networks. *American Journal of Community Psychology, 30*(2), 289–303. Retrieved from http://search.proquest.com

hooks, b. (1982). *Ain't I a woman? Black women and feminism.* London: Pluto Press.

hooks, b. (1994). *Teaching to transgress: Education as the practice of freedom.* New York, NY: Routledge.

Hull, G., Scott, P. B., & Smith, B. (eds.). (1982). *All the women are White, all the Blacks are men, but some of us are brave: Black women's studies.* New York: The Feminist Press.

Jones, A. (1993). *Wade in the water: The wisdom of the spirituals.* Maryknoll, NY: Orbis Books.

Jones Thomas, A., Hoxha, D., & Hacker, J. (2012). Contextual influences on gendered racial identity development of African American young women. *Journal of Black Psychology, 39,* 88–101. http://dx.doi.org/10.1177/0095798412454679

Kupchik, A. (2009). Things are tough all over: Race, ethnicity, class and school discipline. *Punishment & Society, 11*, 291–317. http://dx.doi.org/10.1177/146 2474509334552

Morris, E. W. (2007). "Ladies" or "Loudies"? Perceptions and experiences of Black girls in classrooms. *Youth & Society, 38*(4), 490–515. http://dx.doi.org/10 .1177/004418X06296778

Reeve, C. D. (ed.). (1992). *Plato: Republic.* (G. M. Grube, trans.). Indianapolis, IN: Hackett Publishing.

Robbins, R. (2000). *Literary feminisms.* New York, NY: St. Martin's Press.

Sherman, A. L. (2003, January/February). Faith in communities: A solid investment. *Society, 40*(2), 19–26. http://dx.doi.org/10.1007/s12115-003-1048-2

Simkins, S. B., Hirsch, A. E., Horvat, E. M., & Moss, M. B. (2004, Winter). The school to prison pipeline for girls: The role of physical and sexual abuse. *Children's Legal Rights Journal, 24*, 56–72. Retrieved from http://search.proquest.com

Simpkins, S. D., Vest, A. E., & Becnel, J. N. (2010). Participating in sport and music activities in adolescence: The role of activity participation and motivational beliefs during elementary school. *Journal of Youth and Adolescence, 39*(11), 1368–1386. Retrieved from http://search.proquest.com

Spencer, R., & Liang, B. (2009, March 13). She gives me a break from the world: Formal youth mentoring relationships between adolescent girls and adult women. *J Primary Prevent, 30*, 109–130. http://dx.doi.org/10.10007/s10935 -009-0172-1

Townsend, T. G., Neilands, T. B., Jones Thomas, A., & Jackson, T. R. (2010). I'm no Jezebel; I am young, gifted, and Black: Identity, sexuality, and Black girls. *Psychology of Women Quarterly, 34*, 273–285. http://dx.doi.org/10.1111 /j.1471-6402.2010.01574.x

U.S. Department of Education. (2012). *State dropout and completion data file* (Table 125). Retrieved from National Center for Education Statistics: http://nces .ed.gov/programs/coe/indicator_coi.asp

Wigfield, A., Eccles, J. S., Schiefele, U., Rosner, R., & Davis-Kean, D. (2006). Development of achievement motivation. In N. Eisenberg, W. Damon, & R. M. Leiner (eds.), *Handbook of child psychology: Vol. 3, Social, emotional, and personality development*, pp. 933–1002. Hoboken, NJ: Wiley.

Winn, M. T., & Behizadeh, N. (2011). The right to be literate: Literacy, education, and the school-to-prison pipeline. *Review of Research in Education, 35*, 147–173. http://dx.doi.org/10.3102/0091732X10387395

Woodson, C. G. (1933). *The Mis-education of the negro.* Trenton, NJ: Africa World Press.

Part IV

Criminal Justice

Chapter 22

Violated and Victimized: The Juvenile Justice System and Black Girls

Tomasina L. Cook

INTRODUCTION

The rate of juvenile delinquency in America is a growing epidemic. Although boys still comprise the majority of juvenile arrests, the representation of girls in the juvenile justice system is rising (Snyder & Sickmund, 2006). According to the Office of Juvenile Justice and Delinquency Prevention (2012), 1 in 4 youth in the United States is a juvenile, which includes about 73.9 million people. The juvenile justice system is comprised of juvenile law enforcement, the juvenile courts, and juvenile correctional agencies which are components of the criminal justice system that is intended to treat youthful offenders. The history of the juvenile justice system evolved from the needs to keep children safe and protected from the adult criminal justice system. Since the nineteenth century, children who were considered delinquent, neglected, or runaways were treated exactly the same way as adult criminal offenders (Mennel, 1972). As a result, there were several major juvenile justice initiatives that were geared toward protecting children as they go through the criminal justice system. The first major transformation was to separate the criminal justice system offenders, adult and youth. Examples of these separation components were the probation, courts, and law enforcement systems.

The purpose of these separations was to establish a legal framework for a systematic process for youth in the criminal justice system; later this approach was labeled the juvenile justice system. An overall aim of the juvenile justice system is not to punish juveniles like adult offenders, but provide rather rehabilitation options to treat their criminality. Since the inception of the juvenile justice system, there have been some major transformations that revolutionize the way youthful offenders are treated as they go through the criminal justice process.

Initial attempts at reforming youthful offenders were reformatory schools. Social reformers of the nineteenth century felt that troubled juveniles needed an institution for rehabilitation purposes. Unfortunately, at the turn to the twentieth century, these reformatories' practices were geared for White women only, African American women were placed in male prisons, where they were put on chain gangs and were subject to beatings (Rafter, 1990). Additionally, another goal was to separate youthful offenders from adults. New York City's Society for the Prevention of Juvenile Delinquency established the New York House of Refuge to house juvenile delinquents in 1825. The first juvenile court was established in Cook County in the state of Illinois in 1899. In the next few decades, all of the states had established juvenile courts. The purpose of these courts was to align with the legal doctrine parens patriae, which means that it gives the state the power to act as a guardian for children. Therefore, the original goal was to help rehabilitate youthful offenders to a law-abiding adult life. Also, another goal was to view juvenile court as a civil rather than criminal matter.

During the turbulent times of the 1960s, the issue of the legal rights of juvenile offenders became controversial and the United States Supreme Court became involved. At this time, youth in the juvenile court system did not have constitutional legal rights. In the landmark case of *In re Gault* (1967), the U.S. Supreme Court ruled that despite juvenile court proceedings being civil, juveniles have rights under due process of law; meaning that juveniles have the same rights under the Fourteenth Amendment, which gives protection of due process of law and equal protection clauses that are identical to adult offenders. Post *In re Gault*, there were major changes that occurred involving comprehensive services to juveniles. In 1968, Congress passed the Juvenile Delinquency Prevention and Control Act. The purpose of the act was for states to receive federal funding to develop comprehensive plans and programs that would work on a community level to prevent and deter juvenile delinquency. Later, in 1974, the federal government changed this act to the Juvenile Justice and Delinquency Prevention Act, which is monitored by the United States Department of Justice and the National Institute for Juvenile Justice and Delinquency.

During the 1980s and 1990s, juvenile crime rates dramatically increased (Siegel & Welsh, 2014). Also, during the time period, there was an increase of African American girls involved in the juvenile justice system. According to the National Children's Defense Fund (2011) the number of girls arrested has grown by 50% since 1980; African American girls are three times more likely to be incarcerated than White girls.

EXTENT OF BLACK GIRLS IN THE JUVENILE JUSTICE SYSTEM

There are various causes of juvenile delinquency. However, the causes for African American girls are quite complex; they are typically both the victim and offender in the juvenile justice system. First, they are overrepresented in the system and in the inequitable treatment services. Unfortunately, they are more likely to receive harsh sanctions, such as incarceration and no mental health and/or addiction treatment options. According to Lauristen (2003) data from the Department of Justice, African American girls faced much higher risks of nonstranger violence than either Hispanic or White girls, and they are more likely to be victimized by a stranger in their neighborhood. In the beginning of the social reform movement to combat juvenile delinquency, sub-reformer women groups were formed, such as White women reformers and the African American women reformers. These women reformers wanted to focus on the victimization of girls. However, there was a major difference in their concerns regarding White girls' well-being and regarding girls of color, particularly African American girls (Odem, 1995). The White women reformers' focus was more on the sexual victimization of White girls involved in the juvenile justice system, such as what contributing factors led to their initial involvement. As a result of this inquiry, it was discovered that current laws at the beginning of the last century did not protect White girls. Therefore, statutory rape laws were created to protect girls, but primarily White girls, not African American girls from sexual perpetrators (Belknap, 2007). Due to these controversial issues regarding the sexuality practices of young African American girls, they were left particularly vulnerable to sexual exploitation, with no protection from the law (Smith Brice, 2011).

Currently, the juvenile justice system has two distinct categories of offender: delinquents and status offenders (Senna & Siegel, 1992). Often, African American girls are initially involved in the juvenile justice system due to status offenses rather than criminal offenses. Status offenses are activities that are viewed as offenses when committed by juveniles because of their age at the time of the activity. Bartol and Bartol (2013) state that status offenses are not illegal if done by an adult, therefore they are not criminal in nature to adults. Examples of status offenses are truancy, running away from home, breaking curfew laws, and defiance towards parents. However, despite the passing of a new legislative act in 1994 designed to protect women called the Violence Against Women Act (VAWA), many juvenile courts have circumvented the legislation by relabeling status offenses as delinquent acts. For example, family conflicts can now be viewed as family violence; in the past these family conflicts that might have led to status offense charges now can result in delinquency charges of assault and harassment (Buzawa & Hotaling, 2006). African American girls due to the various strains in the home are more susceptible to being arrested for family violence–related criminal acts. The juvenile justice system has a tendency to judge these acts as antisocial behaviors that are criminal. The system is failing to see that this is a youth in crisis and needs help in processing her traumatic experiences. When the juvenile justice system fails to recognize and treat these trauma issues, they are re-victimizing African American girls in their system.

Therefore, in order to understand the complexity of African American girls in the juvenile justice system, there is a need to understand the dynamics of the African American girls by taking a critical look at the unique factors that play an integral role in the nature and extent of their involvement in the juvenile justice system.

VIOLATED AND VICTIMIZED

The juvenile justice system plays an integral role in the violation and victimization of African American girls. Several feminist scholars argue that girls are not only the victims of injustice at home, but also risk being victimized by agents of the juvenile justice system (Siegel & Welsh, 2014). Tracy, Kempf-Leonard, and Abramoske-James (2009) took a further look at this dynamic by utilizing national data and found that girls were handled more punitively than males at almost every stage of the juvenile justice system. In general, juveniles are more likely to be a victim of a crime than adults. The juvenile justice system was built of paternalistic and racist views. As a result of these sexist, racist, and classist views, African American girls are feeling the brunt of the juvenile justice system in various aspects. Despite being in the system for less violent crimes and status offenses than their counterparts, they are more than likely to be treated harsher with unfair arrests, dispositions, and treatment services.

African American girls have substantially higher victimization rates than White juvenile girls; the rate for African American girls was approximately four times greater than the rate for White girls. In addition, the homicide victimization rates for African American girls were higher than the rates for White males. Generally, African Americans girls are more likely to suffer violation of their individual rights that are guaranteed by the United States Constitution and be victimized by perpetrators and the juvenile justice system. The juvenile justice system is harsher towards girls, but especially to African American girls due to the nature of their involvement in antisocial behaviors. Unlike their counterparts, African American girls' contacts with the juvenile justice system are often due to running away from home (Sharp, 2010). The juvenile justice system has failed to look further into the dynamics of the African American girl home environment. For example, runaways often leave home to avoid further physical or sexual abuse. Instead of the juvenile justice system investigating why the youth is running away from home, they view the youth as a juvenile offender and charge her with a status offense of running away from home. Female adolescents who have a history of exposure to violence have unique needs that must be met in order to successfully prevent recidivism. As a result of their violence exposure, these adolescents may have lingering trauma or mental health difficulties, engage in risky sexual behaviors, and abuse drugs and alcohol.

Additionally, African American girls see themselves as continuous victims in their families, schools, community, and in the juvenile justice system. According to Pugh-Lilley, Neville, and Poulin (2001), African American girls see their delinquent criminality as defending and protecting themselves from victimization.

FAMILY FACTORS

Familial factors are an essential component in African American girls being involved in the juvenile justice system. A major family factor is poor or inconsistent parenting. Oftentimes, African American parents file a person in need of supervision (PINS) or children in need of supervision (CHINS) petition. Generally, the purpose of PINS and CHINS is to supervise a child underage who the court or juvenile probation department has determined does not attend school, engages in at-risk behavior, is dangerous or out of control, or often disobeys his or her parents, guardians, or school officials. In essence, the parents have lost control of parenting their child and are looking for help from the juvenile justice system. African American families have unique characteristics that are different from White families. Some view these unique characteristics as being dysfunctional. One of these characteristics is single parenting. Since President Lyndon B. Johnson declared a "War on Poverty" in 1964, there has been a huge increase of African American single-parented households. The majority of these households are headed by women due to teenage pregnancies, unwed pregnancies, and the male leaving the family, which is called the "black Matriarchy" (Staples, 1970). Some scholars believe that this is due to the remnants of slavery and the long history of oppression of Black women and children. Also, African Americans girls are faced with sexist and racist disparities in the juvenile justice system, such as the high likelihood of being placed in a juvenile detention center as a youthful offender. In the U.S. Census data from 2010, it was reported that the majority of African American families consisted of single-parent mothers.

Teenage pregnancies can cause difficulties for the family; one is the economic stress. Often children born to teenage parents are more than likely to live in poverty and to experience both academic and social problems that can be a precursor to delinquency. These strain factors can cause esteem issues for both the parent(s) and the child. Having low self-esteem can lead to lack of self-worth and an "I don't care attitude." This unhealthy view of self can contribute to problematic behavior in the community, the home, and school. These problem behaviors can be seen as defiant in nature but are actually a cry for attention and help in dealing with environmental factors. Additionally, children who are born to teenage mothers are often involved more in the juvenile justice system, more likely to experiment with alcohol and drugs, and become a teenage parent themselves. As a result of these factors, a vicious cycle continues.

Another concern is the lack of supervision caused by inadequate child care. Lack of supervision varies and may range from the parent(s) not being at home due to work obligations or being neglectful due to their mental health or addiction issues. African American girls are often involved in makeshift child care arrangements that are neglectful and prone to abusive situations. African American girls are more at risk to become victims of childhood sexual and physical abuse due to lack of parental supervision. According to the National Crime Victimization Survey of 2010, African American youth have a significantly higher chance of becoming victims of violent crimes than White American youth. Due to the lack of supervision, these youth are at risk for crime. African American girls are uniquely susceptible to gendered violence and its effects (Tonneson, 2013). Additionally, their high crime neighborhoods put them at risk for victimization or crime-prone behaviors.

As previously stated, African American girls become involved in the juvenile justice system due to family conflict, especially between the parent and child. According to Nye (1958), if there is parental conflict in the home, this is a significant predictor of delinquency. Children living in constantly stressful homes are prone to misbehaving at school and home. Later, they can develop a lack of trust and respect for their family. This maladaptive behavior can lead to more strife in the family, oppositional defiance behavior, and antisocial behavior as well.

EDUCATION

Once African American girls become involved in the juvenile justice system, their education becomes more difficult to obtain. African American girls are five times more likely than White, Hispanic, and Native American girls to be suspended or expelled.

The failure to meet educational needs increases disengagement and dropouts, increasing the risk of later juvenile court involvement. The correlation between lack of educational attainment and school zero-tolerance policies is an essential component to a fast track involvement in the juvenile justice system.

They become stigmatized by the educational institution as being a "criminal" and are more prone to harsh exclusionary disciplinary actions that may result in expulsion and being "aged out" to a general education program (GED). This unfair and unjust concept is known as the "school to prison pipeline." The school to prison pipeline concept is based on several practices, policies, and conditions that promote criminalization within educational environments that results in the recidivism and incarceration of African American juveniles. Of course, African American girls are their main target. According to Dixon et al., (2008), the pipeline analogy has become a dominant frame to analyze the lived experiences of girls and boys, disproportionately African American, who are being criminalized in their learning environments, ultimately leading to future contacts with juvenile and criminal justice systems. Additionally, the Advancement Project (2010) reported that "arrests in school represent the most direct route into the school-to-prison pipeline, but out-of-school suspensions, expulsions, and referrals to alternative schools also push students out of school and closer to a future in the juvenile and criminal justice systems" (pp. 4–5). Morris (2013) highlighted that African American girls represent the fastest growing segment of the juvenile justice population, and they have experienced the most dramatic rise in middle school suspension rates in recent years. Also, among the nation's 10 highest suspending districts, Black girls with one or more disability experienced the highest suspension rate of all girls (Losen & Gillespie, 2012). Frequently, these suspensions are the result of zero-tolerance policies. The original purpose of a zero-tolerance policy in schools was to enforce detention, suspension, and expulsion policies in response to drugs and weapons in violent acts. When children are repeatedly suspended from school they lack supervision, which can cause them to get in additional trouble and also this can cause them to fall behind in academics. However, over time, these zero-tolerance policies began to target minority children specifically, who eventually disengage from school due to this inequality from school administrators. To illustrate, African American girls are affected by the stigma of having to participate in identity politics that marginalize them or place them into polarizing categories—"good" girls or girls that behave in a "ghetto" fashion—which exacerbate stereotypes about Black femininity, particularly in the context of socioeconomic status, crime, and punishment (Jones, 2009). Furthermore, Blake, Butler, Lewis, and Darensbourg (2011) suggested that African American girls were being criminalized for qualities that have been associated with their survival as Black females; for example, to be "loud" or "defiant" which are typical infractions that lead to the use of exclusionary discipline in schools. Not only can this pipeline cause a lack of education and increase criminality, but it can be a precursor to teenage pregnancy.

CHILD ABUSE AND NEGLECT

African American girls have a higher chance of being a victim of child abuse and neglect compared to White girls, where the perpetrator is the parent. The most common form of abuse is neglect. Neglect is often misunderstood due to cultural reasons. However, a basic definition of neglect is the repeated failure of a parent or guardian with responsibility for the child to provide the necessary food, clothing, shelter, medical care, or supervision to the degree that the child's health, safety, and well-being are threatened with harm. The next form of abuse is sexual abuse. In a study conducted by Black Women's Blueprint (2011), 60% of African American girls have experienced sexual abuse at the hands of African American men before reaching the age of 18. In a previous study, conducted by the Black Women's Health Imperative (2004), over seven years the rate of sexual assault was approximately 40% among African American females. This type of pervasive trauma can lead African American girls to mental health disorders, addiction, abusive relationships, and running away from home.

A major cause for child abuse and neglect is high stress within the families. As a way of coping with the stress, often parents self-medicate with alcohol and drugs. There is a strong relationship between child abuse and parental alcoholism. Additionally, other substances, such as cannabis, cocaine, and opiates often play an important role in the neglect and abuse of children. Lastly, children that are raised by addictive parents are more often prone to becoming addicted themselves. Lederman, Dakof, Larrea, and Li (2004) reported that 34% of girls who enter the juvenile justice system have a substance abuse disorder. Also, many of them will develop a cycle of violence. Basically, when African American girls experience childhood violence they are more prone to become violent adults due to previous victimization.

Many researchers believe that there is a child abuse and juvenile delinquency link. Child abuse victims may run away from home in order to escape the abuse and live on the streets or get involved with gang activity and even prostitution. Children at risk of maltreatment, such as child abuse or neglect, also are at increased risk of experiencing mental health problems (Johnson et al., 2002; Manly, Kim, Rogosch & Ciccheti, 2001). Runaways have a greater chance of getting involved in delinquency and drug abuse (Jung, Tajima, Herrenkohl & Huang, 2009).

MENTAL HEALTH

Mental health issues among African American girls are a huge concern in society, especially in the juvenile justice system. Despite these concerns, many girls in the juvenile justice system have mental health disorders and need mental health services (Petrila, 1998). Grisso (2004) highlighted these concerns in a comprehensive review of the most common mental health disorders of youth in juvenile programs:

- Anxiety disorders, such as obsessive-compulsive disorder and post-traumatic stress disorder.
- Disruptive behavior disorders, such as conduct disorder and oppositional defiant disorder.
- Mood disorders, such as bipolar disorders, dysthymia, major depression, and other depressive disorders.
- Substance-related disorders, such as abuse and dependence disorders that are related to chronic and serious alcohol or drug abuse.
- Thought disorders, such as psychotic disorders and schizophrenia.

Rates of depression are highest among African American girls. In 2009, two-thirds (67%) of African American teen girls reported feeling sad or hopeless for 2 or more weeks in a row in the past 12 months compared to the national average of teen girls (34%) (Centers for Disease Control and Prevention, 2009).

As a result of the prevalence of these disorders among African American girls, it is essential for the juvenile justice system to properly use screening and assessment tools to identify and treat mental health disorders. Although mental health screening is increasing, it is still not common in juvenile justice services; most youths with mental health problems in this system are not thoroughly assessed and provided with specialized treatment unless they display severe symptoms or have a history of past mental health treatment (MacKinnon-Lewis, Kaufman & Frabutt, 2002). According to the Coalition for Juvenile Justice (2000), mental health services for youth in the juvenile justice system are fragmented and inadequate. Therefore, it is critical to address these mental health disorders in order to prevent future criminality. African American girls are more at risk to develop mental health disorders than their counterparts due to various biological, sociological, psychological, and familial factors. Furthermore, Herz (2001) estimated that African American girls were, respectively, three times less likely to receive mental health placements than White girls. Unfortunately, African American girls' mental health goes unrecognized due to their disruptive behavior and defiant tendencies. Due to these behavioral concerns, their mental health problems are poorly misunderstood. Prior research has demonstrated that females within the justice system may be especially vulnerable due to their high rates of mental health problems and abuse histories (Abram, Teplin, McClelland & Dulcan, 2003; Fazel, Doll & Langstrom, 2008). Examples of their abuse histories include incest, neighborhood violence, and vicarious traumatization from witness violence in the home and school. While efforts are underway to address the unique mental health needs of girls in the system (Zahn, Hawkins, Chiancone & Whitworth, 2008), very little attention has been given to the complex needs of the African American girl that is involved in the juvenile justice system due to various victimizations.

FAMILIAL FACTORS

Family plays an integral role in the contributing factors that lead African American girls into the juvenile justice system. A major contributing factor is stressors within the family, such as poor interpersonal relationships among family members. The causes of these poor relationships can be lack of communication, unresolved conflict, poor parenting, the family breakup due to abandonment, and divorce. When children experience family breakup they are more likely to demonstrate behavior problems and hyperactivity than children in intact families (Bray, Bray & Zeeb, 1986). A disturbing explanation for female delinquency is girls' problems with their parents due to both physical and sexual abuse. These abuses are the main reasons why they report running away from their dysfunctional home to escape the abuse. Another familial risk factor that criminologists are exploring is the relationship between juvenile delinquency and parental criminality (Crum et al., 1996). African American girls whose parent(s) are participants in criminal behavior have a higher risk of becoming a juvenile delinquent themselves. They engage in delinquent behaviors to support themselves and other family members by selling drugs, prostitution, violent acts, and theft-related crimes. African American girls view their criminality as necessary for survival. Also, for them their parents' criminal behavior is seen as a learned behavior that is somewhat acceptable in their home and environment.

TREATMENT STRATEGIES

The juvenile justice system must provide a comprehensive continuum of individualized formal and informal services that address the emotional, educational, physical, and social needs of African American girls in the juvenile justice system. According to Robinson and Ward (1991), African American girls need to develop effective coping strategies that will promote optimal development. These services must include prevention and intervention strategies, such as early identification by screening properly, using assessment tools that are culturally and gender specific, diversion programs that have programmatic components that address the specific needs of African American girls, and individualized and group mental health and addiction treatment services. Such services must include a coordinated community response or a task force with the cooperation of the juvenile justice system, educational system, child welfare system, and participation from the parents. Services that are the most effective for African American girls must be planned and coordinated at the initial phase of entering the juvenile justice system. For African American girls in the juvenile justice system, a fully developed service continuum of care from prevention to aftercare is vital to ensure that all of their needs are being addressed, and the likelihood of positive outcomes is enhanced. Therefore, the juvenile justice system must take a critical look at the treatment options that are available for African American girls.

Most often African American girls are initially diagnosed with oppositional defiant disorder and conduct disorder. The DSM-IV-TR (American Psychiatric Association, 2000) describes two disruptive behavior disorders, oppositional defiant disorder (ODD) and conduct disorder (CD), as the disorders with which mental health professionals are most likely to diagnose juveniles. Oppositional defiant disorder symptoms are a pervasive pattern of negativistic, defiant, disobedient, and hostile behavior. According to Webster-Stratton, Reid, and Murrihy (2010), there are various risk factors that contribute to the creation of ODD: punitive or inconsistent parenting, family history of mental illness, addiction, and family violence, the temperament of the child, negative peer relationships, and learning disabilities. On the other hand, CD is considered to be more clinically severe. The symptoms for CD are aggression towards people and animals, the destruction of property, serious violations of rules, deceitfulness, and theft. Kazdin (2000) reports that the risk factors for CD are the same as ODD with additional risks being exposure to violence and direct association with antisocial peers.

Due to the nature of risk factors that cause African American girls to become involved in the juvenile justice system, the intervention strategies must address their various issues. The intervention strategies must be evidence-based practices that are race- and gender-specific.

CONCLUSION

African American girls have multiple factors that cause them to be involved in the juvenile justice system. Our educational, mental health, and juvenile justice systems must understand the complexity of African American girls in the nature of their unique victimization characteristics in order to combat this growing epidemic of juvenile delinquency.

REFERENCES

Abram, K. M., Teplin, L. A., McClelland, G. M., & Dulcan, M. K. (2003). Comorbid psychiatric disorders in youth in juvenile detention. *Archives of General Psychiatry, 60,* 1097–1108.

Advancement Project. (2010). Test, Punish, and Push Out: How "Zero Tolerance" and High-stakes Testing Funnel Youth Into the School-to-Prison Pipeline. Washington, DC.

American Psychiatric Association (2000). *Diagnostic and statistical manual of disorders* (4th ed., text rev.). Washington, DC.

Bartol, C. R., & Bartol, A. M. (2013). *Criminal behavior: A psychological approach* (10th ed.). Upper Saddle River, NJ: Prentice Hall.

Belknap, J. (2007). *The invisible woman: Gender, crime, and justice* (3rd ed.). Belmont, CA: Thomson Higher Education.

Blake, J., Butler, B., Lewis, C., & Darensbourg, A. (2011). Unmasking the inequitable discipline experiences of urban Black girls: Implications for urban educational stakeholders. *The Urban Review, 43*(1): 90–106.

Bray, C. B., Bray, J., & Zeeb, L. (1986). Behavior problems of clinic children: Relation to parental marital status, age, and sex of child. *American Journal of Orthopsychiatry, 56*: 399–412.

Buzawa, E. S., & Hotaling, G. T. (2006). The impact of relationship status, gender, and minor status in the police response to domestic assaults. *Victims & Offenders, 1*, 323–360.

Centers for Disease Control and Prevention. (2009). Youth Risk Behavior Surveillance System (YRBSS). Retrieved from http://hdl.handle.net/1902 .1/12521

Coalition for Juvenile Justice. (2000). *Handle with care: Serving the mental health needs of young offenders* (Annual Report). Washington, DC.

Crum, R., Lillie-Blanton, M., & Anthony, J. (1996). Neighborhood environment and opportunity to use cocaine and other drugs in late childhood and early adolescence. *Drug and Alcohol Dependence, 43*, 155–161. doi:10.1016/S0376 -8716(96)01298-7.

Dixon, S. V., Graber, J. A., & Brooks-Gunn, J. (2008). The role of M. Edelman. The cradle to prison pipeline: an American health crisis. *Preventing Chronic Disease, 4*(3), A43.

Fazel, S., Doll, H., & Langstrom, N. (2008). Mental disorders among adolescents in juvenile detention and correctional facilities: A systematic review and metaregression analysis of 25 surveys. *Journal of the American Academy of Child and Adolescent Psychiatry, 47*, 1010–1019.

Grisso, T. (2004). *Double jeopardy: Adolescent offenders with mental disorders*. Chicago: University of Chicago Press.

Herz, D. C. (2001). Understanding the use of mental health placement by the juvenile justice system. *Journal of Emotional and Behavioral Disorders, 9*, 172–181.

Johnson, R. M., Kotch, J. B., Catellier, D. J., Winsor, J. R., Dufort, V., Hunter, W., & Amaya-Jackson, L. (2002). Adverse behavioral and emotional outcomes from child abuse and witnessed violence. *Child Maltreatment, 7*, 179–186.

Jones, N. (2009). *Between Good and Ghetto: African American Girls and Inner-City Violence*. Piscataway, NJ: Rutgers University Press.

Jung, M. K., Tajima, E., Herrenkohl, T., & Huang, B. (2009). Early child maltreatment, runaway youths, and risk of delinquency and victimization in adolescence: A mediational model. *Social Work Research, 33*, 19–28.

Kazdin, A. E. (2000). *Psychotherapy for children and adolescents: Directions for research and practice*. New York, NY: Guilford Press.

Lauristen, J. L. (2003). *How families and communities influence youth victimization.* *OJJDPBulletin.* Washington DC: U.S. Department of Justice.

Lederman, C. S., Dakof, G. A., Larrea, M. A., & Li, J. (2004). Characteristics of adolescent females in juvenile detention. *International Journal of Law and Psychiatry, 27*(4), 321–37. doi:10.1016/j.ijlp.2004.03.009.

Losen, D., & Gillespie, J. (2012). Opportunities Suspended: The Disparate Impact of Disciplinary Exclusion from School. Los Angeles, CA: The Center for Civil Rights Remedies at the University of California, Los Angeles Civil Rights Project.

MacKinnon-Lewis, C., Kaufman, M. C., & Frabutt, J. M. (2002). Juvenile justice and mental health: Youth and families in the middle. *Aggression and Violent Behavior: A Review Journal, 7*, 353–363.

Manly, J. T., Kim, J. E., Rogosch, F. A., & Ciccheti, D. (2001). Dimensions of child maltreatment and children's adjustment: Contributions of developmental timing and subtype. *Development and Psychopathology, 13*, 759–782.

Mennel, R. M. (1972). Origins of the Juvenile Court: Changing perspectives on the legal rights of juvenile delinquents. *Crime and Delinquency, 18*, 68–78.

Morris, M. W. (2013, March). Searching for Black girls in the school to prison pipeline. National Council on Crime & Delinquency. Retrieved from http://www.nccdglobal.org/blog/searching-for-black-girls-in-the-school-to-prison-pipeline

National Children's Defense Fund. (2011). *State of America's Children.* Retrieved from http://www.childrensdefensefund.org

Nye, F. I. (1958). *Family relationships and delinquent behavior.* New York: Wiley.

Odem, M. E. (1995). *Delinquent daughters: Protecting and policing adolescent female sexuality in the United States, 1885–1920.* Chapel Hill, NC: The University of North Carolina Press.

Petrila, J. (1998). Prevalence rates in juvenile justice systems. *Mental Health Weekly, 8*, 4.

Pugh Lilly, A., Neville, H. A., & Poulin, K. L. (2001). In protection of ourselves: Black girls' perceptions of self-reported delinquent behaviors. *Psychology of Women Quarterly, 25*, 145–154.

Rafter, N. H. (1990). *Partial Justice: Women, Prisons, and Social Control* (2nd ed.). New Brunswick, NJ: Transaction Books, pp. 181–182.

Robinson, T., and Ward, J. A. (1991). A belief in self far greater than anyone's disbelief: Cultivating resistance among African American female adolescents. *Women & Therapy*, 89–104.

Senna, J., & Siegel, L. (1992). *Juvenile law: Case and comments* (2nd ed.). St. Paul, MN: West.

Sharp, S. F. (2010). The victimization histories of women prisoners. In V. Garoia and J. E. Clifford (eds.), *Female victims of crime: Reality reconsidered.* Upper Saddle River, NJ: Prentice Hall.

Siegel, L. J., & Welsh, B. C. (2014). *Juvenile delinquency: The core* (5th ed.). Belmont, CA: Wadsworth.

Smith Brice, T. (2011). Faith as a protective factor against social misconceptions of Black girls: A historical perspective. *Social Work & Christianity, 38*(3), 315–331.

Snyder, H., & Sickmund, M. (2006). *Juvenile offenders and victims: 2006 National Report.* Washington, DC: Office of Juvenile Justice and Delinquency Prevention.

Staples, R. (1970). *The myth of the Black matriarchy*. Black Scholar, (1). Jan-Feb; 16.

Tonneson, S. C. (2013). "Hit it and quit": Responses to Black girls' victimization in school. *Berkeley Journal of Gender, Law & Justice*, 1.

Tracy, P. E., Kempf-Leonard, K., & Abramoske-James. (2009). Gender differences in delinquency and juvenile justice processing: Evidence from National Data. *Crime and Delinquency, 55*(2).

U.S. Bureau of the Census. Projected Population by Single Year of Age (0–99, 100+), Sex, Race, and Hispanic Origin for the United States: July 1, 2012 to July 1, 2060.

U.S. Census Bureau. (2011). *African American family income by family size*. Retrieved from http://www.census.gov/hhes/www/income/statemedfaminc.html

Wald, J., & Losen, D. (1999). Defining and re-directing a school to prison pipeline. *New Directions for Youth Development, 99.*

Walker, S., Spohn, C., & Delone, M. (2007). The color of justice: Race, ethnicity, and crime. In Allace, J. M., Goodkind, S., Wallace, C. M., & Bachman, J. G. *Racial, ethnic, and gender differences in school discipline among US high school students: 1991–2005. Negro Educational Review, 59(1-2), 47–62. America* (4th ed.) Belmont, CA: Wadsworth.

Webster-Stratton, C. H., & Reid, M. J., & Murrihy, R. C. (2010) The incredible years program for children from infancy to pre-adolescence. Prevention and treatment of behavior problems. In A. D. Kidman & T. H. Ollendick (eds.), *Clinical handbook for assessing and treating conduct problems in youth*, pp. 117–138. New York, NY: Springer.

Zahn, M. A., Hawkins, S. R., Chiancone, J., & Whitworth, A. (2008). *The girls' study group—Charting the way to delinquency prevention for girls*. Washington, DC: Office of Juvenile Justice and Delinquency Prevention.

Chapter 23

The Big Picture: Black Girls, Adolescents, and Crime Today

Byron Miller

INTRODUCTION

Since 1996, juvenile crime rates have generally decreased but one alarming pattern has emerged. The rates of antisocial and criminal behaviors among adolescents have been decreasing more for boys than girls (Puzzanchera, 2013; Zahn et al., 2008). Nearly every day there is a news report depicting the deviant or criminal behaviors of adolescent girls. A recent video search on the YouTube website using the keywords "girl fights" yielded over 600,000 results, demonstrating the commonality with which female deviance is occurring. Moreover, these antisocial behaviors are increasing most among Black girls.

For instance, in August 2013, a White woman in Pittsburgh was brutally beaten by three teenage Black girls after confronting them for throwing a bottle at her car. The girls kicked and punched the woman as well as kicked her head into the concrete. The three teens were soon arrested and taken to the local juvenile detention center where they were charged with ethnic intimidation, robbery, and conspiracy (Teens Face Ethnic Intimidation Charges). Such images and acts of violence are becoming more common among adolescent females, especially Black girls. But few studies have specifically focused on the deviant and criminal actions of this demographic group. Such an examination benefits from synergizing social, psychological, and historical perspectives. In doing so, this chapter examines the contemporary relationship between adolescent girls, Black girls, and crime.

ADOLESCENT GIRLS, DEVIANCE, AND CRIME

In 2010, nearly half a million (480,000) adolescent girls were arrested in the United States (Puzzanchera, 2013). Delinquent juveniles represent approximately 15% of all annual arrests (Snyder, 2008), and females account for nearly one-third of all juvenile arrests (Puzzanchera, 2013; Zahn et al., 2008). Though adolescent boys engage in more deviant and criminal behaviors than do girls, female delinquency is on the rise (Cauffman, 2008; Dodge, Cole, & Lynam, 2006). In fact, between 1996 and 2004, the caseload for boys decreased 13% while the caseload for antisocial girls increased 14% (Cauffman, 2008; Zahn et al., 2008).

The growing number of arrests for adolescent girls is associated with a multitude of factors including changes in the judicial system. The juvenile justice system was first established when Congress passed the Juvenile Justice and Delinquency Prevention Act of 1974 to decriminalize and divert all status offenders, as well as protect the community, protect the youth in its custody, and provide meaningful interventions that reduce or deter juvenile crime and delinquency. However, in 1980, Congress amended the Juvenile Justice and Delinquency Act of 1974 to enable juvenile courts to incarcerate youth for status offenses (behaviors considered deviant or illegal due to the minor's age). As a result, the system can now use its discretion to transform juvenile status offenders into juvenile delinquents.

Though boys are arrested for a wider variety of deviant offenses, girls are more often arrested for status offenses. Parents and authority figures often use status offenses as mechanisms to control young women, especially those girls suspected of being sexually promiscuous (Taylor-Thompson, 2006). Consequently, adolescent girls typically enter the juvenile justice system for status offenses such as running away from home, underage drinking, truancy, prostitution, and curfew violations (Dalby, 1994; Taylor-Thompson, 2006). Therefore, it appears that status offense laws may be unfairly used to target and discriminate against female offenders.

In addition to status offenses, adolescent girls are also being arrested for numerous other crimes such as burglaries and drug violations, but violent crimes have become most prominent. For example, between 1980 and 2003 the proportion of girls arrested for aggravated assault increased from 15% to 24% (Cauffman, 2008; Snyder, 2008), violent crimes (e.g., robbery and murder) increased from 10% to 18%, and property crimes (e.g., larceny, motor vehicle theft, arson, and burglary) increased from 19% to 32% (Chauhan, Burnette & Repucci, 2010). Moreover, between 2001 and 2010, the proportion of females arrested for robbery, assault, larceny-theft, and disorderly conduct increased more than boys (Puzzanchera, 2013). As a result, girls now account for approximately one-third (34%) of all juvenile arrests for assaults.

Race and the Juvenile Justice System

Race-related issues have long been a major concern in the adult and juvenile justice systems (Pope & Snyder, 2003). Black youth are disproportionately overrepresented in the juvenile justice system compared to Whites (Chauhan et al., 2010), and the rate at which Blacks are referred to juvenile courts for delinquency offenses is more than 150% greater than the rate for Whites (Knoll & Sickmund, 2012). In fact, encounters with police, arrests, convictions, and waivers for adult court are consistently higher for Blacks than Whites (Piquero, 2008). Data from the National Council on Crime and Delinquency show that, not only are Black youth more likely to be charged, sentenced, and confined longer (even for the same offense) than their White counterparts (Piquero, 2008), but adjudicated Black youth are also less likely to receive probation but more likely to be placed in secure detention (Words, Bynum & Corley, 1994). As such, although Black adolescents only comprise 16% of the general population of youth, they make up 38% of juveniles in residential facilities, and 58% of youth sent to adult prisons (Knoll & Sickmund, 2012; Piquero, 2008).

Though the racial disparities at each step of the juvenile system are clear, the causes of these differences are not apparent. There are several theoretical perspectives that are not mutually exclusive, which are used to explain the racial differences in juvenile delinquency and crime. The *Differential Involvement Theory* posits that Blacks are overrepresented in the justice system because they are involved in more criminal activities (Chauhan et al., 2010). This perspective is supported by statistics indicating that Black youth offend at disproportionately higher rates (Piquero & Buka, 2002; Puzzanchera, 2013). For example, in 2010, Black youth were involved in the majority (51%) of all juvenile arrests (Puzzanchera, 2013). In contrast, the *Differential Selection Theory* posits that Blacks are selected, targeted, and processed differently by the justice system, which contributes to the higher rates of contact (Chauhan et al., 2010). Therefore activities such as racial profiling increase the risk that Black youth will be arrested.

Another interesting perspective examines the *school-to-prison pipeline*, which refers to the compilation of policies, conditions, and general perceptions that facilitate criminalization within educational institutions that result in the incarceration of adolescents (Morris, 2012). Arrests within schools represent the most direct route into the school-to-prison pipeline, but suspensions and expulsions play a significant part in pushing students out of school and towards criminal activity. However, Black students are more likely to be suspended or expelled from school for disrespect, excessive noise, threats, and loitering (Advancement Project, 2010). This suggests that the school-to-prison pipeline primarily affects Black youth, who in turn face greater risk of criminalization and being in the juvenile justice system.

In addition, using nationally representative data, Pope and Snyder (2003) found that non-White juvenile offenders were more likely to be arrested if the victim of their crime was White than if the victim was non-White. Put another way, non-Whites pay a heavier punitive penalty for victimizing a White than a non-White. This suggests that there are racialized differences in the value of victims, whereby Whites have a greater social and racial value than do non-Whites. This also implies that the juvenile justice system is racially biased in a manner that is unjust to non-White youth, who are punished more severely for victimizing someone who is White. Thus, the racial differences in juvenile justice appear to at least partially stem from the discretion used by authority figures at each stage of the system from arrest to adjudication and disposition.

BLACK GIRLS, DEVIANCE, AND CRIME

Much of the literature examining racial disparities in juvenile delinquency and juvenile justice in the United States centers on the troubles of young men of color. However, girls represent the fastest growing segment of the juvenile justice population (Taylor-Thompson, 2006) and, as with boys, non-White girls are disproportionately overrepresented in the juvenile justice system. Although White girls make up 65% of the juvenile population, non-White girls make up nearly two-thirds of the female juvenile justice population (Piquero & Buka, 2002; Taylor-Thompson, 2006). Yet, the greatest increase in adolescent girls' arrest rates, secure confinement, and residential placement is among Black girls, who represent 36% of the female population in the juvenile justice system (Puzzanchera, Adams & Sickmund, 2010; Taylor-Thompson, 2006).

As discussed by Ambrose and Simpkins (2001), a study conducted by the Philadelphia Defender Association in 1999 found that the typical female juvenile offender is an African American who has a history of involvement in dependency court, been placed in foster care multiple times, has a history of running away, has at least one parent with a substance abuse history, and has suffered some form of abuse herself. This suggests that Black girls are more likely to come from dysfunctional social backgrounds, which in turn puts them at greater risk of being deviant and entering into the juvenile justice system. More importantly, these risk factors primarily stem from the social environment in which Black girls are nurtured. From this perspective, it is essential to make a more thorough investigation into the social milieus of adolescent Black girls to gain a better understanding of the risk factors associated with their higher rate of delinquency and criminal behaviors. A number of environmental factors have been shown to be associated with an adolescent girl's vulnerability to delinquency. In particular, research indicates that family characteristics, neighborhood contexts, schools, and history of abuse strongly predict the criminal and deviant behavior of Black girls.

Family

Family is the primary source of socialization and plays a significant role in predicting an adolescent's antisocial behavior. Parental supervision is an important part of protecting youth from delinquency, and adolescent girls are more likely to be delinquent when they are not consistently monitored or disciplined by their parents (Schlossman & Cairns, 1993). The ability for parents to adequately supervise their children and deter deviant behavior is strongly related to the structure of the family. Research shows that youth who reside with both biological parents are less likely to be delinquent than those in other family structures (Zahn et al., 2010). Although youth in female-headed households are more likely to display aggressive behaviors (Kowalski-Jones, 2000), the highest rates of juvenile delinquency are for youth in father-only households (Zahn et al., 2010). However, Black girls are more likely than other girls to live in female-headed households given that two-thirds of Black children are raised in single-parent households (Kids Count, 2013), which suggests their family structure is one factor that places these girls at greater risk for being delinquent, especially violent.

Families of delinquent girls tend to exhibit more dysfunction and experience higher rates of intra-family conflict than the families of delinquent boys (Taylor-Thompson, 2006). More delinquent Black girls report being in dysfunctional families than their White counterparts (Gavazzi, 2006), which further suggests that dysfunctional family backgrounds increase the risk for delinquency among Black girls. Such dysfunction may include parents who are abusive or use drugs, which puts those adolescents at high risk for antisocial behavior (Zahn et al., 2010). Girls who are victims of physical, sexual, or emotional abuse at home are also more likely to display violent behavior (Molnar et al., 2005; Zahn et al., 2008). For example, girls who are chronic runaways document significant levels of sexual and physical victimization, which suggests these girls may be trying to escape their abuse and victimization (Huizinga et al., 2013; Zahn et al., 2010). Another form of dysfunction involves adolescents having family members with criminal backgrounds who not only place youth at greater risk for delinquency (Rowe & Farrington, 1997), but also encourage their juvenile family members to display criminal behaviors themselves (Giordano & Mohler-Rockwell, 2001). Given that Black girls are more likely than their peers to have a family member with a criminal background due to the disproportionate number of incarcerated Black adults, this suggests that the propensity of familial criminality further places Black girls at greater risk for deviant and criminal behaviors.

Neighborhoods

A growing body of literature indicates that neighborhood factors explain a significant portion of the racial disparity in antisocial behavior (Chauhan et al., 2010; Sampson, Morenoff & Raudenbush, 2005). Disadvantaged neighborhoods are typically classified by their higher prevalence of persons who are impoverished, receive public housing or financial assistance, and live in female-headed households (Chauhan et al., 2010). Not surprisingly, compared to Whites, Black girls are more likely to live in disadvantaged neighborhoods (Chauhan et al., 2010).

Neighborhoods can contribute to racial disparities in juvenile offending through several mechanisms. First, youth in disadvantaged neighborhoods have more opportunities to be deviant, which supports the previously described differential involvement theory. Research shows that persons in disadvantaged neighborhoods are more likely to engage in antisocial and criminal acts (Sun, Triplett & Gainey, 2004). A study by Molnar and colleagues (2005) found that girls in Chicago were more likely to commit violent acts if they lived in neighborhoods with a high concentration of poverty. Girls in disadvantaged neighborhoods may also use violence to prevent or stop violent attacks on themselves. Second, there tends to be greater police surveillance in disadvantaged neighborhoods as posited by the differential selection perspective. Such surveillance increases the likelihood that youth in those neighborhoods will be encountered and arrested by law enforcement officials. Third, Blacks are more likely than Whites to live in disadvantaged neighborhoods that are characterized by higher crime rate behavior (Chauhan et al., 2010). Lastly, Blacks are less able to leave these disadvantaged neighborhoods (Chauhan et al., 2010), which increases the odds that such trends will continue inter-generationally.

Neighborhoods with structural disadvantage or concentrated poverty have higher rates of violence, exposure to violence, and arrests for property and personal crime (Molnar et al., 2005; Zahn et al., 2010). In turn, youth in neighborhoods perceived as having higher levels of crime, violence, and joblessness are more likely to have aggressive behaviors (Kowalski-Jones, 2000). Moreover, girls living in communities with high rates of poverty or violent crime are much more likely to act violently than girls in other neighborhoods (Molnar et al., 2005; Zahn et al., 2010). That

Black girls are more likely to live in neighborhoods with these characteristics suggests they are more likely to be violent themselves as a result of living in an environment that exposes them to violence and other types of criminal behaviors.

Schools

Schools are closely tied to neighborhood contexts because most youth attend schools near their residence, so school and neighborhood demographics are often closely aligned. Looking more closely, the extant literature shows an inverse relationship between academic performance and juvenile delinquency (Hawkins et al., 2009; Zahn et al., 2010). However, schools with higher proportions of minorities tend to have, on average, lower academic performance (Kao & Thompson, 2003), which suggests that such schools have higher rates of delinquency. Moreover, schools with higher proportions of minority students tend to have greater punitive discipline in response to disruptive and problematic student behaviors (Welch & Payne, 2012). These findings suggest that Black girls are more likely to attend schools characterized by low academic performance, greater delinquency, and more severe punishments that collectively increase their risk for deviant and criminal behaviors.

Research also indicates that the school suspension rates of Black girls have increased more than their male counterparts (Losen & Skiba, 2010). The high rates of school suspensions among Black girls appear to be a multifaceted phenomenon attributed to a variety of factors. For example, Morris (2012) found that some teachers perceive Black girls as being loud and defiant, and Black girls were more likely than White or Latino girls to be reprimanded for being "unladylike." Such negative evaluations of Black girls by predominantly White teachers may reflect attitudes of misunderstanding due to the cultural mismatch between students and teachers (McGrady & Reynolds, 2013). Being stigmatized as not being "good girls" or being girls that behave in a "ghetto" fashion may lessen a Black girl's feelings of belongingness to school, which in turn increases their likelihood of being deviant (Zahn et al., 2010).

Abuse

Regardless of race, female offenders have higher rates of both internalizing and externalizing mental health problems than do boys (Cauffman, 2008). Girls in the juvenile justice system are also more likely to have a history of abuse and neglect than their peers who are not in the system, and such stressors are strongly associated with risk-taking behaviors (Zahn et al., 2010). It is estimated that the prevalence of mental disorders in the juvenile justice setting is about 25%, which is much higher than the

15% of the general U.S. population (Ferrell, 1999), and 70% of girls in the justice system have histories of physical abuse compared to 24% of the general teenage girl population (Taylor-Thompson, 2006).

Adolescent girls are more than twice as likely to engage in violence if they have a history of physical or sexual assault or were otherwise violently victimized (Molnar et al., 2005; Zahn et al., 2010). Experiencing such victimization can, in turn, lead young girls to engage in various forms of delinquent behaviors such as substance abuse as a form of self-medication (Taylor-Thompson, 2006), as well as stealing, drug dealing, or prostitution as a means of earning money to purchase drugs or alcohol, and being independent to escape their abusive environment. Furthermore, most girls who experience some type of physical or sexual abuse are between the ages of 12 and 15 (Taylor-Thompson, 2006). Given the association between abuse and the timing of their delinquent acts, it seems possible that many of the antisocial and criminal acts of juvenile females are actually cries for help. For example, a girl may run away from home to escape an abusive environment, but may subsequently be arrested and enter the juvenile justice system as a status offender. Collectively, these findings suggest that girls in general, and Black girls in particular, are being deviant and arrested for status or violent offenses as a means of externalizing the distress associated with their above-average rates of mental disorders and abuse.

PROPOSED SOLUTIONS

Although a number of delinquency risk factors affect both boys and girls (e.g., family dynamics, school involvement, and neighborhood environment), others such as early onset of puberty, abuse, and mental disorders directly increase a girl's risk of delinquency (FBI Law Enforcement Bulletin, 2011). Since the juvenile justice system is now dealing with a sizable proportion of female offenders, efforts must be made to make the juvenile system more responsive to the gender-specific needs of girls (Cauffman, 2008). Still, the prevention efforts of the juvenile justice system continue to focus on boys and do not provide adequate services and solutions to handle the diverse issues and underlying social mechanisms associated with female juvenile delinquency and rehabilitation (Zahn et al., 2010).

It is apparent that the juvenile justice system needs to incorporate novel strategies that can be implemented to seriously reduce the deviant and criminal behaviors of adolescent girls generally, and Black girls specifically. The extant literature shows there are a number of protective factors that deter adolescent girls from becoming juvenile offenders including the involvement of a caring adult, school connectedness and success, and religiosity (FBI Law Enforcement Bulletin, 2011; Hawkins et al., 2009; Zahn et al., 2010). Future strategies should therefore incorporate protective factors as well as address known risk factors related to a girl's family, neighborhood and school contexts, mental disorders, and experiences with abuse.

Female adolescents who are in the juvenile justice system need to be provided with developmentally appropriate support and resources for rehabilitation that help them become healthy and productive members of society (Goltesman & Schwarz, 2011). Rather than placing juvenile offenders in a large residential placement facility, one alternative is to employ community-based centers that punish delinquent girls as well as provide treatment within their community. Such facilities enable female offenders to receive the help they need while also allowing easier access to familial and friend support systems (Goltesman & Schwarz, 2011).

Mentorship is another significant source of social support that would help improve the lives of adolescent girls in either residential or community-based facilities. Many young girls revere celebrities because they lack direct connections with appropriate adults to model themselves after. However, antisocial youth who receive adult mentorship are not only less delinquent, but also tend to have better relationships with their parents, earn better grades, are more confident in their school work, miss fewer school days, and express fewer internalizing and externalizing behaviors than those who do not (Grossman & Garry, 1997; Keating et al., 2002; Rhodes, Grossman & Resch, 2000). Therefore, implementing mandatory mentoring programs in both residential and community-based facilities could significantly improve the life chances of at-risk girls, reduce their possibility of recidivism, and also lessen their costs to the state and society. Black girls, in particular, could benefit from the National Cares Mentoring Movement that has strategic partnerships with a multitude of national organizations.

Lastly, when addressing the problems associated with the delinquency of juvenile females, especially Black girls, we first need to keep in mind that adolescence is a developmental stage in the life course when young girls sometimes make mistakes. As such, at each stage of the juvenile justice system, authority figures need to treat youth like youth, not as adults. This means everyone from law enforcement officers to judges needs to take the processes of adolescent development into account when deciding whether to arrest, criminally charge, or sentence juveniles for their antisocial behaviors.

REFERENCES

Advancement Project. (2010). *Test, Punish and Push Out: How Zero Tolerance and High Stakes Testing Funnel Youth into the School-to-Prison Pipeline.* Washington, DC.

Ambrose, A. M., & Simpkins, S. (2001). Improving conditions for girls in the justice system: The Female Detention Project. Retrieved from http://www.njdc.info/pdf/factsheetgirls.pdf

Cauffman, E. (2008). Understanding the Female Offender. *The Future of Children*, *8*(2), 119–142.

Chauhan, P., Burnette, M., & Repucci, N.D. (2010). Racial Disparities among Female Juvenile Offenders: The Contribution of Neighborhood Disadvantage and Exposure to Violence in Antisocial Behavior. *Court Review*, *1-2*(46), 10–15.

Chauhan, P., Reppucci, N., Burnette, M., & Reiner, S. (2010). Race and Neighborhood Disadvantage, and Antisocial Behavior Among Female Juvenile Offenders. *Journal of Community Psychology*, *38*(4), 532–540.

Dalby, C. (1994). Gender Bias Towards Status Offenders: A Paternalistic Agenda Carried Out Through the JJDA. 12 *Law and Inequality*, 429.

Dodge, K. A., Cole, D. C., & Lynam, D. (2006). Aggression and Antisocial Behavior in Youth. In N. Einsber, W. Damon, & R. Lerner (eds.), *Handbook of Child Psychology*, Vol 3: *Social, Emotional, and Personality Development*. Hoboken, NJ: John Wiley and Sons.

FBI Law Enforcement Bulletin. (2011). Retrieved from http://www.fbi.gov/stats-services/publications/law-enforcement-bulletin/june_2011/bulletin-report.

Ferrell, J. (1999). Cultural Criminology. *Annual Review of Sociology*, *25*, 395–418.

Gavazzi, S. M. (2006). Gender, Ethnicity, and the Family Environment: Contributions to Assessment Efforts Within the Realm of Juvenile Justice. *Family Relations*, *55*, 190–199.

Giordano, P. C., & Mohler-Rockwell, S. (2001). Differential association theory and female crime. In S. Simpson (ed.), *Of Crime and Criminality: The Use of Theory in Everyday Life* (pp. 3–24). Thousand Oaks, CA: Pine Forge Press.

Goltesman, D. D., & Schwarz, S. (2011). Juvenile justice in the U.S.: Facts for policymakers. *National Center for Children in Poverty Fact Sheet*, 1–7.

Grisso, T. (2008). Adolescent Offenders with Mental Disorders. *The Future of Children*, *18*(2), 143–164.

Grossman, J. B., & Garry, E. M. (1997). Mentoring—A proven prevention strategy. *U.S. Department of Justice, Office of Juvenile Justice and Delinquency Prevention.* Retrieved from https://www.ncjrs.gov/pdffiles/164834.pdf

Hawkins, S. R., Graham, P. W., Williams, J., & Zahn, M. (2009). Resilient Girls—Factors That Protect Against Delinquency. *U.S. Department of Justice, Office of Juvenile Justice and Delinquency Prevention.* Retrieved from https://www.ncjrs.gov/pdffiles1/ojjdp/220124.pdf

Huizinga, D., Miller, S., & the Conduct Problems Prevention Research Group. (2013). Developmental Sequences of Girls' Delinquent Behavior. U.S. Department of Justice, Office of Juvenile Justice and Delinquency Prevention. Retrieved from http://www.ojjdp.gov/pubs/238276.pdf

Kao, G., & Thompson, J. (2003). Racial and Ethnic Stratification in Educational Achievement and Attainment. *Annual Review of Sociology*, *29*, 417–442.

Katz, R. S. (2000). "Explaining Girls' and Women's Crime and Desistance in the Context of Their Victimization Experience." *Violence Against Women*, *6*(6), 633–660.

Keating, L. M., Tomishima, M. A., Foster, S., & Alessandri, M. (2002). The Effects of a Mentoring Program on At-Risk Youth. *Adolescence, 37*(148), 717–734.

Kids Count data. Retrieved from http://datacenter.kidscount.org/data/tables/107-children-in-single-parent-families-by#detailed/1/any/false/867,133,38,35,18/10,168,9,12,1,13,185/432,431.

Knoll, C., & Sickmund, M. (2012). Delinquency Cases in Juvenile Court, 2009. *U.S. Department of Justice, National Report Series Fact Sheet*. Retrieved from http://www.ojjdp.gov/pubs/239081.pdf

Kowalski-Jones, L. (2000). Staying Out of Trouble: Community Resources and Problem Behavior Among High-Risk Adolescents. *Journal of Marriage and the Family, 62*, 449–464.

Losen, D., & Skiba, R. (2010). Suspended Education: Urban Middle Schools in Crisis. Los Angeles CA: The Center for Civil Rights Remedies at the University of California, Los Angeles Civil Rights Project. Retrieved from http://www.splcenter.org/sites/default/files/downloads/publication/Suspended_Education.pdf

McGrady, P., & Reynolds, J. R. (2013). Racial Mismatch in the Classroom: Beyond Black-White Differences. *Sociology of Education, 86*(1), 3–17.

Molnar, B. E., Browne, A., Cerda, M., & Buka, S. I. (2005). Violent behavior by girls reporting violent victimization. *Archives of Pediatric and Adolescent Medicine, 159*, 731–739.

Morris, M. (2012). Race, Gender and the School-to-Prison Pipeline: Expanding Our Discussion to Include Black Girls. *African American Policy Forum*. Retrieved from http://aapf.org/wp-content/uploads/2012/08/Morris-Race-Gender-and-the-School-to-Prison-Pipeline.pdf

Piquero, A., & Buka, S. (2002). Investigating race and gender differences in specialization in violence. *Criminology at the Millennium*. In R. A. Silverman, T. P. Thornberry, B. Cohen., and B. Krisberg (eds.). Boston: Kluwer Academic Press.

Piquero, A. R. (2008). Disproportionate Minority Contact. *The Future of Children, 18*(2), 59–79.

Pope, C. E., & Snyder, H. N. (2003). Race as a Factor in Juvenile Arrests. U.S. Department of Justice, Office of Juvenile Justice and Delinquency Prevention. Retrieved from http://cj-resources.com/CJ_Juvenile_Justice_pdfs/juvenile%20justice%20and%20race%20-%20Pope%20et%20al%202003.pdf

Puzzanchera, C. (2013). Juvenile Arrests 2010. U.S. Department of Justice, Office of Juvenile Justice and Delinquency Prevention. Retrieved from http://www.ncjj.org/pdf/242770.pdf

Puzzanchera, C., Adams, B., & Sickmund, M. (2010). Juvenile Court Statistics 2006–2007. Report. Pittsburgh, Pa: National Center for Juvenile Justice. Retrieved from http://www.ncjj.org/PDF/jcsreports/jcs2007.pdf

Rhodes, J. E., Grossman, J. B., & Resch, N. L. (2000). Agents of Change: Pathways Through Which Mentoring Relationships Influence Adolescents' Academic Adjustment. *Child Development, 71*(6), 1662–1671.

Rowe, D. C., & Farrington, D. P. (1997). The familial transmission of criminal convictions. *Criminology, 35*, 177–201.

Sampson, R. J., Morenoff, J. D., & Raudenbush, S. (2005). Social Anatomy of Racial and Ethnic Disparities in Violence. *American Journal of Public Health, 95*(2), 224–232.

Schlossman, S., & Cairns, R. B. (1993). Problem girls: Observations on past and present. In G. H. Elder Jr., J. Modell, & R. D. Parke (eds.), *Children in Time and Place: Developmental and Historical Insights* (pp. 110–130). New York, NY: Cambridge Press.

Snyder, H. N. (2008). Juvenile Arrests 2005. U.S. Department of Justice, Office of Juvenile Justice and Delinquency Prevention. Retrieved from https://www.ncjrs.gov/pdffiles1/ojjdp/218096.pdf

Sun, I. Y., Triplett, R., & Gainey, R. R. (2004). Neighborhood Characteristics and Crime: A Test of Sampson and Groves' Model of Disorganization. *Western Criminology*, 5(1), 1–16.

Taylor-Thompson, K. (2006). Girl Talk—Examining Racial and Racial Gender Lines in Juvenile Justice. *Nevada Law Journal*, 6, 1137–1164.

Teens face ethnic intimidation charges after brutally beating woman in North Side. Retrieved from http://www.wpxi.com/news/news/local/teenage-girls-accused-beating-robbing-woman-north-/nZc8W/

Welch, K., & Payne, A. A. (2012). Exclusionary School Punishment: The Effect of Racial Threat on Expulsion and Suspension. *Youth Violence and Juvenile Justice*, 10(20), 155–171.

Words, M., Bynum, T. C., & Corley, C. J. (1994). Locking up youth: The impact of race on detention decisions. *Journal of Research in Crime and Delinquency*, 31(2), 149–165.

Zahn, M., Agnew, R., Fishbein, D., Miller, S., Winn, D., Dakoff, G., . . . & Chesney-Lind, M. (2010). Causes and Correlates of Girls' Delinquency. U.S. Department of Justice, Office of Juvenile Justice and Delinquency Prevention, 2–18.

Zahn, M., Brumbaugh, S., Steffensmeier, D., Field, B., Morash, M., Chesney-Lind, M., . . . & Kruttschnitt, C. (2008). Violence by Teenage Girls: Trends and Context. U.S. Department of Justice, Office of Juvenile Justice and Delinquency Prevention. Retrieved from https://www.ncjrs.gov/pdffiles1/ojjdp/218905.pdf

Chapter 24

Pathways to Delinquency and Imprisonment

Catherine Fisher Collins

In America as of this writing there are approximately 70 million children. This number will increase to 78 million by 2020. Between 1946 and 1964 the number of teens increased; it then declined in the 1970s and 1980s, then began to increase in the 1990s again. By 2020, children will make up 24% of the American population. With so many children projected as part of the American population, have we prepared ourselves to meet their needs and demands? Marian Wright Edelman, executive director of the Children's Defense Fund, reported on the state of African American children who are currently among millions of American children who are living in poverty (Children's Defense Fund, 2013):

Each Day in America for Black Children[1]

3 children or teens are killed by firearms.

20 babies die before their first birthdays.

105 children are arrested for violent crimes.

---

[1] Statistics that contribute to the Cradle to Prison Pipeline cycle, according to the Children's Defense Fund 2007 and CDF research library.

111 children are arrested for drug abuse.

218 babies are born at low birth weight.

219 babies are born to teen mothers.

763 high school students drop out.[2]

390 children confirm abuse or neglect.

740 babies are born into poverty.

336 public school students are corporally punished.[2]

1,172 babies are born to unmarried mothers.

1 child or teen commits suicide.

6,191 public school students are suspended.

1,385 children are arrested.

1 child is killed by abuse or neglect.

If these daily occurrences haven't shocked you, July 2011 and December 2009 Children's Defense Fund reports on moments in an African American child's life will:

Moments in America for Black Children

Every 4 seconds a public school student is suspended.[2]

Every 57 seconds a public school student is corporally punished.[2]

Every 27 seconds a high school student drops out.[2]

Every minute a child is arrested.

Every minute a baby is born to an unmarried mother.

Every 2 minutes a baby is born into poverty.

Every 3 and a half minutes a child is abused or neglected.

Every 4 minutes a baby is born without health insurance.

Every 4½ minutes a baby is born to a teen mother.

Every 6 minutes a baby is born at low birth weight.

Every 15 minutes a child is arrested for drug abuse.

Every 15 minutes a child is arrested for violent crimes.

Every 2 days a child commits suicide.

What can we expect from these African American children who, from birth, are faced with a wall of social and political barriers? Some are able

---

[2] Based on calculations per school day (180 days of seven hours each). All calculations by the Children's Defense Fund.

to meet these challenges and manage to survive, while others are destroyed by social ills and involvement with the juvenile justice system. The Children's Defense Fund's report "America's Cradle to Prison Pipeline" (2007) states, "It is not right, sensible or necessary to have 13 million poor children in a $13.3 trillion economy" (p. 6). I strongly agree and in this chapter, I will focus on African American children and adolescent girls' struggle to survive in America.

CHARACTERISTICS OF JUVENILE GIRLS

Early Juvenile Justice System

Today's juvenile justice system is currently not equipped to deal with the behavioral changes and issues of African American adolescent females. In America's early history, when children broke the law they were treated like adult criminals. However, by the twentieth century, 32 states had developed a separate juvenile court system. From then on, the goal of the U.S. criminal justice system, as it related to children, was rehabilitation, education, and return to the community as good, law-abiding citizens (an attitude that appears to no longer exist). Through most of the 1950s, these juvenile courts had jurisdiction over all children under 18 years of age. In the 1960s and 1970s, a series of laws regarding juveniles were passed, including the Juvenile Delinquency Prevention and Control Act of 1968 and the Juvenile Justice and Delinquency Prevention Act of 1974. These acts gave money to cities that reformed their juvenile justice system to address violent youth/crimes with a focus on prevention.

However, what has emerged out of this effort are 50 states, each with a different juvenile justice system, and a return by many state governments to the earlier attitudes of treating juveniles like adults and confining them to adult prisons. Currently, there are over 2,400 children under 18 serving life sentences in adult prisons, where they are reported to be abused by older inmates and staff.

America's Response to Juvenile Girls

Presented here are various behavioral aspects of African American juvenile girls that may lead them down various pathways that increase their risk of imprisonment. It's imperative that the reader be exposed to how faulty systems (gangs, family violence, poor public schools) have failed this fragile population, making these young girls vulnerable to exploitation by others, such as pimps and drug dealers.

To understand the seriousness of the problems faced by African American youths, we must explore in more detail those social/political/

economic factors that affect their life stability. To this end, I will discuss previously mentioned conditions, drawing on research from the Children's Defense Fund's report (2007) and research by Bloom et al. (2003) on the "common characteristics of an at-risk adolescent female" (pp. 519–520). These characteristics will serve as the framework to discuss how African American girls are affected. These characteristics are as follows:

- Age 13 to 18
- History of victimization, especially physical, sexual, and emotional abuse
- School failure, truancy, and dropout
- Repeated status offenses, especially running away
- Unstable family and social life, including family involvement in the criminal justice system, lack of connectedness, and social isolation
- History of unhealthy dependent relationships, especially with older males
- Mental health issues, including history of abuse
- Overrepresentation: communities of color in the justice system
- Economically marginalized population.

An examination of each of these characteristics will include a discussion and statistics that, as applied to African American adolescent girls, will show that the results form the foundation for criminal behavior. Also, where applicable, major risk factors that Cass and Curry identified in the CDF report (2007, pp. 17–18), if applicable, will be noted.

FRAMEWORK FOR ANALYSIS

The following are Bloom's characteristics along with my discussion of specific relevance to African American female juveniles.

Ages 13 to 18

According to Wallman (2008), "In 2007 there were 73.9 million children in the United States, 1.5 million more than in 2000. This number is projected to increase to 80 million in 2020. In 2007, there were approximately an equal number of children in each of these age groups: 0–5 (25 million), 6–11 (25 million), and 12–17 (25 million) years of age" (p. 14). The U.S. Census Bureau estimated that in 2002 there were "72,894,500 persons under the age of 18—the group commonly referred to as juveniles" (Snyder & Sickmund, 2006, p. 2). The racial makeup in America shows approximately 40 million White and 9 million African American youth age 5–17, and by 2020 there will be 78 million children in America. This population is the fastest growing and will require more attention and resources. A Florida newspaper article, "Our View: Girls Gone Awry," reported an incident in which a 12-year-old and three other girls in Brevard County beat and kicked another girl, and stated that "Florida's juvenile justice system isn't prepared to handle increasing numbers of girls guilty of assault and other offenses" (p. 1). Girls are increasingly showing violent behavior, and adolescent girls have been arrested in increasing numbers. Another example of this aggressive and violent behavior occurred in upstate New York in 2005, when 16-year-old Evony S. Capps was charged with second-degree murder. It was reported that Capps was fighting with a 14-year-old over a pair of earrings when a bystander, Arthur Boyd, attempted to break up the fight and was stabbed in the throat and neck by Capps. It has also been reported that U.S. female juvenile assaults rose from 200 for every 100,000 girls to 750 between 1980 and 2003.

America must address the demands that this increasing population will require—not only immediately but in the future as well. Rather than spending money on the "back end" ($44,000 to $50,000 per juvenile for confinement in a juvenile detention center), America should invest in the "front end" for public education that on the average costs a mere $8,701 per American student (*USA Today*, 2007). If we fail to heed the warnings, many children and teenagers will become victims of America's failure.

History of Victimization, Especially Physical, Sexual, and Emotional Abuse

Even though sexual abuse spans all racial and ethnic groups, the impact of the abuse, when coupled with racism and other social factors, takes a severe toll on African American children during their formative years, with significance for shaping inappropriate adolescent and adult behaviors. There have been numerous studies that document the physical, sexual, and emotional abuse of American children. In one of these studies, girls made up a greater share of victims of maltreatment (52%) as compared to boys (48%) (Snyder & Sickmund, 2006).

Also, a study by Mount Sinai School of Medicine found that low birth weight and childhood abuse boost the risks for depression, social dysfunction, and other psychological problems in adolescence and adulthood (Science Daily, 2007).

Further, a CDF report (2007) states that "low birth weight is a risk factor for later physical, developmental and learning problems" (p. 17). And in 2003, there were 906,000 referrals. In 2004 there was a slight reduction to 872,000 victims of child abuse and neglect (Hopper, 2007, p. 1). Of the 2004 victims, more than 60% were referred for neglect by parents or caregivers, 18% referred for physical abuse, 10% for sexual abuse, and 7% for emotional maltreatment. These data reflect the seriousness of the problem. African American children had the highest rates of victimization.

New York City "recorded more than 65,000 reports of child abuse and neglect in 2006 . . . and in the first 11 months of that year, 40 of the children suspected of being abused died—though not necessarily because of that abuse" (Copolo, 2007, p. 1).

Parents of these abused children are at the top of the perpetrators' list at a horrifying 79%. The others who abuse these children are unmarried partners of parents (4.1%), other relatives (6.5%), foster parents (0.4%), residential facility staff (0.2%), day care providers (0.7%), legal guardians (0.2%), other professionals (0.2%), friends/neighbors (0.3%), others (5.1%), and unknown/missing (3.9%). Potential overlap of relationship to perpetrators accounts for a total of more than 100% (Hopper, 2007).

We must always keep in mind that the abuse may escalate to a fatal occurrence. According to Rennison and Welchans (2002), out of all the children under age five who were murdered between 1976 and 2000, 31% were killed by fathers; 30% by mothers; 23% by a male acquaintance; 7% by relatives; and 3% by strangers.

For many children, school may be their only safe haven away from the abuser. However, a growing number of teachers are also sexually exploiting children (Shakeshaft and Cohen, 1995). Shakeshaft and Cohen reported on educators' sexual abuse of children for the U.S. Department of Education. The results revealed that nearly one in ten students nationwide are targets of educators' sexual misconduct. Another report, "The State of School: Safety in American Schools 2004–2005," found that "4.5 million students are the victims of sexual misconduct by school staff members" (p. 4) and "students age 12–18 were more likely to be victims of . . . sexual assault, robbery and aggravated assaults. The total crimes committed [against] this age group are 243,000" (p. 3). It was reported that "485 educators in New York State have had their teaching credentials revoked, denied, surrendered or sanctioned from 2001 through 2005 following allegations of sexual misconduct." The courts are paying close attention and handing out some hefty sentences, as in the case of Pam Rogers. This elementary education teacher was convicted of sexual assault of a 13-year-old male student. She could have received 100 years for 13 counts of rape and sexual assault, but Judge Bart Stanley gave her less than 10 years (Grace 2006, 2007).

As these children attempt to survive after the abuse, many experience serious problems, as Banyard and Williams et al. (2002) report in "The Women's Study," which began in 1970 and investigated the consequences of sexual assaults on a sample composed primarily (84%) of African American girls who ranged in age from 10 months to 12 years at the time of the assault. The survivors were interviewed in 1990–1991 to gain information on the consequences of sexual abuse. The sexual abuse of these survivors involved sexual contact by force, threat of force, or misuse of authority by a person who was five or more years older than the child, whether or not force was used. The sexual abuse of these children ranged from genital fondling to sexual intercourse, and the perpetrators were fathers, stepfathers, other family members, friends and acquaintances, and male strangers (p. 47). Of the survivors interviewed, 86% were African Americans, 64% were unemployed, 50% never married, 29% had a high school diploma/GED. As adults, they had mental health issues, anxiety, and depression (p. 48). Other researchers have investigated the negative consequences of child abuse on girls and found that survivors have trauma-induced symptoms like amnesia, multiple personality, and desensitization (Mullen & Fleming, 1998). Also found have been aggressive behavior and physical fights with partners; Chesney-Lind and Sheldon (2004) found that many girls in correctional settings have experienced "physical and sexual abuse, and nearly 4 out 5 have run away" (p. 236) apparently to escape the abuse. The issue of child sexual abuse came to the attention of U.S. Attorney General Alberto Gonzales when a Justice Department official showed him seized Internet child pornography. There were explicit pictures of "fathers sexually assaulting their daughters, some younger than 10. Another segment showed men defecating on screaming babies whose tiny hands and feet were tied down with bath towels" (Johnson, 2006, p. A13). It has also been reported that at a hospital a three-month-old infant was being treated for a venereal disease of the throat (Bass, 1983, p. 24).

Following these reports of torture of America's innocent children, *Time* magazine noted that "10 years of probation [was] given to a Nebraska man for sexually assaulting a child, by a judge who said he was too small to survive in prison." Abused adolescent girls whose fragile psychological state may trigger inappropriate behavior are often brought before the courts. I hope that, before rendering decisions, the courts take into account the social history of African American women who may have been sexually assaulted.

School Failure, Truancy, and Dropout

Educators and policy makers agree that public education is in crisis. Investigators Robert Balfanz and Nettie Legters discuss this issue in their 2004 report, "Locating the Dropout Crisis," quoted in Hardy (2006, p. 18). They report that "nearly half of the nation's African American students, and almost 40% of Hispanic students, attend high schools in which graduation is not the norm." It has also been well documented that high school dropouts are almost three times as likely to be incarcerated as youths who graduated from high school (Harlow, 2003). This is further supported by statistics that show 75% of state prisoners and 59% of federal prisoners are high school dropouts. Further, in another article, "Dropout Nation" (Thornburgh, 2006), it was reported that nearly 1 in 3 public high school students won't graduate; for African Americans and Latinos, the rate is "an alarming 50%" (p. 32). For girls in 2002, the dropout rate was 9.9%, as compared to 12% for boys (Snyder & Sickmund, 2006). When students believe that they will not be successful in school, they tune out the teacher, becoming angry and frustrated, which may lead to reduced self-esteem, which in turn contributes to inappropriate actions that may result in delinquent behavior. If these children happen to attend an elementary school in one of this nation's 21 states that allows paddling, their aggressive behavior could be exacerbated. According to Dr. Alvin Poussaint, "Children as young as 6 months are paddled and last year Texas paddled 50,000 children" (Poussaint, 2008).

Schools play an important role in determining the path that their student body will take: "Research commonly finds that school failure is a stronger predictor of delinquency than . . . racial or ethnic background . . . and those leaving school without a diploma were significantly more likely to become involved in chronic delinquency than graduates." When teachers blame the parents for not being responsible and parents blame the teachers for not teaching, no one wins, and the children become the losers. With 75% of state prison inmates and 59% of federal inmates high school dropouts, by now the picture should be clear. The proliferation of education regulations and testing standards, such as the No Child Left Behind (NCLB) Act, may not be addressing the underlying issues of public education, which comprise myriad social factors. NCLB testing in the public schools will not fix a broken school district. In addition, while testing under NCLB may tell the federal government that African American children's test scores are failing, it does little to address "the cultural competence of teachers to work effectively with children from diverse racial and cultural backgrounds" (Howard, 2006, p. 2). Also critical are teachers' attitudes about their students. One study quoted a student as saying, "It was hard for me to get along with teachers. Some were prejudiced and one had the nerve to tell the whole class he didn't like Black people" (Arnold, 1995, p. 140).

While school districts struggle to close financial and academic achievement gaps, educators must keep in mind external attacks, such as sexually explicit lyrics that have been shown to have a "strong influence on [youths'] sexual behavior" (Tanner, 2006, p. A7). Equally explicit are music videos, such as one in which a young African American female performer turns her buttocks toward the male rapper, who swipes a credit card between her buttocks.

Dr. Johnnetta Betsch Cole, a former president of Bennett College, a college for young women, tackled this subject in her article "What Hip-Hop

Has Done to black Women" (2007): "What value can there be in descriptions of black girls and women as 'bitches,' 'ho's,' 'skeezers,' 'freaks,' 'gold diggers,' 'chickenheads,' and 'pigeons'? What could possibly be the value to our communities to have rap music videos that are notorious for featuring half-clothed young black women gyrating obscenely and functioning as backdrops, props and objects of lust for rap artists who sometimes behaves as predators?" (Cole, 2007, p. 96). Dr. Cole continues with a discussion of how these kinds of messages and images affect "the future of our young women and men, for their chances of building healthy relationships and, ultimately, for building strong black families" (p. 96).

Further, these derogatory negative lyrics and images are not confined to the eyes/ears of the Black community. We must ask ourselves what impact these images and lyrics have on the opinions and attitudes of teachers, police officers, lawyers, public defenders, juries, and correctional officers when they encounter African American women and adolescent girls. With the number of children entering American school systems from homes where they have been exposed to rap and hip-hop music—compounded by parents or guardians who are not present to filter out negative exposures—teachers and administrators must keep in mind that these growing numbers of American children will be entering their classrooms in need of their understanding and social and psychological services.

Repeated Status Offenses, Especially Running Away

An estimated 1.7 million youths ran away or were thrown away (kicked out by parents or guardians) in 1999. Of these teenagers, 68% were age 15–17, 57% were Whites, 17% were Blacks, and 15% were Hispanics, with an equal number of male and females (Snyder & Sickmund, 2006, p. 45).

In some jurisdictions, some types of behaviors once categorized as "status offenses"— like sexual behavior, running away, truancy, incorrigibility, and disorderly conduct—are now being labeled as felonies and therefore grounds for detention (Steffensmeier et al., 2005, p. 355). An example of how the courts are handing out severe penalties is the case of a 15-year-old Texas teen, Shaquanda Cotton. This African American high school student was accused of shoving a teachers' aide hall monitor and was given a year in a high-security detention center. Then, her sentence was extended for another year because she was found with contraband: an extra pair of socks and a plastic foam cup. This high school student is one of the 4,562 juveniles held by the Texas Youth Commission. Supporters of Cotton "say a White judge who gave a White 14-year-old girl probation after she was convicted of burning down her family's home treated Shaquanda unfairly" (Moreno, 2007, p. 1). In addition, in Buffalo, New York, a 13-year-old African American female was charged as an adult with second-degree murder for setting her step-grandfather's house on fire (Herbeck, 2007, p. A1). It is these types of disparities in the disciplinary treatment of African Americans that may account for their overrepresentation in the criminal justice system.

Each year, over 2 million youths are arrested for various crimes. Some of these reported crimes were committed by African American female gang members. In America, there are more than 30,000 gangs with a total of over 800,000 members (Urban Advocate, 2008, p. 3). According to a 2004 survey, the racial/ethnic makeup of these gangs is: Hispanic, 49%; Black, 37%; White, 8%; Asian, 5%; and other, 1% (Snyder & Sickmund, 2006, p. 73). Today's American gang membership is primarily male, with girls serving as an auxiliary or in coed gangs to do the bidding of male gang members, which may include sexual favors, concealing and carrying weapons for boys, selling drugs, and fighting with girls in rival gangs. In the past decade, however, there has been an increase in girls who are join-ing male gangs or starting their own gangs. Some girls join gangs as early as 12 or 14 years old, and they join for a variety of reasons. The Arts and Entertainment Network reported that there are 65,000 girls in American gangs.

For the African American female runaway, joining a gang gives her sanctuary from sexual abuse and violence in the home. In Jody Miller's (2001) study, she compared girls who join gangs with those who do not. Her study found that girls who joined had witnessed physical and sexual violence, were abused by family members, saw drugs/alcohol used in their home, and had family members in jail.

Half of the girls in Miller's study had been sexually assaulted by a member of the family or someone to whom they were exposed by a family member (p. 46). Further, a 1995 study of African American girls in the Vice Queens, a Chicago gang, found that these girls lived in low-income com-munities plagued by poverty, unemployment, and high crime rates (Fishman, 1995). By joining the gang, they gained status and protection. Some of these girls formed relationships with other neighborhood girls so they could earn money selling drugs to increase their status and enhance their lifestyle.

Miller (2001) notes that some scholars have argued that some young women on the inner-city streets operate with greater autonomy, allowing them greater participation in the drug trade. These young women may have been runaways or forced out of their homes before they developed the intellectual foundation and decision-making skills needed to survive. This makes them prime targets for gang membership. Coming from homes where sexual abuse exists can push these young girls out into the waiting arms of gangbangers and a life of sexual exploitation by male gang mem-bers. In the 21st century, gangs use sophisticated means to attract these young girls. They "often use cell phones and the Internet to communicate their illicit activities. Street gangs typically use the voice and text messaging capabilities of cell phones to conduct drug transactions and pre-arranged meetings with customers. Members of street gangs use multiple cell phones that they frequently discard while conducting their drug trafficking operations. For example, the leader of an African American street gang operating on the north side of Milwaukee used more than 20 cell phones to coordinate drug-related activities of gang members. . . . Gang members use social networking Internet sites such as MySpace, YouTube and Facebook" (National Gang Threat Assessment, 2009).

As previously mentioned, some of these African American teenagers leave home because of sexual abuse; however, they are further sexually exploited by the gang initiation rite called "sexing-in," whereby girls are forced to have sex with multiple male gang members as entry into the gang life. Often, these sexual acts are performed without the use of a condom. Also most disturbing is the rumored "HIV initiation," in which females have sex with an HIV-infected male; there is, however, no data to support this claim" (Chesney-Lind & Sheldon, 2004, p. 81).

In another sexual initiation called "rolls-in," a pair of dice is rolled and whatever number comes up determines how many males have sex with [a girl]" (Chesney-Lind & Sheldon, 2004, p. 81). Another initiation, which is very violent, is the "beat-in": a group of girls beat the would-be gang member for several minutes, and if she survives, she's in the gang. Many young African American girls live in neighborhoods where gangs are allowed to flourish. If a family member is already a member of a gang, a girl may hang out with people who participate in gang activities. This early exposure, coupled with school violence, leads some of these girls to seek protection while in school. According to USA Today (2006), the percentage of students ages 12–16 who reported street gangs present at school during the previous six months were: Whites 14%, Blacks 29%, Hispanics 37% and others 22% (p. 1). Rounding accounts for the total percentage equaled more than 100.

As Snyder and Sickmund's (2006) report of students' fistfights in school shows, girls appear to be the major offenders. When young women fight in school, it appears to be more common among Blacks and Hispanics. Fighting among groups showed Whites, 22%; Blacks, 34%; Hispanics, 29.5%, and others, 14.5%, with the majority of fights occurring in 9th grade (31.9%), followed by 10th grade (25%), 11th grade (23%) and 12th grade (17.7%) (p. 73). The Bureau of Justice reports that 2.7 million crimes are committed at school each year. Teachers were victims of 1,603,000 violent crimes from 1996 to 2000, and juvenile girls are the largest group of victims of sexual assaults. Once these girls are on the streets, they must secure resources to support themselves and sometimes their parents. The longer these girls are exposed to street life, the more opportunities arise for them to begin using drugs in an attempt to ease their pain. Drug dependency may cause girls to become drug mules or sell drugs. Some may turn to prostitution, violence, or shoplifting to support their habits. With an annual new crop of runaways numbering about 1.3 million to 1.4 million, gang membership will continue to be difficult to refuse for girls who are addicted, hungry, and homeless.

Another growing gang problem is M-13. This gang originated outside America with members from El Salvador, Guatemala, Honduras, and Mexico (Castaneda, 2006, p. B6). It was reported that there are 100,000 M13 gang members worldwide, of which 2,000 are in the United States (Fox News, 2007). These gang members want to be recognized, so they mark their territories with graffiti and wear gang colors. Most gangs' racial makeup is reflective of their neighborhood. For African American girls who, like others in their communities, struggle to deal with the racism and sexism that keep them in economic bondage, gang membership may provide a sense of escape. However, if a girl decides to leave gang life, she may be subject to a ritual called "beat-out," where other gang members take turns beating the girl who asked to quit the gang. In some instances, members kill those who want to leave or a gang member's relative. It is rare but it happens.

Unstable Family and Social Life, Including Family Involvement in the Criminal Justice System, Lack of Connectedness, and Social Isolation

Parents are the primary source of influence on their children. When children grow up in violent environments, exposed to external gang violence or intimate dating violence, parents must be prepared to handle how these violent acts will affect their child. Aggressive behavior often results. As Comer and Poussaint (1992) explain, "Aggression in everyday language is interpreted to mean an unjust attack of some kind, ranging from personal argument to large-scale war. But at the same time aggression is really a kind of life energy. It is much like gasoline—a spark on the ground can be destructive to everything nearby. But the gasoline in your fuel tank provides the energy necessary to run the car. Human beings need this energy to make their way in the world. But it must be notified and channeled, much like crude oil is refined and put in the gas tank. Whenever a child is faced with an obstacle or problem he attacks it with raw physical energy (aggression). If this response is not [channeled], conflict and chaos result. Parents, caretakers, teachers, and others must help the young child to gradually turn raw aggression energy into the fuel for curiosity, determination, learning, work and play" (pp. 57–58).

Without adequate parenting, the child could channel this aggression into unhealthy behavior, aided by gang members, drug dealers, and others who prey on their vulnerability. Further, "permitting early negative behavior, anger and aggression to be expressed without any check or effort to turn it into socially acceptable, useful energy is just as harmful as trying to suppress it" (Comer & Poussaint, 1992, p. 60). Teachers and others who interact with African American children must understand how children feel when they see the adults in their lives—no matter how capable—encounter difficulty in gaining education and work. What can a child conclude about his future in such a situation (Keinston, 1977), while at the same time faced with racist acts that create more anger and frustration? It is a very delicate balancing act. Many African American children live in neighborhoods where they witness frequent shooting and other violent acts. Thus they may admire the perpetrators and imitate their violent behavior. That's why it's critical that teachers must be knowledgeable about the social conditions forced on these children that create anxiety and anger resulting in inappropriate classroom behavior. Research shows that teachers who believe certain children can't learn are one of the major deciding factors in a student's academic achievement. Yet there are others who do not have a clue as to why some children fall behind and eventually fail. In a workshop described in Gary Howard's book *We Can't Teach What We Don't Know* (2006), "A white elementary teacher, with a tone of intense frustration in her voice, said to the group, 'I don't understand all of this talk about differences. Each of my little kindergarten students comes to me with the same stuff. It doesn't matter whether they're Black, Hispanic, or White, they each have a brain, a body, and a family. They each get the same curriculum. I treat them all alike. And yet by the end of the year, and as I watch them move up through the grades, the Blacks and Hispanics fall behind and the White kids do better. They all start with the same basic equipment. What happens?'" (p. 29).

When African American children are behind closed classroom doors with a teacher for five to seven hours a day, if they sense an attitude that does not support learning, they will eventually be turned off to learning rather than turned on—the mission of a committed educator. However, "Research in both classical psychology and educational psychology has long shown that the expectations that others have for us—especially those who act as important influences in our lives—affect the way in which we view ourselves. The way we view ourselves in turn affects our own expectations for ourselves. Finally, the expectations we hold for ourselves impact our performance" (Green, 2005, p. 19).

Equally important, parents must help their children to manage their aggression and keep them from becoming victims of multiple social ills. When a child shows aggressive and destructive behavior at home, the chances are he/she may exhibit similar behaviors at school. If this occurs, the child may be referred for psychological testing that may lead to special education classification and medication. Once children enter the special education path, some become discouraged and leave school before graduation, released to the waiting arms of the gangs, drug dealers, and pimps. Because so many African American children are harmed by the poverty and lack of education, it is often difficult for them to survive.

We know that in America, wealth is unequally distributed. As Reason et al. (2003) point out, "When we look at the distribution of wealth in the United States, we see even more glaring disparities. The top 1% of wealth holders control 39% of total household wealth. The share of wealth held by the bottom 80% of Americans is only 15% of the total wealth. The richest 1% of households own 48% of financial wealth, and the top 20% of households control 94% of total financial wealth in the United States" (pp. 6–7). In other words, a few Americans control the majority of the wealth in America. They further point out that "the average white family has twenty times the wealth of the average nonwhite family. In dollar terms, the average net worth of a white person is $43,800, while the average net worth of a Black person is $3,700" (p. 7). You see, when you have wealth/money you can accumulate more by investing in home/property and educate yourself/kids and pass the wealth on to your heirs. The burden of poverty is even harder for African Americans because so many families are headed by single females with limited skills and education, making it difficult to accumulate family wealth or gain an education. A Children's Defense Fund report (2007) states, "A child with an incarcerated parent is six to nine times as likely as a child whose parent was not incarcerated to become incarcerated [herself]" (p. 17). We must interrupt the intergenerational cycle of crime where an estimated ten million children have experienced having a parent incarcerated at some point in their lives by addressing the root causes that disproportionately take African American mothers and fathers out of our community, leaving millions of vulnerable children to the waiting arms of criminal predators. Further, studies by Rosenbaum (1989) and Owen and Bloom (1997) of girls held by the California Youth Authority found 70% and 89% of these females had family members who had been arrested. Another "survey found that 41% of teenage children of incarcerated parents had been suspended from school and 31% had run-ins with the police. It is no surprise that approximately 40% of incarcerated adults have an immediate family member who has spent time in prison" (Margolies & Kraft-Stolar 2006, p. 9).

This is very significant for African American females where the incarceration of the males in their community has reached crisis proportions, resulting in limited or no opportunities for a loving relationship. Faced with both gender and racial biases, the African American female may slip down the road to street prostitution, drug trafficking, and gang membership.

History of Unhealthy Dependent Relationships, Especially with Older Males

In an effort to escape some of life's unpleasant events, young African American females may turn to behaviors that make them feel better or cope with horrible life events. Sometimes, those who offer love are male companions whom they select to make them feel better but who may be the facilitator (e.g., a pimp) of inappropriate behaviors. These young women may also turn to gangs that model a family's role where older gang male members protect and abuse them at the same time. They also become easy prey for older males who can be high school classmates or the pimps in the neighborhood. In high school, an older boyfriend is perceived as giving an adolescent girl status and recognition. Gowen and Feldman (2004) found that in these types of relationships, in an effort to please the older male, girls may engage in certain sexual behavior (e.g., oral and anal sex) before they are ready. Also, 54.8% of these girls had sex while under the influence of drugs and alcohol and 52.4% reported not using condoms consistently, exposing them to unwanted pregnancies and sexually transmitted diseases (p. 171). In 2004, there were 6,789 births to girls under 15 and 420,000 babies born to teen mothers (Realityworks, 2006, p. 1). Gowen and Feldman (2004) also found that African American girls who date a boy three or more years older are more likely to be influenced by this male to have sex and drink alcohol. Young naive girls who want to make an impression will also engage in other risky behavior like smoking marijuana, crack cocaine, or meth. As previously mentioned, sometimes this behavior leads to older males convincing younger girls to have sex without the use of a condom, potentially resulting in HIV/AIDS. Teen girls are contracting HIV/AIDS at a fast rate (Lamendola, 2007, p. 1; Mero, 2007, p. 1).

Mental Health Issues, Including History of Abuse

Young women have many physiological and psychological developments that they must learn to adjust to. The onset of menarche, hair growing where it was once bare, clothing that suddenly doesn't fit correctly in the bust and buttocks areas, and the dreaded acne, may affect self-esteem and self-worth. When these events are combined with other stressors like parental sexual assault, poor grades, pressures to join gangs, sexual advances from both sexes, or parents who are physically absent due to incarceration or emotionally absent due to drug abuse, psychological problems can ensue. Sometimes a mental health diagnosis results, such as depression, panic attacks, or obsessive-compulsive behavior (Teplin & Abrams et al., 2006, p. 11). However, according to Hardy (2008), "Three-quarters of children and youths who need mental health services in the United States do not receive them" (p. 24). According to an article in the *Challenger* newspaper by Marian Wright Edelman (2005, p. 10), 70% of children in the juvenile justice system have mental health problems. In 2003 alone, 15,000 were incarcerated because mental health services were unavailable in their communities (p. 10). When these young women and girls have been victims of sexual and physical abuse, they are more likely to engage in violent or nonviolent crimes (Herres & McCloskey, 2003), followed by interaction with the criminal justice system. Rather than referring these young women for mental health services they are sent to juvenile detention centers.

Kaplan and Busner (1992) uncovered racial biases in the handling of African American adolescents. They reported on research by "Lewis, [who] concluded in two studies that racial bias on the part of the mental health system leads to the incarceration of Black children and adolescents in juvenile offender facilities while White children and adolescents with similar symptoms are more likely to be hospitalized in psychiatric facilities" (p. 758). This is further supported by a 2006 Human Rights Watch report, "Custody and Control," which said, "New York state suffers from statewide healthcare deficiencies including poor access to services for children with mental health needs. . . . This failure can result in girls being confined in juvenile prisons not only because they manifest preventable but untreated behavior problems, but also because overwhelmed parents feel they cannot control their children without state intervention, or because judges recognized that incarceration is the only way to guarantee access to health services." This is totally unacceptable behavior for a state that is spending more on prison construction (discussed later) than on educational and health care.

When African American juveniles are incarcerated, they suffer separation and loneliness. When African American mothers are incarcerated, their children feel abandoned to face life challenges alone. These challenges often lead them down the pathway to juvenile court and sometimes adult prisons, where the abuse may continue.

Overrepresentation: Communities of Color in the Justice System

Snyder and Sickmund (2006) in their "reviews of existing research literature found that minorities (especially Black) youth are overrepresented at most stages of the juvenile justice system" (p. 189). Racial disparities may occur at the point when the decision is made to arrest and prosecute. It appears from their research that the decision to arrest is where the most discretion is, and thus where the greatest potential to affect the overrepresentation of minorities is found. The Snyder and Sickmund report presents various statistical tools (pp. 189–190) for measuring disparity at each decision point. By no means am I suggesting that the individual who has broken the law should not be arrested. What I am suggesting, however, is that police officers play a very important role in creating overrepresentation. Harris (2007) states, "Police are the entry point, the gatekeepers, of the criminal justice system. They make discretionary decisions every day about who is likely to commit a crime and who should be targeted by the criminal justice system; about who should be stopped, questioned, searched, and arrested. These decisions are made on the basis of individual police officers' life experiences—their training, their instincts, their prejudices and biases. And all too often, they are decisions influenced by race" (p. 74). There may even be an incentive to arrest, because some arresting officers may be required to appear in court, which may lead to overtime pay for every court visit beyond their assigned shift. We must be mindful that not all individuals are able to leave their prejudices at the workplace door. This is one important reason for diversity training workshops.

Human Rights Watch (2006) in its report states, "Across the U.S. 70% of delinquency cases involving White girls are dismissed, while only 30% of cases involving African American girls are dismissed. Nationally, 34% of 12- to 17-year-olds in the U.S. are girls of color, yet they account for 52% of those detained for juvenile offenses."

Globally, a report by Amnesty International and Human Rights Watch (HRW) found that at least 2,225 prisoners in the United States are serving life without parole for crimes they committed as minors. These sentences are rare elsewhere in the world, where a total of 12 child offenders are serving life terms in Israel, South Africa, and Tanzania. But in the United States, two decades of mandatory sentencing laws and increasing prosecutorial discretion to try children as adults have created an entire population of young prisoners who will live the rest of their days behind prison bars (Hubner, 2006, p. 17). In America, there are 42 states that can sentence teenagers to life in prison without parole, and Black children are sentenced to life without parole at a rate 10 times more than White youths. And some states continue to drop the age from 18 downward; in one state, a 10-year-old can be seen in adult court. For example, "in Mississippi children as young as 13 years old can be sentenced to prison for the rest of their lives" (Thomas, 2008, p. 5). In addition, "of the 6,629 youths who entered the custody of California's Department of Corrections for an offense committed prior to their 18th birthday, 70% were African American and Latino and 10% were white; and African American youth are 4.7 times as likely to be transferred to adult systems than white youths" (p. 4); and in Illinois "over a three-year period (2000–2002), 99% of the youths automatically transferred to adult court in Cook County were African American and Latino" (p. 7). Another study, by Bartollas (1993), of institutional placement in the Midwest found that Black adolescent girls were placed in public facilities 61% of the time, while White girls were always sent to private facilities (p. 236) where rehabilitation and services were considerably better. Further, "Research has shown that juveniles incarcerated with adults are five times more likely to report being victims of sexual assault than in juvenile facilities and the suicide rate of juveniles in adult jails is 7.7 times higher than that of juvenile detention centers" (www.spr.org 7/30/07).

From this analysis it is apparent that in the United States embedded social/economic factors are in place that facilitate this overrepresentation of minorities, specifically African American children.

Economically Marginalized Population

Poverty is one measurement that shows how well or poorly a particular group is doing. According to the Juvenile Offenders and Victims 2006 National Report, in 2002 almost one-third of Black juveniles lived in poverty and one-fifth of Black children under age five lived in extreme poverty (Snyder & Sickmund, 2006). The U.S. Census tracks a poverty rate for Blacks of 24.9%, Whites 8.3%, Hispanics 21.8%, and Asians 11.1%. Recognizing the impact of poverty on children was the recent subject of a Harvard University School of Public Health report, "Children Left Behind" (Garcia et al., 2007), which paints a more current view of how America once again is failing African American and Hispanic children. The report presented the best and worst neighborhoods for children. The worst are:

- For Black children: Buffalo, Chicago, New York
- For Hispanic children: Bakersfield, Providence, Springfield (Massachusetts)
- For White children: Bakersfield, New York, El Paso
- For Asian children: New York, Bakersfield, Fresno (Garcia et al., p. 2)

As this report acknowledges, "Early life experiences are critical to human development and opportunities for advancement throughout life" (pp. 2–3). Poverty status is but one more indicator of America's failure to protect children, its most vulnerable citizens. In an article from *American School Board Journal* (Hardy 2006), the author noted, "Social scientists have identified six primary risk factors, all of which are common in low-income households. They are poverty itself, welfare dependence, absent parents, one-parent families, unwed mothers, and parents without a high school diploma" (pp. 17–18).

Poverty among children is recognized as one of the most important indicators for health and academic achievement (Barton, 2004) and must be considered as an important factor in a child's survival. However, when you add racism into the poverty equation, as William Julius Wilson has done, you end up here: "whites believe that African Americans are responsible for their own inferior economic status because of cultural traits. Because even affluent whites fear corporate downsizing, they are unwilling to vote for governmental assistance to the poor. whites are continuing to be suburban dwellers, further isolating poor minorities in central cities and making their problems distant and unimportant."

Some White Americans are also disenfranchised by the same government that allows Black children to live in poverty. Because some White Americans are not gaining the levels of education needed to fully understand the social and political structure of this nation, they become equally vulnerable. Some may believe resources are being shifted to Black children, and this keeps the racism fueled.

The U.S. Census reveals income disparities between African American households and others. The median income for Black families is $30,939. For Whites it is $50,622, Asians, $60,637, and Hispanics $36,278. There are myriad problems that these children encounter that are due to their poverty status, and the ripple effects of poverty are life threatening.

When you look at disparities utilizing Bloom's at-risk characteristics and the work of other scholars like James Bell (2007), you will see this rush to incarcerate African Americans as a "network of legislation, policy, practice, and structural racism that has fostered blacks being incarcerated at unconscionable levels . . . for increasingly minor acts" (p. 49). Bloom's, Edelman's, and Bell's analyses point out where the economic, social and political factors intersect in these institutionalized processes that guarantee that some Americans will be propelled into the waiting arms of American's criminal justice system.

REFERENCES

Arnold, R. (1995). Process of victimization and civilizations of Black women. In P. B. Sokolofy, *The Criminal Justices System* (2nd ed.). New York: McGraw Hill.

Banyard, V. L., Williams, L. M., Siegel, J. A. & West, C. (2002). Childhood sexual abuse in the lives of Black women: Risk and resilience in a longitudinal study. In C. West, *Violence in the Lives of Black Women*. New York: The Hansworth Press, pp. 45–58.

Bartollas, C. (1993). Little girls grown up: The perils of institutionalization. In C. Cutlier (ed.), *Female Criminality: The State of the Act*. New York: Garland Press.

Barton, P. E. (2004, November). Why does the gap persist? *Educational Leadership,* 62(3) 8–13.

Bass, E. (1983). Introduction: In the truth itself, there is healing. In E. Bass & L. T. Thorton (eds.), *I Never Told Anyone.* New York: Harper Row, pp. 23–61.

Bell, J. (2007). Correcting the system of unequal justices. In T. Smiley, *The Covenant with Black America.* Chicago: Third World Press, 47–71.

Bloom, B., Owens, B., Deschenes, P., & Rosenbaum, J. (2003). Developing gender-specific services for delinquency prevention. In P. Muraskin, *It's a Crime: Women and Justices* (3rd ed.). Upper Saddle River, NJ: Prentice Hall, 517–543.

Castaneda, R. (2006, October 18). Gang members describe life inside M-13. *Washington Post,* p. A6.

Chesney-Lind, M., & Sheldon, R. G. (2004). *Girls, Delinquency and Juvenile Justices.* Belmont, CA: Thomson/Wadsworth.

Children's Defense Fund. (2005). Stand up for children now: State of America's children action guide. Washington DC.

Children's Defense Fund. (2007). America's cradle to prison pipeline. Summary Report. Washington, DC.

Children's Defense Fund. (2008, 2009, & 2013 November). Moments in America for children: Washington, DC. Retrieved from http://www.childrendefense .org/data/momersion

Cole, J. (2007, March). Sex, violence, disrespect, what hip-hop has done to Black women. *Ebony* 62(5), 90–96.

Comer, J. P., & Poussaint, A. (1992). *Raising Black Children.* New York: Plume Books.

Copolo, D. (2007, December 3). Helping young mothers help their babies and themselves. *Gotham Gazette.* Retrieved from http://www.gothamgazette .com

Edelman, M. W. (2005, April 13). Injustices of the juvenile justice system. Reprint. *Buffalo Challenger,* 42(15), 10.

Edelman, M. W. (2007). America's cradle to prison pipeline: A report of the children's defense fund. Washington, DC.

Fishman, L. T. (1995). The vice queens: An ethnographic study of Black female gang behavior. In M. Klein, C. Maxsom & J. Miller (eds.), *The Modern Gang, Reader.* Los Angeles: Roxbury, 83–92.

Garcia, D. A., McArdie, N., Osypuk, T., Lefkowitz, B., & Kringold, B. (2007). Harvard school of public health, children left behind, how metropolitan areas are failing America's children, center for the advancement of health.

Gowen, J. K., Feldman, S., & Dommovon, Y. (2004). A comparison of sexual behavior and attitudes of adolescent girls with older versus similar aged boyfriends. *Journal of Youth and Adolescence,* 33(2), 167–176.

Grace, Nancy. Televison broadcast aired (10/2/07 & 10/3/07). Interview with Amber Hill's aunt.

Grace, Nancy. Televison broadcast aired (1/11/07 & 5/5/06). CNN.com/ Transcripts.com.

Green, R. (2005). *Expectations: How Teachers' Expectations Can Increase Student Achievement and Assist in Closing the Achievement Gap.* Columbus, Ohio: McGraw Hill.

Hardy, L. (2006, December). Children at risk, mental health. *American School Board Journal*, 17–21.

Hardy, L. (2008, March). Children at risk, mental health. *American School Board Journal*, 24–27.

Harlow, C. F. (2003). Educational and correctional populations, U.S. Bureau of Justices, Offices of Justices Programs, Bureau of Justices Statistics, January 2003, ncj195670, Washington DC.

Harris, M. (2007). Fostering accountable community-centered policing. In T. Smiley, *The Covenant with Black America*. Chicago: Third World Press.

Herbeck, D. (2007, June 24). Did girl's revenge fuel fatal arson? *Buffalo Newspaper*, p. A1.

Herres, V., & McCloskey, L. (2003). Sexual abuse, family violence and delinquency. Findings from a longitudinal study. *Violence and Victims* 18, 319–334.

Hopper, J. (2007, September 26). Child abuse, statistics, research and resources. Retrieved from http://www.Jimhopper.com

Howard, G. (2006). *We Can't Teach What We Don't Know*. New York, New York: Teachers College Press.

Hubner, J. (2006, Spring). Discarded lives: Children sentenced to life without parole. *Amnesty International Journal*, 16–21.

Human Rights Watch. (2006, September). Custody and control, conditions of confinement in New York's juvenile prisons for girls, 18(4). Retrieved from http://www. hrw.org/reports/2006/us0906

Johnson, K. (2006, December 14). Gonzales concentrates on child abuse. *USA Today*, pp. A13–14.

Kaiser, K. (2008, February 7) Assistant director FBI congressional testimony on before House Committee on Foreign Affairs. Retrieved from http://www .fbi.gov/congress/congress08/kaiser020708.htm

Kaplan, S., & Busner, J. (1992, June). A note on racial bias in admission of children and adolescents to state mental health facilities versus correctional facilities in New York. *American Journal of Psychiatry*, 149(6), 768–772.

Keinston, K. (1977). *All Our Children*. New York: Carnegie Corporation.

Lamendola, B. (2007, March 12). AIDS educator focus on teens, *South Florida Sun-Sentinel*. Retrieved from http://www.orlandosentinel.com/news /local/state/orl-teens/207mar12

Margolies, K. J., & Kroft-Stolar, T. (2006, February). When free means losing your mother: the collision of child welfare and the incarceration of women in new york state. correctional association of New York State: Women prison project.

Mero, R. (2007, February 27). Man sentenced for sex with teen. *The Morning Star*. Retrieved from http://www.nwaonline.net/article/2007/03/news/022807

Miller, J. (1991). *Prostitution in Contemporary American Society: Sexual Coercion*. Lexington, Mass.: Lexington Books.

Miller, J. (2001). *One of the Guys: Girls, Gangs and Gender*. New York: Oxford University Press.

Miller, L. (2004). Illinois prisoners reentry: Building a second chance. Annie E. Casey Foundation.

Moreno, S. (March 29, 2007). Texas teen's imprisonment sparks protest. *Washington Post*. Retrieved from http://www.washingtonpost.com

Mueller, R. (2003). U.S. Department of Justices, Federal Bureau of Investigation (FBI), Uniform Crime Report, Crime in the United States 2003, Special Report, Violence Among Family Members and Intimate Partners, Section V, Number of Confrontations Between Victims and Offenders by Relationship, Table 5.4, U.S. Department of Justices, Federal Bureau of Investigation Uniform Crime Reports. Retrieved from http://www.fbi.gov/uce/03cius.htm

Mullen, P., & Fleming, J. (1998). Long term effects of child sexual abuse: Issues in child abuse. Number 9 Autumn. National Child Protection Clearing House. Retrieved from http://www.aifs/gov.au/nch/issues9.html

Mumola, C. (2006). Drug use and dependence, state and federal prisoners, 2004. U.S. Department of Justices, Bureau of Justices Programs, Bureau of Justices Statistics, Special Report. Washington, D.C. October 2006.ncj213530

Mumola, C. (2007). Medical cases of death in state prisons, 2001–2004. U.S. Department of Justices, Bureau of Justices Programs, Bureau of Justices Statistics. Washington D.C. January 2007 ncj 216340

National Gang Threat Assessment 2009. (2009, January). U.S. Department of Justices, Product 2009:mo335-001. Retrieved from www.uddoj.gov/ndic/pubs32/32146/index/htm

Owen, B., & Bloom, B. (1997). Profiling the needs of young female offenders: Final report to executive staff of the california youth authorities, Washington, DC: National Institute of Justice.

Poussaint, A. (2008, October 23). Speech before Council of Great City Schools, Hilton American Hotel, Houston, Texas.

Realityworks Inc. (2006). 2709 Mondavi Road, Eau Claire, Wisconsin. Retrieved from http://www.Realityworks.com

Reason, C., Conley, D., & Debro, J. (2003). *Race, Class, Gender and Justices in the United States*. Boston, MA: Allyn & Bacon, 1–19.

Rennison, C. M., & Welchans, H. (2002, August). U.S. Department of Justices, Offices of Justices Programs, Bureau of Justices Statistics, Criminal Victimizations, 1998–1999.

Rosenbaum, J. (1989). Family dysfunction and female delinquency. *Crime & Delinquency, 35*, 31–44.

Science Daily. (2007, February 6). Retrieved from http://www.sciencedaily.com

Shakeshaft, C., & Cohen, A. (1995, March). Sexual Abuse of Students by School Personnel. *Phi Delta Kappan, 76*(7), pp. 513–520.

Smith, B. (2001). *Sexual Abuse Against Women in Prison*. ABA Criminal.

Snyder, H., & Sickmund, M. (2006, September 22). Time of day. In OJJDP Statistical Briefing Book (Juveniles as Offenders). Retrieved from http://ojjdp.ncys.gov/ojstatbb/offenders

Snyder, H., & Sickmund, M. (2006). Juvenile offenders and victims: 2006 national report. U.S. Department of Justices, Office of Justice Program, Office of Juvenile Justices and Delinquency Prevention. Washington DC.

Steffensmeier, D., Schwartz, J., Zhong, H., & Ackerman, J. (2005). An assessment of recent trends in girls' violence using diverse longitudinal sources: Is the gap closing? *Criminology, 43*(2), 355–405.

Tanner, L. (2006, August 27). Teenage sex linked to lewd music. *Buffalo News*, p. A7.

Teplin, L. A., Abram, K. M., McClelland, G. M., Merecle, A., Dulcan, M., & Washington, J. (2006, April). Psychiatric disorders of youth in detention. U.S. Department of Justices, Offices of Justices Programs, Office of Juvenile Justices Delinquency Prevention, pp. 1–16.

Thomas, A. H. (2008). No chance to make it right. The NAACP Legal Defense and Educational Fund, Inc.

Thornburgh, N. (2006, April 7). Dropout nation. *Time* 30–40.

Urban Advocate Publication of the National School Board Association Council of Urban Boards of Education (CUBE). (2008, April/May). As youth gangs evolve, urban schools must respond too, p. 3.

USA Today. Snapshots, organized trouble at school, July 7, 2006.

Wallman, K. (2008). Americas' children in brief: Key national indicators of well-being, 2008, Federal Interagency Forum on Child and Family Statistics. Retrieved from http://www.nichd.nid.gov/publication/pub/upload/Americas'_children_in_in_brief_report2008 pdf

Chapter 25

Raising the Age of Criminal Responsibility in New York: A Judge's Observation

Juanita Bing Newton

A judge . . . is more than a moderator; [a judge] is affirmatively charged with securing a fair trial and a judge must intervene *sua sponte* to that end, when necessary. . . . Justice does not depend upon legal dialectics so much as upon the atmosphere of the courtroom, and that in the end depends primarily upon the judge. (Learned Hand, *Brown v. Walter*, 1933)

These words, written by a great American jurist, have both guided me and haunted me for the 28 years I have served as a Judge in the New York State court system. The quote has been a constant source of encouragement and a reminder that, in the end, justice in my courtroom, in my sphere of influence, depends on me. In meeting the often difficult challenges of the daily resolution of cases and controversies, this sentiment has encouraged and permitted me to look beyond the "legal dialectics" and to see the people behind, and often hidden from, the legal proceedings. Through this prism of promoting justice, I particularly have become passionate about the condition and status of the teenagers who have appeared before me as criminal defendants, charged as adults and attempting to navigate a perilous adult criminal justice system. These children exhibit in the courtroom every range of emotion, from scared to cocky. But mostly, the children present as children lost in an adult world. In this misplaced world of child-adults, ensuring justice was mostly always difficult, only sometimes successful.

Adolescents, as young as age 16, are treated as adults for all purposes in the New York criminal justice system. They have the right to remain silent after arrest but they don't have the right to call their parents. They are housed in jails and prisons with adults and are not provided with any protection from older, more violent offenders. They can be subject to police interrogation techniques identical to those employed to break down the more savvy repeat offenders. Some of these techniques are so psychologically severe that they have recently been condemned by New York's highest appellate court in *People v. Thomas* (2014). There are no protocols to protect their vulnerability. Yet, we know that children need protection and that there are numerous safeguards in place for children in the justice system who have not yet reached age 16. Those 16 and older are adults for all purposes. Except, as a mother at a public hearing concerning these issues once told me, she was notified of her 16-year-old son's arrest when a police officer called her, after the arrest, after the lineup had been conducted, after the confession had been obtained, after the booking had been completed, to ask permission to give her child an aspirin. The child was complaining about a headache and medication could not be dispensed without parental permission due to his age. It is ironic that the government acknowledges the need for parental involvement in the most minor health issues while concluding that the same child should be subject to a life-changing criminal justice process, alone and as an adult. In New York State, 16-year-olds can't vote, can't join the military, and can't buy cigarettes or alcohol. But they are treated as adults for all purposes in the criminal justice system (Schuyler Center for Analysis and Advocacy, 2010). In this chapter, my goal is to discuss the policy decisions which lead to an inordinately low age of criminal responsibility in New York, the ways juvenile and adult criminal adjudications differ, the consequences for youth in the adult system, and suggestions for change.

In the minds of a growing chorus of policy makers and others, the outcome of this long ago policy making—that 16-year-olds are deemed adults in the criminal justice system—has created an unfair and unjust justice system for those adolescents, who along with the public at large, would be better served if they were no longer adjudicated as adults but rather in the juvenile justice system.

In most jurisdictions and in the Federal courts, the age of responsibility for treatment as an adult is generally age 19 or older. Only New York and North Carolina prosecute 16-year-olds as adults. In New York State, all

16-, 17-, and 18-year-olds who are charged with a crime, regardless of the nature of the charges, are treated as adults. Even though more than 74% of crimes committed by 16- and 17-year-olds are misdemeanor level charges, the youths are nonetheless treated as adults in a system designed not for them but for adults (Justice Policy Institute, 2007). However, for the first time now in more than fifty years, the state of New York is in the midst of a serious discussion on the appropriateness of this policy and whether to raise the age of criminal responsibility in order to be in line with the other 48 states and, more important, to provide better process and better outcomes for children while ensuring continuing public safety.

Most agree that New York settled on age 16 as the age for criminal prosecution as an adult in an indirect manner and as a by-product of the establishment of the New York Family Court in 1962. The decision was intended and expected to be a temporary determination of the age of responsibility. After extensive discussion, the 1961 constitutional convention which recommended the new court entity concluded that children age 15 and under would be deemed juvenile delinquents (considerations for this determination included existing rules, past practices, and fiscal concerns) and placed under the protective jurisdiction of the newly-established family court. The extensive debate on the age of responsibility, however, failed to result in a strong consensus on the appropriate age for adult jurisdiction, and the convention deferred the "final" decision for future debate and legislative action. While a Joint Legislative Committee again thoroughly reviewed the issue and completed a study in 1963, again no firm consensus or agreement was reached on the age of responsibility and the committee tabled the issue again for future debate and study. The comprehensive discussion required to bring closure to the debate on whether this 16-year-age cut-off was appropriate or not was again left for another day. And thus, all children age 16 and older were transformed into adulthood for purposes of criminal liability, prosecution, and punishment (Sobie, 2010). Now after a more than fifty-year delay and with an abundance of data and scientific evidence in hand, there is a new and broad effort to finally and definitively resolve the issue of whether matters involving adolescents aged 16 and 17 should be appropriately adjudicated in adult criminal courts.

In the years since 1963, the appropriateness of the 16-year-old cut-off point and its effect on children and public safety has been a marginal topic for sentencing and only occasionally discussed and debated. The official language of criminal responsibility is contained in Article 30 of the New York Penal Law and is couched in the notion that infancy is a defense to responsibility. Section 30.00 provides that "a person less than sixteen years old is not criminally responsible for conduct." By application, all persons age 16 and older are criminally responsible and must be prosecuted, as mandated by the Penal Law, in the adult criminal court. Interestingly, the only changes in New York law since 1963 have had the effect of actually lowering the age of criminal responsibility. Downward movement of the age of responsibility occurred in the 1980s, when horrific crimes committed by a small number of juveniles under the age of 16 led to the lowering of the age of criminal responsibility to as low as age 13 for juveniles charged with the most serious and violent crimes such as murder, rape, robbery, and arson. To facilitate the change, the statutory scheme was amended and an exception added to Penal Law Section 30.00, subdivision 1 to provide that "a person thirteen, fourteen or fifteen years of age is criminally responsible for acts" of certain designated crimes.

Further, Penal Law Section 30.00, subdivision 3 provides that "in any prosecution for an offense, lack of criminal responsibility by reason of infancy . . . is a defense." Because infancy is an absolute defense to adult prosecution, the statute places children age 16 and older in the adult court and those less than 16, with specific exceptions, in the juvenile court known in New York as the Family Court. These exception cases involving 13-, 14-, and 15-year-olds are prosecuted in adult criminal court but make up a relatively small number of matters annually. These cases also are statutorily subject to removal from the adult criminal court to the family court for juvenile delinquency proceedings and findings when mitigating factors exist to support that transfer (NY Family Court Act Section 301.1).

Why does the jurisdiction of the court (adult versus juvenile) matter? In simple terms, the entire focus of case adjudication in these two courts is different, resulting in dramatically different and life-altering outcomes. While the primary purpose of criminal justice sentencing in the adult court is continuously debated, it is clear that retributive punishment has taken center stage ahead of deterrence and rehabilitation. On the other hand, by definition, the outcome focus for the juvenile or family court is rehabilitation, which is deemed to be in the best interest of the child. As a result, in the juvenile court there are numerous programs, services, and support for the child in the form of productive intervention that is not available to the youth in the adult criminal court (Corriero, 2011–2012).

Equally important, even at the pre-court stage of a case, there are rights and protocols in place for juveniles age 15 and under that provide specific protections not available to older youths. For example, upon the arrest or detention of adolescents under age 16, a parent or guardian must be contacted immediately. If detained at a police facility or station house, the youth must be placed in a room apart from adult offenders and in a designated space that has been pre-approved by child welfare officials. Adolescents must be protected and treated as the children they are. Such services are not available to older adolescents once they reach their 16th birthday.

In New York, the adjudications for juvenile cases are handled in the Family Court, created by the Family Court Act Section 301.1, where the focus is on the outcome that serves the best interest of the child.

The concept of least restrictive punishment is applied, with rehabilitation as the goal. Adjudications do not result in a criminal record; results are sealed. In contrast, the process for the adolescent age 16 and older is a public adult system that leads to public criminal records. The focus of sentencing is not necessarily and, certainly not exclusively, on rehabilitation of the offender. Incarceration can lead to potential placement with older offenders, and the collateral consequences of a public record can serve as a deterrent to a successful and rehabilitated future (Corriero, 2011–2012).

Clearly, the consequences for youths prosecuted in adult versus juvenile courts are significant both in direct response to the adjudication but also in ways collateral to the final court judgment. A child aged 16 and older with a matter in adult criminal court may have her case disposed of in an arguably favorable non-jail sentence. A sentence of restitution in a minor larceny case or a sentence to pay a fine in a case involving possession of a small amount of marijuana may be considered a benign outcome. These direct consequences to a conviction seem relatively insignificant. But attending collateral consequences may ruin the minor child's future. She will have a public record that could materially affect opportunities for education (both admission to colleges and financial aid options), employment, housing, and consumer credit ratings. Moreover, the danger of a negative collateral consequence is exponentially greater in this day and age of technology and the internet when criminal information, even sealed information, is readily accessible. The danger of public punishment and the prospects of dire collateral consequences are antithetical to the best interests of children and to the needs of the community. The consequences both direct and collateral are not minor (Justice Policy Institute, 2007).

Who are these children at risk of adult adjudication in New York State? A recent report, *Advancing a Fair and Just Age of Criminal Responsibility for Youth in New York State* (Governor's Children's Cabinet Advisory Board, 2011), provides a statistical snapshot of these youth and describes some of the dimensions of the problem:

- During 2009, there were 47,339 youth ages 16 and 17 years arrested in New York State. Over half of those arrests (26,802) occurred in New York City.

- During 2009, there were 7,391 youth admitted to county jails in New York State who were under the age of 18 years at admission (excludes New York City jail admissions): 2,883 youth age 16 years and 4,508 youth age 17 years.

- During 2008, there were 3,570 youth admitted to jails in New York City who were under the age of 18 years at admission: 1,277 youth admitted at age 16 years and 2,293 youth admitted at age 17 years.

- On January 1, 2010, 687 youth ages 16 to 18 years were in the custody of the New York State Department of Correctional Services (DOCS).
- On October 24, 2010, there were 5,726 youth under adult probation supervision in New York State who were under the age of 18 years at sentencing.

These startling numbers are not inconsequential and are compounded by the fact that the impact of treating too many youth as adult criminals also falls disproportionately on youth of color. The result is increased traffic on what the Children's Defense Fund describes as the "Cradle to Prison Pipeline" which "leads children to marginalized lives and premature deaths." Citing detailed statistical data, the Advisory Board found that:

Youth of color are represented in New York's justice system in numbers that are disproportionately greater than their representation in the general population and that exceed any differences in offending rates. Youth of color experience differential treatment at each decision point in the criminal justice process that in turn amplifies their disproportionality among juvenile arrestees at later stages. In addition to exposure to harsher treatment in the adult system, youth of color are also at great risk of becoming systematically disadvantaged as an adult criminal record reduces lifelong opportunities for education, employment and housing. (Governor's Children's Cabinet Advisory Board, 2011)

Fortunately, these disturbing findings have fueled the push for change. Now, for the first time in fifty years, there is serious debate and discussion about moving the age of criminal responsibility upward to age eighteen. The focus on the 16- and 17-year-old defendant is a focus on fairness and justice, as many recognize that both the social and scientific evidence point to the conclusion that adult treatment for adolescents of 16 and 17 is inappropriate and contrary to the needs of children and to public safety.

So what in fact has fueled this shift in thinking and propelled an old issue into the limelight? Moving the debate forward are two related developments, one based in science and the other in law. Previously unknown or unrecognized, scientific research about the adolescent brain and brain development has demonstrated that our earlier thinking about adolescents was wrong. Adolescents are really more closely aligned with traits of children than those of adults. The clear evidence suggests that despite the full physical development of adolescents, their brains are not fully developed but continue to grow well past age 18. Equally important to the shift in thinking is the legal recognition of the new scientific evidence in determining criminal culpability of the adolescent as delineated by the United States Supreme Court. The Court's recognition and application of brain science has legitimized the issue as one deserving review and response. In *Roper v. Simmons* (2005), the Supreme Court was called upon to determine if an adolescent younger than 18 could be subject to the death penalty. In resolving the issue in favor of the youth, the court relied heavily on adolescent brain science, stating:

> Three general differences between juveniles under 18 and adults demonstrate that juvenile offenders cannot with reliability be classified among the worst offenders. First . . . [a] lack of maturity and an underdeveloped sense of responsibility are found in youth more often than in adults and are more understandable among the young. . . . The second area of difference is that juveniles are more vulnerable or susceptible to negative influences and outside pressures, including peer pressure. . . . The third broad difference is that the character of a juvenile is not as well formed as that of an adult. . . . These differences render suspect any conclusion that a juvenile falls among the worst offenders. . . . From a moral standpoint it would be misguided to equate the failings of a minor with those of an adult, for a greater possibility exists that a minor's character deficiencies will be reformed. . . . For the reasons we have discussed . . . a line must be drawn. . . . The age of 18 is the point where society draws the line for many purposes between childhood and adulthood.

The highest court in the land has spoken and definitively drawn the line for criminal and moral adult responsibility at 18. In doing so, it relied heavily on the developing brain science as well as our long jurisprudential view of morality, rehabilitation, and justice. The relied-on brain science informs us that the brain continues to develop beyond ages 16, 17, and 18. We now know that the portion of the developing brain that monitors judgment, the prefrontal cortex, is in fact one of the last areas to develop. We know that anatomically the adolescent is not as equipped as adults to make sound, deliberate, and intentional decisions. Adolescents are simply less able to make thoughtful and rational choices than adults (Baird, Fugelsang & Bennett, 2005). An important corollary with the inability to make sound choices is that adolescents are more susceptible to succumb to the power and suggestion of others, especially adults. The knowledge and teachings on the anatomy and physiology of the adolescent brain permit us to now better appreciate the unique functioning of the brain as an explanation of the often curious and inexplicable behavior of teenagers.

Some years ago at a judicial education conference, a judge in the group offered that he would "never listen to that junk" as an unsolicited comment to my statement that I often looked at MTV, VH1, BET, and similar television programming that appealed to teenagers and young adults. I replied, "You would if you were trying as I am to understand their behavior and attitudes in response to the important issues inherent in their criminal matters before me." At that time I was sitting as a trial judge and presiding over felony criminal matters. I often searched for understanding in every source available to me, whether it was medical science, educational literature, or even MTV. Indeed, I learned a great deal about my 16-, 17-, and 18-year-old defendants from simply speaking with them. I discovered that they responded well to someone caring about them. In response to that need, I instituted a quarterly "report card day" when the adolescent defendants were required to appear and present their report cards to me. It was not designed to be punishment or a controlling sword of Damocles. Rather, it was an opportunity for them to show someone who cared the evidence of their hard work, their successes, and often their needs. Interestingly, whether armed with good reports or not-so-good reports, my young defendants always made their court appearances on report card day. They were searching for caring.

Critical to our understanding of this brain phenomenon and evolving national best practices are recent developments in neuroscience suggesting that teenagers are neither as mature as adults nor as blameworthy for their actions. Brain imaging studies comparing adults and adolescents confronted with difficult situations show, for example, that adolescents take more time than adults to form a judgment that something is bad and are slower to respond appropriately. Adults also have been found to have more activity in the parts of the brain that create mental imagery and signal internal distress. This has led researchers to believe that adults who are confronted with a potentially dangerous scenario are more likely to create a mental image of possible outcomes than children are and to have an adverse, preemptive response to those images. Other studies have confirmed significant age-related differences in cognitive processing affecting adolescents' ability to make sound judgments (Baird, Fugelsang & Bennett, 2005).

A review of these many studies supports conclusions learned from my courtroom encounters—that adolescents exhibit short-sighted decision making, poor impulse control, and vulnerability to peer (and other) pressures. Additionally, there are solid findings that the parts of the brain that govern impulse control, planning, and thinking ahead continue to develop well beyond age 18. There also are several studies indicating that the systems governing reward sensitivity are "amped up" at puberty, which would lead to an increase in sensation-seeking and in valuing benefits over risks. And there is emerging evidence that the brain systems that govern the processing of emotional and social information are affected by the hormonal changes of puberty in ways that make adolescents more sensitive to the reactions of those around them and thus more susceptible to the influence of peers (MacArthur Foundation Research Network on Adolescent Development and Juvenile Justice, Issue Brief 3).

Based on the foregoing, it is evident that simple biology places 16- and 17-year-olds at severe risk in the adult criminal justice system, and assignment to that system sadly squanders the opportunity to improve public safety by securing a better outcome for children.

Another issue related to the age of responsibility is whether there is a gender difference between the male adolescent brain and the female adolescent brain. Are there specific findings in the brain science that enlightens our understanding of the brain of adolescent girls? Indeed there are and these findings show differences between girls' and boys' brains. Important to the application of this science to both genders is an understanding of some of its important revelations.

In the joint report *Justice by Gender* (American Bar Association & National Bar Association, 2001), the authors conclude that the pathway to female delinquency is punctuated by factors directly related to female adolescent development. "Research and evidence suggests that a key component of girls' development is the relationships and connections they develop with others. Additionally, a noted clinical psychologist, Dr. Marty Beyer, has found that as girls move into adolescence, many report significantly lower levels of self-competence (perceived self-worth, physical appearance, social, academic, and athletic competence) than boys, which may drive their associations with antisocial peers."

Additional studies of girls in the justice system (Riehman, 2004) find that two-thirds of them are children of color, primarily Black and Latina. More important, studies (Riehman, 2004) find that female adolescent offenders have high levels of:

- Family dysfunction
- Trauma and sexual abuse
- Mental health and substance abuse problems
- High-risk sexual behaviors
- School problems
- Affiliation with deviant peers

After years of addressing criminal adjudication of adolescents in adult court, I can affirm that all of the social and biological science statistics, findings, and conclusions, converge with a vengeance on the young people who appear in a court that is not cognizant of their needs. They are misplaced children.

The criminal case of AB who appeared before me years ago is illustrative of the power of peers or others on an adolescent Black girl's decision making. That case informs my thinking even today. AB was a 16-year-old living in a single-parent household in a very poor and crime-ridden community with a mother who worked full-time to make a modest home and give her daughter things designed to make her happy, keep her safe, and keep her at home and in school. While mother worked, AB was of course easy prey to the fast-talking, handsome drug dealer who became both father figure and boyfriend. Add to this situation a dose of danger and excitement, protestations of love and devotion, and there was the predictable outcome of an adolescent well in over her head. She became the dealer's "helper" and was the person designated to hold the "stash" (small amount of cocaine) in a low level drug sale (two vials) operation. AB could not have been more vulnerable: an economically and emotionally poor, adolescent female, without a father and, because of work, also without a mother. It is not difficult to conclude that this 16-year-old may not have been equipped to make a thoughtful decision about her involvement with a drug dealer who she thought cared for her. During the course of her criminal matter in my court, I often questioned whether intervention in the Family Court would have been better for AB. Clearly, little societal benefit would be achieved by treating her as an adult. Was she an adult in this situation or really a vulnerable child saddled with mental, physical, and societal baggage? Her presence in my court was exceedingly troubling to me. The appropriate disposition for the adult (age 24) male co-defendant with a prior felony conviction was easy. But what would I do with AB?

A felony conviction for this child at age 16 would have made her ineligible for so much that a successful future would require. She would be shunned in the academic, economic, and employment world. She also would likely succumb to more criminal activity, as evidenced in studies comparing the recidivism rates of youth processed in the juvenile system with those handled in the adult system. Youth processed in the adult system are likely to re-offend more quickly and at higher rates. This is largely due to the focus of the adult system. In contrast, the juvenile justice system is typically characterized by higher staff-to-youth ratios, staff who are philosophically oriented toward treatment and rehabilitation, and programming that facilitates the development of social competencies. Youth in adult facilities, meanwhile, do not have access to such services and are particularly vulnerable to depression, sexual exploitation, and physical assault (Corriero, 2011–2012).

AB's case outcome could have left her in a challenged situation but for the intervention from a court and judge who would not be bound by "legal dialectics" but looked to justice for a child. Fortunately, after engaging social service and academic professionals, we were able to rescue AB from the bad and uninformed choices she made. She was placed on probation and entered a progressive high school from which she graduated. Importantly, her concerned mother was brought into the process as a partner and deserved credit for the success of the collaborative effort between mother, child, and judge. I attempted to replicate with success the juvenile family court model for AB. She was adjudicated a youthful offender (N Y Criminal Procedure Law, Article 720) and was relieved of the burden of a criminal conviction.

AB was one among many that appeared in my courtroom and who daily appear in great numbers in the adult courts throughout New York State. In the near future, New York will be forced to resolve this important question of what is the appropriate age for criminal responsibility in the 21st century. New York Chief Judge Jonathan Lippman has suggested a compromise approach which would create Adolescent Diversion Parts to be held within the current criminal courts. In those parts, cases involving youths aged 16 and 17 would be adjudicated in a manner similar to those prosecuted in the juvenile family courts. Youths who complete the program would be given the opportunity to have their cases dismissed and to receive much needed social services. The program has seen some initial successes (Rempel, Cadpret & Franklin, 2013). The Governor's Children's Cabinet Advisory Board, in response to its report, is calling for the establishment of a Governor's Task Force that, among other things, would undertake a study to examine the implications for courts, law enforcement, probation, corrections, and public safety for raising the age of criminal responsibility in New York.

Hopefully, the current steps, taken more than fifty years after the 1961 convention, will lead to a strong consensus for change. The uncontroverted adolescent brain science, in conjunction with the precedent of the United States Supreme Court and numerous studies and anecdotal reality, supports the need to raise the age of criminal responsibility and provide better outcomes and justice for adolescent teens. This critical issue impacting the lives and future of our children cannot be tabled again. We must act now.

REFERENCES

American Bar Association and National Bar Association, *Justice by Gender: The Lack of Appropriate Prevention, Diversion and Treatment Alternatives for Girls in the Justice System.* Available at http://stoneleighfoundation.org/content/justice-gender-lack-appropriate-prevention-diversion-treatment-alternatives-girls-justice-sy

Baird, A., Fugelsang, J., & Bennett, C. (2005). *What Were You Thinking? An fMRI Study of Adolescent Decision Making.* Available at http://faculty.vassar.edu/abbaird/PreviousSite/dev/archives/conferencePubs/CNS_05_ab.pdf

Corriero, M. (2011–2012). *Judging Children as Children: Reclaiming New York's Progressive Tradition,* 56 N. Y. L. Sch. L. Rev. 1413-30.

Governor's Children's Cabinet Advisory Board. (2011, January). *Advancing a Fair and Just Age of Criminal Responsibility for Youth in New York State.* Available at / documents/Advancing_a_Fair_and_Just_Age_of_Criminal_Responsibility_for_Youth_in_NYS.pdf

Justice Policy Institute. (2007). *The Consequences Aren't Minor: The Impact of Trying Youth as Adults and Strategies for Reform.* Available at www.justicepolicy.org/research/1965

MacArthur Foundation Research Network on Adolescent Development and Juvenile Justice. *Less Guilty by Reason of Adolescence,* Issue Brief 3. Available at http://www.adjj.org/downloads/6093issue_brief_3.pdf

People v Adrian P. Thomas, ____ NE3d ____, 2014 WL 641516 (NY), 2014 NY Slip Op 01208 (February 20, 2014). *People v. Walter,* 62 F.2d 798, 800 (2d Cir, 1933), Criminal Procedure Law, Article 720 Family Court Act Section 301.1

Rempel, M., Lambson, S., Cadpret, C., & Franklin, A. (2013). *The Adolescent Diversion Program: A First Year Evaluation of Alternatives to Conventional Case Processing for Defendants Ages 16 and 17 in New York.* Available at http://www.courtinnovation.org/research/adolescent-diversion-program-first-year-evaluation-alternatives-conventional-case-processing

Riehman, K. *Adolescent Girls in the Juvenile Justice System: Issues for Treatment,* presented at Women Across the Life Span: A National Conference on Women, Addiction and Recovery, July 13, 2004, Baltimore, MD. Available at http://womenandchildren.treatment.org

Schuyler Center for Analysis and Advocacy. (2010). *Raising the Age: Why 16- and 17-Year-Olds Don't Belong in New York State's Adult Criminal Justice System.* Available at www.scaany.org/documents/cpa_policybrief_raisingtheage_sept2010.pdf

Sobie, M. (2010). *Pity the Child: The Age of Delinquency in New York,* 30 Pace L. Rev. 1061.

Chapter 26

Aggression and Violence in Teen Girls

Chiquita D. Howard-Bostic

The primary goal of this chapter is to use a "life-course-persistent" developmental process to identify pathways of early and ongoing risk factors to consider their role in explaining later criminal and violent behavior (Schaeffer et al., 2006). The trajectory shows divergent pathways of aggression among African American girls through elementary school years leading into their teenaged years. Some studies predict a high risk that early onset aggression performed exclusively or routinely by African American females will augment over their lifetimes (Xie, Cairns & Cairns, 2002). Also proposed is that some behaviors are not as prevalent or disappear completely as the individual reaches adulthood and learns alternatives to physical aggression (Tremblay, 2003). These findings also explore what sociologists know about sociocultural and structural influences that inhibit Black girls' physical, verbal, and relational aggression. Finally, intervention options are introduced in support of future research on this subject matter.

AGGRESSION TYPES

Three distinct types of aggression are reported in studies on African American female-perpetrated violence and victimization: relational, verbal, and physical aggressions. Current research also confirms frequent use of both overt and subtle forms of aggression among African American girls (Xie, Farmer & Cairns, 2003). Current research reports that Black girls are more physically and relationally aggressive than White girls (Crick, Ostrov & Werner, 2006). But in general, studies show that African American girls exhibit similar rates of relational aggression and less physical aggression than boys of all ethnicities. Relational aggression, a more subtle aggression type, is less open and more manipulative than are verbal and physical aggression types. Social and direct relational aggression types are forms of socially manipulative aggression that can injure victims psychologically (Xie et al., 2003). Direct relational aggression consists of episodes in which aggressors seek to damage the self-esteem or social standing of their peers. Studies are more likely to survey Black female teens' use of relational aggression to complement reported patterns showing that African American elementary students are more likely than Caucasian children to use overt and relational aggression (Xie et al., 2002).

Social relational aggression is non-confrontational social interaction. Social relational aggression is also especially common among more assertive girls and is branded in studies by its role in the process of maintaining prominent status in peer groups (Rose, Lockerd & Swenson, 2002). However, when interrelated delinquent acts are considered, gendered findings may differ. For example, Farrell, Kung, White, and Valois (2000) report that girls are no more relationally aggressive than are boys who use illicit drugs. Social forms of relational aggression include argumentative assertiveness, overt androgyny, and use of defensive tones. Other examples include social exclusion, such as excluding people from a group, and social isolation, which involves deliberately ignoring others. Alongside the aforementioned types, African American girls are also reported to use social alienation as a form of relational aggression such as telling others they are not welcome (Xie et al., 2002).

Similarly, verbal aggression occurs when an individual uses a hostile tone and/or hurtful words. Most research on bullying behavior compares aggression of girls to that of boys with a focus on taunting or teasing that accelerates physical or psychological harm of others. Findings that reflect Black girls' use of verbal aggression include acts such as gossiping, writing notes about individuals, insulting others, talking about someone behind their back, the betrayal of trust, humiliating others, giving verbal threats, name calling, yelling, and arguing (Xie et al., 2003).

Physically aggressive behavior typically includes hitting, pushing, kicking, fighting, jumping someone, throwing a chair at someone, or using a weapon. Physical aggression is generally expressed actively or passively, but also entails intent to cause harm, increase relative social dominance, or intimidate others. Miller-Johnson, Moore, Underwood, and Coie (2005) offer data on patterns of female-perpetrated assault, which illustrate African American girls' performance of physical aggression. They report that female-perpetrated assault rates are slightly higher for African Americans than those of other ethnicities, but almost half of the female population in detention is Black (p. 76). Differential treatment among female populations who perpetrate physical aggression is a current research initiative that should not be overlooked since African American girls are overrepresented in the juvenile justice system.

SOCIAL MOTIVATIONS FOR AGGRESSIVE CONDUCT

Universal depictions of gender often fail to consider applicable racial, feminine, and gendered contexts of Black girls' socially aggressive conduct. In several childhood aggression studies, gender is conceptualized as "white adolescent female" and ethnic-minorities are generalized as African American males. It appears that African American girls' aggression is best characterized in more complex analyses that associate intersectional dimensions of social relationships (McCall, 2005). Social motivations for Black girls' aggression include gendered socialization processes, constructions of historical identity, and empowerment tactics.

Social Motivation 1: Gendered Socialization Processes

Blake, Lease, Olejnik, and Turner (2010) contradict claims that girls in general are socialized to avoid conflict. Their sentiment is mirrored in multiple studies arguing that unlike Caucasian girls, African American girls are taught aggression as a way to build self-esteem and self-confidence (Damon & Lerner, 2008). This finding also patterns ongoing claims that early on socialization processes prompt Black women to have higher self-esteem and fewer mental health issues than other women (Holsinger & Holsinger, 2005, p. 236). These aggression studies embody how African American girls should act, respond, and negotiate conflict as children, teenagers, and later in their adult years. Studies claim that African American girls perform various types of aggression in ways that are distinct from girls in other race categories (Hamlett, 2011).

In Blake et al. (2010), the parents of fourth- and fifth-grade girls actually admit to encouraging their daughters to be aggressive by motivating them to be firm, liberated, and emotionally resilient. The authors note that early on, these African American parents are compelled to socialize their daughters to withstand harsh criticism, and contingent upon community conditions, these parents may also train their daughters to challenge adversity or to defend themselves (Blake et al., 2010, p. 396). Henceforth, as compared to other White working-class parents, African American parents are documented as being less disapproving of their daughters' aggressive behavior.

African American parents who encourage their daughters to behave aggressively may inadvertently inspire other inappropriate acts of aggression. It is also presumed that parents of African American children use less sex-specific socialization patterns, which encourages a loose, masculine interpretation of Black girls' aggression. Perhaps the relevant truth is that African American girls are encouraged or expected to behave as aggressively as boys and to use overt aggression. They are then positioned to defend themselves and to mask relatively hurt feelings later in life (Blake 2007, p. 78).

Social Motivation 2: Constructions of Historical Identity

Since slavery, a process of identity construction has produced a unique characterization of African American girls as social beings. Alice Walker's compilation of work *In Search of Our Mothers' Gardens: Womanist Prose* warns that depreciated Black feminine concepts stem from historical experiences of slavery, humiliation, and a lack of sensitivity toward African American females from childhood to adulthood (Walker, 1983). Equally stated in a poetic interpretation from Smith (1983), McCray writes: "black girls, mean and too-loud-laughing, can never walk with their heads down and never care that their brand of beauty is not popular" (p. 57). McCray's poem best symbolizes a Black feminist interpretation of African American girls' alleged angry voice and demeanor. "Loudness" is a metaphor that characterizes this type of Black aggression and femininity (Lei, 2003). Although McCray's depictions reject stereotypes of young African American girls as naturally and unconsciously aggressive young women, by some means, these depictions show that Black girls run the risk of taking on a traditional dichotomous definition of femininity. Similar to the ideas presented in McCray's poem, Fordham (1993) goes so far as to offer a much bolder reference of African American girls as the "good girl–bad girl, virgin-seductress, angel-whore, " which presents such an unfortunate representation of Black girls in a unique context that frames their victimization and violent performance (p. 4).

Furthermore, Mahiri and Conner (2003) urge that the media socially constructs Black girls' criminalization via the discourse of rap and hip-hop music. Through song, dance, and video, stigmatized images revisit ancient cultural stereotypes of Black identity and sexual proclivity (p. 123). African American girls are often stereotyped using aggressive and flamboyant definitions when they engage groups and relationships. Media, texts, and research characterize attitudes about Black female aggression using a *race- and class-prescribed definition of femininity*, which typecasts Black girls as loud, disruptive, aggressive, and therefore potentially threatening.

Social Motivation 3: Empowerment Tactics

African American females are reported to be aggressive as a form of resistance, as an act of liberation, and to assume responsibility for their own survival. An ethnographic study, "Fighting to Be Somebody: Resisting Erasure and the Discursive Practices of Female Adolescent Fighting," describes the experiences of five at-risk female middle school students, two of whom are African American (Adams, 1999). The author redefines Black girls' aggression as a symbol of power and self-empowerment. In Adams (1999), one teen claims, "she will fight someone if they're messing with her boyfriend" (demands respect) and the other teen says "she will fight if someone calls her a bad name" (defends her character) (p. 115). Other studies describe ways that teenaged African American females adopt "bad girl identities" by exaggerating toughness in order to seek independence and respect (Laidler & Hunt, 2001, p. 659).

RISK FACTORS AS PATHWAYS TO AGGRESSION

Considerable research reports instances where children and teenagers model aggressive conduct or become angry as a result of family conflict, condescending treatment by teachers, or being teased by peers (U.S. Department of Health & Human Services, 2001). Different pathways and risk factors such as individual, peer, home, and neighborhood characteristics are shown to influence aggressive behavior of teenaged African American females.

Pathway 1: Individual Characteristics

Individual characteristics such as poor problem-solving skills, focusing attention, temperament balance, and low intelligence are shown to increase risks for aggressive behavior among African American girls. These traits place the aggressive child at risk of misinterpreting behavior of others, which may lead to conflict and potential acts of violence (Pepler & Slaby, 1994, p. 39). Unlike most studies, research entitled "Aggression and Fighting Behavior among African American Adolescents: Individual and Family Factors" links African American girls' performance of relational aggression to weapon carrying, perceptions of their families' views toward violence, and their participation in fights at school. In this study, Cotten and colleagues (1994) survey Black female students using a continuum of relational aggressiveness that correlates the degree of African American girls' performance of relational aggression and influences on their attitudes about violence. Violent attitudes significantly correlate with girls' use of violent conduct and weapon carrying (for confidence and security): Fourteen percent of the female sample were suspended from school and 16% carried a weapon (p. 620). Cotten et al. (1994) find that aggression displayed in adolescent years by African American girls who report individual level characteristics is likely to accelerate as they grow older.

Pathway 2: Peer Relationships

Zimmerman and Messner (2010) propose that females who lack adult guidance and control, foster weaker emotional bonds between friends and family. Lack of supervision increases the likelihood of Black girls' exposure to and contact with violent peers. Moreover, African American girls who are violent tend to bond in groups that accompany and support their physically aggressive acts against others. Talbott, Celinska, Simpson, and Coe (2002) argue that group interaction among violent Black girls encourages relational, verbal, and physical aggression. Girls using these aggression types are less likely to bond with others and are more susceptible to victimization, which increases their likelihood of being bullied by peers.

African American females also experience high levels of victimization in forms of bullying, neglect, abuse, physical assault, and homicide. National research indicates that African American youth report being bullied more often than White American youth (Nansel et al., 2001). A study about the characteristics of child maltreatment victims provides evidence that "in 2010, slightly fewer than one-half (45%) of all child victims of maltreatment were White, 22% were African American, and 21% were Hispanic" (Office of Juvenile Justice and Delinquency Prevention, 2012). Even more severe, an analysis of national homicide data by *Violence Policy Center* in Washington, DC reports that, "in 2009, 928 (14%) of 6,505 Black homicide victims were female and 5,576 (86%) were male" (2012, p. 2). Correspondingly, large samples of African American girls report acting out aggressive conduct toward peers, family, and friends to retaliate against abuse and ill-treatment (DeHart, 2008).

Pathway 3: Home Environment

Research finds that a disproportionate number of single-mother families, increasing divorce rates, and an increase in non-marital childbirths have negatively impacted the health and wellness of African American girls (De Bell, 2008). Concurrent studies argue that adolescents who reside in homes where families provide limited social support or minimal involvement with youth are also shown to be at risk for aggressive behavior (Pepler et al., 1994). Hamlett (2011) confirms that father-figure status and psychosocial variables such as parenting style and relationships impact Black girls' aggression (p. 88). Hamlett provides evidence that fathers' residency influences aggression among girls who reside in single-parent households.

Parenting behaviors such as disciplining, involvement, engagement, emotional connection, and guidance are also strong predictors of children's emotional development and future involvement in criminally aggressive activities. McLoyd and Smith (2002) report that "African

American and poor parents rely on spanking their children as a form of punishment or discipline" (p. 45). Studies also compare parental disciplinary measures performed across different jurisdictions. For example, in Singer, Anglin, Song, and Lunghofer (1995), "compared with 5.5% of the girls living in small cities, 10.3% of urban girls reported being 'beaten' by their parents." Since the 1990s, it has become popular for studies to examine aggression among lower-income African American girls whose parents carry out harsh or inconsistent physical discipline (Hamlett, 2011).

Regardless of a parent's justification for spanking their child, experts suggest that physical discipline entails long-term risks and potentially deleterious side effects. Judith Graham, a human development specialist, says, "spanking teaches a child that they are a victim who deserves discomfort and suffering" (Graham, 2001, p. 1). In turn, the punishment incites uncontrolled fits of violent anger, suppressed self-worth, and challenges forming lasting relationships. Spanking may also instigate types of relational aggression such as testing boundaries, pushing limits of reasonable control, and engaging in power struggles with others. Professionals recommend that "parents develop disciplinary strategies other than spanking for managing undesired behavior" (American Academy of Pediatrics, 1998, p. 723).

Lansford and colleagues (2004) tracked patterns of parental discipline used for 585 children (ages 5 to 16) from elementary to high school. They found that African American parents are more likely to use physical punishment to address hostile conduct. Interestingly, parents in the study reported using harsh and strict discipline when they worry that the youth will have an at-risk future. Lansford et al. recognize the parents' reported intent to discipline or punish their children rather than to promote negative behavior. Given their findings, it is probable that some parents consider spankings as a more effective, direct, and immediate form of discipline. Related nonviolent disciplinary options include linking bad behavior and the relative consequences, offering rewards to motivate good behavior, and encouraging youth to build healthy relationships. In contrast, spanking advocates argue that spanking is "a sign of nonpermissiveness, anticipatory socialization, God's will, a morally neutral childrearing tool, and a psychic release" (Davis, 2003, p. 7). Depending upon the context, findings on traditional defenses of spanking indicate that spanking may alter the course of the violent child's aggression (Davis, 2003).

Pathway 4: Neighborhood Factors

In social environments characterized by social disorganization, society anomie, and high levels of poverty and unemployment, there are considerable exposure to violence and a high probability of personal victimization. Although the impact of societal factors is quite unpredictable for assessing the outcomes for all African American girls, "disadvantaged neighborhood dynamics are known to increase the likelihood that children will misbehave as a result of exposure" (Hann & Borek, 2002, p. 100). In a dissertation on self-regulation of aggression among African American adolescent girls, Hamlett (2011) finds that girls from urban, low-income communities are disproportionately at risk due to factors such as low socioeconomic status (SES), neighborhood violence, and an overrepresentation of peers in the juvenile justice system.

In communities characterized by high levels of neighborhood crime, chaos, and social disorganization, disruptive behaviors may be more normative or expected (Schaeffer et al., 2006). Hence, persistent use of confrontation-inflicted physical aggression may also reflect living in a low-income urban setting in which certain levels of violence are to a certain extent acceptable (Lockwood, 1997). It is important to note that some studies caution against using a "deficit model" (emphasizing problem behavior as a causal factor), over-pathologizing, or stereotyping minorities as victims of slavery (Holsinger et al., 2005, p. 212).

African American girls who fight often suffer "triple jeopardy," an interacting hierarchy of class, gender, and race discrimination and victimization (Russell-Brown, 2004). The burden of each status builds from numerous social biases that put Black girls at risk of a poor quality of life. African American girls are deviant adolescents who fight to meet an alleged code of the streets in their communities. Simultaneously, these girls are typecast as unnaturally strong, abnormal girls who implement inappropriate feminine behavior. Ultimately, Black girls are also plagued by a gender neutral interpretation of aggression that feminizes Black masculinity.

"Girls can and do fight with far more than words and tears when necessary," says Jones (2008, p. 63). Using fists to fight can prove publicly that young Black girls are not scared. The element of toughness that stems from fighting lessens a need to "look over one's own shoulder," which serves as code for accountability, strength, and a fearless presentation of self. Consistent with findings about "boys in the hood" in Anderson (1999), Jones (2008) offers a girl's literary account of the book *Code of the Streets*. Jones conducts field research such as interviews, home visits, and observations with teenaged African American girls in the inner-city of Philadelphia. In this study, the participants frame fighting as a "tough front" used to deter potentially aggressive future challenges. They report sharing the lived experiences of their male peers in the streets of Philadelphia. For example, African American girls recall being "rolled on, jumped, or having a friend who has been shot, robbed, or stabbed" (p. 69). However, Jones does not associate the use of guns with urban adolescent girls' illustration of their power or lack thereof. In tandem, Lockwood (1997) reports that physical aggression via street fighting is typically a result of engaging in direct confrontation with others as opposed to using subtle forms of relational aggression. Fighting in school is another way that anger is unleashed on others in a community setting (Lines, 2006).

ANGER AS PHYSICAL VIOLENCE

Winn (2013) suggests that in late adolescence or early adulthood, many African American females learn that physically aggressive behaviors have high stakes and are too risky as a means for resolving conflict. As a result, no strong relationship exists between Black girls' onset episodes of violent, verbal, or relational aggression and any alleged *future* performance of deviance. Studies on dating violence and suicidal behavior demonstrate the extent to which aggression presents predicted short-term risks for African American girls' involvement in physically violent and delinquent behavior.

Physical Aggression 1: Dating Violence

Dating abuse is common in relationships of African American male and female college students. Nearly one-third of Black college students sustain or inflict physical aggression in a dating relationship (Clark, Beckett, Wells & Dungee-Anderson, 1994). Correspondingly, among subjects in West and Rose (2000), more than 90% of both African American male and female college students report experiences of verbal aggression as an aggressor or victim throughout their dating relationships (p. 472). As adults, aggressive girls are more at risk of becoming perpetrators and victims of domestic violence (Smith & Thomas, 2000).

Relational and physical aggressions are commonly performed among Black female college student populations. First, it is common for dating partners of African American females to make them feel inferior or to degrade them (Clark et al., 1994). Relational aggression has been performed in response to disrespect. By the same token, no matter the race, class, or ethnic orientation of the couple, an unhealthy dating relationship that entails limited respect is more likely to involve psychological or physical violence than is a relationship where verbal aggression is not present. Secondly, Black females are said to be aggressive in response to a full range of violence in relationships and are significantly more likely than White females to threaten, slap, hit, or throw objects at their partners. In line with research on stereotypes about Black girls' attitudes (the bad girl analogy), potential justifications for Black girls' "acting out" and experiencing dating violence include: lacking conflict resolution skills, responding aggressively to victimization, and seeking dominance in the relationship after adopting a relatively androgynous role as both a wage earner and a caretaker (Lines, 2006).

West et al. (2000) investigate the prevalence of aggression experienced by young African American college students from low-income families. The treatment of Black girls by their partners explains how and why they sustain or inflict aggression during dating relationships. Although Black girls hit as often as their partners, very few studies explore motivations for female-perpetrated intimate partner violence (Howard-Bostic, 2011). West et al. posit that Black women are punished by African American males in dating relationships because they have greater access to economic resources than do their partners. African American girls who believe "black women have more opportunities than black men" are likely to experience more types of psychological abuse in their dating relationships than Black females who do not subscribe to this belief (p. 484).

Abused African American girls are more or less portrayed by academics as aggressive victims who are trapped in cycles of abuse. The historically marginalized status of African American girls also makes them at risk for violence, with an increased number of risks escalating the probability for victimization. African American girls are often framed in studies as victims who fight in self-defense or who perform aggression because they are not taught alternative responses. Black teens' ability to sustain or use less aggression also influences their experiences of dating violence. Black females may take the blame for their partner's lesser position, or deny their own economic stress or hardship in order to reduce conflict in the relationship (West et al., 2000, p. 475). For that reason, Black teens are said to be more tolerant of abuse and more willing to retaliate with physical violence. Consequently, use of aggression signifies their oppression and invisibility.

Physical Aggression 2: Sexual Violence

Few studies examine sociodemographic variables and the sexual health of African American teenaged girls. However, Silverman, Raj, Mucci, and Hathaway (2001) report that Black female high school students appear to be more likely than individuals from other groups to report sexual violence in absence of a dating relationship. Reported victimization types include being shoved, slapped, hit, or forced into any sexual activity. Common responses of African American girls in the study include "Yes, I was hurt physically and sexually" and "I was not hurt on a date" (p. 574). The study also notes that lower-income Black girls are vulnerable to their boyfriends, but they should also be wary of men on the streets. Silverman et al. warn with great caution that African American girls are at a greater risk than others of being sexually abused by males whom they are not dating. Furthermore, young Black girls living in disadvantaged neighborhoods may lack access to support and resources to deal with trauma. Hence, their victimization is magnified because lower-income residents are also less likely to receive protection from law officials following instances of abuse (Schaffner, 2007).

Silverman et al. (2001) also correlate sexual dating violence with all assessed forms of substance use (alcohol, tobacco, and cocaine), unhealthy weight control, and suicidality. Jones (2008) connects "staying pretty" to aggressive attitudes that influence an African American girl's role in potential acts of violence. Jones says "a young Black girl's ability to have a light-brown skinned complexion, 'straight' or 'good' hair, and a slim figure is directly influenced by Black girls' involvement in interpersonal aggression or violence" (p. 75). Hence, these young ladies may be prone to fight in order to protect a certain "look"; they may also be hit as a response to their bodily images.

Wingood and colleagues (2001) conducted a unique study of Black adolescent females who reported having a physically abusive boyfriend. The study, "Dating violence and the sexual health of Black adolescent females," includes a sample of 522 Black females ages 14 to 18, 18.4% who reveal a history of physical dating violence. The study positively associates girls' history of violence with their sexual health outcomes and sexual behavior. The authors acknowledge that African American female adolescents have a higher prevalence of dating violence and higher rates of unintended pregnancy and sexually transmitted diseases (Wingood et al., 2001). They also remind the reader that sexually violent experiences influence negligent choices such as "dreading the consequences of negotiating condom use, accepting lesser control over sexuality, and having anxiety about pregnancy prevention options" (p. 4). The findings in Wingood et al. confirm that prevalence of sexual victimization among African American female teens is associated with increased performance of physical and relational aggression.

Physical Aggression 3: Self-harm

The scope of self-injurious violence explored in research on African American girls' suicide is limited to occurrences of chronic self-cutting, suicide attempts, and successful suicide. Self-cutting includes penetration of jewelry into eyebrows, lips, tongues, nares, nipples, or genitals. Suicide attempts are less common among African American girls than among other youth. However, Borowsky, Ireland, and Resnick (2001) report record increases in suicide rates among African American and other minority groups. Suicide rates for African American children ages 10 to 14 years old increased 126% from 1980 to 1995 (p. 485). Future research is needed to develop culturally responsive prevention and intervention strategies.

Studies relate suicidal tendencies to issues of interpersonal safety, anger, and emotional needs. Holsinger and Holsinger (2005) warn that African American youth tend to mask symptoms of suicidal behavior by acting out in high-risk ways (e.g., substance use or abuse and becoming pregnant). Thus, parents, mentors, and health advocates should be mindful of circumstances such as having a friend commit suicide, illicit drug use, and history of mental health treatment that predict suicide attempts of Black youth (Holsinger and Holsinger, 2005, p. 486). Reported risk factors for self-harm (childhood abuse, violence perpetration, and weapon carrying) relate more closely to physical abuse and violence (Borowsky et al., 2001). A previous suicide attempt, violence victimization, violence perpetration, alcohol use, marijuana use, school problems, and ease of access to guns at home are also significantly associated with Black girls' suicide.

Silverman et al. (2001) report that "recent suicide ideation and actual suicide attempts are approximately 6 to 9 times as common among female teens who report being sexually and physically hurt by dating partners" (p. 578). Silverman et al. mention that the pain and humiliation of teens that experience dating violence may predispose them to suicidal thoughts and behavior. There is a need for additional research that specifically considers African American teen girls' experiences of suicidality.

AGGRESSION AND DELINQUENT ACTS

In recent public discourse and media, African American girls are increasingly represented as "dangerous others" (Mahiri et al., 2003). Whether it is an issue of violence, crime, or sex, these African American girls are burdened with escaping high expectations for violence and brutal images projected of them as whores. Relationships vary between Black female teens' aggression and forms of delinquency such as high school dropout, sex/pregnancy, drug/alcohol use, and detention/arrests.

Delinquent Act 1: High School Dropout

Although dropout rates differ dramatically by state, the dropout rates for African American girls are troubling. The National Women's Law Center reports that approximately 40% of the Black female population of the class of 2003–2004 dropped out of school (2007, p. 6). High rates of high school dropout are associated with an array of individual (low achievement), social (antisocial peers), family (low educational aspirations), and cultural, socioeconomic, and institutional factors. These dynamics enhance the likelihood of students' loss of interest or detachment from the learning/socialization process (Kokko et al., 2006).

Kokko et al. (2006) find that developmental trajectories of physical aggression predict both school dropout and physical violence. Ultimately, high aggression levels and problem behaviors at school impact cognitive capacities and chances of completing school. They also project an increased risk of school dropout among the highly aggressive compared with the moderately aggressive (p. 415). In contrast, relational (prosocial) or aggressive attitudes and relative conduct aggression do not have additive or protective long-term effects on occurrences of high school dropout. No preexisting research (longitudinal studies on life course and dropout rates) specifically demonstrates how African American girls' use of aggression directly correlates with their failure to complete high school. Thus, the issue requires further research.

Delinquent Act 2: Sex/Pregnancy

It is well documented that aggression places girls at concurrent risk for early sexual activity, teen pregnancy, and early childbearing (Hamlett, 2011). A growing body of literature suggests that limited opportunities and social disorganization increase the likelihood that African American girls will engage in sex at an early age and become pregnant. Current research also links teen decisions not to use contraception to feelings of hopelessness and a perceived lack of personal opportunities in the future (Kogan et al., 2013).

Waddell, Orr, Sackoff, and Santelli (2010) report that teen pregnancy rates among NYC residents are more than four times higher among Black females (122/1,000) (p. 427). African American female students are also most likely to be currently sexually active (35.4%), followed by Hispanics (32.7%), and White females (23.4%) (p. 430). Furthermore, Black girls are said to engage in risky sexual behaviors that later develop into violent intimate relationships (Moffit, Caspi, Rutter & Silva, 2001). It is not unlikely for African American girls to replicate this cycle of abuse as future mothers.

Delinquent Act 3: Drug/Alcohol Use

Drug use, relational aggression, and delinquency during adolescence are a considerable focus of research. Findings showing a direct association between African American girls' aggressive misconduct and drug and alcohol use are inconsistent. Farrell et al. (2000) consider Black girls' attitudinal changes that result from drug use and predict a strong correlation between Black girls' use of relational aggression and drug use. Wells et al. (1992) add that antisocial behavior and attitudes are stronger predictors for initiation of drug use for Asian children than for Black and White adolescents. Nevertheless, studies confirm lesser drug use problems among African American girls and increased criminality as compared to other youth, but arrest rates for drug offenses are more prevalent among Black female teens (Snyder, 2002).

Both welfare recipiency and lower socioeconomic status are closely examined in research on drug and alcohol using behavior. Epstein, Botvin,

Baker, and Diaz (1999) find that adolescents with two parents residing in highly urbanized New York City have significantly lower levels of delinquency and illicit drug use than do adolescents with single parents. Such research raises specific concern about the potential mental health and quality of life outcomes for African American girls residing in single-parent households.

Unlike studies on drug use, representation of inner-city minority youth remains very small in national surveys of alcohol use. Among studies that consider racial/ethnic minorities, drinking status of friends, parental use, and perceived attitudes of others are strongly associated with alcohol use (Epstein et al., 1999). There is no significant relationship presented regarding aggression and alcohol use such as binge drinking, alcohol misuse, or alcohol consequences (Walton et al., 2010).

Delinquent Act 4: Detention/Arrests

Chesney-Lind (2010) speculates that Black girls are targets for relational aggression, which is oftentimes falsely confused and replaced with assumptions about their role in more serious types of violence. Chesney-Lind does not ignore bullying programs that protect victims from "mean girls." Nevertheless, female aggression has generated a public debate regarding the corresponding changes in administrative discretion with regards to arrests of African American girls. More young African American girls are brought into detention, typically being framed as aggressive liars, manipulators (overemotional and needy), or "bad girls" (Gaarder, Rodriguez & Zatz, 2004). However, it is estimated that over 90% of girls in the juvenile justice system report prior experiences of child victimization (Schaffner, 2007, p. 8). In tandem, the reported reputational findings about young female delinquents rarely consider links between juvenile offending and violence against girls such as sexual, physical, and emotional abuse.

Whether the roots of female violence are systematic, gendered, or individually based, African American girls' overall involvement in crime has continued to increase. Between 2003 and 2007, female/youth-perpetrated homicide increased by 51.3%, and girls' performance of larceny-theft increased by 13.9% as compared to a 3.5% increase for boys (Gage, Josephs & Lunde, 2012, p. 604). Relative studies confirm that race and ethnicity are salient predictors for female delinquency and representation in the juvenile justice system (Tracy, Kemf-Leonard & Abramoske-James, 2009). In 2004, data showed that 31% of African American girls were arrested. At that time, 17% of all juveniles were African American females. Also, rates of injuring another individual badly (requiring bandages or medical care) increased significantly among the population of African American females (Gage et al., 2012, p. 605). Ultimately, more recent criminally delinquent behavior among these girls has been characterized as "merciful victimization, brave and liberated aggression, conduct void of decent morals, out of control performance, and cold hearted killing" (Schaffner, 2007).

CONCLUSION: INTERVENTIONS

African American girls who are violently aggressive face increased risk of behavioral, social, and emotional problems. *Four* intervention efforts (building relational skills, acknowledging distress, encouraging counseling, and challenging differential treatment) can include, but not be limited to outreach, education, early intervention services, specialized youth services, public education, and media campaigns. However, success of each intervention depends on whether the processes centralize each African American girl's safety, enhances their accountability, improves their ability to build a positive peer network, and works to change the climate in the community.

First, to **build relational skills** and target use of relational aggression, *mentorship programs* can be designed and implemented to: (1) enhance relational skills and Black girls' propensity to resolve interpersonal conflict (DuRant et al., 1994); (2) reinforce positive and nonviolent attitudes of girls and boys of all race and ethnic groups (Adams, 1999); (3) teach them to listen, understand, and bond with others; (4) minimize defensiveness and encourage cooperation and reception to the ideas of others; (5) devise creative solutions that genuinely address mutual concerns; and (6) regulate emotions and manage difficult situations, which can ultimately preserve the emotional safety.

Secondly, to **acknowledge distress** and better explore violence against Black girls, stakeholders should consider a *gender-specific intervention program* that acknowledges signs of distress and is designed and implemented to: (1) target types of distress that are commonly triggered by emotional and behavioral problems; (2) show concern via support and encouragement during or following stressful situations; (3) acknowledge behavioral changes to draw attention to potential source(s) of their problems; and (4) offer necessary recommendations for professional counseling to help African American females cope with challenging situations. As a third intervention, parents, teachers, and mentors should **encourage counseling** because *treatment*: (1) safely manages, prevents, or slows the rate of negative outcomes; (2) is a form of support; (3) points out adverse consequences that aggression presents for Black girls and others; and (4) helps girls hear similar stories that focus on positive ways to address challenges.

To conclude, practitioners, authorities, researchers, and policymakers should **challenge differential treatment** of African American females by: (1) acknowledging that studies over-exaggerate Black girls' involvement in sexual promiscuity, drug and alcohol use, and violent crime; (2)

avoiding use of discriminatory stereotypes that cause a large number of innocent African American girls to be subjected to disrespect and humiliating assumptions about being "bad girls"; (3) reporting data showing the disproportionality of court involvement among African American females; (4) reexamining measurement bias and using better documented reasons for suspension and punishment in schools (Gage et al., 2012, p. 619); and (5) better addressing racial and sexual justice.

REFERENCES

Adams, N. G. (1999). Fighting to be somebody: Resisting erasure and the discursive practices of female adolescent fighting. *Educational Studies, 30*(2), 115–139.

American Academy of Pediatrics Committee on Psychosocial Aspects of Child and Family Health. (1998). Guidance for effective discipline. *Pediatrics, 101*, 723–728.

Anderson, E. (1999). *Code of the street: Decency, violence and the moral life of the inner city.* New York: W.W. Norton.

Blake, J. J. (2007). Gender-normative and non-normative aggression in preadolescent girls. (Doctoral dissertation). Retrieved from University of Georgia Theses and Dissertations. http://hdl.handle.net/10724/10022

Blake, J. J., A. Lease, S. P. Olejnik, and T. L. Turner. (2010). Ethnic differences in parents' attitudes toward girls' use of aggression. *Journal of Aggression, Maltreatment and Trauma, 19*(4), 393–413.

Borowsky, I. W., M. Ireland, and M. D. Resnick. (2001). Adolescent suicide attempts: risks and protectors. *Pediatrics, 107*(3), 485–493.

Chesney-Lind, M. (ed.). (2010). *SUNY Series in women, crime, and criminology: Fighting for girls: New perspectives on gender and violence.* Albany, NY: SUNY Press.

Clark, M. L., J. Beckett, M. Wells, and D. Dungee-Anderson. (1994). Courtship violence among African American college students. *Journal of Black Psychology, 20*(3), 264–281.

Cotten, N. U., J. Resnick, D. C. Browne, S. L. Martin, D. R. McCarraher, and J. Woods. (1994). Aggression and fighting behavior among African-American adolescents: Individual and family factors. *American Journal of Public Health, 84*(4), 618–622.

Crick, N. R., J. M., Ostrov, and N. E. Werner. (2006). A longitudinal study of relational aggression, physical aggression, and children's social-psychological adjustment. *Journal of Abnormal Child Psychology, 34*(2), 131–142.

Damon, W., and R. M. Lerner. (2008). *Child and adolescent development: An advanced course.* Hoboken, NJ: Wiley.

Davis, P. W. (2003). The changing meanings of spanking. In *Social problems: constructionist readings,* ed. D. R. Loseke and J. Best, 6–12. New Brunswick, NJ: Transaction.

De Bell, M. (2008). Children living without their fathers: Population estimates and indicators of educational well-being. *Social Indicators Research, 87*, 427–443.

DeHart, D. D. (2008). "Pathways to Prison: Impact of Victimization in the Lives of Incarcerated Women." *Violence Against Women, 14*(12), 1362–1381.

DuRant, R. H., C. Cadenhead, R. A. Pendergrast, G. Slavens, and C. W. Linder. (1994). Factors associated with the use of violence among urban Black adolescents. *American Journal of Public Health*, 84(4), 612–617.

Epstein, J. A., G. J. Botvin, E. Baker, and T. Diaz. (1999). Impact of social influences and problem behavior on alcohol use among inner-city Hispanic and Black adolescents. *Journal of Studies on Alcohol and Drugs*, 60(5), 595.

Farrell, A. D., E. M. Kung, K. S. White, and R. F. Valois. (2000). The structure of self-reported aggression, drug use, and delinquent behaviors during early adolescence. *Journal of Clinical Child Psychology*, 29(2), 282–292.

Fordham, S. (1993). Those loud Black girls: (Black) Women, silence, and gender "passing" in the academic. *Anthropology and Education Quarterly*, 24(1), 3–32.

Gaarder, E., N. Rodriguez, and M. Zatz. (2004). Criers, liars, and manipulators: Probation officers' views of girls. *Justice Quarterly*, 21(3), 547–578.

Gage, N. A., N. L. Josephs, and K. Lunde. (2012). Girls with emotional disturbance and a history of arrest: Characteristics and school-based predictors of arrest. *Education and Treatment of Children*, 35(4), 603–622.

Graham, J. (2001). Spanking. *Cooperative Extension Publications*, University of Maine. http://umaine.edu/publications/4357e/

Hamlett, N. M. (2011). An examination of predictors of relational and physical aggression among African American early adolescent girls: The role of father involvement, temperament, and self-regulation. *Dissertation Abstracts International*, 72, 1–161.

Hann, D. A., and N. Borek. (2002). *Taking stock of risk factors for child/youth externalizing behavior problems*. Bethesda, Maryland: National Institute of Mental Health.

Holsinger, K., and A. M. Holsinger. (2005). Differential pathways to violence and self-injurious behavior: African American and White girls in the juvenile justice system. *Journal of Research in Crime and Delinquency*, 42(2), 211–242.

Howard-Bostic, C. D. (2011). *A Qualitative Analysis of Intimate Partner Violence* (Doctoral dissertation, Virginia Polytechnic Institute and State University).

Jones, N. (2008). Working "the code": On girls, gender, and inner-city violence. *Australian and New Zealand Journal of Criminology*, 41(1), 63–83.

Kogan, S. M., J. Cho, K. Allen, M. K. Lei, S. R. Beach, F. X. Gibbons, and G. H. Brody. (2013). Avoiding adolescent pregnancy: A longitudinal analysis of African-American youth. *Journal of Adolescent Health*, 53, 14–20.

Kokko, K., R. E. Tremblay, E. Lacourse, D. S. Nagin, and F. Vitaro. (2006). Trajectories of prosocial behavior and physical aggression in middle childhood: Links to adolescent school dropout and physical violence. *Journal of Research on Adolescence*, 16(3), 403–428.

Laidler, K. J., and G. Hunt. (2001). Accomplishing femininity among the girls in the gang. *British Journal of Criminology*, 41(4), 656–678.

Lansford, J. E., K. Deater-Deckard, K. A. Dodge, J. E. Bates, and G. S. Pettit. (2004). Ethnic differences in the link between physical discipline and later adolescent externalizing behaviors. *Journal of Child Psychology and Psychiatry*, 45(4), 801–812.

Lei, J. L. (2003). Necessary toughness?: Those "loud black girls" and those "quiet Asian boys." *Anthropology and Education Quarterly*, 34(2), 158–181.

Lines, D. (2006). Aggressive youth. *Therapy Today, 17*(7), 13–6.

Lockwood, D. (1997). *Violence among middle school and high school students: Analysis and implications for prevention.* Washington, DC: National Institute of Justice Research in Brief, Department of Justice.

Mahiri, J., and E. Conner. (2003). Black youth violence has a bad rap. *Journal of Social Issues, 59*(1), 121–140.

McCall, L. (2005). The complexity of intersectionality. *Signs, 30*(3), 1771–1800.

McLoyd, V. C., and J. Smith. (2002). Physical discipline and behavior problems in African American, European American, and Hispanic children: Emotional support as a moderator. *Journal of Marriage and Family, 64*(1), 40–53.

Miller-Johnson, S. M., B. L. Moore, M. K. Underwood, and J. D. Coie. (2005). The development and treatment of girlhood aggression. In *The Development and Treatment of Girlhood Aggression*, ed. D. J. Pepler, K. C. Madsen, C. Webster, and K. S. Levene, 75–95. Mahwah, NJ: Lawrence Erlbaum Associates Publishers.

Nansel, T. R., M. Overpeck, R. S. Pilla, W. J. Ruan, B. Simons-Morton, and P. Scheidt. (2001). Bullying behaviors among U.S. youth: Prevalence and association with psychosocial adjustment. *Journal of the American Medical Association, 285*, 2094–2100.

National Women's Law Center. (2007). When girls don't graduate we all fall: A call to improve high school graduation rates for girls. Retrieved November 30, 2013. http://www.nwlc.org/sites/default/files/pdfs/when_girls_dont_graduate.pdf

Office of Juvenile Justice and Delinquency Prevention. (2012). *OJJDP Statistical Briefing Book* (Washington, DC: U.S. Department of Justice), "Characteristics of child maltreatment victims, 2010." Retrieved November 29, 2013. http://www.ojjdp.gov/ojstatbb/victims/qa02102.asp?qaDate=2010&text=

Pepler, D. J., and R. B. Slaby. (1994). Theoretical and developmental perspectives on youth and violence. In *Reason to hope: A psychosocial perspective on violence and youth*, ed. L. D. Eron, J. H. Gentry, P. Schlegel, 27–58. Washington, DC: American Psychological Association.

Rose, A. J., E. Lockerd, and L. Swenson. (2002). Disliked and "popular" relationally aggressive youth: Differences in adjustment and manifestations of relational aggression. Paper presented at the *Biennial Meeting of the Society for Research on Adolescence*, April 11–14, New Orleans, LA.

Russell-Brown, K. (2004). *Underground codes.* New York: New York University Press.

Schaeffer, C. M., Petras, H., Ialongo, N., Masyn, K. E., Hubbard, S., Poduska, J. and S. Kellam. (2006). A comparison of girls' and boys' aggressive-disruptive behavior trajectories across elementary school: Prediction to young adult antisocial outcomes. *Journal of Consulting and Clinical Psychology, 74*(3), 500–510.

Schaffner, L. (2007). Violence against girls provokes girls' violence: From private injury to public harm. *Violence Against Women, 13*, 1229–1248.

Silverman, J. G., A. Raj, L. A. Mucci, and J. E. Hathaway. (2001). Dating violence against adolescent girls and associated substance use, unhealthy weight control, sexual risk behavior, pregnancy, and suicidality. *JAMA: The Journal of the American Medical Association, 286*(5), 572–579.

Singer, M., T. Anglin, L. Song, and L. Lunghofer. (1995). Adolescents' exposure to violence associated symptoms of psychological trauma. *Journal of the American Medical Association, 273,* 477–482.

Smith, B. (ed.). (1983). *Home girls: A Black feminist anthology.* New Brunswick, NJ: Rutgers University Press.

Smith, H., and S. P. Thomas. (2000). Violent and nonviolent girls: Contrasting perceptions of anger experiences, school, and relationships. *Issues in Mental Health in Nursing, 21,* 547–575.

Snyder, H. (2002). *Juvenile arrest trends by race 1980–1999.* Rockville, MD: National Center for Juvenile Justice.

Talbott, E., D. Celinska, J. Simpson, and M. G. Coe. (2002). Somebody else making somebody else fight: Aggression and the social context among urban adolescent girls. *Exceptionality, 10*(3), 203–220.

Tracy, P. E., K. Kemf-Leonard, and S. Abramoske-James. (2009). Gender differences in delinquency and juvenile justice processing. *Crime and Delinquency, 55,* 171–215.

Tremblay, R. E. (2003). Why socialization fails: The case of chronic physical aggression. Pp. 182–224 in B. B. Lahey, T. E. Moffitt, and A. Caspi (eds.), *Causes of conduct disorder and juvenile delinquency.* New York: Guilford Press.

U.S. Department of Health and Human Services. (2001). Youth violence: A report of the surgeon general. Washington, DC: U.S. Department of Health and Human Services, 12.

Violence Policy Center. (2012). Black homicide victimization in the United States: An analysis of 2009 homicide data. Washington, DC. Retrieved November 29, 2013. http://www.vpc.org/studies/blackhomicide12.pdf

Waddell, E. N., M. G. Orr, J. Sackoff, and J. S. Santelli. (2010). Pregnancy risk among Black, White, and Hispanic teen girls in New York City public schools. *Journal of Urban Health, 87*(3), 426–439.

Walker, A. (1983). *In search of our mothers' gardens: Womanist Pros.* Houghton Mifflin Harcourt: Orlando, FL.

Walton, M. A., S. T. Chermack, J. T. Shope, C. R. Bingham, M. A. Zimmerman, F. C. Blow, and R. M. Cunningham. (2010). Effects of a brief intervention for reducing violence and alcohol misuse among adolescents. *JAMA: The Journal of the American Medical Association, 304*(5), 527–535.

Wells, E., D. M. Morrison, M. R. Gillmore, R. F. Catalano, B. Iritani, and J. D. Hawkins. (1992). Race differences in antisocial behaviors and attitudes in early initiation of substance use. *Journal of Drug Education, 22*(2), 115–30.

West, C. M., and S. Rose. (2000). Dating aggression among low income African American youth: An examination of gender differences and antagonistic beliefs. *Violence Against Women, 6*(5), 470–494.

Wingood, G. M., R. J. DiClemente, D. H. McCree, K. Harrington, and S. L. Davies. (2001). Dating violence and the sexual health of Black adolescent females. *Pediatrics, 107*(5), 1–4.

Winn, K. L. (2013). African American girls and physical aggression: A resilience study on how adult African American women overcame physically aggressive adolescence. *Doctorate in Social Work (DSW) Dissertations.* Paper 49, 1–147.

Xie, H., R. B., Cairns, and B. D. Cairns. (2002). The development of social aggression and physical aggression: A narrative analysis of interpersonal conflicts. *Aggressive Behavior, 28*(5), 341–355.

Xie, H., T. W. Farmer, and B. D. Cairns. (2003). Different forms of aggression among inner-city African-American children: Gender, configurations, and school social networks. *Journal of School Psychology, 41*(5), 355–375.

Zimmerman, G. M., and S. F. Messner. (2010). Neighborhood context and the gender gap in adolescent violent crime. *American Sociological Review, 75*(6), 958–980.

Chapter 27

African American Adolescent Females in the Criminal and Juvenile Justice Systems

E. Jeannette Ogden

African American adolescent females in the criminal and juvenile justice systems are confronted with unique challenges that affect their status and treatment. A historical perspective of the roles, functions, and responsibilities of the courts in these systems, as well as perceptions and assumptions about African American adolescent females in this country, is critical to understanding these challenges and how they relate to crime and delinquency.

Adolescence is a transitional stage of physical, sociological, and psychological human development that generally occurs during the period from puberty to legal adulthood (Merriam-Webster, 2012). Adolescents begin to examine themselves, recognize influences on their behavior as well as the perceptions of others, during this stage. They also formulate self-esteem, thoughts and feelings about themselves and their individual identity. Adolescents often define themselves based on the opinions of others, such as their peers, society, and their environment. An adolescent from an urban environment, high crime, or impoverished area is more likely to be exposed to an environment that can be detrimental to their development than an adolescent from a more affluent, privileged area who is exposed to more opportunities and better situations. Coping devices, social media, and economic status are also factors that contribute to their developing identity during adolescence. This is a challenging time for adolescents. Their full sense of self-identity may not develop until the end of the period of adolescence, if at all.

The period of adolescence is frequently associated with the teenage years and the onset of puberty. However, the physical, psychological, and cultural expressions of adolescence may begin earlier and end later. For example, although puberty has been historically associated with the onset of adolescent development, it typically begins prior to the teenage years, occurring in preadolescence, particularly in females (*Psychology Today*, 1991). Although there is no precise chronological age definition for adolescence, the age span of 12–21 will be used herein to espouse the concepts and principles relating to African American adolescent females in the juvenile and adult criminal justice systems.

African American adolescent females appear in both the juvenile and criminal justice systems, depending on their biological age upon entry. No consideration is given to their psychological age or stage of development. There are distinct differences between the roles and responsibilities of courts in the juvenile and criminal justice systems. Both systems involve the policing, prosecuting, defending, adjudicating, and sentencing of those who are accused and/or convicted of a criminal offense. The stakeholders (police, prosecutors, defense attorneys, probation, and corrections officers) and decision makers (judges) are the same in both systems. However, the goal of the juvenile justice system is rehabilitation and treatment rather than punishment alone. Juvenile Court proceedings are civil and enable judges to focus on the individual juvenile rather than solely on the alleged offense. The courts in the criminal justice system are primarily adversarial and judges impose punitive sanctions upon conviction for criminal offenses.

The treatment received by African American adolescent females is quite similar in both systems because the perceptions and assumptions attributed to them by system stakeholders and decision makers in both systems are similar, although the roles and responsibilities of the systems differ.

Stakeholders and decision makers have certain biases, prejudices, assumptions, and perceptions about African American adolescent females that are derived from their own life experiences, culture, and backgrounds. Their perceptions and assumptions result in unconscious biases against African American adolescent females which reflect historical societal perceptions. These perceptions, assumptions, and resulting biases of stakeholders and decision makers adversely impact the treatment of African American adolescent females before, during, and after their involvement in the criminal and juvenile justice systems and contribute to their overrepresentation among those who are in contact with both systems.

HISTORICAL REFLECTION

The institution of slavery predestined the roles and responsibilities of African American adolescent females as well as their socialization and created a caste system that relegated them to the lowest social, political, and economic status in society. Their identities were defined by their societal roles and their sense of self was shaped by and depended on the fulfillment of those roles. They were confronted with the challenges associated with adapting to a new environment and adjusting their lifestyles in order to survive.

The initial role of the African American adolescent female was that of laborer. Identified as property, her purpose was to provide labor, breed, and provide sexual gratification for slave owners and/or overseers, most of whom were men, without complaint, compensation, or consideration. She was expected to perform the same types of manual labor as her male counterpart, despite age and gender differences. She was denied any proprietary interest in her own body or offspring. Her psychological and emotional needs were disregarded and her developmental needs were considered only in the context of her ability to perform various forms of labor. Since slaves were considered property and not people, she had no protection against wrongs perpetrated against her.

Experiences of enslavement were different for African American adolescent females and males. Enslaved females were not only exploited for their physical labor, they were also exploited for their reproductive capabilities. Their reproductive function was crucial to the economic interests of slaveholders, especially after the importing of slaves from Africa to America was outlawed by Congress in 1801.

The perceptions and expectations about African American adolescent females in society continued after slavery ended under the concept of convict leasing. Convict leasing was a system of penal labor (peonage) practiced in the Southern United States. It began with the emancipation of slaves at the end of the American Civil War in 1865, peaked around 1880, and officially ended in 1928, although it persisted in various forms until World War II (Litwack, 1998).

Convict leasing provided prisoner labor to private parties, such as plantation owners and corporations. Corruption, lack of accountability, and racial violence resulted in one of the harshest and most exploitative labor systems known in American history (Mancini, 1996).

Vigorous and selective enforcement of laws and discriminatory sentencing resulted in African Americans making up the vast majority of the convicts leased (Litwack, 1998). African American adolescent females were included among the leased convicts with no regard to their age or gender.

Stereotypic images and complex challenges arose as a result of the historical experiences of African American adolescent females. On one hand, they were viewed as Black amazons—strong, sinister, dangerous, and contemptuous. On the other hand, they were viewed as maids who were expected to provide for the health and welfare of White children, even if it meant the neglect of the health and welfare of their own children. If problems arose involving their children, they were deemed to be negligent, unfit parents.

They were also characterized as immoral, sexually depraved, loose, and permissive. These images became more prevalent from 1969 to 1989 when America declared a War on Drugs and their images were linked to crack addicts, welfare queens, and baby mamas (mothers of illegitimate babies).

Current images of African American adolescent females, especially those depicted in rap music and videos, where they are viewed as vibrating buttocks, scantily dressed, voiceless sex objects, continue to perpetuate negative perceptions and assumptions. These images assault the integrity of African American adolescent females and contribute to their disproportional representation within the criminal and juvenile justice systems.

My experience, derived from judicial observations, conversations, and working with African American adolescent females, convinces me that the impact from absorbing these images has a direct link to their socioemotional development and criminal conduct. It also affects peer influence and responsive peer pressure which in turn affects judgment, self-esteem, and risk taking. This impact is greater during adolescence than it is during adulthood.

JUVENILE JUSTICE SYSTEM

Throughout history children who were accused of committing crimes were imprisoned as adults. They were preyed upon, exploited, victimized, abused, assaulted, and sometimes killed while imprisoned in adult facilities.

The need to protect imprisoned children has been recognized since feudal times. The King of England exercised his royal prerogative and acting as "Father of the Country" appointed a Chancellor to act on his behalf and assume responsibility for the custody, care, and treatment of children who committed crimes. This authority, designed to provide protection and rehabilitation for juvenile offenders, became known as the doctrine of "*parens patriae*," a Latin term meaning "parent of the nation." Parents had no legal way to challenge or change decisions made by the Chancellor and the juveniles had no rights under the doctrine of "parens patriae."

Today the doctrine of "parens patriae" refers to the public policy of the state to act as parent of any child or person who is in need of protection. It operates in the juvenile justice system where the state is considered to be the parent of all juveniles within its jurisdiction, and state courts have the inherent power and authority to intervene to protect the best interests of the juveniles. The doctrine has been expanded with limited authority to include school principals as parent of students within their jurisdiction.

The fate of a juvenile who commits a crime is now in the hands of a judge rather than a Chancellor. Great discretion is given to judges and principals in the decision-making process. Although there is a process for parents to challenge and/or change judicial decisions, there are significant limitations and change is difficult to obtain.

Research and scientific studies on the developmental differences between juveniles and adults and their relationship to behavior led to the creation of a separate justice system for juveniles with a goal of rehabilitation and treatment, rather than punishment, as a response to their conduct.

Changes in outward physical appearance, faster body growth, sexual maturation, and the development of secondary sexual characteristics occur during adolescent development simultaneously with social, emotional, and cognitive development. In addition, the brain of an adolescent is evolving in its ability to organize, regulate impulses, and weigh risks and rewards. This renders the young adolescents more vulnerable to engaging in risky behaviors such as unsafe sexual behavior, reckless driving, substance abuse, and impulsive acts of violence.

The first juvenile court in the United States was established in 1899. In the late 1960s, juveniles in the juvenile justice system were given constitutional rights. Today, the juvenile justice system is a mirror reflection of the criminal legal system, dealing with offenses committed by minors, usually between the ages of 10 and 18 years, rather than adults. The age for determining eligibility for adjudication of a juvenile as an adult in the juvenile justice system is determined by the laws of each state, although all states and the District of Columbia allow prosecution of juveniles as adults under certain circumstances. The age for processing juveniles in criminal court in New York and North Carolina is 16 years, regardless of the type of offense or criminal history of the accused. The age ranges from 17 to 18 years in all other states.

The juvenile justice system involves special courts, commonly referred to as Juvenile or Family Courts. Those courts deal solely with minors charged with crimes and minors who are neglected or out of the control of their parents. The proceedings are deemed civil in nature and may or may not be adversarial. The Court can involve parents, social workers, and probation officers in the predisposition process to achieve positive results.

The Court also has various postdisposition sentencing options to meet both the safety needs of society and the treatment needs of the juvenile. Sentencing options include educational and/or therapeutic programming in the child's community, residential placements outside of the community, and sentences of prison terms with transfers to state prisons upon reaching adulthood for serious and/or repeat offenses. In cases of parental neglect or loss of control, the Court may sentence juveniles to foster homes, reform schools and/or correctional facilities, or treat them as wards of the Court.

Juveniles enter the juvenile justice system by way of arrest for committing violation, misdemeanor or felony level offenses, or by petition filed by parents, guardians, or schools for committing "status offenses." A "status offense" is an offense that can only be committed by a juvenile because of their age at the time of the activity. Examples are underage alcohol possession and/or consumption, curfew violations, and truancy. Juveniles convicted of status offenses or violations are adjudicated as Persons in Need of Supervision [PINS].

Juveniles convicted of an offense, which if committed by an adult would be considered a misdemeanor, punishable by up to 1 year in jail, are adjudicated as juvenile "delinquents" rather than as convicted criminals. The juvenile could be incarcerated in a juvenile correctional facility, placed on probation or sentenced to a conditional discharge wherein the juvenile is required to comply with conditions imposed by the court for a designated period of time.

Juveniles convicted of an offense, which if committed by an adult would be considered a felony, punishable by more than 1 year in jail, are adjudicated as "juvenile offenders." They are incarcerated in juvenile correctional facilities until they reach the age of majority and then transferred to adult criminal facilities.

Rehabilitation and treatment, in addition to community protection, are considered to be primary and viable sentencing goals.

Limitations are placed on public access to juvenile court records because of the belief that juvenile offenders can be successfully rehabilitated. Criminal convictions in the criminal justice system are a matter of public record. Although limitations exist, juvenile records are not automatically expunged or sealed. As a result, juveniles often face collateral consequences from involvement in the juvenile justice system such as difficulty obtaining employment, serving in the military, or obtaining financial aid for college.

In the 1980s and 1990s, juvenile crime across the nation rose dramatically. In response, states across the nation enacted "get tough" laws that required law enforcement and the courts to automatically charge youths as adults if they were alleged to have committed certain violent crimes and weapons offenses. These laws deprived juveniles of the protections traditionally afforded them in the juvenile justice system. African American adolescent females and males were disproportionately subjected to these laws and disproportionately subjected to the failure to have their records expunged and sealed, thereby disproportionately subjecting them to the collateral consequences of involvement in the juvenile justice system.

States also adopted different ways of moving from juvenile to adult criminal court for trial and punishment. In some cases, these new laws subjected juveniles to the most severe sentences, leading the U.S. Supreme Court to strike down state laws that imposed the death penalty or life without the possibility for parole for juveniles as cruel and unusual punishment.

Many of the new state laws exposed juveniles to the dangers and potential abuses attributed to incarceration with adult offenders—much like they'd experienced before the establishment of juvenile courts.

By 1988, the majority of juveniles in the juvenile justice system were African American adolescent females and males. Not only were they overrepresented, they were overrepresented at every major decision point in the system. A decision point is an action that occurs at the point of the decision to (1) make an initial arrest or file a petition, (2) hold a juvenile in detention pending investigation, (3) refer a case to juvenile vs. criminal court, (4) waive a case pending in juvenile court to adult criminal court, (5) formally petition a case into court vs. probation diversion, (6) impose a particular sentence, and (7) impose sanctions.

The disproportionate representation of minorities at all stages of the juvenile justice system, as well as the fact that their rates of overrepresentation increase as they proceed through the system, is a trend known as Disproportionate Minority Contact (DMC). The federal law known as the Juvenile Justice and Delinquency Prevention Act, in efforts to reduce DMC (National Council on Crime and Delinquency, 2007), requires states to create plans to reduce the number of minority youth in the juvenile justice system. It also prohibits states from sentencing juveniles who commit "status offenses" such as curfew violations, truancy, and alcohol possession, to placement in adult detention facilities.

Statistics show that African American adolescent females and males are more likely to experience harsher dispositions and penetrate further into the juvenile justice system than White youth (National Council on Crime and Delinquency, 2007).

In 2009, African American youth made up 31% of all youth arrested in that year, an arrest rate nearly twice that of White youth. The arrest rate for African American adolescent females was also greater than that of their White female counterparts (Snyder, 2011).

Unfortunately, additional studies in this area specifically addressing arrest and offense rates for African American adolescent females are scant.

All of the decisions impacting the overrepresentation of African American youth in the juvenile justice system, including African American adolescent females, are influenced by the decision maker's perceptions and assumptions about African American adolescent females. These decisions often reflect a bias on behalf of the decision maker and neglect to consider the impact of social, mental and/or emotional distress, societal exclusion, and exposure to trauma, often faced by African American adolescent females (Rachlinski, Johnson, Wistrich & Guthrie, 2009).

A study on race and the fragility of the legal distinction between juveniles and adults examined the effects of race on the perception of juvenile culpability. The study found that race had a significant effect on White Americans' support for severe sentences, such as life without the possibility of parole for youths, and their perceptions of juveniles' blameworthiness relative to adults (Rattan, Levine, Dweck & Eberhardt, 2012).

Researchers in said study manipulated the race of the offender from African American to White in a number of case studies about support for and opposition to life without parole sentences for youth in non-homicide cases in order to examine the impact of race on the participants' perceptions of youth as a mitigating factor in this context. Even when controlling for the participants' political ideology and evidence of racial bias, the researchers found that study participants were more likely to impose harsher sentences when researchers explicitly primed participants to believe that the offender was African American, than when researchers primed participants to believe that the offender was White (Rachlinski, Johnson, Wistrich, & Guthrie, 2009).

When courts transfer youth to the adult system, it is documented that Black youth receive significantly more punitive sentences than White youth (Jordan & Freiburger, 2009).

These studies support the position that juvenile justice policies have been applied unequally to African American adolescent females based on distorted perceptions of race. Also, that they receive harsher and more punitive sentences than their White counterparts, particularly those who were transferred from juvenile to criminal court, and that unconscious racial bias of judges contributes to this disparity.

Negative racial stereotypes, assumptions, and attitudes of decision makers in all stages of the juvenile justice system tend to reduce sympathy for African American adolescent female offenders. Negative stereotypes and assumptions about African Americans generally as a group are sometimes attributed to individual African American adolescent offenders.

Although the extent to which negative stereotypes, bias, and prejudice shape opinion and practice is unclear, research evidence supports the position that it plays a pernicious role in the juvenile and criminal justice systems.

CRIMINAL JUSTICE SYSTEM

The criminal justice system is the system of law enforcement directly involved in apprehending, prosecuting, defending, sentencing and punishing those who are suspected or convicted of criminal offenses. Adversarial by design, it operates under the principle that anyone can accuse another of committing a crime. However, the accused is presumed innocent of the accusations until proven guilty beyond a reasonable doubt at a trial in a court of law.

This presumption of innocence is a fundamental principle of criminal law and applies to everyone accused of committing a crime. In reality, the presumption of innocence is not always afforded to African American adolescent females accused of committing crimes. On the contrary, they are frequently presumed guilty long before they go to trial. They are also more likely to be presumed suspects in criminal investigations and presumed more likely to commit crimes in general.

Sometimes their exuberant hand/arm gestures, head shaking, or other attitudinal expressions contribute to police perceptions that they are angry, violent, threatening, and dangerous. If they are outspoken or opinionated, they are presumed to be disrespectful. If their voices elevate because of the excitement of the moment, they are perceived as loud-mouthed troublemakers. Additional perceptions include images of African American adolescent females as welfare queens, violent thugs, and promiscuous whores, images synonymous with criminality.

These presumptions and perceptions inform the way the police respond to African American adolescent females. Police officers may respond by being more aggressive, insensitive, callous, and/or by treating African American adolescent females with disrespect. Said police responses are not limited to African American adolescent females suspected and/or accused of committing a crime, they are also directed at African American adolescent females who are victims of crime. These responses are contributing factors to the disproportionate number of African American adolescent females who have contact with the criminal justice system.

More than 1 million women were under the supervision of the criminal justice system—either in prison, jail, or on probation or parole supervision—as of 2010 (Guerino, Harrison & Sabol, 2012). African American females generally and African American adolescent females implicitly are over-represented in all stages of the criminal justice system, particularly in the prison system.

A national survey of imprisoned women in the U.S. found the majority to be young, women of color, and single mothers (American Correctional Association, 1990). Most were convicted of drug and property-related offenses. Many of them did not have skills to be productive members of society when they were arrested. Locking them up upon conviction guarantees that they will not gain the skills needed to better themselves.

According to the Bureau of Justice Statistics (BJS), African American women constituted 23% of the total number of women in prison but their rate of imprisonment was 6 times higher than their White counterparts (Minton, 2011).

African American adolescent females are confined in patriarchal institutions whose primary purpose is to punish rather than rehabilitate. They are subjected to high levels of racial and sexual violence, as well as to a lack of professionalism and humanitarianism perpetrated against them by prison staff. Sexual abuse, domestic violence, mental illness, illiteracy, poverty, and homelessness also affect them at a profound rate.

A consequence of incarceration is the loss of their children. According to a 2008 Bureau of Justice Statistics Special Report, nearly two-thirds of women in prison are mothers, 77% of incarcerated mothers reported being the sole caregivers for their children before incarceration, and 11% reported their children being placed in foster care, compared to only 2% of fathers (Glaze & Maruschak, 2010).

In addition to the devastating impact of a mother's imprisonment on the stability of the family, African American adolescent females also face severely limited access to social resources such as public housing, transitional income, and sustainable employment upon re-entering the community. Promoting excessively punitive responses to crime without considering the needs of these young women only further limits their ability to successfully reintegrate into their communities and rehabilitate their lives.

African American women generally, and African American adolescent females implicitly, are one of the largest disenfranchised groups in America. Collateral consequences of their involvement in the criminal justice system result in a loss of intimate partners, employment, social contacts, and eligibility for certain public benefits—marginalizing them in mainstream society.

Many African American adolescent females enter the criminal justice system from economically and socially depressed communities. Income inequality affects outcomes in the criminal justice system. Persons accused of crimes with financial resources to retain high-priced attorneys and investigators often get better results than those who have overworked and underpaid attorneys without the means to pay for investigative services. They are also more likely to experience bias based on race, gender, and class.

SUGGESTED RESPONSES

Appropriately addressing disproportionate treatment of African American adolescent females in the criminal and juvenile justice systems must begin with an acknowledgement, by decision makers at all stages, of the existence of the problem and acceptance of the fact that they have an obligation to alleviate it.

Educating system stakeholders such as police, prosecutors, defense attorneys, judges, probation and parole officers, and all other decision makers who interact with African American adolescent females about attitudes, perceptions, and actions that may not be motivated by a discriminatory intent, but definitely have a discriminatory effect on the treatment of said adolescents, is an essential first step toward attaining equality in the criminal and juvenile justice systems.

African American adolescent females are incorrectly deemed to be more mature and calculating than their White counterparts, less likely to be forgiven or excused, less likely to be seen as amenable to treatment, and more likely to be deemed deserving of punishment. Identifying these implicit biases and fostering relationships between the adolescents and stakeholders will help to dispel these biases.

Increased attention must be paid to environmental factors that affect the conduct of African American adolescent females such as exposure to domestic violence, trauma, normal adolescent fighting with parents, and other social problems including poverty, poor education, and mental health. The increasing acceptance of conduct, in certain segments of society, such as carrying and/or using weapons and teen pregnancy are additional factors that affect their conduct.

Examining such contributing factors to criminal conduct utilizing interdisciplinary models that place behaviors in social, psychological, and biological context for African American females can aid in understanding and responding to their contact with the criminal and juvenile justice systems. Culturally appropriate evidence-based assessment and treatment is essential to their ability to adapt and grow.

Trauma and exposure to trauma is another contributing factor that affects their conduct. Many African American adolescent females suffer from trauma at high rates, particularly those who have contact with the criminal and juvenile justice systems. Unaddressed trauma can negatively impact them throughout their lives.

Assisting African American adolescent females to understand and deal with peer and parental responses can offset some of their biological and emotional disconnections. Differentiating between African American adolescent females whose actions are more of an affront to parental and local authority than violations of law from those whose actions are purely criminal in nature will play a significant role in determining the appropriateness of their contact, entry, and movement through the criminal and juvenile justice systems. Identifying and providing adequate resources to navigate and remedy conflicts with parents and persons of authority will better serve them, their families, and society.

Positive school involvements, fair and equitable enforcement of rules, recognition of mental health problems such as anxiety and depression, recognition of substance abuse and co-occurring disorders, and understanding that punitive, zero-tolerance policies that push marginalized African American adolescent females out of schools and into the criminal and juvenile justice systems without investigation and/or consideration of the root of their problems by teachers and principals will reduce school-generated petitions into the juvenile justice system.

Coordinating responses between law enforcement, schools, support staff, families, and communities to work together to develop targeted, coordinated, culturally relevant, and comprehensive transition plans for African American adolescent females is a critical component of any solution.

Addressing the perceptions and assumptions of African American adolescent females about decision makers and stakeholders within the criminal and juvenile justice system is also necessary. Sometimes African American adolescent females perceive support or assistance from police, schools, families, probation officers, or other community representatives as unhelpful and counterproductive. As a result, they reject the assistance and respond in ways that exasperate the decision makers and make their situations worse. They wrongfully rationalize that physical aggression is an appropriate and efficient strategy for dealing with their problems.

There is a pervasive misunderstanding about African American adolescent females and the nature of delinquency. Their plasticity should be molded by an understanding of how vulnerable they are and responding to their vulnerability by holding them accountable in more therapeutic ways. We must understand that they do not have the same capacity to engage in abstract thinking and cognitive reasoning as older adults, nor the ability to weigh the pros and cons of certain courses of action. We must realize that they are more susceptible to peer influence, have poor impulse control, difficulty regulating moods and emotions, and their concern for immediate rewards and self-gratification is matched by their lack of concern for long-term consequences.

Although cognitive differences between adults and adolescents eventually even out, psychosocial differences persist into late adolescence and early adulthood, making these recommendations applicable to African American adolescent females in both systems. Once ingrained in the criminal and/or juvenile justice system, their cognitive capacities may be further compromised by fear, fatigue, learning difficulties, and victimization.

The good news is that they may acquire new skills as they mature and through instruction and experience their cognitive, neurological, psychological, and psychosocial capacities improve. They will then make better choices, learn to resist peer pressure, become less impulsive, and acquire new values.

Actions of African American adolescent females are no different than the actions of other adolescents, male or female. The difference is the way they are treated in response to those actions.

CONCLUSION

The impact of disproportionate treatment and resultant social disadvantage is underappreciated in the research on the lives of African American adolescent females in the criminal and juvenile justice systems. Endemic social distress and exclusion make compliance with social norms very challenging.

American law is replete with evidence of racial discrimination against African American adolescent females because of their sex, race, and economic status. Poverty is greater among African American females and children than any other class of people in the United States. As a result, they are confronted with a social triple jeopardy: race, gender, and class. This social triple jeopardy, coupled with accompanying biases, negative perceptions, and assumptions, continues to challenge African American adolescent females.

Understanding their societal status and the origins of the negative perceptions and assumptions which lead to implicit and/or explicit biases against them is critical to understanding the challenges they face both in and out of the criminal and juvenile justice systems.

"Equal Justice Under the Law" is a foundational principle of our legal system which is often depicted by a statue of a blindfolded lady holding equally balanced scales which represent a process that only takes objective factual findings into consideration when dealing with those accused of committing crimes. She is referred to as "Lady Justice" and represents a concept of equality and justice applicable to all in the juvenile and criminal justice systems.

Unfortunately for African American adolescent females in the criminal and juvenile justice systems, equal justice is evasive. They are rarely viewed as ladies and regularly receive unequal treatment, regardless of their roles in the system. Unconscious and implicit biases adversely affect them whether they are victims of crimes, perpetrators of crimes, or employees of the systems. Many of them have fallen through the cracks designed to assist them. They are disproportionately detained and incarcerated in both systems and are at risk for non-stranger violence at a higher rate than any other group, including their African American male counterparts. They are perceived as sexual deviants, delinquents, and/or criminals prior to the adjudication of their legal actions. Their dignity and humanity is frequently forgotten and their importance to mainstream society is often ignored.

African American adolescent females must not allow negative societal images and perceptions of them by others define who they really are. They must not lose sight of their potential nor confuse images with personal vision. When they do, they can successfully avoid the pipeline from the juvenile to criminal justice system. How they define themselves will determine how they are confined.

Although we cannot lose sight of the relevance and importance of the blindfold worn by "Lady Justice," which envisions and symbolizes the principle of equal justice under law, perhaps we should remove the blindfold and allow her to take a good look at the treatment of African American adolescent females in the criminal and juvenile justice system. She will see that much work must be done to obtain "Equal Justice." After all, looks can be deceiving.

This chapter may be used for research, teaching, and private study purposes. Any substantial or systematic reproduction, redistribution, reselling, loan, sub-licensing, systematic supply, or distribution in any form to anyone is expressly forbidden.

REFERENCES

American Correctional Association. (1990). Female Offender: What Does the Future Hold? Retrieved March 8, 2014, from https://www.ncjrs.gov/App/Publications/abstract.aspx?ID=127562

Glaze, L., & Bonczar, T. (2011, November 1). Probation and Parole in the United States, 2010. Retrieved March 8, 2014, from http://www.bjs.gov/content/pub/pdf/ppus10.pdf

Glaze, L., & Maruschak, L. (2010, March 30). Parents in Prison and Their Minor Children. Retrieved March 8, 2014, from http://www.bjs.gov/content/pub/pdf/pptmc.pdf

Guerino, P., Harrison, P., & Sabol, W. (2012, February 9). Prisoners in 2010. Retrieved March 8, 2014, from http://www.bjs.gov/content/pub/pdf/p10.pdf

Jordan, K., & Freiburger, T. (2009, December 16). Examining the Impact of Race and Ethnicity on the Sentencing of Juveniles in the Adult Court. Retrieved March 8, 2014, from http://cjp.sagepub.com/content/21/2/185.abstract

Litwack, L. (1998). *Trouble in mind: Black southerners in the age of Jim Crow.* New York: Knopf.

Mancini, M. (1996). *One dies, get another: Convict leasing in the American South, 1866–1928.* Columbia, S.C.: University of South Carolina Press.

Minton, T. (2011, June 28). Jail Inmates at Midyear 2011—Statistical Tables. Retrieved March 8, 2014, from http://bjs.gov/content/pub/pdf/jim10st.pdf

National Council on Crime and Delinquency. (2007, January 1). And Justice for Some: Differential Treatment of Youth of Color in the Justice System. Retrieved March 8, 2014, from http://www.nccdglobal.org/sites/default/files/publication_pdf/justice-for-some.pdf

Psychology Today. (1991, January 1). Adolescence. Retrieved March 8, 2014, from http://www.psychologytoday.com/basics/adolescence

Rachlinski, J., Johnson, S., Wistrich, A., & Guthrie, C. (2009, April 8). Does Unconscious Racial Bias Affect Trial Judges? Retrieved March 8, 2014, from http://papers.ssrn.com/sol3/papers.cfm?abstract_id=1374497

Rattan, A., Levine, C., Dweck, C., & Eberhardt, J. (2012, May 23). Race and the Fragility of the Legal Distinction between Juveniles and Adults. Retrieved

March 9, 2014, from http://www.plosone.org/article/info:doi/10.1371/journal.pone.0036680

Snyder, H. (2011, September 1). Arrests in the United States, 1980–2009. Retrieved March 9, 2014, from http://www.bjs.gov/content/pub/pdf/aus8009.pdf

About the Editor and Contributors

EDITOR

CATHERINE FISHER COLLINS, D.Ed., earned her doctoral degree from the State University of New York at Buffalo, where she also received her Master's Degree in Allied Health Education and graduated from the School of Nursing, Nurse Practitioner's Program.

Collins is a respected author of many published books, including *Sources of Stress and Relief for African American Women* (2003), *The Imprisonment of African American Women: Causes, Conditions and Future Implications* (1997, winner of the 1997 Outstanding Academic and Scholarly Award), *African American Women's Health and Social Issues,* first edition (1996), *African American Women's Health and Social Issues,* second edition (2006), *The Imprisonment of African American Women: Causes, Experiences and Effects,* second edition (2010), and *African American Women's Life Issues: Today's Vital Health and Social Matters* (2013). In 2011, she launched *Women's Health Radio* show that airs on WWWS 1400 AM every other Saturday with a focus on women's health issues and wellness. Collins has also held positions in health care and education administration and served as Director of a Registered Nursing Program.

Collins has received more than 50 awards and honors. Among them are the Western New York Women's Hall of Fame, SUNY Outstanding Faculty Fellow, honors from governors of New Jersey (outstanding service), New York (Attica Prison Health Initiative), and Kentucky (Coronial), and the 2014 Jane Altes Prize for Exemplary Community Services.

Currently, Collins is an associate professor at State University of New York, Empire State College, Department of Community and Human Services.

CONTRIBUTORS

Sheila Marie Aird, PhD, MA, is an associate professor and academic coordinator of Global Studies at SUNY's Empire State College. Dr. Aird is actively engaged with mentoring, teaching, and the creation and development of global studies courses inclusive of the African Diaspora. In addition, she is a standing board member of the Image Initiative Inc., an organization that works to empower young African Diaspora and Latina young woman in the Syracuse, NY, school district. She received her PhD in Latin and Caribbean History and MA from Howard University. During her final year of research at Howard University, she was awarded the prestigious Sasakawa Fellowship from the Nippon Foundation in Japan. Aird also holds a BA in Anthropology and an MA in Anthropology with a focus on Historical Archeology from the Maxwell School of Citizenship and Public Affairs at Syracuse University. Aird has presented on her work in many venues both domestically and internationally. Most importantly, Dr. Aird's passion lies in promoting the history and culture of members of the African Diaspora while educating the public through the medium of documentary film, photography, and museum exhibits. Her areas of interests are colonial enslavement, Public History, pop culture, and issues of race in the African Diaspora community. At present she is working on a documentary and a photography exhibit.

Funmi Aiyegbo-Ohadike (pronounced IYABOW), RN, DNP, FNP-BC, is a family nurse practitioner who has established herself as an expert clinician with over 17 years of experience. Aiyegbo graduated from Rutgers University with a BS in Nursing in 1995; received her MS from Columbia University in 1998; and DNP from Rutgers University in 2010. As a faculty member at Sacred Heart University and UMDNJ, she prepared nursing students on both the baccalaureate and graduate level for entry to practice. She has particular expertise in geriatrics, family practice, pharmacology, and home care. Aiyegbo has presented at both regional and national conferences on various topics in health care.

Te Cora Ballom is a board certified osteopathic family physician currently serving as a captain in the United States Public Health Service. A graduate of Bishop College, she attended medical school at the University of North Texas Health Science Center and completed postgraduate training at Detroit Osteopathic Hospital. Capt. Ballom has practiced medicine for twenty-nine years and currently serves as the Regional Medical Director for the South Central Region overseeing the Health Services of 16 federal prisons and 44,000 inmates. As a family physician her special interests are in preventive medicine and nutrition.

Ursuline R. Bankhead was born and raised in Buffalo, NY, and is a graduate of Buffalo Public Schools. She received her undergraduate degree in

Psychology from Pennsylvania State University–Behrend College, a Master's in Marriage and Family Therapy from East Carolina University, and her Doctorate in Counseling Psychology from the State University of New York at Buffalo. Her dissertation *Man-Up: African American Men Discuss Race, Masculinity, and Coping with Stress* explored the perspectives of African American men across three generations, solidifying her interest in issues facing people of color across generations. Bankhead has worked as a substance abuse counselor, a family mediator, and an in-home family therapist. Currently, she works as a licensed psychologist with the VA Western New York Healthcare System in Buffalo, in a primary care setting. Additionally, she works as an adjunct professor for the State University of New York at Buffalo, teaching a graduate level Multicultural Counseling course, is a member of the Minority Veterans Committee, and the Psychology Training and Diversity Committees. Bankhead has participated in and led several cultural competency and diversity-related training projects for the VA.

Lindamichelle Baron, EdD, is an author, educator, professional developer, and entrepreneur. She is the president of a publishing house that also supports professional development for educators, Harlin Jacque Publications. Her poetry collections have been used extensively for over 30 years in classrooms throughout the tri-state area and the United States. Her poetry and other narratives resonate with themes of self-empowerment, love of self and others, and critical literacy. Her doctorate in Cross Categorical Studies, and master's in Reading are both from Columbia University, Teachers College. Among her collections are *The Sun Is On, For the Love of Life,* and *Rhythm & Dues*. She also co-authored a 1st through 8th grade Language Arts textbook series for Pearson Learning, *The Write Direction*. Her journal publications focus on the social and emotional intelligences, culturally responsive pedagogy, and artistic and critical literacy. Baron is currently Chairperson for the Department of Teacher Education at York College, City University of New York, where she teaches undergraduate courses in educational psychology, literacy and the arts, content area literacy, and human development. She has received numerous awards as an author, educator, literary exemplar, entrepreneur, and social activist.

Virginia A. Batchelor, PhD, is an associate professor in the School of Education at Medaille College. She has received numerous awards for community service. She earned her PhD in the sociology of education from the State University of New York at Buffalo in 2001, and has taught at Medaille since 2001. She teaches courses in diversity, research methods, and foundations of education. Her publications include: *Breaking the Code: Minor Sex Trafficking and School Children* (2013), *Creativity* (2009), *Women in the Shadows: Seeking Health, Seeking Self* (2006), *Culture Change* (2006), and *A Soul's Reunion*

(1995). She provides professional development training on cultural competencies and cultural sensitivity. She presents at international, national, regional, and local conferences on topics such as Community Preservation in connection with the Underground Railroad, African American Womenhood, African American History, sex trafficking, online teaching, the mis-education of public education, and culturally responsive teaching.

Betty Boyle-Duke, RN, C-PNP, is the Director of Clinical Services for the College of Nursing's Mobile Health Van Program at New York University (NYU), where she is also an adjunct faculty member. Her undergraduate and master's degrees in nursing are from Simmons College in Boston, MA, and she is currently pursuing a Doctor of Nursing Practice at NYU. Throughout her career as a nurse practitioner she has worked with the adolescent population, specifically youth from socially disadvantaged backgrounds. She has held several positions as a clinician and administrator providing primary care and health education in the foster care system as well as school-based health. She holds membership in several local and national professional organizations. In addition to her professional pursuits, she mentors and counsels high school and middle school students of color on accessing college and health careers.

Kellie Bryant, DNP, WHNP, is currently the Director of Simulation Learning and Clinical Assistant Professor at New York University College of Nursing. She oversees the day-to-day operation of NYU's Clinical Simulation Learning Center where she works with faculty in the development, implementation, and integration of over 75 simulation sessions a week for the undergraduate and graduate programs. Bryant has presented extensively and published in the areas of simulation and teenage pregnancy. She has received a March of Dimes grant to implement a series of teenage pregnancy and childbirth classes for pregnant teenagers in foster care. She is currently among key personnel on 2 HRSA grants that focus on increasing use of simulation in the classroom setting, and teaching oral and systemic health to Nurse Practitioner students through the use of simulation. Bryant has over 11 years of teaching experience including teaching health as assessment and women's health courses for undergraduate and graduate programs. In addition, Bryant has 10 years of experience as a Perinatal/Women's Health Nurse Practitioner. She practiced at Jamaica Hospital Women's Health Center providing care for women across the life span with a special interest in teenage pregnancy. Bryant received her associate degree in nursing from Hudson Valley Community College. She then continued her education at SUNY Stony Brook where she received her bachelor's and master's degrees. In 2006, she completed her Doctorate of Nursing Practice (DNP) from Case Western Reserve University. She has received her certificate in simulation from Drexel University.

Tomasina L. Cook is the Department Chair of Criminal Justice at Erie Community College. She has completed her doctoral work in Counselor Education and Supervision and holds master's degrees in Criminal Justice Administration and Mental Health Counseling. She is a Licensed Mental Health Counselor and has a private counseling practice where she specializes in counseling offenders and victims in the criminal justice system. Additionally, she is an adjunct counselor educator at Empire State College, Medaille College, and Niagara University. Her areas of research include domestic violence, violence against women, victimology, juvenile delinquency, forensic counseling, homicide survivors, and women in the criminal justice system. She has written articles and presented on several topics related to victims of crime. In addition, she has provided consultation to criminal justice and human service agencies and has received numerous awards in the fields of criminal justice and counseling. Outside of academia, she has worked for the Niagara County Sheriff's Department and Niagara Falls Police Department in the State of New York.

Cassandra E. Dobson, PhD, MS, RN-BC, PHc, is an assistant professor at Lehman College, City University of New York in the Bronx. Dobson believes in the delivery of optimum patient care. She is an efficient nurse who always goes above and beyond to meet the needs of the patients. Dobson's vision for the future is to educate and empower patients to seek appropriate health care in a timely manner. She is an advocate for the promotion of self-management for individuals with sickle cell disease. Dobson has worked in several different positions during her nursing career, from LPN, staff nurse, Senior Clinical Preceptor, Clinical Instructor, Home Care Nurse, Clinical Care Coordinator, Administrative Nurse Manager, Assistant Director of Nursing, Quality Management Analyst in Research, and adjunct professor. She also works per-diem as an Administrative Nurse Manager at Montefiore Medical Center, Bronx, N.Y. Dobson completed a postdoctorate in Epidemiology and Public Health at Albert Einstein College of Medicine at Yeshiva University in May of 2010. She is active in several community organizations, where she has sat on the Board of Directors for Coalition of Concerned Medical Professionals (CCMP) since 1998 and Queens Sickle Cell Advocacy Network (QSCAN) in 2006–2008. She has served as a nurse consultant to persons with sickle cell disease in the tri-state area. Dobson has received acknowledgements for her work with sickle cell disease from various organizations. She has also received a scholarship from Columbia University to complete her dissertation, "Guided Imagery for Pain Management by Children with Sickle Cell Disease Ages 6 to 11." Dobson's goal is to continue to touch the lives of children and families who suffer with sickle cell disease and other chronic diseases through research, education, and public health programs.

Hope E. Ferguson is the senior writer for the State University of New York's Empire State College. She's been a daily newspaper reporter and has written for a number of publications and publishers including *Christianity Today, Today's Christian Woman, Herlife* magazine, *Diversity & the Bar* and *Scholastic, Inc.* She is the recipient of the 1996 Print Media Award for excellence in coverage of mental health issues from The Alliance for the Mentally Ill of New York State, and other awards. She began her career at Harcourt Brace and Harper & Row Publishers in New York. She studied art at Oberlin College in Ohio, and received a bachelor's degree in U.S. History from Howard University in Washington, DC.

Aquilla Frederick, MBA, MSW, LCSW, currently works as a private practitioner, teacher, and writer. Earlier, she worked as an accounting/financial professional and held roles as an associate producer and adjunct faculty at CUNY. She received a BS and MBA from Long Island University, and a MSW from New York University. Frederick completed postgraduate training as a family and couple therapist at the Ackerman Institute for the Family and is currently on faculty. Her interests include working with and generating clinically relevant ideas about relational trauma in families of color, and the experiences of racism and invisibility among young intellectually gifted females at elite schools. She co-authored *The Role of a Mentoring Group for Family Therapist Trainees of Color.* Prior to Ackerman, she was a staff psychiatric social worker and family therapist for HIP Manhattan Mental Health. She worked extensively with diverse individuals, couples, and families with both acute and chronic psychological problems, and facilitated adolescent and women's trauma groups. Frederick was an associate producer for *Frontiers in Psychotherapy TV*, a weekly cable TV program where she hosted and produced shows focusing on diverse issues and modalities in psychotherapy. She has presented at the Psychotherapy Networker Symposium, AFTA, local organizations, and CUNY. Aquilla Frederick maintains a private practice in New York City.

Gloria A. Gibson earned her PhD in Social Foundations of Education with a minor in Sociology of Education from SUNY Buffalo. She also received an MBA and MS degrees in Human Resource Management from SUNY Oswego. Gibson has conducted research on Black Adolescent Females and their identity formation while they attend and suburban public high schools in the Western New York area. She has worked with and interviewed Black single women raising their children, exploring how they incorporate literacy in their homes. In addition, Gibson's research focus is framed in Critical Cultural Ethnography, which investigates how social reality and lived experiences are socially and culturally constructed and operate at different levels of human agency. Specifically, she focuses on how race, class, and gender in society and educational institutions marginalize individuals.

Mary Harley Gresham is the Vice Provost for Educational Collaboration and Engagement at the University at Buffalo (UB). Her responsibilities include expanding and supporting the campus-wide infrastructure to promote and enable university-community engagement, developing policies and opportunities for university-community collaborations; facilitating P-16 relationships with area schools, and she is the campus supervisor for Millard Fillmore College, the Educational Opportunity Center and the Office for University Preparatory Programs. Formerly dean of the Graduate School of Education at UB, Dr. Gresham has spent most of her professional career developing or managing programs that create academic support and access to higher education for nontraditional students. A psychotherapist, with expertise in multicultural issues, she holds a PhD in Counseling Psychology, and is a clinical professor in the Department of Counseling, School, and Educational Psychology. Gresham has held leadership positions on an array of community boards and initiatives. Her other interests include higher education leadership and the P-16 continuum.

Yvette R. Harris is a professor of psychology at Miami University. She received her PhD in psychology from the University of Florida with a specialization in cognitive development. For the past 20 years her research has focused on exploring the environmental contributions to preschool and school age cognitive development, and more recently has taken on applied focus examining the learning/teaching patterns of African American mothers transitioning from welfare to work and the challenges of family reunification as mothers reenter society from prison. She has presented her work at both national and international conferences, her research has appeared in a variety of educational and developmental journals, and her work has been funded by the National Science Foundation, Proctor and Gamble, Miami University, and the Harvard/Radcliffe Murray Research Center. She has co-authored several books: *The African American Child: Development and Challenges* (1st and 2nd editions); *Children of African Origin: A Guide for Educators and Caregivers; Developmental Science: An Introductory Approach;* and *Children of Incarcerated Parents: Theoretical, Developmental and Clinical Implications.* She has discussed her work on National Public Radio, Voice of America, *Knowledge for Life,* and *Sunday Mornings with Rodney Lear.*

Chiquita D. Howard-Bostic, PhD, is a professor, grant writer, offender treatment/intervention facilitator, and a community mentor. She is an Assistant Professor of Sociology and Criminal Justice Studies, and also serves as the Criminal Justice Internship Coordinator at Shepherd University in Shepherdstown, West Virginia. Dr. Howard-Bostic teaches online and face-to-face courses in the academic disciplines of sociology, criminal justice studies, psychology, and communications. Her current research and journal publications have advanced the study of online teaching pedagogy, cross-cultural motivations for aggression, and emotive-based treatment for perpetrators and victims of mutually performed domestic violence. Over the past fifteen years, she has generated social change as a university administrator and a community developer. Alongside her research, Dr. Howard-Bostic facilitates university service learning projects, community-based youth programs, and international learning initiatives. She has participated in international projects in Cuba, Jamaica, and Vancouver. She also works with women's centers, politicians, and professionals on restorative justice initiatives that service first-time drug offenders. Howard-Bostic is a former college director of institutional assessment and has served as an executive director of housing and human services. She received her PhD in Sociology, teaching certificate in Women's Studies, and a Race and Social Policy research certification at Virginia Polytechnic Institute. She earned a master's degree in Urban Planning at the State University of New York at Buffalo.

Portia Johnson has been an assistant professor at Seton Hall University College of Nursing in South Orange, New Jersey, since 2007. She has an AAS degree from Mercer County Community College, a Bachelor of Science (BSN) from William Paterson University, Master's in Nursing (MSN) from Hunter College of the City University of New York and an EdD from Columbia University, Teachers College, New York City. Prior to her faculty position at Seton Hall she was employed at Hoffmann La-Roche Pharmaceutical Company as a Drug Safety Associate for 18 years. After completing her doctoral education she decided to change her career and become a nurse educator. Dr. Johnson teaches a variety of foundational courses such as Health Promotion, Introduction to Professional Nursing, Gerontology, Health Assessment lab instruction, and has taught online in the RN to BSN Program. She is chairperson of the Obama Obesity Initiative for Concerned Black Nurses of Newark, local chapter of the National Black Nurses Association. Her current research is a meta-analysis on childhood obesity. In addition, she is writing a chapter on obesity.

Jessica J. Jones, MA, is an instructor of English and Humanities at the University of Louisiana–Lafayette and associate faculty at the University of Phoenix. She obtained her bachelor's degree in English from Louisiana State University and her master's degree in English from the University of Tennessee. She is currently pursuing her PhD from the University of Phoenix in higher education administration. Her research focus involves issues of equity and inclusion, leadership development, spirituality in academia, and mentoring experiences of students and faculty of color in higher education. In addition to her academic work, she serves as a mentor at her former elementary school by encouraging young girls to strive for independence, empowerment, and positive identity development.

Illana R. Lane, PhD, is the Dean of the School of Education at Medaille College in Buffalo, New York. She is a former New York City elementary school teacher. Her doctorate and master's degrees are from the State University of New York at Buffalo. She serves on the Amherst Central School District Board of Education and is President-Elect of the New York Association of Teacher Educators (NYSATE). She is also a member of Jack and Jill of America Inc., Buffalo Chapter. In addition to presenting at local, national, and international conferences on educational issues, she has also received recognition from Madison Who's Who of Executives and Professionals and Who's Who among Students in American Universities and Colleges and received the Sojourner Truth Leadership Award in 2011. Articles she has authored include "Breaking the Code: Domestic Minor Sex Trafficking and School Children" (2013), and "Good Teaching: Truth or Fiction" (2006). Her juried academic presentation topics include human rights vulnerabilities and young people, sex trafficking, transparency and community engagement, culturally relevant pedagogy, and learning styles of children of African descent.

Denise Linton, DNS, FNP-BC, is a family nurse practitioner, educator, researcher, editor, local, national, and international speaker and a writer. She began writing in order to disseminate information about cervical cancer screening and prevention. Her doctorate is from the Louisiana State University Health Sciences Center School of Nursing in New Orleans and her master's of science in nursing and a family nurse practitioner certification are from Columbia University School of Nursing in New York. She has authored a book chapter, "Promoting Cervical Cancer Prevention among African American Women," in C. F. Collins (ed.), *African American Women's Life Issues: Today's Vital and Social Matters* (2013). Her publications in various peer-reviewed nurse practitioner and nursing journals include, "Diagnosing and Managing Predisease States in Women's Health" (2013), "Primary-Care Prevention of Cervical Cancer" (2013), and "Cervical Cancer Vaccines: What We Need to Know" (2012). She is a member of various nursing and nurse practitioner organizations such as Sigma Theta Tau International Honor Society of Nursing, American Nurses Association, and National Black Nurses Association. She is also an abstract and manuscript reviewer and the editor of "Southern Connections," the Southern Nursing Research Society newsletter. She was the recipient of the National Black Nurses Association's Nurse Educator of the Year award (2012), the Baton Rouge

District Nurses Association's Celebrate Nursing Top 25 Nurses award (2012), and the University of Louisiana at Lafayette Black Faculty and Staff Caucus's Distinguished Faculty award (2010). Linton is an assistant professor and the nurse practitioner coordinator in the College of Nursing and Allied Health Professions at the University of Louisiana at Lafayette.

Byron Miller, PhD, MAT, earned a master's and doctorate degree in sociology from Florida State University. He also earned a master's in teaching secondary social studies from the University of South Florida. He is a former high school social studies teacher, and currently an assistant professor with a dual appointment in the Sociology & Gerontology Department and the Black World Studies Program at Miami University in Hamilton, Ohio. He teaches a variety of courses including Social Problems, Research Methods, Race and Ethnic Relations, and Race and Criminal Justice. Miller is also a social epidemiologist who has conducted research on the effects of racial discrimination on the mental health of African Americans (*Coping with Racial Discrimination: Assessing the Vulnerability of African Americans and the Mediated Moderation of Psychosocial Resources*), the impact of family support on adolescents' psychological well-being (*Racial and SES Differences in Depressive Symptoms Among Black and White Youth: An Examination of the Mediating Effects of Family Structure, Stress, and Support*), and the social factors that influence the health of persons in interracial relationships (*What Are the Odds: An Examination of Adolescent Interracial Romance and Risk for Depression*).

Jamesetta A. Newland, PhD, RN, FNP-BC, FAANP, DPNAP, is a clinical associate professor at New York University College of Nursing where she teaches in the doctor of nursing practice program. In addition to teaching, she maintains an active practice as a family nurse practitioner in the College's Nursing Faculty Practice, providing primary care to a diverse group of patients in an urban setting. She has been a consultant nationally and internationally on nurse practitioner education and practice, nurse-managed health centers, and faculty practice, with continuing professional affiliations in Botswana and Japan. Her passion for scholarly endeavors finds an outlet through service on editorial boards, presentations and publications, mentoring, and involvement in community and professional organizations. Her contributions have been recognized by honors such as the Nurse Practitioner State Award for Excellence for New York from the American Association of Nurse Practitioners in 2011 and the Dr. Martin Luther King Jr. Excellence in Social Justice Award from Pace University in 2007. For eight years, she has been editor-in-chief of *The Nurse Practitioner* journal and has also contributed book chapters about sickle cell disease in two of Dr. Collins's previous books, *African American Women's Health and Social Issues* (2006) and *African American Women's Life*

Issues: Today's Vital Health and Social Matters (2013). Dr. Newland strives to make a small difference in the lives of everyone she meets.

Juanita Bing Newton is a judge of the New York State Court of Claims and the dean of the New York State Judicial Institute. The Judicial Institute is the educational arm of the New York State court system and provides educational programming for the judges as well as all court system attorney employees. She began her judicial career in 1986 when she was appointed to the Court of Claims by Governor Mario Cuomo. During her 27-year judicial career she has served in numerous assignments including felony trial judge, civil matrimonial and motion judge, and as a court administrator charged with the operation and management of the Manhattan Supreme Court, the five boroughs of the Criminal Court for the City of New York, and the statewide access to justice programming.

Prior to her appointment to the bench, Judge Newton worked as a prosecutor in Bronx County, as the executive director and counsel to the New York State Committee on Sentencing Guidelines and as a non-judge court administrator.

In both 2003 and 2007, she was found highly qualified and recommended as a candidate for appointment to the state's highest court, the New York Court of Appeals, by the Commission on Judicial Nominations.

Judge Newton was a member of the Commission on Judicial Conduct, the disciplinary body for judges, for five years. Over the years she has served on many committees, and currently sits on the statewide Permanent Commission on Sentencing and the Court Interpreter Advisory Committee.

She was a member of numerous professional associations including the New York County Lawyers' Association Task Force to Increase Diversity in the Legal Profession, which she chaired; the Board of the City Bar Justice Center; and the American Bar Association's Standing Committee on Legal Aid and Indigent Defense. She was a member of the Board of the Institute for Faculty Excellence in Judicial Education and the Leadership Institute of the University of Memphis.

Judge Newton, a native of the Bronx, New York, received her undergraduate degree from Northwestern University and law degree from the Catholic University of America Columbus School of Law. She has received honorary degrees from the Law School of the University of the City of New York and the College of Mount St. Vincent.

E. Jeannette Ogden has been admitted to practice law for over 30 years. She has served as a judge for almost 20 years on the Buffalo City, Erie County Criminal and Family Courts. Prior to serving on the bench, she worked as a prosecutor, civil attorney, and private practitioner. She earned her JD Degree from SUNY at Buffalo Law School where she presently instructs courses in Trial Technique and Mental Health Issues in Criminal

Law. She is also an adjunct instructor at Daemen College. Her professional affiliations include memberships on the New York State Advisory Committee on Judicial Ethics, the NYS Bar Association House of Delegates, Character & Fitness Committee of the NYS Supreme Court Appellate Division 4th Dept. and the ABA Commission on Youth at Risk. Judge Ogden is the Chair of the Gender and Racial Fairness Committee for NY Courts in the 8th Judicial District, a Vice President of the NYS Association of Women Judges and member of numerous community and Bar Associations. She regularly appears as a speaker for civic and community organizations, public schools, and churches. Her message and her motto is to "lift as you climb."

Marianne E. Partee, PhD, is a Professor of Economics at The State University of New York Erie Community College South Campus. She has a PhD from The State University of New York at Buffalo. Her research/teaching focus is Economics and Sociology. During her tenure along with the teaching responsibilities she has served as the Social Science Department Chairperson for 2 terms in a department of twelve full-time faculty members and on average 20 part-time faculty members. Under her leadership the department broadened the course offerings to reflect current social concerns. She created the Women's History Course that sequentially was approved by the curriculum committee. Partee was the first full-time female in the department. Over the years she has served on various committees at the college, including the curriculum committee, the appointments committee, the President's Blue Ribbon Diversity committee, as well as participated in the campus council. Currently, Partee is a member of the SUNY at Erie Faculty College Senate, a reappointments committee member for the Faculty Federation of Erie Community College, is active with the Faculty Council of Community Colleges, and an Academic Advisory Board member for Annual Editions: Economics for McGraw-Hill Publishers. She conducts research in macroeconomic policy and its impact on economic inequality. In her work she emphasizes the significances of socioeconomic forces that shape lives. Her last publication was *The Industrial Revolution*, discussing how its aftermath expanded social inequalities that remained in the 21st century.

Caryn R. R. Rodgers, PhD, is a clinician and researcher. She received her doctorate in clinical psychology from St. John's University in Jamaica, New York. She completed a fellowship in Adolescent Medicine at the Harvard Medical School through the Leadership Education in Adolescent Health (LEAH) Fellowship. She also completed a fellowship in community-based participatory research through the W. K. Kellogg Fellowship at Johns Hopkins University Bloomberg School of Public Health. She has published several articles and co-authored a book chapter entitled

"Resilience and Protective Factors for African American and Latina Girls" in Dr. Jen Lau Chin's edited series *Diversity in Mind and in Action*. She is a member of the American Psychological Association where she has served in several leadership roles. She was a member of the APA Task Force on Resilience and Strength in Black Children and Adolescents and a board member for Division 29, Division of Psychotherapy for two terms. Now, she is on the American Psychological Association Committee on Youth and Families (CYF). Rodgers' research focuses on adolescent health promotion in low-income urban communities of color through intervention and program development. Through the employment of community-based participatory research and mixed-method approaches, she works with communities, families, and youth to further understand contextually relevant protective factors that promote resiliency, strength, and adaptive functioning. Her work is currently funded through the National Institute of Child Health and Development (NICHD). Rodgers is currently an Assistant Professor in the Department of Pediatrics at Albert Einstein College of Medicine at Yeshiva University. She is a licensed psychologist who works primarily with adolescents and their families.

Leslie R. Walker, MD, is the Chief of the Division of Adolescent Medicine, and Professor and Vice Chair of Faculty Affairs in the Department of Pediatrics at the University of Washington and Seattle Children's Hospital. At Seattle Children's Hospital, she also co-directs the Adolescent Substance Abuse Program (ASAP). She received her undergraduate degree at Stanford University and medical degree from the University of Illinois. After finishing her Pediatric Residency at the University of Chicago she went back to her home state of California to complete her adolescent medicine fellowship at the University of California, San Francisco. She has worked nationally and locally to improve the health and well-being of adolescents and young adults, focusing her research on health risk behaviors like substance abuse, early teen pregnancy, and parent interventions to improve adolescent health. She serves on many national boards and committees and recently served as the President of the Society for Adolescent Health and Medicine (SAHM). She has also served on multiple committees at the National Academy of Sciences, Institute of Medicine, focusing on improving the missed opportunities for adolescent health and young adult well-being. She has authored many chapters and research articles, most recently focusing on adolescent and young adult substance abuse and workforce diversity. She is a frequent guest on NPR's *Tell Me More* with host Michele Martin, as well as other national and local media sites.

Yvonne Wesley, RN, PhD, FAAN, is an independent health consultant, while directing the Leadership Institute for Black Nurses at New York University's College of Nursing. A nurse for more than 35 years, she has contributed much to the fields of nursing and health promotion. With her PhD in nursing from New York University, where her focus was Research and Theory Development, Wesley has authored numerous publications in peer-reviewed journals. With her master's degree in nursing from Rutgers University in Newark, she specialized in maternal/child health and created community-based programs to reduce Black infant mortality in New Jersey. In adjunct positions at both Kean University and New York University, she has served on the STEM program development and faculty search committees. She is a sought-after speaker regarding minority health and nursing leadership.

Index

Capps, Evony S., 317
CD4 cell count, 4
celebrity endorsements, 84
Celinska, D., 354, 367
Center for American Progress, 61
Center for Children in Poverty, 62
Center for Epidemiological
    Studies—Depression Scale, 8
Center for Substance Abuse
    Prevention, 57
Centers for Disease Control and
    Prevention (CDC): on childhood
    obesity, 87; and chlamydia, 42;
    definition of obesity, 77, 122; on
    gonorrhea, 43; on HIV and STD
    prevention programs, 4–5, 252; on
    HIV infections among youths, 137;
    on HPV vaccine, 164–165; on
    intimate partner violence, 139; on
    pneumocystis carinii pneumonia
    (PC), 4; on poverty, 239; on
    prenatal care, 69; sexual history,
    guide for taking a, 165; on syphilis
    and gonorrhea, 20; on use of birth
    control among African-American/
    Hispanic teen girls, 136; website
    address, 5; Youth Risk Behavior
    Surveillance System (YRBSS), 156
Centers for Disease Control on
    highest rates of HIV infection
    (2013), 6–7
Champion, J. D. and colleagues,
    41, 47
Chaney, Evan, 85
Chesney-Lind, M., 296, 319, 332,
    362, 364
child abuse and neglect, 294
child murder, 318
child pornography, 225, 319
child poverty, 62
Child Protective Service (CPS), 183.
    See also foster care and Black
    adolescent girls
child welfare, 183, 184, 185, 189, 193
childhood obesity, 75–76
children, prison terms of, 329–330
children in need of supervision
    (CHINS), 291

Children's Defense Fund, 314, 316
Childs, G. D., et al., 158, 167
Chin, H. B., and colleagues, 9, 10, 12
chlamydia trachomatis, 41, 42, 45, 47
CHOICES program, 260
Chuang, J., 222, 235
cigarette use, 50, 51, 55
Clinton, Bill, 157
Coalition for Juvenile Justice (2000),
    295, 298
Code of the Street (Anderson), 262,
    266, 356
Coe, M. G., 354, 367
Coie, J. D., 350, 366
Cole, J., 320, 321, 332
Collins, Catherine Fisher, 385
Collins Hill, P., 202, 209
colorblindness, 177–178
Comer, J. P., 324, 332
commercial sex industry, 222, 227,
    234. See also sex trafficking
Community Reinvestment Act, 68
community-based rehabilitation
    centers, 309
Comprehensive Sexuality Education
    (CSE), 240
condom use, 8–9, 20, 139
conduct disorder (CD), 297
confrontation-inflicted physical
    aggression, 356
Conner, E., 352, 366
constitutional rights of juveniles, 373
consumerism, 72
contraceptive devices, 139
contraceptive use, 20
convict leasing, 371
Cook, Tomasina L., 389
Cormier, S., 253, 254, 255
Cose, E., 215, 219
Cotten, N. U., et al., 353, 364
Cotton, Shaquanda, 321
"Cradle to Prison Pipeline," 313n1,
    315, 342
Craigslist, 226
Crawford, P., 5, 17
criminal and juvenile justice systems,
    African American adolescent
    females in: adolescence defined,